RECESSION CHRONICLES

WHAT OTHERS HAVE SAID

"Bill Pittenger is, in my opinion, the best real estate market analyst in the private sector. I look forward to reading his periodic reports on Florida's economy, real estate market, and how it is linked to the national and global economies."

Grant Ian Thrall, Ph.D
Former Professor, University of Florida
Fellow, Homer Hoyt Institute
Past President American Real Estate Society

"During the Great Recession there was a dearth of market data. Commercial real estate appraisers still needed to tell the story and estimate value. My firm relied on economic data and projections produced by Bill Pittenger. His forecasts and viewpoints were like a beacon in rough economic seas."

Walter Duke, MAI
President, Clobus, McLemore & Duke
Mayor, City of Dania Beach

"For 30 years Bill Pittenger has dazzled me with his insight, intellect and accurate market analysis. His writings and presentations are readily understandable and logical. He made sense out of a horrible economic situation—The Great Recession. Many of his recession era writings are now memorialized in this book—*Recession Chronicles.*"

Steven L. Marshall, MAI, SRA
Corporate Partner, Clayton, Roper & Marshall, Inc.

"There are five books that belong on every lender's book shelf. Two of them are by Bill Pittenger: *It All Matters: An Appraisal Anthology* and *The Bankers' Guide to Federal Appraisal Regulation. Recession Chronicles* is sure to be another."

Frank DiLorenzo
Senior Vice President, Commercial Real Estate –
Suntrust Bank, Atlanta, Georgia

RECESSION CHRONICLES

WILLIAM L. PITTENGER

THE GREAT RECESSION

CHRONICLED IN 150

CONTEMPORANEOUSLY

WRITTEN ESSAYS

Recession Chronicles
The Great Recession Chronicled In 150 Contemporaneously Written Essays
All Rights Reserved
Copyright © 2014 William L. Pittenger
V 1.0 First Printing September 2014

Cover design, layout and formatting:
Tom Hinson / Brand Cultivation, LLC
Atlanta, Georgia
brandcultivation.com

Bill Pittenger Real Estate Economics, LLC
billpittenger.com
ISBN: 978-0-578-15039-0

PRINTED IN THE UNITED STATES OF AMERICA

ABOUT THE AUTHOR

William "Bill" Pittenger is a Business and Real Estate Economist as well as a professionally designated (MAI and SRA) real estate appraiser. He has over 43 years of diverse experience in real estate, economic analysis, forecasting and valuation in private practice and on behalf of both private and public sector organizations.

He has held senior positions at a $44 billion (assets) super-regional bank (corporate chief appraiser) as well as at two of the nation's federal banking agencies.

In addition to this book, he is the author of the book *It All Matters: An Appraisal Anthology* as well as five other books including *The Bankers' Guide to Federal Appraisal Regulation*.

He is also the author of over 300 articles, whitepapers, e-books and monographs. He has taught bank examiners at the Federal Financial Institutions Examination Council (FFIEC) and at all of the federal banking regulatory agencies. He has testified before committees of the United States Congress as well as before the Florida Governor and Cabinet. He is a Fellow and Economist Roundtable member at the Economic Development Research Institute (EDRI) and a member of the Florida Economic Research Network (FERN) of Enterprise Florida. He writes and presents extensively and his work has been published in a wide variety of professional journals as well as news and trade publications.

ALSO BY WILLIAM L. PITTENGER

- *It All Matters: An Appraisal Anthology* (January 2014)

- *Federal Appraisal Regulation from the Lenders' Perspective*

- *The Bankers' Guide to Federal Appraisal Regulation*

- *Eighteen Timeless Appraisal Ideas*

- *Readings in Fair Lending and the Appraisal Process*

- *Appraising for Lending Purposes—Focusing On Fundamentals*

Learn more or order online at BillPittenger.com

DEDICATION

This collection of essays is dedicated to the many consumers and businesses that struggled through the Great Recession; the broadest and deepest economic downturn since the Great Depression of the 1930s.

ACKNOWLEDGEMENT
OF OUR SPONSORS

The author extends his sincere gratitude to our sponsors. Their
generosity makes it possible for us to distribute books free of
charge to many universities, libraries, appraisal schools, agencies,
professional organizations and instructors who are shaping the
next generation of leaders in our field. Sponsors of this book are:

- *Integra Realty Resources*

- *RealWired!*

- *Axiom Bank*

More information about each sponsor appears on the following pages.
We encourage you to thank each of them and to use their services.

We know value ⅂ when we see it.

realwired!

RealWired! is a technology and consulting firm that focuses on streamlining the business of commercial real estate with processes and technology.

The company provides a commercial appraisal suite of software including **DataComp**, a comparable sales and lease tracking database, **Edge**, an appraisal report writing software and **Manager**, an appraisal management workflow application.

RealWired! also offers financial institutions **YouConnect**, a web based enterprise class request and vendor management solution. YouConnect automates and streamlines the residential and commercial real estate appraisal process while satisfying federal and state examination and auditing requirements. YouConnect handles appraisals, reviews, BPO's, evaluations, environmental studies, construction inspections, vendor management including licensing verification, workflow, status tracking, storage and reporting.

RealWired! is owned by Brenda Dohring Hicks, MAI and Jeff Hicks MAI and is based in Tampa Florida.

RealWired!
518 N. Tampa Street
Suite 300
Tampa, FL 33602

realwired.com
813-349-2700
brenda@realwired.com
Jeff@realwired.com

Axiom Bank®

Axiom Bank is a federally chartered community bank that provides value-oriented consumer and commercial banking services through an extensive network of branches in Florida. Axiom Bank is headquartered in Central Florida and has 20 branch locations, with 19 branches located inside select Walmart Supercenters®, offering our customers the convenience of banking and shopping under one roof.

Our bankers are empowered to engage with customers, developing relationships that improve lives and strengthen communities. Our branches are open late on weekdays and open on Saturdays to accommodate busy schedules—all part of our unwavering commitment to exceed customer expectations with the highest level of service and involvement in thet communities we serve.

Axiom Bank
258 Southhall Lane
Maitland, FL 32751-7449
www.axiombanking.com
800-584-0015

Member
FDIC

CONTENTS

SECTION ONE
2007: PRELUDE TO RECESSION

SECTION TWO
2008: OVER THE EDGE AND INTO THE DEPTHS OF RECESSION

SECTION THREE
2009: RECESSION WITH A CAPITAL "R"

SECTION FOUR
2010: RECOVERY BEGINS

SECTION FIVE
2011: RECOVERY AT
GLACIAL SPEED

SECTION SIX
2012: MORE GLACIAL
SPEED RECOVERY

SECTION SEVEN
2013: THE NEW NORMAL?

FOREWORD

William "Bill" Pittenger is not a prophet, but as my late partner Michael Y. Cannon (and close friend of Bill Pittenger) might have said, "We are not appraisers—we are real estate economists!" Indeed, Bill is one of the premier real estate economists working in Florida. He continues to be a singular practitioner of well-researched and reasoned forecasting, combining dedicated economic scholarship with a level of personal and professional integrity that has made his reputation the gold standard in the real estate community.

I began my working relationship with Bill after I relocated to Florida in 2004, by which time he was already a giant within the appraisal profession. To put it mildly, the subsequent decade has been a time of interesting trends. Through it all, Bill has been a consistently insightful member of the real estate community as an expert on both local and national trends, and is an oft contributor to national and regional news outlets, to help explain economic happenings to a wider audience.

A highly important facet of Bill's career has been his consistent insistence on objective and reasoned appraisal valuation practices. Whether instructing federal bank examiners or testifying before the United States Congress, his insistence marks not only his dedication to ethical conduct, but also his commitment to ensuring greater trust and resiliency in this nation's banking system. This same tenacity helped limit his clients' exposure to fallout from the real estate collapse during the Great Recession, and contributed greatly to my professional relationship with him during his time as Chief Commercial Appraiser at Seacoast Bank in Stuart, FL.

Indeed, this insistence on quality appraisal work has been a defining characteristic of my own two and a half decades in the appraisal business. In my ten years as an appraisal and valuation practitioner in Florida, Bill has been one of an elite group of clients who has always demanded the most thorough analysis backed by the very best data.

Whether managing the commercial division of a local real estate appraisal company, owning and running my own commercial appraisal firm, or serving as the regional manager of a national appraisal corporation, I've been able to look to Bill's high standards and dedication to objectivity and strive to make them the cornerstones of my professional endeavors. I credit Bill among my peers for reinforcing (and paying for) these qualities. Over the past decade I have seen other firms in the real estate business—including brokers, agents, and appraisers—succumb to the fallout of a quickly changing market and their own willingness to ignore the fundamentals of good business practice. In 44 years of practice in this field, Bill Pittenger has earned an unassailable reputation and the metaphorical high ground from which he has been able to take the long view and advocate for the best in our industry.

I have had the pleasure of reading his previous books, and Bill's writings will serve any reader looking for greater insight into the important role that real estate plays in our economy. His most recent previous work, *It All Matters: An Appraisal Anthology*, is an excellent read for anybody wishing to understand the premium placed on good real estate information by financial institutions. Additionally, it presents good arguments that nothing we do in this field exists in a vacuum, as Bill lays out the consequences appraisals can have on the very financial institutions upon which we all rely every day. The Great Depression may have seen an overhaul in the financial system that guarantees average Americans safety in their checking and savings accounts, but one of the important lessons from the last decade has been the inescapable nature of the interconnected relations which exist within our economy.

In certain respects, Bill's new book, *Recession Chronicles*, may be considered a continuation or sequel to *It All Matters: an Appraisal Anthology*. A copy of Bill's previous work sits on a readily accessible shelf of reference material in my office, and for good reason. *It All Matters* is an anthology of articles written by Bill that focuses primarily on the issues that banks, and the appraisers they engage, must face on a continuing basis, as well as deeply insightful recommendations and explanations of the approaches that successful financial institutions employ. *Recession Chronicles*, however, reads as in real-time, developing a view of the Great Recession as seen from the author's eyes and experience. The collected writings within this book have been reproduced without revision, appearing as they did at the time of each articles' original publication. This serves the simultaneous purpose of demonstrating how Bill was able to anticipate the troubles facing the economy, and how the implications of the collapse were greatly underestimated. It is easy to look back and see with clarity, but within these articles you will see how at least one wise man forecast the dangers that were ahead of us.

Even as I write this in 2014, I am still being engaged on assignments resulting from the Great Recession, as the balance sheets of toxic assets continue being processed and litigated while the reforms of the Dodd-Frank Reform Act have changed the landscape for appraisal yet again. It is no coincidence that I bring up this recent and rather important piece of legislation affecting the business of appraisal. Bill has written a freely available article on the subject, one that any person seeking an introduction to this legislation will find helpful. He has linked it to updates on the guidelines of interagency appraisals, a fully amended Title XI of FIRREA (one of the most important regulatory laws in the appraisal business) as related to Dodd-Frank, as well as progress reports for the reader interested in the continuing evolution of this legislation.

In addition to these works on the regulatory and structural importance that appraisals have in the current financial market, Bill has written practical and functional guides on the writing and review of appraisals for those looking to improve their own practices within the business. He has written guides on effective management and development of appraisal firms, aids for anyone who wishes to gain a deeper appreciation of good appraisal practice, whether for self-enrichment or for the practical purposes of knowing what to look for when engaging an appraisal firm.

With four decades of experience and success in this field, Bill Pittenger remains a veritable font of wisdom for anyone who seeks a deeper understanding of our financial system and the professionals who research and evaluate real estate. I recommend this present book to you, and once again extend my profound thanks to Bill for all the service he has done to inform, educate, and support our industry and our economy.

I have had the good fortune to have met and developed a strong professional relationship with Bill Pittenger, to experience his successes, and to emulate his ethics and persistence to continually elevate our shared profession. Whether this colors my appreciation for his work is something I leave for the reader of this book to determine, but I am confident that Bill's work—the most recent example of which you now hold in your hands—speaks for itself and will stand the test of time.

Scott M. Powell, MAI, is the Managing Director of Integra Realty Resources' (IRR) Miami/Palm Beach office. He can be reached in Stuart, FL at (772) 463-4131 ext. 210, or by email at spowell@irr.com. For more information, please visit www.irr.com or blog.irr.com.

PREFACE

"In the ruin of all collapsed booms is to be found the work of men who bought property at prices they knew perfectly well were fictitious, but who were willing to pay such prices simply because they knew that some still greater fool could be depended on to take the property off their hands and leave them with a profit."

Chicago Tribune Editorial,
April 1890

Before exploring recession details, it may be instructive to understand the origin and development of the recent housing crisis. Indeed, virtually no community was untouched by what became an extraordinary downturn. What started as a housing bubble, evolved into the deepest and broadest recession since the Great Depression of the 1930s.

The Great Recession as it has come to be known officially began in December 2007 and ended in June 2009 although its seeds were being sown as early as 2002 and recovery is still a work in progress in 2014. It began with the bursting of an $8.0 Trillion dollar housing bubble. The bursting bubble contributed to chaos in banking as well as a sharp decline in housing wealth and a resultant contraction in consumer spending.

As both consumer and business spending dried up huge job losses followed. In 2008 and 2009 which were the depths of the recession, the labor market lost 8.4 million jobs which equated to over six percent of the nation's payroll employment. This was the most dramatic employment contraction since the Great Depression of the 1930s. By comparison, the second most severe contraction in modern times was the recession of 1981. Even then, employment contraction was 3.1% or roughly half that of The Great Recession.

Bubbles are not new to the U.S. economy. Indeed they are often a byproduct of free market capitalism. American financial history is replete with stories of good ideas getting out of control and ending with disastrous results. In the 1850's, for example, the emerging technology was the telegraph. Investors funded too many miles too soon resulting in 10 times the needed capacity and the industry temporarily wilted.

Then came railroads connecting the east and the west. Quickly, too many miles of track were built with too few people or too little freight to use them. A full 25% of railroad miles went bankrupt.

During the 1920's stocks were the big story. Again, too much exuberance led to irrational run up of prices and the crash in 1929. In recent history there was the dot-com frenzy of the 1990's and the bursting of that bubble in 2000. In every bubble, investors were seduced by the opportunity for quick money. Today, we benefit from the innovation of new industry and technology but at the time it was too much, too fast, with an absence of *real* economic demand and the result was financial ruin for many—especially those who joined the frenzy at its peak.

For the last five years, we have been picking up the pieces of a residential real estate bubble. Like all bubbles, it too will have some future benefits that are not fully apparent now. Benefits may take the form of improved lending, underwriting, risk management and regulatory models. That knowledge is little comfort to those who entered the frenzy late and experienced financial distress or disaster.

The U.S. economy was recovering after the dot-com bubble burst in 2000 when he terrorist attacks of September 11, 2001 occurred. The Federal Reserve sought to revive a shocked economy by reducing the federal funds rate from 3.5% to 1.75% and later in June 2003 to 1.0%. Mortgage interest rates then dropped from about 8% to 6% in 2003 following the last Federal Funds rate adjustment.

Residential supply and demand relationships were in balance in 2002. The extraordinarily low Federal Funds rate however led to *"cheap money"* and eventually to excess liquidity. That cheap money quickly found its way to the highly leveraged real estate industry.

Fueled in part by cheap money, new home sales rose from 5.25 million in 2001 to 6.175 million in 2003 and 8.357 million in 2005. At the same time, the median home price rose from $147,500 in 2001 to $178,800 in 2003 (+21%) and new home construction starts rose from 1.6 million in 2001 to 1.85 million in 2003. At that time however, home prices were rising faster than incomes and new home construction was increasing faster than population growth. These conditions were recognized as early as late 2003 when it was apparent that continued unconstrained growth was unsustainable.

Despite what was fast becoming a tidal wave of excess liquidity, housing expansion had a profoundly *positive* (albeit short lived) effect on the local and the broader economy. Employment was growing, inflation was under control, consumers were spending and economic life was generally good. The so-called "sand states" such as Florida, Arizona, California and Nevada were among the biggest beneficiaries. Nevertheless the seeds of housing collapse and recession were being sowed even as the economy grew.

As employment expanded, the fastest growing occupations included mortgage brokers who originated loans and mortgage bankers who packaged them into securities for ultimate sale. The largest secondary purchasers were Fannie Mae and Freddie Mac, both shareholder owned companies but because they were chartered by Congress, are known as government-sponsored enterprises (GSE). Neither is backed by the full faith and credit of the U.S. government although many consumers and real estate practitioners believe otherwise. By 2008, however, both entities had been nationalized and are now under the control of the federal government with a new regulator, the Federal Housing Finance Agency (FHFA), a pumped up version of its predecessor, the Office of Federal Housing Enterprise Oversight (OFHEO).

Because Fannie Mae and Freddie Mac were chartered to enhance home ownership for low and moderate income households, both enterprises had mortgage limits. The limits were not tied to inflation or income but rather to housing prices. As a result, the GSEs became unintended bubble enablers. In 2003 and 2004, home prices were increasing faster than Fannie and Freddie's limit. As a result, numerous households in high cost areas—specifically east and west coasts—were shut out in the sense that neither Fannie nor Freddie could purchase their mortgage.

For years, both organizations also had carefully crafted underwriting standards which often meant that another group of borrowers was left out—those with blemished credit or those with properties that did not conform to the GSE standards. What followed was both agencies began ratcheting down their underwriting standards under Congressional and Administration pressure to make home ownership more readily available to more consumers.

Fannie Mae and Freddie Mac were only a part of the lending universe. Banks, thrifts and mortgage companies could tap the same cheap money and sell loans into the vast mortgage-backed securities market that Fannie Mae had pioneered. And tap the cheap money they did. The ranks of mortgage brokers swelled to over 55,000—many of whom were untrained, most unlicensed and most also unregulated. Mortgage brokers who were regulated were only loosely regulated by the states. Brokers originated loans and mortgage bankers packaged them into securities. They filled the void created by Fannie Mae and Freddie Mac loan limits as well as that created by their underwriting standards.

Securitization became a double-edged sword. It helped make home ownership available to more people. Indeed, home ownership reached a high of 69.4% in 2004. Securitization also spread the risk but at the same time it obscured the risk as those who "originated to sell" had no so-called "skin in the game." Most originations during the bubble era were, in fact, originate to sell with virtually nothing being held in portfolio. As an aside, over 70% of all loan originations during the time period were done by loosely or unregulated mortgage brokers with no capital at risk. Banks and other heavily regulated institutions with capital at risk originated only 30% and lost market share for several years.

With home prices escalating rapidly, there was a vast untapped market for loans over the Fannie and Freddie limit and for borrowers with impaired credit. The private sector tapped that with so-called subprime loans and with a variety of new and creative options. Sub Prime lending, once a small lending niche intended to serve those who may be temporarily credit impaired increased dramatically. Beyond its originally intended purpose, it morphed into a vehicle for financing investors and flippers who wanted to finance multiple homes or units. Add to that exotic and high risk mortgage instruments accompanied by declining loan underwriting standards that often allowed borrowers to be approved with little or no documentation and the subprime mortgage market evolved into a disaster in waiting.

Subprime quickly became the fastest growing mortgage sector. In 2001, for example, originations totaled $160 Billion. By 2003 originations nearly doubled to $310 Billion and by 2005 originations doubled again to $625 Billion. The dollar amount of loans outstanding logically followed the same pattern. From 2001 to 2003, outstandings increased 46% from $479 Billion to $699 Billion. By 2005 (the peak year) outstandings increased another 77% to $1.240 Trillion. As the market collapsed, both new originations and outstandings slid precipitously. By 2008, outstandings had declined by nearly one-third and new originations were nil.

During the subprime run up, innovation out ran both financial regulation and financial institution risk management. Mortgage instruments were introduced which had not been tested in times of economic stress, if at all.

Ownit Mortgage, for example, (which subsequently failed) introduced a 45 year mortgage while other companies introduced no documentation or low documentation loans—sometimes referred to pejoratively as *"liar loans."* Another variation on the adjustable rate mortgage was the so-called "Option Payment ARM" that allowed borrowers to pay less than the full amount of interest which was then added to the loan balance resulting in negative amortization and a growing loan balance. That instrument was widely used in California and Florida, where values and prices were increasing dramatically, and to a lesser extent in other states. Indeed, as long as values were increasing these instruments worked. When values began to slide, however, widespread disaster resulted.

With such liberal terms and a widespread belief that house prices could only rise, many home buyers could purchase and finance more home than they could actually afford. Similarly, investors and flippers could purchase *more* homes than they could afford.

Nevertheless, the feeding frenzy continued. Greed, combined with a herd mentality took over the market. The frenzy was fueled by builders, lenders, sales agents and others who sought to fill the apparent demand for housing. It would not be long however, before it became apparent that the demand was not *real* demand but rather artificial and bubble driven.

Record low interest rates spurred the housing and credit industries in three fundamental ways. In markets where homes and land were limited, consumers could *pay* more. They did and prices spiked. In markets where land was plentiful, builders and developers could *build* more.

They did and prices spiked. Everywhere, the boom led to rising prices, mortgages and mortgage related debt. Similarly, investors could not get enough subprime mortgage bonds. Many originally bought only the most secure tranches of the securitized offerings. As the market grew, investors went in search of yield and began accepting the lower rated tranches.

No Tree Grows to the Sky. The ancient proverb says it all. Nothing goes on forever. By late 2005, the real estate cycle had run its cyclical course and the bubble was losing air. So many market participants (builders, lenders, sales agents, buyers, sellers and more) lost sight of the fundamental economic fact of life that for every house built, there must be a user—either owner or tenant. By 2005 however, it was too late. Somewhere between 25 and 40% more homes had been built than there were people to occupy them. Predictably, prices declined. Owners—at least those who bought at the peak—were left with a value less than their mortgage balance. As an aside, CoreLogic, an economic research and forecasting firm, estimated that in November 2010, 42% of Florida homeowners were underwater on their home mortgage.

Credit quality deteriorated and, by mid-2008, foreclosures reached record highs. According to the Mortgage Bankers Association (MBA), at the end of the third quarter of 2008, Florida foreclosures for prime fixed rate loans hit 3.8% while subprime fixed rate loans soared to 17.49%. The story with adjustable rate mortgages (ARM) was even worse. Prime ARMs soared to 15.19% while subprime reached a staggering 40.18%.

By the end of 2007, the nation was officially in recession. Unlike most recessions (at least those since World War II) that began with some type of monetary policy issue or economic shock, and eventually rolled into housing, this one actually began with housing and rolled into the broader economy.

The destruction from the recession was enormous financially and in human terms. Almost no one escaped the recession. By its end, existing home sales volume had declined roughly 50% from its 2005 peak while new home sales volume had declined 80% from its peak in 2006. Median price declined 33% nationally and 53% in Florida.

Construction employment declined 65% reaching an all-time high sector unemployment high of 20%.

Commercial real estate followed by losing a full 50% of its aggregate value during 2008 and 2009. The value decline was faster and steeper then residential.

Over 8.0 million jobs were lost during the recession before finding a bottom in 2010.

Today (2014) the economy has returned to growth but the growth has been painfully slow and erratic—and is likely to remain that way through the current decade.

William L. Pittenger
Saint Cloud (Orlando) Florida
Summer 2014

ABOUT THIS BOOK

This book is a collection of articles and essays written contemporaneously from 2007 through 2013. Because each one was written as events were unfolding, they are not viewed through a prism of history. When

Recession Chronicles is a contemporaneous walk through The Great Recession from beginning to end.

we look back at any event, especially one as broad, deep and far reaching as the Great Recession, our views sometimes become distorted. Perhaps not egregiously so but often to the extent that we view what happened as being more or less severe depending on our point of view.

As I re-read each of the 150 articles and essays included herein, I considered filtering them through the lens I have today. I considered changing forecasts that, when the fog cleared or more facts became known (as they always do), turned out a little differently. I even considered eliminating certain pieces all together. As an aside, when I missed the mark it was almost always by underestimating the severity of an event or understating the recovery time period.

Every word of what you are about to read was based on careful research of information known at the time. After all, that is the essence of forecasting: using known or knowable contemporary information to make inferences about the future.

The essays in this book are largely about the macro economy. For reasons that may be obvious, Florida entered the analysis. Florida is my home and was one of the economically hardest hit states during the recession. As a result, you will see many references to Florida recessionary events. Additionally, for several years during the recession, I was employed as chief real estate economist at Stuart, Florida based Seacoast

National Bank. Rather than eliminating those references, I left them intact. Seacoast National Bank is located in what is known as Florida's Treasure Coast. Indeed, to a significant extent, the Treasure Coast is a microcosm of Florida which, in turn, is a microcosm of the nation.

This book is organized in seven major sections plus a postscript. Section one is a Prelude to Recession in 2007. The nation fell into the depths of the recession in 2008; stayed there for most of 2009 and began to show modest signs of recovery in 2010. Recovery occurred at glacial speed throughout much of 2012 and what began to emerge in 2013 might be characterized as the new normal. The PostScript is a brief forecast for the economy from mid-2014.

Every word of what you are about to read was based on careful research of information known at the time.

In total context, *Recession Chronicles* is a contemporaneous walk through The Great Recession from beginning to end. I hope you, my valued reader, will find it to be a useful tool and historical reference.

William L. Pittenger

2007
PRELUDE TO RECESSION

The seeds of recession were being sown as early as 2002 when home prices began rising faster than household income. That brought new construction to a virtual halt. That was followed by inventory growth and extraordinary existing home sales volume decline, price decline, employment decline and distress throughout the mortgage industry and the broader economy.

As 2007 dawned, evidence was still not convincingly apparent that wide spread recession was only months away. The true depth and breadth of the ultimate recession was also not apparent. Indeed, many geographic markets and product sectors remained relatively healthy well into 2007. The threat began to show itself when Mortgage giant Freddie Mac announced on February 27th that it would no longer buy the most risky subprime loans. That was followed in April by the bankruptcy of New Century Financial and in August by the bankruptcy of another giant American Home Mortgage Investment. Investment bank, Bear Stearns was later forced to liquidate two hedge funds that had invested in risky securities backed by subprime loans. Finally, Fitch Ratings cut the credit rating of another mortgage giant, Countrywide Financial. Its rating was cut to the third lowest grade possible.

By August, the subprime mortgage market had imploded. The housing crisis was deepening almost by the day as foreclosures mounted and subprime lenders were left with worthless underlying assets. The crisis was no longer a consumer crisis but one that reached the top echelons of Wall Street, specifically its investment banks.

Housing starts, permits and sales all began to decline precipitously in late summer. Nevertheless, commercial real estate was holding up reasonably well causing many observers to wonder if the commercial sector had dodged the bullet. Only a few months later, it would become

I

apparent that it had not. In fact, as you'll read later, the commercial real estate market collapse which followed residential by around 18 months turned out to be faster, steeper and even more severe that residential.

The nation was clearly in recession. While many consumers and businesses strongly believed the nation was in recession, that fact was not announced by the Business Cycle Dating Committee (BCDC) of the National Bureau of Economic Research (NBER) until December 2008. Indeed, that announcement came a full 12 months after the group claimed the recession had started in December 2007.

AUGUST 7, 2007

IT'S BEEN A BRUTAL TWO WEEKS FOR HOUSING

Both new and existing home sales fell, the rate of home ownership fell, subprime woes grew and credit tightened. Let's take a look at the indicators, decide what they mean, how they affect us and what to watch for going forward.

Existing home sales fell 3.8% to a 5.75 million annual rate while new home sales declined 6.6% in June. Expectations were for more moderate decline in both measures. In the last 12 months sales of new homes have declined 22% and are now running 40% below their July 2005 peak.

The nation's home ownership rate has also fallen to its lowest level since 2003. The Census Bureau puts the rate at 68.4%. That is down from its peak of 69.4% in 2004. The two fundamental drivers are affordability and credit standards. The effect of tightening credit standards could, however, be offset by affordability as more home sellers slash their asking prices.

An often overlooked piece of data from the Census Bureau is the number of finished but vacant homes. That statistic puts vacant homes nationally at 2.04 million which is down slightly from the first quarter when the rate was pegged at 2.18 million—the highest vacancy since the bureau began tracking it some four decades ago. The dramatic increase in the first quarter is almost certainly the result of *flipper-spec-*

ulators in the market which led to far more homes being constructed than there were occupants—either owner or tenant. The good news is vacancies appear to have peaked and may be receding—a sign that the excess inventory is being absorbed.

The indicators for the general economy were not nearly as bleak. Second quarter GDP rebounded to 3.4% after anemic 0.6% growth in the first quarter. Most observers believe that the second half of 2007 will show relatively strong growth of about 2.6% (annualized). Housing continues to be a drag on the GDP but it is still being supported by full employment and solid consumer spending.

Clearly the strongest factor in the economy is the tight labor market with unemployment remaining low at 4.3%. Five percent is generally considered inflation neutral in a full employment environment.

Core inflation risks are fading. At 1.9%, core inflation is within the Fed's zone of tolerance however there is still well founded concern over non-core components which include food and energy. The Fed is under increasing pressure to measure total inflation as most economists believe it is a more realistic measure.

Last week The Conference Board reported a surprising upward bounce in its consumer confidence index perhaps suggesting that consumer spending is not likely to retreat significantly despite the continued housing slump.

The Labor Department also reported that non-farm productivity rose 1.8% annualized in the second quarter. That is more than double the first quarter annualized rate.

So far there has been no significant spillover from the housing market to the broader economy however distress in credit markets which began with sub-prime mortgage problems could quickly change that. Subprime defaults have sky rocketed and billions of dollars more in sub-prime loans are set to adjust by the middle of 2008. Given lower collateral values and higher interest rates, industry observers put forecast losses as high as $1.0 Trillion—a staggering number which could have a profoundly adverse effect on the general economy.

As of this writing however, we still do not believe the economy is poised to slip into recession.

Metrostudy released its second quarter 2007 new construction housing data last week. In the six county south Florida area, the number of finished vacant single family units finally fell for the first time since the third quarter of 2005. Miami- Dade experienced the largest decline at 11.7% while Palm Beach and Martin declined at 8.3% and 2.7% respectively. Broward, St. Lucie and Indian River county finished inventory all grew. Quarterly starts fell to only 2,462 which is less than half the pace of a decade ago and only 30.5% of the pace at the peak in the third quarter of 2005.

South Florida housing inventory in the second quarter stood at 14,545 units which is the lowest level since the third quarter of 2003 and at current absorption rates suggests at 9.5 month supply. Inventories fell in every south Florida County except Broward where it rose by 6.4%. The following is a county by county summary of markets served by Seacoast National Bank.

Treasure Coast—Indian River County
The finished vacant home inventory rose for the 11th consecutive quarter. Metrostudy pegged current inventory at 1,023 units which is 5.6% higher than last quarter. At the current absorption rate, that is an 8.4 month supply. Add in units under construction and there is an apparent 13.6 month supply. Equilibrium and recovery are therefore not yet in sight and probably won't be in 2007.

The good news is that the number of units under construction has fallen to 2003 levels and total inventory has declined over the last three quarters. Finally, quarterly starts fell to 191, a level not experienced since 2002.

St. Lucie County
Finished vacant inventory rose *again* to 1,368 units. This represents a 9.5 month supply. Add in under construction inventory and there is an apparent 15.3 month supply. St. Lucie's finished vacant inventory has remained at or near this level of supply for the last year. If there is good news in the numbers it is that total inventory has fallen 8.6% to 2,203 as the number of units under construction fell by 24.3%. Other good news this quarter is that the number of starts (205) is half the number of closings (411) meaning that the market is moving in the right direction but equilibrium is not yet in sight. In 2005, St. Lucie was one of

the nation's fastest growing counties. Today it has one of the nation's largest inventory hangovers.

Martin County

Finished vacant inventory fell modestly (2.7%) in the second quarter. Inventory stands at only 398 units today which, at the current absorption rate is still a 6.7 month supply. The number of units under construction fell by 38.7% to 225 in the second quarter. This is the lowest number in a decade. Total construction starts also fell to only 39 units. Equilibrium is clearly in sight and achievable in 2007.

Gold Coast—Palm Beach County

Finished vacant inventory fell by 8.3% to only 1,199 units—a 2.6 month supply. Add to that, inventory under construction plus models and total inventory is 3,256 which represents a 7.1 month supply. Total inventory may grow in the next quarter or two as a high number of foreclosed properties will enter the market.

Broward County

Finished vacant inventory in Broward County is now at 724 units which is a manageable 3.1 month supply. In an unexpected trend reversal however, quarterly new construction starts out paced move ins. While that reversal is unwelcome, it is probably a benign change as Broward has only 1,525 vacant developed lots in active subdivisions. This is the fewest of any south Florida county and is clearly manageable.

Space Coast—Brevard County

The number of starts in Brevard fell below closings for the first time in the second quarter of 2006. Since then the trend has been positive and inventory has burned off in an orderly fashion. Today, total inventory of 1,559 units equates to a 6.6 month supply. The actual inventory is the lowest since the second quarter of 2003 and the months of supply has dropped to early 2004 levels.

Orlando Tri County Metro—Orange County

Total inventory reached its peak late in the cycle in the third quarter of 2006. As a result, there is still a relatively high total inventory of 17,631 units which represents a 10.2 month supply at the current absorption rate. Orange County also has a huge inventory of vacant developed lots for a 17.2 month supply.

Seminole County

Seminole County to the north of Orange virtually mirrors Orange County with a current inventory of 3,830 units and a 9.0 month supply. Seminole also has a 21.4 month inventory of vacant developed lots.

Osceola County

In 2005, Osceola was one of the fastest growing counties in Florida and the 16th fastest growing county in the nation. Today, it has a significant hangover of inventory estimated to be 9,053 units which represents a 12.7 month supply. Osceola began growing rapidly in 2003. At that time, inventory stood at a relatively manageable 1,789 units. Inventory reached its peak of 8,564 units (15.2 month supply) in the third quarter of 2006—very late in the cycle.

AUGUST 22, 2007

HOUSING STARTS, PERMITS AND BUILDER CONFIDENCE DECLINE

Housing starts declined by 6.1% in July to 1.381 million units—the lowest level in a decade when starts dropped to 1.355 million in January 1997. The drop was more severe than economists forecast and Wall Street expected. Year over year starts were 20.9% lower than July 2006. Predictably, builder confidence is now at its lowest level since 1991 according to a recently released survey of its members by the National Association of Homebuilders.

Is a decline in starts all bad, though? According to most news reports, yes. Nevertheless, inventories, which were in balance as recently as 2003, began to climb in 2004 The Commerce Department reported declines in both new construction starts and building permit activity last week. While that's bad for Wall Street and the building industry, is it truly a blow to the overall economy or just progress on the road to equilibrium?

According to the Commerce Department, housing starts nationwide declined and became seriously bloated by 2005 and 2006. The run up in prices fueled more building until supply outstripped demand. Many players lost sight of, or chose to ignore, the fact that for every home constructed there must be an end user whether it be an owner or tenant. During the run up, an estimated 25-40% more homes were constructed than there were people to occupy them. This is a classic bubble and when it burst in 2006, values declined and record numbers of borrowers slipped into foreclosure. That slide into foreclosure will no doubt continue well into 2008—both locally and nationally.

What the press reports as negative, we see as positive and part of the normal economic cycle. With construction starts decreasing, the market will have a chance to burn off excess inventory and regain equilibrium. Once equilibrium is in sight, construction starts will rebound. While that is not much current comfort to Wall Street, builders and those who support the building industry, it is part of the normal cycle that must occur. The fact that the decline is so steep is the result of the run up also being abnormally steep resulting in a bubble that burst leaving record inventories to be absorbed into the market place.

Construction starts have been declining in all Seacoast markets. Again, we see that as positive event as excess inventory is rapidly burning off. The accompanying table shows second quarter construction starts in Seacoast counties together with the quarter during which starts reached their peak.

Several statistics are noteworthy. First, construction starts are down between 37% and 89% in every Seacoast county. The average decline has been in the 50% range. Seacoast counties that reached their peak early are at or near equilibrium today. For example, Palm Beach County reached peak construction starts in late 2003 (although there was an uptick in Q3 2004).

Today, Palm Beach County has a nearly normal supply of new single family homes. Contrast that with Indian River, St. Lucie, Orange and Osceola which built late into the slow down. Each has a 12– 15 month total supply (finished vacant + under construction). Equilibrium is probably not achievable in any of these counties until the second half of 2008.

The Commerce Department also reported building permits down significantly—also reaching a 10 year low and off 50% from the peak. The same is true locally. That is more troublesome as permits are an indicator of *future* construction. The lower permitting activity suggests that the bottom has not yet been reached in most markets.

ORLANDO ECONOMY REMAINS SOLID

In this county level special report we'll take a fresh look the Metro Orlando economy and how it has fared thus far in the housing slump. We'll look briefly at the county level economy and then explore both residential and commercial real estate markets plus what to watch for going forward.

Orlando (Orange County) and surrounding counties have not totally escaped the economic turmoil resulting from the housing downturn. Nevertheless, it has fared better than some its neighbors as a result of its central location, fundamental economic diversity, perceived quality of life and affordability as well as its continued robust growth.

Metro-Orlando (Orange, Seminole, Lake and Osceola Counties) has an estimated population of 1.96 million persons (2006) in 739,000 households and a labor force estimated to be 1,079,440 persons. The unemployment rate is 3.1% compared to 4.3% for the nation as a whole. These demographics contribute to metro Orlando being one of the nation's top 10 metropolitan areas where it is expected to remain for the foreseeable future. In terms of fastest growing counties nationwide, the U.S. Census Bureau ranks Orange number 19; Lake 43; Osceola 50, and Seminole number 100.

The Housing Sector

Like much of Florida and the nation, Metro Orlando has a residential sector which is significantly overbuilt and seriously impaired. Prices have declined from their peak and more decline is likely. Most of Metro Orlando built longer into the real estate downturn than east central Florida and Treasure Coast counties as far south as, and including, Palm Beach County. As a result, Metro Orlando still a huge residential inventory hangover that must clear before the markets reach equilibrium.

In terms of new housing inventory, which is defined as homes that are finished but vacant plus homes under construction. Orange County

---

experienced "twin peaks" in early 2006. In the first quarter, inventory surged 170% from 7,672 units to 20,709 units has in the first quarter. That was a 25.2 month inventory based upon absorption at the time. Inventory declined slightly in the second quarter but jumped again to 21,535 in the third quarter.

The good news is that closings increased 355% between the fourth quarter of 2005 and the first quarter of 2006. While closings have slowed since, the months of inventory has been reduced from 25.2 to about 10.2 months.

Lake County also spiked in the first quarter of 2006; Osceola County spiked in the third quarter of 2006 but Seminole County kept building and did not spike until a year later in the first quarter of 2007. Today (Q2 2007), Lake has an inventory of 41,956 units which is a 9.1 month supply. Most of these units are finished but vacant (25, 208) while 15,413 are still in the pipeline and under construction.

The Seminole inventory declined in the second quarter and now rests at about 3,830 units and a 9.0 month supply.

Finally, Osceola County, once one of the fasted growing counties in both Florida and the nation has a significant inventory hangover at approximately 9,053 units with a 12.7 month supply.

While Metro Orlando was clearly slow to peak late in the cycle, the strength of the local economy together with forecast robust population growth should allow the market to stabilize in late 2008 barring unforeseen economic shock.

A balanced supply in new residential construction is generally considered to be about three months.

Developed Lots
Metro Orlando has a very significant supply of vacant developed lots which will help fuel a new round of construction at some point in the future. Nevertheless the supply is likely to remain excessive for at least the next two years as this type of product almost never absorbs in an orderly fashion.

Residential Resale Activity
Residential resale activity is occurring but has slowed dramatically. The

following table shows activity in each of the Metro Orlando counties through the end of August 2007.

Housing Affordability

Housing prices rose dramatically in much of Florida during 2004 and 2005 and Metro Orlando was no exception. The rise in prices has clearly priced a significant number of buyers out of the market and Florida—at least temporarily—is no longer recognized for its affordable housing. The following table shows median resale house prices during the first quarter of 2007.

Most sales thus far in 2007 (53%) have been in the $200,000 to $300,000 range. Most offering prices however are in the $300,000 to $400,000 range. This is outside the range typically considered affordable by Metro Orlando's most likely market participants and suggests that additional downward correction is necessary and likely. In our opinion, current asking prices will need to drop another 20% to 25% to meet the marketable price sector. This is consistent with declines actually being witnessed in other demographically similar markets which began correction earlier in the cycle.

The Commercial Sector

In most urban Florida markets, the story of residential and commercial real estate is like a "tale of two cities" where the residential sector has been seriously impaired yet the commercial sector remained strong. The same tale can be told in Metro Orlando. The following are a few Industrial, Retail and Office highlights for Metro Orlando.

Industrial Sector

The Metro Orlando industrial sector is currently stable although there has been evidence of a growing vacancy rate and negative absorption in the flex sector. The warehouse vacancy rate is 6.2% but it is 7.7% in the flex sector. While there was positive net absorption, the flex sector was negative in the second quarter at (130,067) SF and absorption has steadily declined since Q3 2006. Given negative absorption, rising vacancy and slowing absorption in the flex sector, we believe this is a sector to be carefully scrutinized going forward. Warehousing, however, remains strong.

Office Sector

The office sector currently has nearly 2.5 million square feet in the pipeline after absorbing 248,335 square feet in the second quarter but experiencing negative absorption (-153,386)in the first quarter. The sector was exceptionally strong in the second half of 2006 having absorbed over 1.1 million square feet. The suburban markets are clearly the strongest.

Things to Watch Going Forward

The primary commercial product sectors remain relatively healthy. Nevertheless there is evidence of weakening in the form of rising vacancy and slowing absorption. That is curious in the face of increasing rents. Pay close attention. Markets can shift quickly.

SEPTEMBER 27, 2007

INDUSTRIAL SECTOR WEAKENING

The industrial sector—both warehouse and flex space—showed its first signs of weakness this summer as many markets across the country reported negative net absorption and modestly rising vacancy rates. Much of the apparent weakness is a result of the on-going housing slump, loss of jobs in both the construction and manufacturing employment sectors and general economic uncertainty. Is a housing-like crash imminent? No, but the sector is posting the weakest results since emerging from the last recession in 2003. That's enough reason to stay informed and be cautious.

The Society of Industrial and Office Realtors (SIOR) of the National Association of Realtors has tracked industrial and office activity by region and nationally for the last eight quarters. The group's Summer 2007 Commercial Real Estate Index shows that while industrial activity remains positive, there was a steep decline from the previous quarter and the weakest showing in the last eight quarters since SIOR tracking began.

At the same time, the U.S. Bureau of Labor Statistics (BLS) reported a loss of 22,000 construction jobs and 46,000 manufacturing jobs in

---

August. Over the last 12 months, losses in these two sectors have been 96,000 and 215,000 respectively.

While the general economy remains relatively healthy, it too has shown signs of weakness in the last two quarters. All these factors combine to create a wait and see attitude among industrial investor, developer and user groups.

The supply side may be slowing too. The American Institute of Architects (AIA) publishes an architectural billing index which serves as a leading indicator of development activity. The premise of the index is that architectural billings lag construction billings by 9-12 months so a slowdown in billings may portend slower construction in the short-term future. The AIB is quick to point out that while the index has slipped, it does not mean that commercial development is about to dry up.

Nationally, vacancy rates have remained stable at about 8.7%. The warehouse vacancy rate was 8.2% but the flex sector was significantly higher at 12.2%. Quoted rents in the second quarter averaged $5.91 per square foot for warehouse and $10.97 per square foot for flex space.

Demand appears strongest in coastal port areas which serve as distribution centers for imports. The full brunt of residential and construction deterioration has not yet been felt fully in the industrial sector. It is very likely; however, that demand, absorption, vacancy and rents will all be affected in large home building markets—including Florida—as the industry scales back its warehouse leasing requirements.

Most Florida markets have fared better than the national averages. Vacancy rates have only risen modestly. There have been pockets of negative absorption but rents continue to hold up. New construction lease rates have remained firm and even increased modestly in some markets. Lease rates for older space have not been as strong.

Central and South Florida—Market by Market
Occupancy has been strong for the last four years in both Central and South Florida. Space constructed has been readily absorbed at competitive rates and vacancy consistently hovered in the 3.0% range. Vacancy rates have begun to increase modestly and absorption has slowed. Let's look at each market.

Palm Beach County has experienced negative net absorption in three of the last four quarters. Similarly, vacancy rates have increased for the last four quarters. In the warehouse sector, vacancy has increased from 2.6% to 5.7%. The flex sector saw rates increase during the same four quarter period from 4.3% to 5.7%. Palm Beach County closed out the second quarter with nearly 750,000 square feet under construction. We expect absorption to remain negative (albeit less negative) for at least the next two quarters. As an instructional note, negative absorption in all markets needs to be evaluated over multiple quarters to get an accurate reading. In some cases a negative number is a normal time lag and not necessarily evidence of too much inventory.

Going forward, vacancy rates should continue to rise to a level approaching the national level by mid-2008 as markets and the overall economy continue correction. That would put both warehouse and flex space at or near the 8-10% mark.

Broward County absorption turned negative two quarters ago in the flex sector and in the second quarter of 2007 for warehouse. The entire Broward County industrial sector has been strong for about the last four years and has readily absorbed newly created space while maintaining overall vacancy in the mid 3.0% range. Warehouse vacancy has increased from 3.7% to 4.6% since the third quarter of 2006 while flex space vacancy has fluctuated modestly but generally increased from 5.0% to 6.0% in the same four quarter period.

Broward County had nearly 2.6 million square feet of new space in the pipeline at the end of the second quarter.

Broward existing inventory. Nevertheless, it is too much to absorb quickly. As a result, we expect absorption to remain negative for at least the next two or three quarters and the vacancy rate for both warehouse and flex space to increase moderately. Warehouse vacancy of 6-7% and flex vacancy of 7-8% is a reasonable expectation.

Miami-Dade County, like both Palm Beach and Broward counties has had a very strong industrial market. The warehouse vacancy rate reached 8% in the second quarter of 2002 and trended lower until mid-2006 when it began increasing modestly. The vacancy rate for flex space has seen several peaks and valleys but has been consistently higher than warehouse. Flex vacancy peaked at 14% in mid-2001 and began a steady descent to about 5% in mid-2006. Since then it has inched back up to 7%. Absorption was negative in the warehouse sector but positive for flex space in the second quarter of 2007. Flex rents have been relatively high ($15-$16 per square foot) in Miami-Dade—significantly higher than its northern neighbors in Broward and Palm Beach.

Miami-Dade has a significant pipeline of over 3.6 million square feet. Despite high rents and a significant pipeline, we expect this market to remain relatively robust. The vacancy rate will likely increase modestly (6.0—6.5 for warehouse and 8.00—8.5% for flex.

Central Florida—Metro-Orlando (Orange, Seminole, Lake and Osceola counties) has experienced strong absorption, low vacancy and rising rents over the last four years. Absorption in the warehouse sector has consistently remained positive however the flex sector turned negative in the first quarter of 2007. There has also been modest upward movement in flex vacancy however rents are still rising. We would expect rents to stabilize over the short term future.

While the entire sector bears watching, we believe Metro-Orlando will remain solid for the foreseeable future as a result of its continued growth, solid job formation, desirable research and development location as well as its location in the geographical center of Florida. The latter makes it a highly desirable distribution hub as well as a research center.

Economic Indicators, such as overall capitalization rates and discount rates used for valuation and pricing decisions remain low by historic standards in all Central and South Florida markets. That implies that investors continue to have confidence in the geographic market and product sector. The following table sets forth several commonly relied upon rates and ratios which we have gathered from a variety of both published and unpublished sources. We believe that these rates and ratios are indicative of what would be realized in most Central and South Florida markets for new or relatively new warehouse and flex space. Note however, that older space would probably experience rates as much as 100 basis points higher.

ECONOMIC INDICATORS MIXED

Indicators were mixed in September. While housing continues to be a drag on the economy, the nation's Gross Domestic Product (GDP) rose and inflation continued to moderate. Growth in consumer spending remained positive but modest despite housing and credit turmoil. Employment grew in September. Consumer debt rose slightly but credit problems are still largely confined to the housing sector. Consumer prices declined contributing to higher disposable income. While consumer confidence is waning, consumers still remain resilient—at least for now. Despite growing turmoil and uncertainty, most observers continue to believe that the economy has definitely lost momentum but a generalized recession in the near future is unlikely.

New home sales fell 8.3% in August while prices declined by 7% according to data released September 27 by the Commerce Department. Sales declined to a seasonally adjusted annual rate of 795,000—the lowest level since sales dropped to 793,000 in June 2000. Year-to-year sales were also down 21.2%. New home sales have now fallen for six consecutive quarters.

The median price of a new home also fell 7.5% to $225,700. That compares to $246,200 a month earlier and $243,900 a year earlier. The ratio of new houses to total houses sold during the month increased to 8.2% from 7.6% a month earlier. The current supply is estimated to be 529,000 which is an estimated 8.2 month supply.

The National Association of Realtors (NAR) also reported

that pending sales declined 6.5% to the lowest level since 2001. Pending sales, which are based on contracts signed but not yet closed, serve as a leading indicator of existing home sales. Like new home sales, pending sales dropped 21.5% from numbers recorded a year earlier.

Existing home sales declined to 5.5 million, down 4.3% from a month earlier and 12.8% from a year earlier. The median price was $224,500. NAR estimates this to be an approximate 10 month supply based on the current sales pace. NAR considers six months to be a normal supply.

Florida fared no better. Statewide in August, Realtor sales (existing and new) fell 26% from a year earlier. The median sale price was $231,900 which was down six-percent from $246,800 recorded a year earlier.

Local data were consistent with state wide data as shown on the following table (See column 2). Note that not all Seacoast counties have reported data.

The prolonged decline in both sales and prices has clearly had a psychological effect on potential buyers. Many of those who are able to do so are taking a wait and see approach wondering if prices will decline even further. This has clearly slowed sales of both new and existing homes and has contributed

to a larger than normal fallout of pending sales. Housing affordability is out of balance with historical trends as well. Gains in income in recent years were far out stripped by rising home prices. While there has been modest retreat in prices, it will need to be much more significant to jump-start sales.

The psychological effect and affordability are perhaps the two most significant impediments to housing recovery.

Despite the bad housing news, the bottom line for the general economy is that there continues to be no sign that the problems in the housing sector are producing recessionary trends.

Consumer Credit is holding up reasonably well—at least outside of the sub-prime mortgage market. According to the American Bankers Association, consumer delinquency rates across most lines of consumer business have not risen in the last year. One noteworthy exception has been auto indirect loans where delinquencies rose slightly in the second quarter to 2.77%. This is the highest rate in over a decade and the rate has risen modestly for five consecutive quarters. Moreover, the repossession rate has reached 1.87 per 1,000 loans—the highest since 1991. Delinquencies in home equity and second mortgage products declined to 1.99%. Bank card delinquencies also declined modestly to 4.39% of total outstandings.

On the negative side, financial obligations are near a record high and likely to rise further this year. Consumers are generally feeling less wealthy. Home equity borrowing is high and credit card outstandings are growing. The Federal Reserve pegged the consumer financial obligation ratio at 19.29% of disposable income.

Consumer debt coverage ratio was 14.29%—virtually unchanged since the fourth quarter of 2006. Combine that with fragile household budgets and a savings rate near zero and consumer credit will likely deteriorate at least modestly over the next year. While the impact will not be disastrous, it will be measurable, but manageable.

Consumer spending growth rate has weakened. While spending growth remains in positive territory, it has been volatile in recent months and August results were disappointing. Real spending growth dropped to 1.4% on an annualized basis in the second quarter down from 3.5% in the prior two quarters. Growth is likely to remain under two percent for at least the remainder of the year. Growth is under heavy pressure on several fronts including housing, mortgage market uncertainty and energy. Retailers report they are bracing for the weakest holiday shopping season in the last five years.

The weakness in the housing markets and declining values is slowing the growth of household wealth. According to the Federal Reserve's Flow of Funds data, housing wealth has virtually stopped growing. Stock equity wealth continued to prop up household wealth through the second quarter but a slow down there could undermine spending growth. Clearly, most of the factors driving consumer spending have turned more negative and retail sales risks have grown. The importance of consumer spending and the significance of a downturn should not be under estimated as spending accounts for roughly two-thirds of U.S. economic activity.

Looking forward, a downturn in consumer spending may also manifest itself in lower lease rates paid by retailers or slower absorption in—or deferred development of—new retail projects. Retail development has been strong in most Seacoast markets and we'll continue to monitor the retail sector carefully.

Consumer Confidence also declined in August according

to the Conference Board. The index was sharply below expectations and was the lowest reading since November 2005. The Conference Board attributes the sharp decline to weaker business conditions and a less favorable job market.

Employment numbers released today are the bright spot in the economy. Remember the angst last month when the jobs report showed a decline of 4,000 jobs? Today the Bureau of Labor Statistics (BLS) released a revision showing non-farm employment actually *increased* by 89,000 jobs last month. Moreover, employment rose in September by another 110,000 jobs exceeding the consensus of 100,000. BLS now estimates total non-farm payroll at 146.3 million jobs.

A payroll increase of 100,000 jobs represents 1% annual growth. That is below the growth level witnessed in stronger economic times but, by any measure, it is solid. There was also a 2% growth in productivity. Combining the two correlates to a 3% real growth in Gross Domestic Product (GDP).

The BLS also reported today that unemployment remained steady at a still low 4.7%. Five-percent is considered "full" employment so the labor market remains tight.

The nation's service and manufacturing sectors remain strong. While both slowed in September they were still in positive territory. Indeed, according to the Institute for Supply Management (ISM), the service sector hasn't experienced a month of contraction in four years. That's significant as the service sector makes up 80% of U.S. economic activity.

The nation's **Gross Domestic Product** (GDP) rebounded to 3.8% in the second quarter after anemic 0.6% growth in the first quarter. This is a modest 2.2% average. Housing and allied sectors continue to be drags on growth. Modest increase in consumer spending, full employment and business equipment investment all fall on the plus side. GDP growth should still be positive—though modest—at less than 3% and probably nearer 2.5% throughout 2007 and into 2008.

Inflation risk remains benign. Core inflation stands at 1.9% which is within the Fed's zone of tolerance. Core CPI (Consumer Price Index) stands at 2.1%. Labor costs have reached a seven year high of 4.9% but strong profits in most sectors appear to be buffering rising prices and therefore inflation.

Federal Reserve rate cut outlook. On September 18th, the Federal Reserve's Open Market Committee took the bold step of reducing the Fed Funds rate a full 50 basis points in an attempt to bolster housing and credit markets and what appeared at the time to be sagging employment. The Fed's emphasis appears to have shifted from inflation pressures to economic risks. Most observers had forecast another 50 basis point cut by spring of 2008. While the Fed could still do that the most recent employment, GDP and inflation indicators argue against any additional cuts this year.

OCTOBER 27, 2007

HOUSING REMAINS TROUBLED—NO END IN SIGHT

Housing starts nationally hit a 14-year low in September when starts fell another 10%. Still, inventories remain near a 19-year high. With no clear end in sight, the continued slump remains the primary threat to economic health both locally and nationally. While the threat is clear, other sectors are holding up and the overall economy continues to grow as evidenced by a modestly rising Gross Domestic Product (GDP) near 3% and buoyed by low unemployment (4.7%), contained inflation (Core CPI 2.1%) and consumers who continue to spend.

As expected, construction starts fell again in September. Not expected however, was the steep drop of 10% to a seasonally adjusted 1.191 million units annualized. That drop was over twice the 4.2% consensus of some of the nation's leading economists. That's a 14-year low for construction starts. At the same time, the inventory of existing homes offered for sale hit a 19-year high as a homes came on the market much faster than they were being sold. According to the National Association of Realtors (NAR), the current inventory nationally is 4.58 million homes. That's up from 2.15 million as recently as January 2007. Much of that increased inventory, however, is recently finished homes. Just as speculators fueled the run up, speculators are now fueling the growing inventory as they seek to dispose of real estate.

Starts will continue to decline for the next few quarters as builders focus on liquidating bloated inventories and both builders and homeowners adjust to declining prices and inventory imbalance.

Builders are clearly feeling the pain of the housing slump. The downturn has wiped out more than $30Billion in value for the nation's 20 largest builders. Moreover, their share prices are down an average of 65% from the peak and are trading at 0.5% of book value—a level reached only twice before in the last 30 years.

To put some of this in context, on September 25th, Miami based Lennar reported a $513.9 million quarterly loss—the largest in the company's 53 year history. The credit rating firm, Moody's also downgraded Lennar's senior unsecured debt to junk status. Centex and Pulte were also similarly downgraded.

D.R. Horton, the nation's largest builder by number of units recently reported that it's cancellation rate was 48% in its fourth fiscal quarter, up 10% from a quarter earlier. Beazer Homes also announced a 68% cancellation rate.

Both Horton and Beazer cater heavily to entry level buyers—one of the market segments hit hardest by the sub-prime collapse.

There is no clear end in sight—locally or nationally. In Florida, as we've reported previously, builders built 25-40% more homes than there were owners or tenants to occupy them. Building was fueled by lenders eager to lend and buyers who perceived a quick profit opportunity. This was the classic bubble and it burst in 2006 leaving a staggering inventory overhang which will not be absorbed quickly but rather over time.

In addition to the inventory problem, many buyers aren't motivated to buy right now. For some, it is the belief that prices will decline further. For others, it is the inability to sell another home or to obtain financing. For still others, it is affordability.

In-migration to Florida has also slowed as Florida's "feeder markets" in the Northeast and Midwest experience some of the same housing and buyer motivation problems Florida is facing and potential buyers no longer perceive Florida to be a haven of affordability.

Locally in Central and South Florida, builders tell us that selling a production home for delivery in the future is exceedingly difficult if not impossible today. As a result, some have closed sales offices or otherwise suspended sales of all but existing inventory or homes nearing completion.

The inventory problem could also be compounded by foreclosures as roughly $1.0Trillion in adjustable rate mortgages reset between now and mid-2008. Many (though certainly not all) owners may not be able to tolerate what will almost certainly be higher payments. Nationally, foreclosures jumped to 223,538 in September, double the number a year earlier. The foreclosure rate is now 1 for every 557 households and 1 in 7 sub-prime loans is currently delinquent Florida now ranks second (behind California) in number of foreclosures.

Where do we go from here? Many builders have now taken the extraordinary step of slashing prices to jump start sales and hopefully shorten the slump. Depending upon the location and home features, some builders have cut prices from 10% to 30%—most near the upper end of the range. Discounts for higher priced homes have reached into six-digits. This is clearly the first time that builders have taken such aggressive action of cutting prices all at once rather than letting them drift lower over time. As the large production builders now have the collective size and influence to move the market—something they have never had before—they may, in fact, hold the keys to housing recovery.

The new price slashing strategy is not without risk to the builders and not without serious adverse impact on existing homeowners. From the builders' perspective, buyers who contracted earlier and put up a nominal deposit, will almost certainly cancel and sacrifice their deposit. If, for example, a buyer had a 10% deposit at risk and prices are cut 30%, that buyer may sacrifice the deposit and re-contract at a lower price or contract with another builder.

The obvious question becomes how can builders cut that far? As prices were running up and nearly out of control through 2005, builder margins were often as much as 35%. Today, they are virtually nil. Nevertheless, builders must take swift action to get inventory off their books and stop the extraordinary cash outflows which, over time, will do more damage to builders and no doubt prolong the slump prolong the downturn. Liquidating quickly, rather than incurring long-term holding costs is oftentimes the most cost effective strategy.

On the consumer side, rapid price slashing will likely have a profoundly negative effect on property values. Homeowners are typically reluctant to reduce their asking prices hoping that prices will rebound in the short-term.

If builders continue the extreme price slashing strategy, homeowners will be forced to follow suit. A bitter pill, indeed, but an economic reality nonetheless. The excesses of the housing bubble must be wrung out of the market before it can recover. The good news is that despite the almost universal pain, builder price cutting may, indeed, be a critical and much needed step toward a successful and hastened recovery.

While the housing slump clearly has the potential of deepening and spilling over to the general economy, as of this writing, that has not happened and recession is not a foregone conclusion. All of the nation's fundamental economic indicators remain relatively healthy. The nation is enjoying healthy government spending, healthy corporate profits outside of real estate, banking and finance and positive, albeit modest, new job formation. We have low unemployment at 4.7% and inflation appears under control at 2.1%. Both are at the high end but still within the Fed's so-called *zone of tolerance*. The risk for short term inflation is benign largely because the nation is currently producing under-capacity despite the fact that both industrial production and productivity are up modestly.

On the downside, according to The Conference Board, consumer confidence has slipped and builder confidence, as measured by the National Association of Home Builders, is at an all-time low. Retail spending is up very modestly but retailers are bracing for the weakest holiday shopping season in the last five years.

The Gross Domestic Product (GDP) is still firm solid measuring +3.8% (annualized) in the second quarter after a very anemic first quarter. Nevertheless housing, which normally contributes about one-percent to GDP is becoming a drag on economic growth.

NOVEMBER 1, 2007

WILL COMMERCIAL REAL ESTATE FOLLOW RESIDENTIAL?

Nineteenth century author Charles Dickens opened his historical novel, *A Tale of Two Cities* with the words, *"It was the best of times, it was the worst of times ... "* These same words could describe the state of Treasure

Coast commercial and residential real estate the last couple of years. It was the best of times for commercial real estate and the worst of times for residential.

It was the best of times for commercial real estate. Most market sectors were experiencing widespread growth which was both steady and orderly. Newly constructed space was rapidly absorbed into the marketplace. Rents were increasing steadily but modestly while vacancy rates remained low. It was, as Dickens might have said, the best of times.

Contrast that with residential real estate. After several years of unprecedented growth, unrestrained price escalation, and the formation of a classic economic bubble, the market came crashing down when the bubble burst in 2006. Since then, it has been the worst of times.

In the lexicon of real estate economics, the demand for housing is referred to as "primary demand" while the demand for commercial space such as retail, office and industrial is termed "secondary demand." Simply stated, everyone needs housing but not everyone needs retail, office or industrial space. These uses follow residential development. If residential development surges, commercial development will soon follow. Conversely, if residential development slows or stops, the demand for commercial is also likely to follow.

The big fear has been that commercial real estate would meet the same fate as the residential sector. While the commercial sector has slowed and is clearly showing signs of weakness, there is no current evidence to suggest that commercial real estate will experience the same level of distress the residential sector has.

Why? Commercial growth has been much more orderly and restrained. There has not been the extraordinary overbuilding that the residential sector experienced and it follows that any decline will experience a much softer landing. Let's look at the current commercial weaknesses.

During the residential run up, builders and their sub-contractors sought office and warehouse space for their own growing businesses. Some rented, some bought. That led to expansion of both office and warehouse space either for rental or in the form of condominium ownership. Affiliated industries sought space in a similar fashion. Real estate businesses, title companies, mortgage companies and similar services grew. Today there is much less demand as some businesses contract and others cease to do business. Additionally, the rate of job formation has slowed thus undercutting the demand for space. As a direct result, vacancy rates have increased, rental rates have flattened and vacant space tends to remain vacant longer. Owners are currently more willing to offer concessions to prospective tenants. Condominium warehouse and office unit sales are currently slow and many of those units have returned to the rental pool on the Treasure Coast.

Shopping center developers often say that "retail follows roof tops." In other words, retail development goes where the new residential development is. Not surprisingly, retail development has slowed. The slowdown has been further compounded regionally and nationally by slower retail spending by consumers.

While retail spending growth remains in positive territory, retailers are bracing for the slowest holiday selling season in the last five years. Those factors have clearly slowed retail leasing activity which will almost certainly slow retail real estate development.

As commercial development slows, it follows that land for commercial development will also slow. Since the value of land is directly related to the value of the finished product, it follows that if there is no demand for the finished commercial real estate product, there will also be diminished demand for the land. As land is a non-earning asset, values will very likely decline over time.

Since last August, there has been a lot of bad news about the credit markets, both commercial and residential. The commercial problems however, have been largely confined to the Commercial Mortgage Backed Securities (CMBS) market where loans—usually large loans—are packaged into securities and sold to investors. The CMBS market remains tight but there are signs the pressure is easing.

The effect of CMBS market tightening has been felt in a limited way on the Treasure Coast largely because the majority of commercial transactions are neither the size nor the type that are packaged and sold. For the most part, commercial real estate loans are available on the Treasure Coast for creditworthy borrowers and for projects that are economically sound. Borrowers should expect to make a significant equity contribution, have reasonable personal liquidity and if it is a proposed rental project, expect your lender to impose a precon-struction leasing requirement.

Finally, ad valorem taxes, insurance and impact fees are exacerbating an already soft market. The pressure is being felt not only on the Treasure Coast but throughout the state as lawmakers wrestle with tax reform, insurance costs sky-rocket as a result of widespread hurricane losses in 2004 and 2005 and local governments seek to cover expected budget short-falls with impact fees on anything from roads to recreation.

NOVEMBER 26, 2007

TRENDS IN OFFICE REAL ESTATE

Until recently, most commercial real estate sectors seemed almost immune to the residential downturn. Rents and sales prices rose steadily, absorption was consistently strong, financing was readily available and capitalization and discount rates were unusually low. The big fear was—and remains—that the effect of the residential problem would spill over into the commercial sector. To some extent, those fears have been real-ized. All commercial real estate product types and Seacoast geographic markets have shown initial signs of weakness. Most deterioration has been modest but nevertheless caution is warranted. Let's look at the economics driving the office sector today and where today's data sug-gest it is heading into 2008.

Take a snapshot of the office market today and you'll see a picture of overall health and stability. Watch the entire movie though, and you may see a different story— a story that shows emerging signs of weak-ness and unambiguous clues suggesting that tomorrow's commercial market may not be nearly as robust as yesterday's.

Real estate—all sectors—is critically linked to the overall economy so many of the clues to the short term future of commercial real estate lie in the economic indicators.

Employment growth, for example, has slowed significantly this year. According to the Bureau of Labor Statistics (BLS) non-farm job growth was about 100,000 in September and 166,000 in October. The October number will almost certainly be revised down and preliminary indications are that November will be less than 100,000 and December will be at or near 70,000. These lower numbers are dismal when compared to the 2006 and early 2007 monthly average growth of about 189,000 jobs. Why the decline? The residential real estate downturn which was made worse by the sub-prime implosion last summer is now showing up in the job numbers. Housing related job *losses* are now averaging about 30,000 per month. That number, however, may significantly under-state reality. Large numbers of people in or allied to the real estate industry are independent contractors and don't get counted in the BLS numbers. Moreover, they are not eligible for unemployment claims so they are not being counted in jobless claims either.

Many builders, too, have been holding the line on job losses as displaced residential trades people have shown up in the commercial sector. Now it appears unlikely that builders can continue to do so and more cuts appear likely. Job losses, particularly in housing and allied industries, are likely to continue to show up as the full effect of the housing decline takes hold. Many observers forecast that job growth will likely average less than 100,000 per month through 2008. Indeed, Moody's is forecasting significantly subdued growth of about 83,000 per month. Combine that with the *phantom job losses* of currently uncounted independent contractors and the reality may, in fact, be much worse than what is currently reported and forecast for 2008. The effect will likely be more pronounced in Florida where employment is more heavily dependent on the service sector including construction and real estate.

Slowing employment growth ripples through the commercial real estate sector in a variety of ways. One significant impact is that with slower employment growth (or worse yet, negative growth) comes diminished demand for office space. While the full effect has not shown up in the local numbers—and probably won't for several more quarters—there is evidence that growth is slowing throughout most Seacoast markets. That is not surprising since employment is so heavily skewed toward the service sector.

Looking at the tri-county South Florida office market (Palm Beach, Broward and Miami-Dade counties), total office vacancies have risen to 9.0% from their recent (Q1 2006) low of slightly over 3%. Overall absorption also turned negative by 104,235 square feet in the third quarter after showing positive absorption of 504,208 in the second quarter.

Palm Beach County Office. Drilling deeper into the numbers, Palm Beach County experienced negative net absorption of 48,952 square feet. The county ended the third quarter with a slightly higher vacancy of 11.6%. The vacancy rate has been climbing slowly since late 2005 when overall office absorption was about 8%. The highest vacancy rate is now in Class A space in the central business district at 14.1%. That class is experiencing one of the highest quoted average rental rates in south Florida at $32.31 per square foot—second only to downtown Miami at $32.53 per square foot. Suburban office rents are being quoted lower at about $28 per square foot. Additionally, an estimated 19.9% of leased office space will expire in 2008 followed by 21% in 2009.

The total employment growth rate in Palm Beach County dropped from slightly over 5% in 2005 to less than 2% today. The office employment growth rate dropped from about 8.4% to about 1% during the same time period. Countywide, Palm Beach County has over 2.5 million square feet of office space under construction with a reported 1.9 million square feet un-leased at the end of the third quarter Capitalization rates averaged 6.67% in Q3 2007 as compared to 6.51% for all of 2006.

Broward County ended the third quarter with an overall vacancy rate of 8.8% and negative net absorption of 334,167 square feet. All classes (A, B and C) experienced negative absorption in the third quarter after having achieved positive absorption in the second quarter. The central business district fared the best and suburban the worst with nearly all (330,401 square feet) located in the suburbs. The county currently has slightly over 2.0 million square feet under construction.

Quoted rental rates for Class-A space averaged $30.94 per square foot in the third quarter while Class-B and C averaged $23.41 and $20.67 respectively.

Capitalization rates have been trending higher in the last few quarters ending the third quarter at 7.33% as compared to 7.0% in 2006.

According to research by CoStar, approximately 19.2% of leased office (square footage) will expire in 2008 followed by another 18.2% in 2009.

The total employment growth rate in Broward County has fallen from a high of about 4.8% growth in 2005 to about 1.0% today. More significantly, office employment growth has fallen from 7.0% in 2005 to negative 0.5%

Metro-Orlando's vacancy rate also inched up to 9.2% from a recent low of 7.8% in mid-2006. The vacancy trend, though upward, has not been nearly as steep as south Florida counties. The average quoted rental rate in the four county metro areas (Orange, Seminole, Lake and Osceola) was $22.12 per square foot. Class-A space is higher but remains significantly below south Florida at $25.06 per square foot. Class-B and C rates stood at $21.06 and $18.51 per square feet respectively. That is significantly below Palm Beach but not quite as far behind Broward.

Metro-Orlando experienced positive net absorption of 55,350 square feet in the third quarter. While absorption was positive, the total was less than half of what was experienced in earlier quarters in 2007. It was also 88% less than the 475,756 absorbed in the fourth quarter of 2006. That quarter was an aberration, though, as the 419,267 square foot Bank of America building sold for a record $96,250,000 or $229.57 per square foot on a reported cap rate of 5.11%. (The average sale price in Metro-Orlando was $189.91 per square foot with a cap rate of 6.52).

Metro-Orlando currently has an estimated 2,482,125 square feet of office space under construction. By CoStar's count, 12.4% of existing leases will expire in 2008 followed by 19.5% in 2009 and 22% in 2010.

Unlike South Florida where capitalization rates have been inching up, Metro-Orlando rates declined to an average of 6.52% from 7.01% in 2006. On the surface, that might imply a stronger market. More likely, however, the market has not yet begun to correct.

The metro area's job growth rate has fallen from 6.0% to 2.5% at the end of October. The change in the office employment growth rate was much greater having dropped from a recent high of 8% in 2005 to about 1.5% today.

The office sector appears poised for correction. Office pricing has grown too fast and too high and clearly needs to adjust downward. Local South and Central Florida markets appear highly vulnerable to a demand slowdown. It will be driven by slower or non-existent office employment growth together with a high level of inventory under construction, slowing absorption and significant amounts of existing lease space expiring over the next one to three years. These variables will put downward pressure on rents and absorption.

Palm Beach County appears poised for the largest and earliest correction. The average rental rate (all classes) is now $28.88 per square foot and is now among the highest in the state, second only to Miami-Dade ($29.27). Combine that with an 11.6% vacancy rate; 2.5 million square feet of new space under construction; 40% of currently leased space expiring in the next two years and significant impairment by late 2008 seems likely. Factor in modestly rising expenses and cap rate growth of 50 to 100 basis points and an overall value decline possibly as high as 20% appears likely based on today's emerging evidence.

Broward County growth has been significant but more restrained than Palm Beach. Nevertheless, office employment growth is now negative and the county has approximately 2.0 million square feet under construction. That, combined with rising expenses and capitalization rates plus over 37% of currently leased space expiring over the next two years all lead us to believe that a downward correction near 10-15% is likely over the next 12-18 months.

Central Florida tends to lag South Florida anywhere from 12-24 months. The current office market is no exception. Rents continue to increase modestly and capitalization rates have actually declined. Nevertheless, office employment growth has dipped to 1.5% while there is currently almost 2.5 million square feet of new space under construction and 32% of existing leased space is scheduled to expire in 2008 and 2009. Also highly noteworthy is that another 22% of leased space will expire in 2010. That is over 50% of currently leased space expiring over the next three years.

The Metro-Orlando office market should flatten in 2008. Without very significant absorption or some other yet unidentified mitigant emerging in 2008, a significant correction may emerge in 2009 as leases expire and vacancies climb. A downward correction of 10-15% may emerge by mid-2009 and the market will probably remain flat through 2010.

High occupancy existing projects, especially those with long term leases should ride out the emerging dislocation. Established medical and health care facilities where tenants are less likely to relocate are also likely to emerge relatively unscathed.

Financing will be more difficult to obtain as both investors and portfolio lenders return to *"back to basics"* underwriting. Lenders will continue to require significantly more equity as they factor in a high probability of declining values into the underwriting equation.

DECEMBER 18, 2007

ECONOMIC INDICATORS SIGNAL RECESSION

The housing slump continues to deepen as inventories and foreclosures rise. The Gross Domestic Product (GDP) hit a five year *high* when it was revised upward to 4.9% (annualized) for the third quarter. That level of growth, however, is not sustainable. Don't look for a near-term repeat. Inflation accelerated with the Consumer Price Index (CPI) rising 0.8%. Core CPI, which excludes food and energy, rose 0.2% in November. Employment growth is slowing as the effect of the housing slump shows up in the numbers. The spending increase will likely be revised down. Consumers are under stress on almost every economic front. With home equity dissipating and savings near zero, many consumers are turning to credit cards. Could that be the next bubble to burst? Let's look behind the numbers.

The nation's Gross Domestic Product (GDP), widely regarded as the most comprehensive measure of economic activity was revised upward from 3.9% to 4.9% for the third quarter. That was after very anemic growth (0.6%) in the first quarter and a rebound to 3.8% in the second quarter. The surprising third quarter growth, however, was fueled by exports and inventories both of which were unusually high and together added 1.28% to the GDP.

The big plus in revised Q3 GDP could actually be a minus in disguise. Inventories surged at an annual rate of $40 Billion which is nearly double the rate of the previous year. That implies that inventories are not moving as expected which could cause companies to reduce both output and employment in order to reduce inventory.

The nominal GDP in the third quarter totaled approximately $13.927 trillion and breaks down as follows: GDP growth is widely expected to retreat to less than 1.8% the fourth quarter and hover near 2.0% through most of 2008 as both business spending and consumer consumption moderate. While all components of the GDP remain in positive territory, there is significant economic stress. Consumers are now being negatively affected by slower job creation, declining home equity, rising food and energy prices, rising debt levels and slowing wage growth. These pressures have manifested themselves in slightly slower spending growth.

Retail spending also took a surprising jump of 1.2% in November. This is after having virtually stalled (+0.2%) in October. The gains were relatively broad based including department stores and big ticket retailers like furniture and appliances. Sales of furniture, appliances and home improvement items have declined for most of 2007 as the housing crisis has gained strength. The fact that two of the three categories grew could be an aberration caused by an earlier than usual Thanksgiving holiday and a retail sales blitz in advance of *Black Friday*, the traditional start of the holiday selling season. The trend in spending growth has been negative throughout 2007 so the November numbers seem too good to be true. Next month's spending numbers will tell a more complete story.

Business investment, a 10.7% contribution to the GDP, has been volatile all year ranging from an 11% gain in the second quarter to (−1%) thus far in the fourth. Despite the volatility, what is becoming clear is that corporate profits are under pressure, even outside of real estate and financial sectors. Indeed, domestic corporate earnings have steadily (and sharply) declined since the third quarter of 2006 while profits derived from overseas operations have risen. Until recently, companies have enjoyed high liquidity, low debt and strong cash flows—all underpinnings of strong corporate growth and a major impetus for both hiring and capital investment. Thus far in 2007, earnings of domestic corporations have fallen 8.3% which is the biggest decline since the last recession (2002). At the same time, profits from overseas operations have risen sharply—about 35%. This is consistent with the broader U.S.

economy which has under-performed the world economy since 2002. Declining domestic profits clearly puts a squeeze on both employment growth and spending—especially capital spending.

The *Business Roundtable* released its fourth quarter CEO Economic Outlook Survey earlier this month. The Business Roundtable is an association of executive officers of leading corporations representing a combined work force of 10 million employees and $4.5 trillion in annual revenues. Most survey respondents expect steady economic conditions for the next six months despite a variety of pressures on the economy. Indeed, 70% of companies expect their sales to increase in the next six months; 51% expect no change in capital spending and 45% expect no change in employment in their U.S. operations.

Inflation accelerated in November at its fastest pace in 10 months. The CPI jumped 0.8%. That leaves the total CPI 4.3% higher than a year ago and the core CPI, which excludes the volatile food and energy components, up 2.2% from a year ago—slightly exceeding the Fed's comfort zone of less than 2%. That is the first core CPI increase since January.

Individually, gasoline prices jumped 9.3%, electric 0.6%, and food prices increased 0.3%. Medical care prices grew 0.4% while clothing prices were up 0.8%. Transportation jumped 2.9% during the month.

In a separate report, the Labor Department reported that weekly earnings for U.S. workers fell 0.4% while average hourly earnings increased 0.5%.

Employment growth has slowed this year. According to the Bureau of Labor Statistics (BLS) 94,000 new jobs were created in November. That was in line with expectations. October job growth was revised up to 170,000 and 100,000 jobs were created in September. Expectations for December are lower at about 70,000. These lower numbers are dismal when compared to the 2006 and early 2007 monthly average growth of about 189,000 jobs. Nevertheless, they are still positive and further support the forecast that near-term recession is unlikely.

Why the decline? The residential real estate downturn which was made worse by the sub-prime implosion last summer is now showing up in the job numbers. Housing related job *losses* are now averaging about

30,000 per month. That number, however, may significantly understate reality. Large numbers of people in, or allied to, the real estate industry are independent contractors and don't get counted in the BLS numbers. Moreover, they are not eligible for unemployment so they are not being counted in jobless claims either.

Many builders, too, have been holding the line on job losses as displaced residential trades people have shown up in the commercial sector. Now it appears unlikely that builders can continue to do so and more cuts appear likely.

Job losses, particularly in housing and allied industries, are likely to continue to show up as the full effect of the housing decline takes hold. Many observers forecast that job growth will likely average less than 100,000 per month through 2008. Indeed, Moody's is forecasting significantly subdued growth of about 83,000 per month. Nevertheless, job growth has a long way to fall before reaching recession levels. For example, the last time the economy hit bottom was in November of 2001. Then, the change in payroll employment was negative 1.1%

The bottom line is that slower payroll growth plus the phantom job losses of uncounted independent contractors may result in a worse job situation than is actually being reported and forecast for 2008.

Unemployment continues to hover at 4.7% for the third consecutive month. The probable outlook for 2008, however, is for higher unemployment as the economy slows. Look for unemployment to rise to about 5.2% by late 2008.

Home equity has declined significantly as real estate sales slow and values decline. Tighter mortgage standards and higher mortgage related costs combine to decrease the volume of mortgage lending. This has created a significant shift in consumer borrowing. Year over year growth in mortgage borrowing slowed 8.0%—less than two-thirds of the pace a year ago and the slowest pace since 1998. At the same time, consumer borrowing—especially credit card borrowing—has increased. This change in the composition of household liabilities is clearly apparent in the accompanying chart..

Is credit card debt the next bubble to burst? Last summer's sub-prime mortgage implosion involved roughly $900 billion in now suspect securitized debt. That melt down was the result of several years of heavy marketing, uncontrolled and reckless lending coupled with poor or non-existent underwriting.

At the same time, credit card debt—most of which is also securitized—grew nearly $100 billion to a staggering $920 billion today. That total is eerily similar to the subprime total.

Signs of stress in the card sector are starting to appear. Until recently, consumers were able to tap home equity to repay credit card debt. Home equity, however, has declined dramatically coincident with the housing slowdown and there is mounting evidence many consumers have turned to credit cards to make ends meet. Indeed, VISA, Master-Card and American Express all report greater use of cash advances and mounting card debt.

Credit card delinquency rates have not risen … yet. In fact, they have held remarkably steady at, or very near 4.4% for the last 18 months. Nevertheless, the major card issuers appear to be positioning themselves for higher delinquencies. American Express, for example, raised its reserves 44% last quarter in its core US card unit. Washington Mutual, Bank of America and Capital One all reported they expect at least a 20% increase in delinquencies in the near and mid-term. Citigroup also reserved $2.24 Billion last quarter for mounting consumer credit losses.

Why is card debt so important? It is the last source of borrowing power for many consumers. With little or no home equity available, a savings rate near zero and consumers currently spending nearly 100% of income, if cash availability from credit cards dries up, delinquencies will almost certainly increase. Additionally, credit card defaults will increase and consumer spending will slow. That scenario could have an adverse effect on the broader economy.

2008
OVER THE EDGE AND INTO THE DEPTHS OF RECESSION

By 2008, the nation was very clearly in recession. The only questions were how long would it last and how deep would it be? As the year wore on, those answers became apparent. It would be broader, deeper and more severe than any downturn since the Great Depression of the 1930s; some 70+ years earlier. The recession also expanded globally.

With little doubt, 2008 was the worst year of the recession and perhaps arguably, the worst year in American economic history. In what proved later to be a vain attempt to stimulate activity by injecting liquidity into the market, the Federal Reserve lowered short term interest rates to three-percent. That was the fifth time in a mere four months it had taken that action. In fact, as early as September the rate had been 5.25%. By the end of October and several more drops, the rate reached one-percent.

In July, the government took over IndyMac, a California bank that made loans to persons who could not prove their income. These loans became known pejoratively as "liar loans." The IndyMac failure became one of the largest and most expensive thrift failures ($10.7 billion) in American history. That was quickly surpassed by the Washington Mutual failure in September. WAMU branches and assets were sold to J.P. Morgan Chase. A total of 25 banks failed in 2008. That was eclipsed by the 133 that failed the following year in 2009.

The federal government attempted stimulus in a very wide and expensive number of ways including guaranteeing $30 billion of Bear Stearns debt in connection with that company's March 16th failure. It was bought out by J.P. Morgan Chase. Around the same time Bank of America agreed (reportedly with government pressure) to buy Countrywide Financial in a deal valued at about $4 billion. Fines, restitution and other penalties levied against Bank of America since then in connection with the actions of Countrywide eclipse the actual purchase price. On September 15th, Bank of America also agreed to buy Merrill Lynch for $50 million.

On September 7th, the federal government took over government sponsored enterprise (GSE) mortgage giants Fannie Mae and Freddie Mac and put them into conservatorship. Roughly a week later, Lehman Brothers filed the largest bankruptcy in U.S. history and sent global markets into chaos. Only a day later, the Fed bailed out insurance giant AIG and less than three weeks after that President Bush signed into law emergency bailout legislation which became the $7 billion TARP, Troubled Asset Relief Program. At the time the precise purpose of the law and how funds would actually be used were unclear. Nevertheless, the federal government seemed desperate to throw money at an enormous and steadily growing problem. Still more money was thrown at the problem in late November when the Fed created the TALF program or the Term Asset-Backed Securities Lending Facility which was designed to prop up securities backed by credit card debt, student loans, auto loans and small business loans.

For the first time in history, the Fed lowered its benchmark interest rate to zero. Around the same time, the government bailed out both General Motors and Chrysler with an initial $13.4 billion to GM and $4.0 billion to Chrysler. Funds came from which came from the previously approved TARP Program.

By the fall of 2008, the American banking system was in freefall and was arguably near collapse. If allowed to happen, global recession and economic havoc would have been the outcome.

MARCH 3, 2008

RECESSION WATCH

The question in many minds is *"are we in, or are we near"* a recession." The short answer is yes. We are probably in a recession and it probably began in November or December of 2007. For nearly two years we've watched as residential real estate inventories grew to record highs while sales and construction starts tumbled to record lows. We've watched consumer spending as well as business investment and production growth slip and consumer confidence tumble to a 15 year low. We've watched the nation's gross domestic product growth rate slip to 0.6% in the fourth quarter after readings of 3.8% and 4.9% in the second and third quarters respectively. Finally, we've watched the labor market contract for the last year and watched it fall into negative territory with a loss of 17,000 jobs in the fourth quarter of 2007. Let's look behind the numbers.

The Business Cycle Dating Committee (BCDC) of the National Bureau of Economic Research (NBER) is the arbiter of the U.S. business cycle. This group of academics maintains a chronology of cycles and identifies the peaks and troughs that frame an economic expansion or contraction. The period from a peak to a trough is a recession and the period between a trough and a peak is an expansion.

The BCDC does not forecast. Instead, it monitors economic activity and generally does not declare either an expansion or contraction (recession) until the economy is actually in one phase or the other. Given that retrospective view, the committee may not declare the start of a recession for 6-18 months after it begins.

The committee views a recession as a significant and persistent decline in economic activity *across* the economy and not confined to one sector. It views the Gross Domestic Product (GDP) as the single best indicator of broad economic activity. One widely publicized criterion for recession is two consecutive quarters of decline in real GDP. While that is generally true, it is not the only measure the BCDC uses. Rather it uses a variety of measures including income, employment, retail and wholesale spending, industrial production and more.

The housing downturn which began in early 2006, was regarded as a single sector recession as most other economic indicators remained strong into 2007. By mid-year, however, the impact was starting to be felt in the commercial real estate markets as well as in employment and other sectors. In August 2007, the subprime mortgage sector collapsed and the effect flowed into the credit markets in general. Other economic sectors, both locally and nationally, began to weaken and the economy came to a virtual standstill in December 2007.

The downturn has not been universal. While Florida has experienced significant impairment in the housing sector with growing inventories, foreclosures and falling home prices, many other communities have not. Indeed, prices are rising in markets where 65% of the U.S. population lives. Nevertheless, economic stress is widespread and it now seems probable that the committee will declare that a recession began in late 2007.

Gross Domestic Product. The GDP is the total of all goods and services and perhaps the broadest measure of the economy. Over 70% of what the U.S produces is for personal consumption. The remaining 30% is business investment (16%) and government spending at 19% (the total does not add to 100% due to the effect of exports and inventories). Given the large share of GDP which is consumer driven we can conclude that *"as the consumer goes, so goes the economy."* The table to the left shows annualized GDP growth for each quarter in 2007.

The consumer segment of the GDP has grown from 68% in 1999 to a high of 72% earlier in 2007. That is far higher than other developed economies such as Germany where consumer spending accounts for 59% of the GDP; Japan where it is 57%, and the UK at 66%. As American consumers wind down their decade long spending spree, we expect the consumer consumption portion of the GDP to retreat to around 68% over the next 24-36 months. The dollar impact equates to about $125 billion for each 1% decline in consumer consumption.

Also in the fourth quarter, residential outlays declined 24%. While expected, it reduced the GDP by 1.2%. Not expected in the fourth quarter was a contraction in business inventories which took another 1.25% off the GDP. For the year, GDP growth was 2.21%.

Caution is very high for the next few quarters. The housing sector remains a key risk as does tightening credit in general and the continued impairment in the mortgage market in particular. Foreclosures are expected to accelerate until at least mid-2008 as subprime adjustable rate mortgages originated in 2005 adjust. The rate of foreclosure should decline later this year.

Delayed business investment, driven by the slow growth economy, is also an important economic risk and will remain a drag on the GDP for the next few quarters. Finally, consumer spending is under pressure;

especially from food and energy.

While we believe the economy has entered a recession, the good news is most key indicators—though weak—remain in positive territory suggesting that this recession will be shallow and short lived much like March through November 2001. Mortgage market and Given softness in nearly every sector of the economy, however, we expect GDP growth to be modest (about 1.5%) in 2008. Our outlook is for weak but positive growth.

Employment growth steadily contracted throughout 2007. By the third quarter, the economy produced a modest 18,000 new non-farm jobs. By the fourth quarter, however, growth turned negative with a *loss* of 17,000 jobs—the lowest since the end of 2003 when the economy was emerging from its last post-recession slump. To put this in perspective, the country produced about 160,000 jobs monthly throughout 2006. In 2008, job gains are expected to average about 35,000 per month.

Job losses were broad based. The construction industry loss was the most severe (see chart) and is now at its lowest level since the early 1990's during the housing decline of that decade. Wage growth has slowed as well. Average hourly earnings are still rising but much more moderately (+3.7% in January 2007 as compared to +4.3% in January 2006).

Unemployment has increased from its cyclical low of 4.4% in March 2007 to its current high of 4.9%. Historically, a recession has always occurred following unemployment growth of this magnitude. Elevated unemployment is a key driver that touches off the series of events that characterize a recession. Increased joblessness undermines consumer confidence and therefore consumer spending. As consumers slow spending, sales sag, business sentiment slumps and firms cut back on investment and payrolls leading to even greater unemployment. It is a vicious cycle that feeds on itself until the cycle is broken. Unemployment will likely rise to about 6.0% during 2008 as job growth continues to slow and the general economy weakens.

New jobless claims rose to 373,000 last week. That is an increase from 354,000 the prior week. New claims of 400,000 are generally considered recessionary. The rising trend in layoffs appears to have begun in December. Continuing jobless claims lag initial claims by a week but they too are trending upward ending the week of February 16th at 2.807 million.

All of the job numbers clearly suggest that the labor market has weakened. Indeed, employment is probably the single most significant indicator to tip the scale toward recession.

Phantom Unemployment refers to a component of jobless persons not counted in the payroll numbers. These are predominately independent contractors, many of whom were allied to the real estate industry as agents, mortgage brokers, construction trades people and others. Many rode the wave up as housing sales and prices skyrocketed from 2003-2005. Many of those same people, however, are no longer working. Because they were independent contractors, they are not eligible for unemployment compensation and are therefore not counted in the payroll numbers. The precise number of people in this category is unknown but is believed to be significant. The most significant effect of so-called phantom unemployment lies in its negative impact on consumer spending.

Consumer Confidence, as measured by The Conference Board dipped sharply in January. With the exception of the period immediately following the 2003 invasion of Iraq, confidence is now at a 15 year low, clearly indicating that the sluggish economy is taking its toll on consumer attitudes. The decline was driven largely by energy prices, deteriorating housing markets and slower employment growth. Especially noteworthy was the number of respondents saying that jobs were hard to get. This response increased to 23.8%. The deterioration was evident across all questions asked in the survey. Consumer opinions of the labor market fell sharply as did intent to buy a new car. Consumers are also expecting lower inflation and lower interest rates than they were in January. Confidence fell across all age and income groups with the exception of the lowest income group.

The consumer confidence responses correlate tightly with spending and suggest that spending will decline going forward. Finally, the sharp decline in consumer sentiment is consistent with a mild recession.

Core retail sales growth has slowed to its weakest pace in over five years since recovery from the last recession. When spending initially began to slow last year, the decline was sharp but generally confined to big ticket items such as appliances, furniture, building supplies and department store goods and services. Today, consumers are cutting their spending on a much broader list of non-essentials.

Sales at grocery stores posted a strong gain but that was largely due to rapidly rising food prices. That gain also came at the expense of restaurants where sales were down implying that more consumers are eating at home. Electronics and appliance stores posted the weakest results in five years and consumers traded down from department stores to warehouse clubs and other deep discounters. Curiously, Wal Mart reported that gift cards were being redeemed for food and essentials rather than discretionary purchases which is more often the case.

Spending began to falter after housing prices began to decline and home equity virtually dried up. As we've written before, spending was being kept alive by consumer homeowners with home equity lines of credit. When mortgage equity withdrawal (MEW) slowed, so did retail spending. The chart at the right shows the very tight correlation between falling house prices and retail spending.

MARCH 12, 2008

EMPLOYMENT DECLINES NATIONALLY AND IN FLORIDA

The economy lost 63,000 jobs in February following a loss of 22,000 jobs (revised down from −17,000) in January. That is the steepest decline in five years. The loss could have been larger— over 100,000 jobs—had it not been for a significant increase in government employment. The unemployment rate fell from 4.9% to 4.8%. The Labor Department reported that 450,000 people left the labor force in February which accounts for the slight downward movement in the unemployment rate in the face of job losses. Florida had a net loss of 7,300 jobs in January. Construction lost 69,000 payroll jobs year over year (-10.9%). Construction losses accounted for 75% of the job losses in the state over the year. Manufacturing and financial services saw job losses while education, health services and leisure/hospitality saw modest gains. While still unofficial, The *Employment Situation* report leaves little doubt that the economy has slipped into recession.

Perhaps the most important economic indicator is *The Employment*

Situation report published on the first Friday of every month by the Bureau of Labor Statistics (BLS). No other economic release is more revealing of general economic conditions than labor market data. It is the first major report of each month and is closely linked to other economic indicators. The data tell us a great deal about how businesses view the current and short term future economic environment. Employers, for example, will not assume the expense of added payroll if they do not believe they will need the additional workers going forward. Conversely, they will be reluctant to lay off workers if they perceive a need in the near future.

From a consumer perspective, nothing is more important than employment and nothing erodes consumer confidence and subsequently slows consumer spending more than job losses either actual or feared. Because consumer expenditures account for about 70% of economic activity in the nation, the expected employment situation can have a profound effect. Clearly that is why this single economic release is so far reaching and widely watched.

The relationship between employment and the business cycle is a tight one and the relationship between employment and GDP (gross domestic product) are therefore closely linked. The GDP report is a quarterly report with a one month lag whereas *The Employment Situation* is monthly. As a result, those needing a timely read on the economy can infer its growth rate from payroll data prior to release of the quarterly GDP report.

In analyzing the relationship between employment and GDP, the data show that since 1960, there has never been an instance when three consecutive monthly declines in payroll have not been accompanied by an economic downturn.

While employment data is a *leading* indicator of a downturn, it is a *lagging* indicator of a recovery. After a definitive bottom has been reached in a down turn, there is generally a protracted period of joblessness before the numbers begin to rise again. In other words, employment lags a recovery.

The current situation. The 63,000 decline in employment in February and -22,000 in January were the first back to back losses since May and June 2003 when the economy was recovering from the 2001 recession.

The February decline was wide spread throughout the economy. Employment fell in manufacturing, construction, retailing, financial services and a variety of professional and business services. Small gains were realized in healthcare, leisure and hospitality and the government.

Housing is clearly the biggest drag on the economy but weakness has also spread to other sectors as well as the broader economy. Private industries lost 101,000 jobs in February and that represents the third consecutive decline in private sector payrolls. Manufacturing and construction are leading the way to the bottom. Both sectors have shed workers at a rapid pace. The construction decline is still linked to the housing market which has not yet found a bottom. Auto manufacturers and their suppliers lead the way down in manufacturing.

Financial services has also been hard hit. The sector has been losing jobs since peaking in late 2006. Most of the losses are occurring in real estate rental and leasing as well as lending and allied services. While real estate jobs have declined substantially, the loss is difficult to measure as most sales agents are independent contractors. They are not eligible for unemployment and therefore not counted in the unemployment numbers. Losses in construction, finance and manufacturing are not surprising given the downturn in housing and credit markets but service sector losses are. Last month business and professional services shed 20,000 jobs and temporary services shed 27,000 more. All this argues strongly for 100 basis point rate cut when the Fed's Federal Open Market Committee (FOMC) meets next week.

Florida employment data lag national data by 30 days. Accordingly, the January data were released last Friday coincident with the February (national) Bureau of Labor Statistics data. The Florida data showed 423,000 jobless out of a labor force of 9,264,000 indicating an unemployment rate of 4.6%. That rate is up one-percent over the prior year and is the highest rate since October 2004.

Non-agricultural job growth was down –0.1% indicating a loss of 300 jobs; a downward trend that began in September 2007 with declines in construction employment.

Construction employment has declined most significantly having lost 69,000 (-10.8%) jobs over the last 12 months. Construction job losses have accounted for 75% of the job losses in the state—a loss which is

---

WILLIAM L. PITTENGER   43

highly significant but not necessarily surprising given the magnitude of the housing decline. Although commercial construction has absorbed some of the lost residential construction jobs, there is no evidence to suggest employment in the construction sector will improve this year. Indeed, as employment growth typically *follows* a recovery, it seems unlikely that construction employment will grow demonstrably until 2010.

Manufacturing employment was down 5% (-19,800 jobs) while financial services lost 1,900 and information services lost 1,400, largely in publishing.

Conversely, education and health services as well as leisure and hospitality sectors all gained jobs.

The news from South and Central Florida was mixed. Most areas experienced employment declines in the last month with the exceptions of several inland counties such as Okeechobee, Highlands and Glades counties. These three counties experienced slight gains.

Despite the year over year gain in employment, the unemployment rate rose in most counties. The average increase was 1.2%. Hendry County experienced the sharpest gain and now stands at 7.2% unemployed.

Treasure Coast unemployment also rose sharply year over year. Indian River County increased from 4.8 to 6.2%. St. Lucie County increased from 4.9% to 6.5% and Martin increased from 3.9% to 5.1%. Hendry, St. Lucie and Indian River counties are now ranked two, five and eight in terms of high unemployment among the state's 67 counties. St. Lucie and Indian River unemployment is construction related and, like the state level, no demonstrable increase is likely this year.

APRIL 15, 2008

ECONOMIC SLOWDOWN INTENSIFIES

Data delivered the past two weeks have reinforced the growing view that the economy has crossed the line into recession. Spending is quickly losing momentum across most categories. Hardest hit is the auto sector.

Credit quality continues to erode as consumers fall farther behind on their monthly obligations and delinquencies continue to rise. Perhaps the most compelling evidence that the economy is in recession is the recent jobs report where the Bureau of Labor Statistics reported a loss of 80,000 more jobs in March. The economy has now lost 232,000 jobs in the last three months. No longer are job losses limited to construction sector. Instead, losses are now being felt across most broadly defined sectors.

The labor market continued to weaken in March as non-farm payroll jobs declined by another 80,000. Employers also cut 76,000 jobs in both January and February—significantly more than the previously estimated loss of 63,000 jobs in February and 22,000 jobs in January. That brings total job losses to 232,000 over the last three months.

Until recently, construction and manufacturing sectors bore the brunt of job losses. That was followed closely by the financial sector. Today, most broadly defined sectors are losing jobs which provide unambiguous evidence that what was once a single sector problem—housing—has spread to the broader economy and tipped the scales toward recession.

Construction industry losses continue to be concentrated among residential builders and their specialty sub-contractors. There is, however, growing evidence that commercial construction employment has also weakened. Similarly, architects and engineers faced rapidly eroding conditions for the first time as employment in those sectors declined.

The general weakening of the economy is also apparent in the number of temporary workers. The temporary ranks declined by 22,000 in March alone and by 60,000 since the first of 2008. Temporary employment is a good leading indicator of the economy as they support all industries. Temporary workers are usually the first to be released in a down turn and the first to be hired when the economy improves.

Manufacturing payrolls have contracted significantly over the last 12 months losing some 310,000 jobs while government sector employment has risen modestly.

Job creation remains positive in only a few sectors. The recent run up in commodities has boosted mining payrolls but that is expected to be temporary. Hotels and restaurants in the nation's prime tourist areas, including central and south Florida, are still being supported by international tourism. That appears to be largely the result of the sagging dollar against the Euro and other European and Asian currencies.

Employment in professional and many technical services has remained relatively stable. During the last recession, employment among professionals declined nearly 20%. Professional services tend to be more resilient and it seems unlikely that such a decline will be repeated for several reasons.

First, companies have not expanded this decade nearly as fast as they did in the 1990's. As a result, professional payroll growth has been more restrained. Second, outsourcing was the rage in the 1990's. Today, employers are seeing the risks of outsourcing and are less likely to do so this cycle. Finally, the risk of losing skilled workers as baby boomers retire is motivating employers to keep these workers even during a slowdown.

Unemployment is up sharply to 5.1% from its cyclical low of 4.4% a year ago. That upward trend is expected to continue for the next few months, possibly topping 6% before conditions improve later in the year.

Florida employment has traditionally fared a little better than the nation as a whole. Today however, the gap has narrowed. Florida's unemployment rate is now 4.6%—slightly lower than the nation. The state lost 27,700 jobs in February 2008 compared to a year ago. Construction employment led the way down with a year over year loss of 77,400 jobs (-12.3%). Construction jobs have accounted for 72% of Florida's job losses. Manufacturing followed with a net loss of 22,000 jobs (5.6%) and financial services with a loss of 6,900 jobs (-1.3%). Since last year, education and health services grew by 33,000 jobs (+3.3%) while leisure and hospitality services grew by 13,700 jobs (+1.5%).

Unemployment Claims have also risen. In the week ending March 29th, there were 407,000 initial claims; 38,000 higher than the previous week of 369,000. A year earlier, there were 319,000 initial claims. Four hundred thousand is generally considered a pre-recession threshold. Unemployment rates for all Seacoast counties are shown on the table to the left.

The Employment Outlook is expected to weaken further during 2008. Construction job losses, which started in the residential sector and flowed into the commercial sector, have largely been felt. Yet to come are cutbacks in financial services and retail sectors. The financial services sector is still reeling from the collapse of the sub-prime mortgage market last August. That was followed by weakness in commercial mortgage backed securities (CMBS). The result was a serious lack of liquidity. Retail spending has all but stalled and job losses in that sector are almost certain to follow. We expect modest improvement by year-end but it will be a long, slow ride.

Consumers are driving the downturn. With employment down, stock and house prices down sharply, gasoline prices at record highs and consumer debt also at record highs, consumers are pulling back sharply. The latest data show that consumer spending is growing at its slowest pace since 2005 in the aftermath of Hurricane Katrina. Consumer spending is not likely to improve in the near term given the laundry list of drags on consumer spending and sentiment.

Consumer and business confidence. Consumer Confidence, as measured by The Conference Board, fell significantly in March marking the first time the survey has experienced consecutive double digit declines since September and October 1991. Additionally, The preliminary University of Michigan Consumer Sentiment Index for April was lower for the sixth time in seven months thus reaching a multi-decade low. Consumers' outlook for personal income, one of both survey's key components, has never been lower.

At the same time, small business optimism fell. According to the National Federation of Independent Business (NFIB) survey, there was weakness across all major categories and the overall optimism index fell to its lowest level since 1986.

Businesses have curbed spending too. Manufacturers' orders for durable goods fell unexpectedly in February as did capital spending. The first quarter numbers for core capital goods shipments declined from +7% to −2% annualized.

Housing. Existing home sales *increased* nationally 2.9% in February ending six straight months of declines. At the same time new home inventories fell by 2.1% to the lowest level since July 2005. New home sales have also fallen 56% from their July 2005 peak—a sign that inventories are correcting and heading in the right direction. At the current pace, and barring some additional unforeseen economic shock, there is reason to expect that we will see a bottom this year. Despite movement in the right direction, the supply and demand relationship remains unfavorable for prices and it remains a buyers' market. The nationwide median price has fallen 8.6% in the last 12 months thus returning affordability to pre-2005 levels.

New home inventory home prices are generally down 25-30% as builders slash prices. In general, the higher prices went up during the 2003-2005 run up, the greater they are falling now. We continue to believe that prices will fall about 25-30% from their high point and return to 2003-2004 levels. That will bring prices more in line with income levels as well as the natural growth of prices. We also believe that history will show 2003-2005 to be an aberration as the growth was clearly unprecedented and unsustainable.

Architectural Billings Index is published by the American Institute of Architects (AIA). It is a leading indicator of commercial construction activity. The underlying rationale is that the overwhelming number of commercial building projects are designed by architects and that there is a strong correlation between architectural design activity and the start of commercial construction.

All indices have inherent weaknesses and the architectural billing weakness is the inability to take into account the time it takes for government approval and financing—both of which can vary widely. The AIA, however, has 13 years of experience with the index and an extraordinarily large number of data sets drawn from both growth and recessionary periods. As a result, there is a high correlation between design and build times in terms of both timing and amount of commercial construction.

Getting behind the index, because there is so little currently on the drawing boards, we can infer that commercial construction will be extremely slow for the next 18 months. The slowest sector will be retail followed by office. Industrial development will be virtually flat. Institutional construction, which includes hospitals, churches, schools and government buildings, should remain positive. In Florida, however, look for the government sector to also contract due to severe budget constraints.

CURRENT TRENDS IN OFFICE REAL ESTATE

Employment, a key demand driver for office real estate, has been softening for the last three quarters. By the first quarter of 2008, job creation was negative with a loss of 76,000 jobs in each of January and February and a loss of 80,000 in March for a net loss of 232,000 jobs in the quarter. The trend continued in April with a loss of another 20,000 jobs. Florida fared modestly better but is clearly not immune from job loss pressures as losses move from construction into finance, retail and even professional services. To put the current downward trend in perspective, the economy was creating an average of 189,000 jobs throughout 2006 and into early 2007. Demand for office real estate began to plummet in the closing months of 2007 as businesses postponed new lease commitments, the economy inched closer to recession and employers who were holding the line on employment were unable to continue to do so. Net office space absorption fell over 74% between the third and fourth quarters of 2007 and turned negative in the first quarter of 2008 as office employment finally turned negative.

Deteriorating office fundamentals are most apparent in markets where the housing downturn has been most severe and where there was a concentration of jobs in residential construction, mortgage finance and allied industries. This includes virtually every major market in Florida and most notably urban Seacoast markets including Metro Orlando, West Palm Beach and Broward County. As Seacoast does not have a presence in Miami Dade, that county is intentionally excluded from our analysis.

Metro Orlando had negative absorption of 577,331 square feet in the first quarter. That compares to negative 97,440 square feet in the fourth quarter of 2007 when absorption first turned negative. Over half (54%) was concentrated in the Class A sector. Net absorption for Orlando's central business district was negative 96,976 square feet versus negative 480,355 in the suburban markets.

The Metro Orlando vacancy rate increased a full 100 basis points in the first quarter growing from 9.6% to 10.6%. To put that in historical perspective, the vacancy was slightly under 8% as recently as Q3 2006 but as high as 11% in Q3 2003. The class A sector has been the most volatile hitting a high of nearly 20% in Q1 2003 and a low of 8% in Q3 2006.

Metro Orlando rental rates in the first quarter averaged $22.93 per square foot broken down as follows: The composition of tenancy in Metro Orlando (based on square footage of tenants) is heavily skewed toward finance, insurance and real estate at 21.6%. That sector has experienced the greatest net decline in job growth. Moreover, Orlando's decline in office employment has been significantly steeper than the nation as a whole having lost roughly 7% of its office jobs since 2004. Also noteworthy is that 41% of the currently leased space based on square footage is scheduled to expire or come up for renewal in 2009 and 2010.

Capitalization rates have also been trending upward having risen on average from 6.8% in Q4 2006 to 7.12% in Q4 2007. We expect this trend to continue as investors re-price risk and base purchase decisions on what is rather than on future expectations. Financing availability (or lack thereof) particularly in the CMBS (commercial mortgage backed securities) markets will also put upward pressure on capitalization rates.

Palm Beach County also experienced negative net absorption (-402,827 square feet) in the first quarter of 2008. That is over twice the negative rate in the fourth quarter of 2007.

The Class A sector experienced negative net absorption of 181,131 square feet followed by negative 154,958 square feet in the Class B sector and negative 66,738 square feet for Class C. Central business district net absorption was negative 206,793 square feet as compared to the suburban markets where absorption was negative 196,034 square feet. All sectors turned negative in late 2007 after several years of positive net absorption.

Overall Palm Beach County office vacancy stood at 13.9% at the end of the first quarter. That rate is up from 12.6% in the fourth quarter; 11.7 in the third quarter, and 10.7% in the second quarter of 2007 and is now among the highest in the state. The vacancy rate has been climbing since mid-2006 and surpassed the average national rate in the second quarter of 2007.

Class A space at $32.66 per square foot is among the highest in the state and so is the vacancy. A vacancy rate of 20+% was last experienced in Palm Beach County in 1999. Despite the rising vacancy rate, rental rates show no current signs of retreating. Similarly, capitalization rates were *lower* in 2007 averaging 6.63% as compared to 7.11% in 2007.

Palm Beach County office tenancy is skewed toward finance, insurance and real estate at 26.3%. Moreover, a full 34% of currently leased space by square footage comes up for renewal in 2009 and 2010. It is unclear whether tenants will renew or can even afford to renew at current rent levels. The fact that the amount of sub lease space current available in the county rose 33% in the first quarter suggests that many tenants are downsizing and will opt for less expensive space.

Palm Beach County
Sub Market activity varies significantly. Especially noteworthy is Boca Raton with the highest vacancy, negative net absorption yet over 1.4 million square feet of space still under construction. The sub market appears poised for a significant short term correction.

Broward County office absorption turned slightly negative (-40,081) square feet after a small positive showing of +22,249 square feet in the fourth quarter of 2007. Broward County absorption has been erratic for the last year however that appears to be largely the result of timing of deliveries which included several large projects in the last three quarters.

The average vacancy rate in the first quarter of 2008 was 9.4%. It has been inching up modestly every quarter since the second quarter of 2007 when it was 7.7%. The upward trend was consistent through all classes of space and through all submarkets except Hollywood and Hallandale—both of which have experienced a declining vacancy rate and modestly increasing asking rents.

The composition of tenancy in Broward is skewed toward finance, insurance and real estate at 21.6%—identical to Orlando but 5% lower than Palm Beach County. The average rental rate for all classes of Broward office space was $27.00 per square foot. Rates varied widely by sub market as can be seen in the accompanying table. Approximately 18% of the currently leased space in Broward County is scheduled to come off lease in 2009 and another 22% in 2010 for a total of 40%.

There are approximately 1.5 million square feet of office space currently under construction. Slightly less than half of it is pre-leased. The biggest concentrations are in southwest Broward and Pompano (60%). Finally, capitalization rates trended modestly *lower* in 2007 averaging 6.84% as compared to 7.43% in 2006.

Looking Forward.
All markets appear poised for negative correction. Palm Beach County has experienced the steepest growth, which, in our view, is unsustainable. The average vacancy rate is in double digits and has been steadily, though modestly, climbing for the last seven quarters. So far, rental rates have defied gravity and remain among the highest in the state, second only to Miami-Dade. Capitalization rates also appear to have defied trend by decreasing rather than increasing. Digging deeper, the data driving the apparent 2007 downward movement occurred prior to the CMBS melt down last summer. We fully expect capitalization rates to climb in the next few quarters. Palm Beach County also has over 26% of its currently leased space coming up for renewal in the next two years. Combine that with nearly two million square feet of space still under construction and downward value correction, perhaps as much as 20%, seems likely.

Metro-Orlando and Broward County are experiencing similar changes, though not as severe. Look for increasing vacancies and cap rates as well as greater rent concessions in all of these markets as we shift from a landlord to a tenant driven market.

JUNE 9, 2008

LABOR MARKET AND CONSUMER STRESS CONTINUE

Employment fell again in May for the fifth straight month driving the nation's unemployment rate to 5.5%. Job losses have become relatively broad based extending beyond housing and construction and into manufacturing, retail trade and business services. Household wealth has also declined. In the first quarter, the drop was led by securities with real estate value deterioration a close second. Consumer borrowing has clearly shifted from mortgage and mortgage equity borrowing to consumer revolving debt—especially credit cards. Diminished household wealth, labor market deterioration, increased consumer borrowing costs as well as stress over gasoline and food prices contributed to consumer sentiment plunging to a 28 year low and the economy growing at little more than stall speed.

The Bureau of Labor Statistics (BLS) of the United States Department of Labor reported Friday (June 6th) that the U.S. labor market continued to weaken with a loss of 49,000 jobs in May. The May loss was less than consensus estimates of 50,000 to 60,000 At the same time, March and April job loss figures were revised to show slightly larger drops of 88,000 and 28,000 respectively. The national economy has now shed some 319,000 jobs so far in 2008.

The May decline continued to be relatively broad based. Last year, job losses were skewed toward construction and housing related sectors. Today, losses are more widespread in construction, manufacturing, retail trade and business services. Health services continue to defy the trend with modestly increased employment.

At the same time the nations unemployment rate surged from 5.0 to 5.5%—the largest single month rise since February 1986. In absolute numbers, that is 8.55 million people unemployed of which 1.55 million have been unemployed for 27 weeks or longer. Note that unemployment benefits expire after 26 weeks.

Part of the large increase can be explained by young people, including recent high school and college graduates, entering the work force for the first time. Indeed, second quarter employment numbers year-over-year consistently show some volatility for that reason. Despite historic volatility however, there is still unambiguous evidence that the labor market has weakened significantly since the third quarter of 2007.

Weekly initial claims (for unemployment) on a four week moving average are about 370,500. Continuing claims rose 1.2% in May to 3.104 million.

Initial claims above 400,000 are widely considered recessionary. The fact that new claims have been consistently below that threshold is encouraging as it tells us there has not been a significant weakening in the claims trend.

The Florida employment situation may have fared a little better. Data from the Florida Agency for Workforce Innovation (AWI) lag the national numbers by 30 days.

Nevertheless, in *April,* Florida's unemployment rate was 4.9%. When May data are released in mid-June we anticipate the rate will have topped 5% but will remain lower than the national rate for the same period. Nevertheless, in April, Florida had 456,000 people unemployed out of a workforce of 9.23 million. Florida workforce numbers for all Seacoast counties appear on page two of this report.

Florida's April employment growth rate was negative 0.8%. This is slower than the national employment growth rate which was positive 0.3%. Florida's negative growth rate continues a trend begun last September and is largely the result of declines in construction. Indeed, construction losses account for about 84,700 lost jobs which is 63% of the jobs lost in the state. That is a 13.8 % decline year over year.

Florida job losses have been greatest in construction, followed by manufacturing, professional and business services, financial services and information technology. At the same time, health services saw a gain as did leisure hospitality and government. Look for the latter two sectors to enter the loss column in the next quarter as leisure hospitality contracts due to high fuel costs and growing softness in that industry and budget constraints negatively impact local government payrolls.

Putting it in perspective, the current unemployment rates for both Florida and the nation remain relatively low despite their modest increases in recent months. In Florida, employment decline is not nearly as broad based as it is nationally. It appears largely driven by the housing slowdown whose tentacles have reached only moderately into other sectors.

Looking forward, total job losses both nationally and in Florida should be less severe than in previous recessions largely because of conservative hiring practices since emerging from the last downturn in 2001. The private sector averaged only 80,000 new jobs per month nationally for the last six years—a relatively modest number during the growth years.

While employers were slow to hire in the growth years, they have been equally slow to lay off in recent bad times. In the previous two decades, employers were quick to replace experienced and therefore more expensive workers with cheaper and less experienced workers. Today, there is concern about the experience level moving into the next decade. That appears to explain why companies are retaining experienced workers at a higher rate.

Household Wealth. The collective value of household wealth fell by $1.7 trillion in the first quarter. According to the Federal Reserve Flow of Funds Report which tracks both sources and uses of money in the economy, that is the largest decline since 2002 and the second consecutive quarter of decline. The decline was not driven by falling home prices last quarter but rather by the stock market where the value of direct holdings of corporate equities fell by $556 billion. A loss in indirect holdings subtracted further from household wealth. Capital losses on financial assets totaled more than $1.0 trillion for the first time since the third quarter of 2002.

The value of real estate holdings fell $305 billion in the same time period. That drop was nearly three times what it was in the fourth quarter of 2007. Additionally, homeowner equity fell even more at $399 billion leaving home equity as a share of residential real estate value at 46.2%—a record low dating back to 1952 when the information was first tracked. To put that in perspective, homeowner equity was over 70% in 1983 and has steadily trended downward. Not surprisingly, the steepest decline has been since 2006 when home prices began to slide.

Consumer Borrowing. There has been a measurable slowdown in mortgage borrowing which is clear in the Fed data. At the same time, consumers are shifting their borrowing to revolving consumer loan products. Indeed, growth in consumer credit borrowing exceeded growth in mortgage borrowing for the first time since 1991. This shift in borrowing was expected continue and is likely to continue as falling home sales, declining home prices, tighter mortgage lending standards and higher mortgage costs all suggest additional slowing of mortgage borrowing growth.

Diminished home equity leaves consumers less able to tap that equity for cash. Mortgage equity withdrawal has been a major facilitator of consumer spending for much of this decade. Combined with the decline in the value of equities, there is a pronounced negative psychological wealth effect. These factors will further limit consumer spending later in 2008 and into 2009.

Consumer sentiment, as measured by a Reuters/University of Michigan Index has fallen to a 28 year low. This too is not surprising given the weak job market, diminished household wealth, and dramatically rising gasoline and food prices.

Gross Domestic Product. All these factors and more roll into an economy that is growing at a rate not much more than stall speed. The Gross Domestic Product (GDP) was revised upward from 0.6% to 0.9% for the first quarter and consensus estimates are for a similar rate of growth in the second quarter as consumers remain financially stressed. Over 70% of the GDP is consumer driven so we are unlikely to see significant economic growth until consumer activities, including housing, begin to rebound.

The Business Cycle Dating Committee (BCDC) of the National Bureau of Economic Research (NBER) has still not officially declared that a recession has begun. Nevertheless, the consensus is that it surely has and the recovery will be slow.

JUNE 19, 2008
CREDIT QUALITY DETERIORATES

Credit quality continues to weaken as consumers face reduced home equity and household wealth together with rising inflation in energy and food prices. Real income and purchasing power have declined over the last 12 months. Households continue to be squeezed by a harsh job market that is holding down wage increases. Mortgage data released by the Mortgage Bankers Association and the Federal Reserve Board show that both mortgage delinquencies and foreclosures continue to rise at a record pace. The current delinquency rates are now the highest on record and far above what was experienced in the 1990 and 2001 recessions, The effect of foreclosures is also expanding beyond homeowners and is now being felt by homeowner associations, municipalities and others as a full 2.9% of U.S. homes are vacant and for sale—the highest rate since 1956.

First quarter 2008 data from the Mortgage Bankers Association show a startling rise in both delinquency and foreclosure rates. No longer confined solely to sub-prime loans, the total first quarter 2008 delinquency rate for all types of 1-4 family residential mortgage loans in the U.S climbed to 6.35% while foreclosures climbed to one-percent. These rates are now the highest on record and far above 1990 and 2001 recession levels.

The problem is also no longer confined to adjustable rate mortgages (ARM). Fixed rate loans are increasingly under stress as well given the erosion in the underlying collateral value and the fact that even prime borrowers are becoming less willing to pay when they see the value of their property continuing to shrink. The following table shows delinquency and foreclosure rates for Florida 1-4 family residential loans.

As might be expected, fixed rate loans to prime borrowers show the lowest delinquency and foreclosure rates at 3.3% past due and 1.34% in foreclosure. Alternatively, subprime adjustable rate loans are the highest at 19.71% past due and 23.33% in foreclosure. The sub-prime category, which is arguably the cause of the credit crisis that began last August, is especially significant. The spread between prime and sub-prime continues to widen and the astounding level of both delinquency and foreclosure activity clearly under-scores the severity of the sub-prime problem.

In terms of fixed versus adjustable rate loans, the fixed rate delinquencies are near previous recession highs while adjustable rate loan delinquencies are much higher.

Of the total adjustable rate loans facing reset, very few are prime, agency (FHA or VA) or portfolio loans made by local banks. By far the largest shares are securitized sub-prime. A reset does not automatically trigger a foreclosure but many sub-prime loans that have, or will soon, reset were made with so-called "teaser rates." Those interest rates are adjusting upward fairly dramatically now. Additionally, the majority were high ratio (loan to value) loans and collateral values have declined meaning that a significant number of sub-prime adjustable rate borrowers owe more than their property is worth and can no longer sell or refinance. The alternative is usually foreclosure.

The peak in sub-prime loans facing reset occurred in the fourth quarter of 2007. Given the few options sub-prime borrowers have, many are, in fact, facing foreclosure. This combination of circumstances helps explain the recent surge in foreclosures 4-6 months after reset.

The number of borrowers entering foreclosure has declined thus far in the second quarter as foreclosures work their way through the legal process.

There was another (but slightly lower) "twin peak" in resets which occurred in April. As a result we can probably expect to see foreclosures rise again, though not as dramatically, in the fourth quarter of 2008 and first quarter of 2009.

While this analysis would suggest that foreclosure rates will decline in the first half of 2009 as sub-prime resets clear, there is still a wild card. A continued weak economy could easily drive prime borrowers into foreclosure. We see this as a real possibility given diminished household wealth, home prices that continue to decline as well as labor market and inflationary pressures.

Homeowners are giving up in this order. Flippers, speculators, legitimate investors and homeowner occupants. During the extraordinary run up of prices in the era of cheap money, flippers and speculators contracted to buy new residential properties but never expected to close on their purchase. They expected to simply "flip" the contract or the property to another buyer and make a huge profit doing so. When the residential market collapsed, they were unable to flip the property and were forced into foreclosure or some form of settlement with their mortgage lender.

Alternatively, homeowners held on to the end, many striving diligently to *not* go to foreclosure. In the second half of 2007, approximately 56% of foreclosures were flipper, speculator and investor. As those clear the legal process, many more homeowners are going to foreclosure.

Another trend worth exploring is that during 2007, roughly one-third of the properties entering "pre-foreclosure" (the first legal step) actually went through the entire process and ended with the property being returned to the lender. About two-thirds were able to recover or settle with their lender. Today that ratio is approaching one-half as more borrowers exhaust their options to avoid foreclosure.

Other consequences of foreclosure. Besides the obvious effect foreclosure has on property owners and their lenders, the extraordinary level of foreclosure activity is taking its toll in other areas as well.

Approximately 2.9% of U.S. homes are vacant and for sale. While that is only a fraction of U.S. homes, it is the highest rate since 1956. Homes standing empty quickly fall into disrepair if maintenance is not performed as necessary. Code enforcement violations cited by cities and counties are on the rise.

Vandalism is also on the rise as vacant homes are stripped of appliances and anything of value. Sometimes the vandalism is as severe as stripping electrical systems to steal copper wire.

Community associations are finding it harder to collect maintenance and other association fees in order to provide both maintenance and service.

JULY 25, 2008

MORE CONSUMER HEADWINDS

The nation's payrolls have declined for seven consecutive months having shed another 62,000 jobs in June. Florida and most Seacoast counties fared no better. Unemployment in both the state and nation held steady at 5.5% in June while several Seacoast counties rose into the 8% plus range. Inflation, while generally contained in the food and energy sectors is a growing concern and it is widely expected to flow modestly into the broader economy given the far reaching effect of high oil prices. It will, however, remain in check by sagging employment and the inability to realize significant wage increases. The Gross Domestic Product (GDP) was 1.0% in the first quarter but the components are lining up for a better showing in the second quarter—perhaps 2%.

The nation's labor market remains in turmoil as 62,000 more jobs were shed in June. That brings 2008 job losses to 431,000. The nation has now shed jobs for seven consecutive months and there is no short-term end in sight as retail, finance and business service sectors are expected to show more losses in coming months coincident with a generally slow economy. Despite continuing losses, the nation's unemployment rate remained unchanged at 5.5%.

Florida's job market fared no better with an unemployment rate of 5.5% —now equal to the nation but the highest since 2003. Unemployment in Florida has steadily risen for the last year. The current unemployment rate is the product of 78,100 jobs lost statewide over the last year. Florida's job growth rate remains negative by 1.0% continuing a trend that began in September 2007.

Florida's job market is still reacting to declines in the housing market. Construction, for example, lost 81,600 jobs year over year. The sector is down 13.5% and construction losses now account for 52% of the jobs lost in the state over the last year. Manufacturing lost 24,900 jobs (6.4%) year over year.

Business and professional services in the state lost 24,100 jobs, financial activities lost 7,700 jobs and information lost 5,300. These categories are defined by the Bureau of Labor Statistics as office employment and the losses do not bode well for the office real estate sector throughout the state. (See *Economic Perspectives,* May 5, 2008)

Total government led the way up with 31,000 new jobs over the year. This seems counter-intuitive given the well-publicized cut backs in government at both the state and local level. Education and health services also added 29,800 jobs while leisure and hospitality gained 18,400.

The state acquired Clewiston based (Glades County) U.S. Sugar last month. The facility will be closed over the next six years to make room for a water flow way from Lake Okeechobee to the Florida Everglades. U.S. Sugar currently employs 1,700 people which is 37% of the Glades County work force. If the jobs expected to be lost are not replaced, Glades County as well as other rural counties around Lake Okeechobee would clearly be adversely affected.

Looking forward, we continue to expect softness in employment at all levels well into 2009. Florida will likely reach 8-9%% before slowly trending downward. The Treasure Coast (Indian River, St. Lucie and Martin Counties) and Space Coast (Brevard) will likely reach the higher end of this range with Metro Orlando and the Gold Coast nearer the lower end. Overall, we expect a jobless recovery from the current economic downturn much like the recovery after the 2001 recession. While employment is always a leading indicator on the downside, as employers are often quick to reduce employment, it is a lagging indicator on the upside as employers are slow to re-hire.

Employment arguably adds the greatest amount of uncertainty to the economic outlook as it is a key driver of consumer and retail spending.

The strength in retail spending did not extend far beyond the discounters in June. Households cut back sharply on big ticket discretionary purchases including appliances, furniture, building materials and autos. Grocery stores and gasoline stations siphoned off a larger share of the consumer dollar. Retail sales rose a disappointing 0.1% in June. Gasoline is consuming a larger share of each consumer dollar and if these sales were taken out, retail spending would have actually declined by about 0.5% in June—a level widely considered recessionary.

As the effect of rebate checks wanes in the third quarter, spending is unlikely to sustain even its paltry second quarter gains.

Inflation is a growing concern for the U.S. economy. The CPI (consumer price index) rose at its fastest rate since June 1982. Total or "headline inflation" rose 1.1% last month. Excluding food and energy, the two most volatile components, core inflation rose by 0.3%. Both figures were substantially higher than consensus estimates of 0.7% headline and 0.2% core. Year over year headline (total) inflation has increased 5% and core inflation (not including food and energy) has increased 2.4%. Both figures are well over Federal Reserve targets.

Today's economic circumstances raise the question of whether *stagflation* is likely. Stagflation is an ugly word used to describe an even uglier condition in which economic stagnation and inflation occur simultaneously and remain unchecked. The two conditions are usually mutually exclusive but can occur when there is an unfavorable and unusual supply shock such as we are experiencing today with rapidly rising oil prices which tend to raise prices at the same time they slow the economy. The term stagflation is thought to be attributable to British Member of Parliament, Iain MacCloud who used it in a speech to 1965. The last time stagflation occurred in the United States was in the early 1970's. It is extremely difficult to fix as the monetary policy response cure is the opposite for each component. To stimulate the economy and hopefully relieve the stagnation, one might expect the Federal Reserve to lower the Fed Funds rate. To relieve inflation, they might raise the rate. Obviously both can't be done concurrently and the cure can be extremely complicated monetarily.

Looking forward at inflation, we do not expect the economy to fall into a state of stagflation. At this writing, the inflationary effects of oil and food prices have not flowed heavily into the broader index or the broader economy. Wage increases, for example, are largely being contained by sagging employment in which employees can't effectively make large wage demands. Nevertheless, fuel prices will clearly play a role in producer prices and there will come a time when manufacturers start raising prices. As long as wages are contained, however, producer price increases should not lead to out of control inflation. We therefore expect inflation to remain higher than Fed target rates for the next few quarters but not grow to the point it is out of control or becomes "stagflation."

Gross Domestic Product. The GDP is the broadest measure of goods and services produced in the economy. In the 4th quarter of 2007 it sank to 0.58%, its lowest level in five years. The final number for the first quarter of 2008 was 1.0%—hardly stellar but still in positive territory. The second quarter advance estimate will be released next week (July 31st) and the components are lining up for growth nearer 2%. As the consumer is about 70% of the GDP, economic growth as measured by the GDP will likely be near stall speed well into 2009.

AUGUST 2, 2008

ECONOMY SHEDS MORE JOBS

The Bureau of Labor Statistics of the U.S. Department of Labor reported on Friday that non-farm payroll employment continued its downward trend in July when the economy shed another 51,000 jobs. So far in 2008, some 463,000 jobs have been lost. At the same time, the nation's unemployment rate rose to 5.6%. Construction, manufacturing and several service sectors—including financial services—continued to lose jobs while both healthcare and mining added jobs. Leisure and hospitality remained flat.

Construction continues to slide with 22,000 jobs lost in July. The sector has lost 557,000 jobs since the sector peak in September 2006. Nearly three-quarters of that decline has occurred since October 2007.

Job losses in the professional and business services sector have accelerated. Employment services lost 34,000 jobs in July with nearly all of it in the temporary help sector.

Employment in the retail sector continues to trend down. Since its peak in March 2007, retail has lost some 211,000 jobs. This correlates tightly with the decline in retail spending. Not surprisingly, employment with motor vehicle dealers has also declined. That too is largely attributable to consumers pulling back on discretionary purchases particularly large ones such as automobiles, furniture and appliances.

Healthcare and mining saw employment gains in July. The healthcare industry has added 368,000 jobs over the last 12 months. Mining employment has expanded 45% (222,000 jobs) since its last low point in April 2003. Much of the growth has been in oil and gas extraction or in support industries.

Look for significant revisions to the employment data when the preliminary and final numbers are delivered over the next 30 and 60 days. The fact that the advance estimate was delivered so early in the month leaves a lot of room for forecasting error.

The Florida Employment Situation is not much different. Florida's employment numbers are compiled and released monthly by the Agency for Workforce Innovation. The numbers, however, lag the national figures by a month. Florida's June employment data were released on July 18th and indicated 508,000 jobless out of a workforce of 9,245,000 for a 5.5% unemployment rate. That rate is down slightly from May's revised 5.6% but is up 1.5% over the year.

The number of jobs in Florida is down 78,000 year over year. Construction leads the way with 81,600 jobs lost since last year. Manufacturing follows with a loss of 24,600 jobs or 6.4%. Total government leads the way up with 31,000 new jobs over the last 12 months. This increase continues to defy well publicized assertions that government entities are strapped for cash due to declining tax revenue.

Looking Forward: We expect employment to continue to trend down over the next two quarters both nationally and in Florida but at a slower rate. We continue to expect Florida unemployment to reach 6.0% and several Seacoast counties to flirt with 8.0+%. Note from the table at the left that several Seacoast counties have already reached or surpassed that level. Hendry County appears largely seasonally related while Indian River and St. Lucie continue to experience the effects of the housing downturn.

MIXED SIGNALS FROM THE HOUSING SECTOR

The housing sector is sending mixed signals. The National Association of Realtors reported that sales of existing single family detached homes as well as their median sale price were down across the country in June. New home sales were also down to a near record low of 512,000 units annualized. At the same time, foreclosures doubled in June begging the question of whether the bottom is even remotely near. Look behind the Florida numbers, though, and we see a different picture. In many areas, existing home sales volume is up modestly and median prices are down only slightly. New home sales in Seacoast counties are also moving in the right direction. While inventory levels remain too high and it is too early to call a bottom to the housing problem, local markets are sending some hopeful signals.

Look behind the local housing numbers —both existing and new construction—and some hopeful signs begin to emerge. The chart at the bottom of the page shows all Metropolitan Statistical Areas (MSA) in the Seacoast Market area. In the Ft. Pierce, Port St. Lucie MSA, which includes St. Lucie and Martin counties, sales have increased month over month through the first half of 2008. Since June 2007, sales volume has increased 43%. The median price however declined over 32% in the same time period. The volatility appears to be driven by Port St. Lucie sales activity. Once one of the most affordable and fastest growing counties in the nation, it now has one of the largest inventory and foreclosure hangovers in the nation. While prices have fallen to the level where they are once again affordable—down 41% from their September 2005 peak—there is now a high level of vacancy and foreclosure activity with an estimated one in 115 households in some stage of foreclosure. That compares to 1 in 483 nationwide.

Other MSA's in south Florida have experienced modest growth this year however volume is down slightly from a year ago. Median prices are also down 15-20% year over year but the trend month over month has been modestly upward.

Sales activity is clearly skewed toward foreclosures and short sales. Inferring from a sample of local sales, it appears that about 35% of existing home sales have been re-sales of foreclosed properties plus a small number of short sales—sales wherein the lender agrees to accept less than the amount of the debt in repayment.

This relatively high number of foreclosure sales is positive in the sense that it is helping clear an extraordinarily over-supplied market. Nevertheless, it does not bode well for future sale prices and we expect that prices will continue decline modestly for the next few quarters even as sales volume continues its modestly upward trend.

Prices are now approaching levels last seen in 2003 and 2004. That level appears to be one point of equilibrium as it brings prices in line with housing's natural long term growth rate as well as household income. Look for modest improvement in 2009 but renewed growth, as evidenced by rising prices, will be a long, slow process Seacoast MSA's are no exception. Indeed, the volumes are small enough that the percentages become distorted and don't yield much meaningful trend information. In all MSAs, June prices were down year over year as were transaction volumes in most, but not all MSA's. Month over month data, however, were inconsistent among

According to Metro study, there is a very significant supply of newly constructed condominiums or units under construction throughout South Florida. Most of it, however is located in the tri-county area of Palm Beach, Broward and Miami Dade counties.

On the Treasure Coast, new inventory decreased 30% from the first quarter. About 54% of the finished vacant supply is located in St. Lucie County where there is still a 14.6 month supply of units.

Palm Beach County had 3,654 condominium units either finished and vacant or still under construction at the end of the second quarter. That is about a 28 month supply. About 32% of that inventory is located in three down-town projects (City Place South—420 units; Two City Plaza—467 units and City Palms—288 units. All are nearing completion and should begin to close this quarter. The good news in the county is that closings have outpaced starts for six quarters. The bad news is that there is still likely to be a significant amount of contract fall out as unit values decline.

In **Broward County** condominium inventory continues to decline with 2,001 finished units or units under construction. About 1,066 (53%) are finished but unsold. Inventory months of supply has *increased* over the last three quarters and currently stands at 12.3 months.

Miami-Dade County is the epicenter of condominium overbuilding. While Seacoast does not have a presence, the numbers are interesting, if not startling. While inventory levels are down for the fourth consecutive quarter, there are still 22,077 units under construction or finished but vacant. The months of supply has actually declined for the first time in 10 quarters but there is still a 36.5 month supply of units.

Single family detached new construction inventory is continuing its decline and is clearly moving toward equilibrium. Starts and inventory are down however, sales are lagging keeping inventories from descending more rapidly. Indian River County is the only Seacoast county to defy the sales trend having experienced upward movement in Q2. In fact, Indian River and Brevard counties appear to be within reach of equilibrium at 6.6 and 7.9 months of supply respectively. At the opposite end of the supply range are Orange and Seminole counties in Metro Orlando that have 17.6 and 18.5 months of supply respectively. Metro Orlando peaked later than most South Florida counties and will be slower to recover. Nevertheless, construction starts and inventory are down but sales need to rise significantly to clear the market.

AUGUST 11, 2008

HOUSEHOLD WEALTH DECLINES

Household credit quality continues to deteriorate as consumer fundamentals remain extremely weak. Household liabilities nationwide totaled $775 Billion at the end of the second quarter. At the same time, the delinquency rate on household liabilities increased to 4.6% of dollar balances outstanding. For perspective, that is nearly double its low of 2.4% at the end of 2005 and well above its last peak of 3.0% in the wake of the 2001 recession. The default rate also rose to 2.05% which is double the rate when credit quality was at its best in 2005. The data point to a continued rise in defaults well into 2009.

Eroding credit quality is apparent in all regions of the country although the extent of erosion is not uniform. Florida and other Sunbelt states which have sustained the full force of the housing downturn have seen all areas of consumer credit quality deteriorate at a faster rate than those areas less affected by housing stress.

The mortgage market continues to be the most seriously impaired. To illustrate the extreme stress, first mortgage delinquencies have now exceeded auto delinquencies and will probably surpass unsecured credit card delinquencies in the third quarter for the first time in history. This is a direct result of deteriorating home equity, mortgage loan resets and a steadily weakening labor market all of which combine to put unprecedented stress on homeowners continued ability to pay. Since consumers turned to credit cards after their home equity dissipated, we expect credit card delinquencies to rise later this year as many consumers run out of alternatives. Not only will the effect on card delinquencies be apparent but retail spending will also likely turn negative in the third and fourth quarters. Retail spending is only running positive at 0.1% today and that is with some lingering help from economic stimulus checks.

Household wealth has continued to deteriorate. The decline in the first quarter was 11.3% annualized—a decline of $2.8 Trillion from the record high of $58.2 Trillion in the third quarter of 2007. A large portion of the decline came from falling house prices and, somewhat remarkably, increased borrowing. Indeed, net home equity has declined for the last three quarters and is now at its lowest level since its measurement began in 1952. Mortgage borrowing has slowed to 5.5%—barely a third of its growth rate two years ago.

The decline in household wealth was also augmented by a decline in stock and mutual fund holdings. When the final second quarter results are counted, this combination will likely be repeated but with less decline in stocks and mutual funds but offset by more decline in housing.

Some emerging consumer credit trends. Consumers are slowing down their repayment of debt and are carrying larger balances longer. Additionally, there is significant evidence of "distress borrowing" particularly against credit cards and particularly in areas—including Florida—with the largest house price declines and weakest economies.

Risks to household balance sheets remains high. The higher than normal risk is the result of declining wealth, declining home prices and job losses which continue to rise. One upside is the recent and sharper than expected decline in energy prices.

AUGUST 18, 2008

HOUSING REDUX: ARE WE THERE YET?

How many times have you heard that from children in the back seat of the car? Today it's more often asked by those wondering if the housing downturn has finally hit bottom. Last week we distributed a report on the housing markets in counties and MSAs (Metropolitan Statistical Areas) served by Seacoast National Bank. There were some hopeful signs. Existing home sales volume is up this year. New home starts and finished inventories are down. All are clear signs that our markets are heading in the right direction—a direction that leads to recovery. This week we'll add a little color to the data and perhaps offer a little more insight into where we are, where we're going and whether today's positive signs are real or just a mirage.

Three years have passed since the first clear signs of downturn began to emerge and two and a half years since the economy fell into the grip of what is clearly the worst housing down turn in decades. Finally, however, there are at least a few *tentative* signs that we may be approaching bottom.

Recent trends in two key indicators—inventories and prices—suggest that the excesses are beginning to dissipate. According to local data by Metro study and the Florida Association of Realtors as well as national data from the Census Bureau, the level of vacant home inventory is ratcheting down. While inventories are still far too high, the direction of change and the fact that the change has been with us for a few months are a good start.

Declining house prices are also bringing affordability back into the marketplace. Nationally, the decline has averaged about 16% since its peak in the second quarter of 2006 according to the Case-Schiller Index, a widely watched and highly regarded index of house prices. In most Seacoast markets from Orlando on the north and along the east coast from Brevard County south to Broward County, the decreases have been more severe with declines as much as 25–30%. Put in perspective, prices in many submarkets doubled in the three year period 2004 and 2006. In those markets, a 30% decline is more tolerable. Those who purchased at the peak—and builders who built after the peak and well into the downturn—however, were clearly hurt in the price collapse.

Another indicator of improvement is the National Association of Realtors Affordability Index. It has improved 22% since 2006. Similarly the average house price-to-rent ratio is down 28% once again confirming that affordability has improved. Be aware however, that neither index is down to its long-term average and that suggests the possibility of further declines.

Pending home sales also offer a hopeful sign. Last week the National Association of Realtors reported pending home sales rose 5.3% in June over the May level. Moreover there were increases in all regions of the country with the largest (+9.3%) in the South. Despite the hopeful sign, there is still some volatility in the numbers which makes it impossible to draw meaningful conclusions. In March pending sales were down 1.0% but up 7.1% in April. They were down 4.9% in May but now up in June. Despite the volatility, the pending sales count suggests that closed sales will be up again in July and August when those figures are released over the next few weeks.

The Florida Association of Realtors also reported encouraging signs. Existing single family home sales increased in the second quarter over the first. Nevertheless, both sales volume and median price, as shown in the accompanying chart declined from a year earlier. The only exception was the Ft. Pierce-Port St. Lucie MSA (St. Lucie and Martin counties) which showed a 34% *increase* in sales volume.

While several hopeful signs are evident, they are tentative at best. Housing recovery is being buffeted by strong headwinds including foreclosures, continued supply and demand imbalance, tight money, turmoil in the secondary markets, declining employment, declining household wealth and low consumer confidence.

As we opined last week in this forum, the fact that existing home sales have increased is a positive sign as it helps clear the excess inventory. The flip side is that prices are declining which suggests, at least in part, that sales are heavily skewed toward foreclosures and short sales. Indeed, our research suggests that about 35% of existing home sales are in that category. Foreclosures are high and will likely to remain high by historical standards well into the next decade. At worst, that alone will drive house prices lower. At best, it will suppress increases for several more years.

The first large wave of subprime mortgage resets (about $385 Billion) occurred in 2007. It peaked in the third quarter. While a reset does not automatically mean a foreclosure many do given the composition of loans and borrower profile. Most subprime loans made during 2006 were "2-28" loans meaning that payments were fixed at a very low interest rate for the first two years and then adjusted to track the six month LIBOR (London Interbank Offered Rate) rate. Payments increased from as little as $350 per month to as much as $1,500 per months—too much for most borrowers to handle. Many of those loans were made to flippers and speculators who were still trying to ride the wave of house price increases.

Predictably, foreclosure filings jumped in the first quarter of 2008. At the end of the first quarter, 23.33% of subprime adjustable rate mortgages in Florida were in foreclosure according to the Mortgage Bankers Association.

The second wave of resets is occurring now as is the first wave of Alt A and payment option ARM resets. The volume is smaller than the first wave but will still result in another surge in foreclosures in late 2008 and early 2009. The chart at the bottom of this page shows both volume and composition of resets through 2009 as forecasted by Moody's Economy.Com.

There are still an estimated 10.5 million subprime loans in existence nationwide and roughly half of those are believed to be in negative equity positions. The flipper and speculator wave of defaults may have passed but conditions are still ripe for future default by homeowners. Owner occupants are not as likely to give up as quickly as flippers and speculators, however it is clear that negative pressures are many.

Household credit conditions are likely to weaken into the next decade as more consumers deal with rising inflation, limited credit availability, a growing potential for job loss and negative home equity driven by more foreclosed homes coming back on the market at what will almost certainly be lower prices.

Recapitalization of Fannie Mae and Freddie Mac by the U.S. Treasury (under new powers granted under the recently enacted housing legislation) is looking more and more likely. If that happens, management of both enterprises will almost certainly change, holders of common stock could be wiped out and many activities performed by both organizations could grind to a virtual halt. That will leave both GSEs (Government Sponsored Enterprises) in turmoil for many months if not longer.

What that means for consumers is fewer choices and more limited credit availability. Portfolio lenders will pick up some of the slack but their resources too are limited and growing more limited as they too struggle with the after-effects of mounting household debt and default.

So where are we and where are we going? To answer the "are we there yet" question raised at the beginning of this piece—clearly no. It will likely be several more quarters before the housing market finds a bottom. The forces working against recovery far outweigh the positives. At worst, there is still plenty of opportunity for more price declines. At best, prices and values will remain flat into the next decade.

AUGUST 25, 2008

ECONOMY CONTINUES TO SHED JOBS

The nation's payrolls have declined for eight consecutive months having shed another 51,000 jobs in July. That's nearly one-half million so far in 2008. At the same time, the unemployment rate increased modestly to 5.7%. In Florida and most Seacoast counties, unemployment rates have now surpassed the nation's rate. Hendry County's unemployment rate surged to 13.6% in July while St. Lucie jumped to 9.5% and Indian River and Okeechobee moved to 9.2%. With so many months of job losses, sector trends are becoming apparent. Clearly, construction and real estate are the most negatively affected but even within those industries, lower paid workers are impacted the most.

The economy continued to shed jobs last month. Over the last 12 months the number of unemployed persons has increased by 1.6 million to a total of 8.8 million persons out of a civilian labor force of about 154.6 million. The number of persons who moved to part time employment for economic reasons also rose by 308,000 to 5.7 million. That number has risen by 1.4 million over the last 12 months. This category is persons who indicated they would like to work full time but cannot find full time employment.

There were also 461,000 workers classified as "discouraged workers"—those who were no longer actively looking for work because they believed no jobs were available for them.

The composition of private sector job losses is now becoming apparent. Some of the top paying corporate management jobs were lost in the 2001 recession from peak in early 2001 to trough in early 2003. Approximately 130,000 jobs or 7% of jobs were cut at the time and employers have been slow to rehire since then. As a result, fewer higher paying jobs are being lost today. Indeed, the majority of industries that generally hire better educated and better paid workers, such as education and health services, continue to expand albeit at a much weaker pace than years past.

Following the credit crisis that began with the sub-prime meltdown in August 2007, financial services began shedding jobs, predominately at Wall Street investment banks that were heavily involved in packaging loans and marketing the securities.

The Bureau of Labor Statistics (BLS) classifies financial service jobs as "credit intermediation" and reports about 41,000 jobs lost this year. This may be understated as many more employees received severance packages and are still technically on company payrolls. According to the employment firm, Challenger, Gray & Christmas, financial service firms have announced 101,000 job losses in recent months, so the BLS number is likely to rise significantly after severance benefits stop.

The only hard hit industries that typically pay above average wages include publishing and to a lesser extent telecommunications. In the publishing sector, losses are not all recession related as there are structural changes in the industry with the flight of advertising dollars from print media to the internet and the resultant decline in newspaper publishing.

Clearly, the majority of jobs being lost in this downturn are real estate and construction related but the effect has been felt most in lower paying jobs across all industries. The following chart shows the industries that have seen the largest job losses since December 2007.

All of these categories except one are likely to bounce back as housing markets stabilize and the general economy begins to improve across the country. The exception is transportation equipment which includes highly compensated workers in the automotive industry. Unlike the construction industry, the outlook in the U.S. auto industry is much more dire. The entire industry is undergoing a wrenching downturn and jobs lost today are unlikely to be replaced even when the economy improves.

Florida has generally tracked the nation in employment but the downturn has become more pronounced. Florida's economy is heavily driven by the construction and real estate service industries. As a result, when those industries are strong, employment is strong. When those industries are weak, however, employment and the broader economy become seriously impaired as they are now.

Florida Employment. Florida's unemployment rate grew to 6.1% in July. This represents 572,000 jobless out of a labor force of 9,333,000. The number of Florida payroll jobs is down 96,800 since last year at this time. Construction and allied industries continue to lead the way down with 79,200 jobs (-13.4%) lost. While residential construction jobs were lost early in the employment downturn, losses in the commercial building sector held up temporarily. Today, however, job losses are occurring in the commercial sector as well. Real estate and construction fuel Florida's economic engine. With unprecedented downturn in that sector, fallout is widespread and felt in many areas of the state's economy.

Job losses are now being felt in allied industries such as building and garden supply as well as furniture and appliance wholesalers and retailers.

Business and Professional services, allied to housing and construction are not immune and are now experiencing job losses. These include title companies, designers and decorators, engineers, architects and even lawyers whose specialty was real estate and construction but who have not transitioned to foreclosure and other types of work. Financial services has lost 10,300 jobs over the last year. At just 1.9% of the sector work force in Florida, the numbers are comparatively small but likely to grow. Education and healthcare services continued to defy the downward trend having grown by 33,600 jobs. Total government also grew by 14,000 jobs continuing to defy assertions that jobs would be lost due to shrinking tax revenue.

Florida's unemployment rate is up 0.6% from June and up a full 2% from a year ago. It now exceeds the national unemployment rate of 5.7%. Significantly, Florida's unemployment rate is now at its highest level since January 1995 when it hit 6.5%. Moreover, Florida's non-agricultural job growth rate is now negative 1.2% and it continues to trend downward, largely a continuing result of declining employment in construction, real estate and allied industries. The unemployment rate in all Seacoast counties continues to trend upward—a trend begun in mid-2007.

OCTOBER 13, 2008

ECONOMY SHEDS JOBS AT FASTER RATE

The nation's economy shed another 159,000 jobs in September bringing the 2008 total to 725,000 and leaving the unemployment rate at 6.1%. Job losses were widespread by both employment sector and geography leaving little doubt that the nation's economy is in recession.

Florida job numbers lag the national numbers by 30 days however the downward employment trend continued in August. The state has lost 99,100 jobs over the last 12 months—47.3% related to construction and nearly all reacting in some way to the housing slump which is now in it's third year. The state's unemployment rate is now 6.5%, a full 2.3 percentages points over a year earlier and the highest since January 1995. Unemployment in every Seacoast county is up both month over month and year over year. Indian River and St. Lucie Counties topped 10% in August while Hendry topped 14%.

The September jobs report showed labor market weakness intensifying with 159,000 jobs lost—a number nearly double the month before. Payrolls experienced their steepest decline in over five years. Weakness was widespread, affecting nearly every employment sector. The unemployment rate remained unchanged from August at 6.1%.

Looking behind the numbers, payroll weakness was reinforced by a 0.5% decline in aggregate hours worked in September. Some 1.3 million people worked fewer hours or could not work at all. The unusually high decline—about double what would be expected—may be linked to hurricanes Ike, Gustav and other weather events in September. We doubt the effect was significant as people would have had to be off work an entire pay period to be counted in the September unemployment numbers. Nevertheless, October numbers will solve that mystery assuming no similar weather events the remainder of the month.

Additionally, 337,000 persons who claim to be seeking full time employment settled for part time work instead. That group is about 1.5 million more than it was 12 months ago. A different measure which counts this group of part time employees as *"under-utilized labor"* rather than fully employed, would suggest unemployment at 11.3%, the highest in 11 years.

JOLTS, an acronym for **J**ob **O**penings and **L**abor **T**urnover **S**urvey, is a survey by the U.S. Bureau of Labor Statistics which measures hires and separations using both quantitative data and qualitative survey findings. The changes are oftentimes small but over time the trends become apparent and are useful in forecasting employment changes especially at times like this in the business cycle.

The "job openings" rate was flat from August 2006 through September 2007 at which time it began trending down. At the same time the "job hires" rate has been trending down and is now at its lowest level since May 2003. Moreover, the "separations" rate (voluntary, involuntary and retirement) has remained essentially flat.

What is becoming apparent is that weakness in employment is now being driven more by layoffs than by slow hiring as it was until July

---

2008. That is supported too by rising initial (unemployment insurance) claims which have been hovering in the high 400,000 range. As a benchmark, 400,000 is widely considered to be recessionary.

Finally, The Conference Board released its Employment Trends Index last week. The index has trended down for the last few months and deterioration is now very pronounced. That offers additional insight and suggests that still weaker employment and a higher unemployment rate lie ahead.

Shrinking consumer spending, compounded negatively by tight credit, is now the leading driver of economic weakness. In technical terms, an *adverse feedback loop* now exists. In more understandable terms, that means that payroll cutbacks now contribute measurably to weaker spending which contributes to more payroll cutbacks and the cycle repeats. It will repeat until something breaks the cycle.

Looking Forward. Job losses averaged 70,750 per month through the first eight months of 2008. The rate of job loss was consistent with a generally slowing economy. In September, however, job losses spiked to 159,000—a staggering 125%. Overall the U.S. economic outlook has deteriorated as financial market stress and a "full blown credit crunch" interact with an already weak U.S. economy and a weakening world economy. Indeed, global business sentiment is reeling from the financial turmoil and confidence has fallen to a level consistent with a contracting global economy. There is no remaining doubt that the economy is in recession and it may be more severe than originally thought.

Job losses are likely to continue and rise over the next few months as employers wrestle with rising expenses, slowing sales and severely restricted access to credit both short and long term. Indeed, the employment picture is not likely to change anytime soon. Look for unemployment to top 7% in early 2009 and perhaps 8% before the trend is reversed.

As credit availability normalizes in response to the Emergency Economic Stabilization Act of 2008 (so called bailout bill).

Employment will improve however any significant improvement is not likely until 2011. While employment is a leading indicator on the way down in a softening economy (employers are slow to lay off), it becomes a lagging indicator on the way up as employers are usually slow to rehire.

Florida Employment. Historically, Florida's usually robust economy has exceeded national rates in employment growth and other key economic attributes. Clearly that was a direct result of real estate and construction fuelling the state's economic engine. When that fuel ran out, the state began to lag the nation in employment growth. Today, Florida's non-agricultural employment growth rate is negative 0.2% continuing a trend that began in September 2007. The state's unemployment rate of 6.5% exceeds the national rate of 6.1%.

The state has lost 99,100 jobs year over year to reach an employment level of 7,924,400. Construction lost 76,400 jobs which accounts for 47.3% of job losses in the state.

Other sectors have not been immune to job losses. The professional and business services sector lost 31,200 jobs year over year while manufacturing lost 23,400, trade, transportation and utilities lost 17,600 jobs and the financial services sector lost 5,700 jobs. The state saw growth in education and healthcare employment in August (+37,400 year over year) and in total government.

Looking forward, we expect business and financial services to contract and continue to shed jobs through 2009. The pace of total government employment growth is slowing and we expect that sector to move to the job loss column in 2009 due to shrinking tax roles state wide. Health services will continue to grow but at a more modest rate. One of many troubling by-products of the recession is more consumers are losing insurance benefits and are, by economic necessity, not getting as much care. Leisure and hospitality remain marginally in the plus column and are expected to grow with an improving economy.

Seacoast Markets have not been immune from employment pressures either. Indeed, St. Lucie and Indian River, two formerly fast growing counties now have unemployment rates over 10%. Their growth has been critically linked to construction in general and housing in particular. Nevertheless, the fundamentals in both counties remain solid and that tells us they will bounce back coincident with improvement in the housing sector. Hendry County has now topped 14% unemployment. That appears to be in part due to seasonal declines in agriculture and allied industries.

Unemployment in Historical Perspective—The Great Depression Years

Year	Unemployment Rate
1929	3.14%
1930	8.67
1931	15.82
1932	25.53
1933	24.75
1934	21.60
1935	19.97
1936	16.80
1937	14.18
1938	18.91
1939	17.05
1940	14.45
1941	9.66%

SOURCE: *Bureau of Labor Statistics*

OCTOBER 20, 2008

CONSUMERS STRUGGLE WITH HOUSEHOLD CASH FLOW

Consumer spending and related activities account for about 70% of the nation's Gross Domestic Product (GDP)—the broadest measure of economic growth. For the last year, consumer finances have been under stress. Household wealth, driven by primarily by home equity and stock ownership has declined significantly. Consumer borrowing has recently begun to slow and unemployment is an ever increasing threat. Consumer credit quality has also deteriorated measurably as disposable income becomes a shrinking part of household budgets. None of these factors bode well for consumers or the broader economy.

Cash flow in the context of consumer spending is the sum of disposable income, consumer credit borrowing, mortgage equity withdrawal and realized capital gains. Consumer cash flow is clearly shrinking and consumers are now struggling to find the cash to support their spending needs.

Tax rebates earlier this year had a positive but modest effect on consumer spending however the impact is all but gone. Without another similar government led stimulus, consumer spending will likely shrink further. Let's look at the components of consumer cash flow.

Mortgage Equity Withdrawal (MEW) was a strong support for household cash flow and consumer spending. Indeed, it was probably more than just a support as it caused homeowners who had home equity lines of credit (HELOC) to spend more than they earned. The savings rate among this group of consumers was negative 13% in fourth quarter of 2007. Mortgage equity withdrawal peaked in early 2006. At that time, it's share of disposable income was 9.5%. It has been trending down since that time.

According to the economic consulting firm Kennedy/Greenspan, mortgage equity withdrawal turned negative in the second quarter of 2008 for the first time since 1992. Moreover, the share of disposable income attributable to mortgage equity withdrawal is now about 0.4%. Net equity withdrawal has declined due to a combination of falling home prices and tighter credit. This combination of events has affected all segments of mortgage lending and has not been limited to just subprime or other so-called exotic mortgage lending.

Much of the decline in second quarter mortgage equity withdrawal was "passive." In other words, it was equity extraction as a result of home turnover. This component fell $140 billion on an annualized basis. That is down 90% from a year earlier.

Alternatively, "active" mortgage equity withdrawal is the sum of cash-out refinancing and home equity loans. Decline in this component was much less severe than the passive component. Cash out refinancing fell $17 billion. Home equity loan volume actually rose in the second quarter although it remained negative year over year. Overall, the decline in active mortgage equity withdrawal fell by $4 billion to $109 billion but still down 71% year over year.

Looking forward, refinancing volume is, and will continue to be, hurt by several factors. First on the list is falling home prices which limit the dollars available to homeowners when they refinance. In mid-2006, for example, 88% of refinances were for a loan amount at least 5% higher than the original loan amount. By the second quarter of 2008, that ratio had fallen to 66%.

In addition, the total number of refinances declined significantly. This too is a product of several inter-related factors including an inability to re-finance, credit impairment, lending standards and reduced overall liquidity in the financial system, especially in the secondary markets.

There is a very tight relationship between mortgage equity and retail spending which is visually obvious on the chart on the preceding page. As home equity declines so does spending. That relationship is more pronounced in this business cycle than in previous cycles.

Consumer credit borrowing declined in August 2008 for the first time in more than a decade. This means that more debt was paid off than was originated. Behind the numbers, however, "perceived demand" for consumer products may still exist but it is not backed by the necessary purchasing power (therefore not true demand).

Non-revolving credit led the decline. Auto sales, which were down approximately 20%, played a big part. Revolving credit declined by less but still experienced its second decline in the last three years. Outstanding consumer credit must show an increase of at least $2.6 billion when September numbers are released. If it does not, we'll see the first quarterly decline since 1991. To put that in perspective, $2.6 billion does not seem like a huge gain particularly since the average gain thus far in 2008 has been about $7.0 billion. What puts it in doubt are already released data which show that vehicle sales and chain store sales are growing much weaker thereby suggesting additional drag on both revolving and non-revolving consumer credit growth. The American big three automakers, for example, have already announced sales down more than 30%.

Credit card holders are now paying off a smaller share of their balances each month and are carrying larger balances longer. That trend started in late 2007 but was interrupted by tax rebate checks earlier in the year. Nevertheless, the trend has resumed and it will be a negative that will persist into the foreseeable future.

Perhaps more ominous is an apparent trend toward distress borrowing. Reacting to less disposable income, fewer capital gains and diminished home equity, consumers are more often financing consumption with credit cards. Although revolving credit growth will decelerate coincident with slowing consumption and a generally slow economy, many purchases—even necessities—will be put on credit cards as other forms of consumer cash flow dry up. Data suggest that this trend is more prominent in areas hardest hit by the housing recession—including Florida.

Nevertheless, we expect the card component of revolving credit to slow significantly by the second quarter of 2009 barring improvement in other areas of consumer cash flow or additional government led stimulus. We also expect defaults to surge as consumers tap out their last source of easy cash flow. That will lead to additional spending decline which is likely to further damage an already fragile economy.

Realized Capital Gains are another source of borrower cash flow however they are difficult to measure precisely as data are limited. The latest information is from the *IRS 2006 Statistics of Income Bulletin*. Even that misses a very large share of gains from sale of real estate. Nevertheless, given slower growth in equity markets this year; value declines of 30%± in residential real estate markets and difficulty selling real estate in general, it is reasonable to expect that capital gains income will remain down significantly even if equity markets improve. If we use previous recessions as a guide, it is likely that capital gains income will be down at least 50-60%. The 2001 recession, for example, saw reduced capital gains income of 50% for about two years.

Disposable income is the largest share of consumer cash flow. Without the temporary effect of tax rebate checks, fundamental income trends are weak but certainly not disastrous. Unemployment has risen and wage and salary growth have decelerated. These trends are expected to continue for at least the next several quarters. We expect significant weakness through the fourth quarter of 2008 and well into 2009.

Looking Forward. The consumer cash flow outlook is pessimistic from virtually any view. Disposable income, the largest and currently strongest component, will likely deteriorate over the next few quarters in response to declining employment and general weakness in the labor markets. Mortgage equity withdrawal is already weak and we expect no demonstrable improvement until 2011. Continued weakness in the credit markets plus foreclosures continuing to hold prices down will constrain any meaningful equity growth. In fact, foreclosures are expected to be a drag on real estate markets and the broader economy into 2011. Capital gains are likely to remain depressed on the real estate side even if we see improvements in the equity markets in 2009. Auto sales, together with slower sales of other big ticket items will constrain non-revolving credit growth while less card lending to tapped out consumers will constrain revolving credit. Consumers are increasingly cash constrained and that will remain a measurable weight on household finances for the next few quarters. In addition to the direct effect on consumers, these forces will combine to adversely affect consumer and retail spending in the aggregate for the next few quarters. We are also likely to see structural change as well. Consumers are being forced to alter spending habits and will move toward savings.

OCTOBER 28, 2008

FORECLOSURES CONTINUE AT RECORD PACE

Florida home foreclosures have been setting new records month over month for over a year. September was no exception. According to RealtyTrac, Florida's foreclosure rate jumped nine-percent over August with 47,956 new filings during the month and 127,306 new filings during the third quarter. Today, one in 178 Florida housing units is in some stage of foreclosure. That compares with a national rate of one in 475. Florida's foreclosure rate now ranks second in the nation—behind only Nevada. Not surprisingly, sun belt cities had the highest foreclosure rates in the third quarter. Cities with the highest rates were all located in California, Florida, Arizona and Nevada. Two Florida cities made the unenviable top 10 national foreclosure cities. Ft. Lauderdale came in at number five with 2.3% of its housing units in foreclosure and Orlando at number eight with 1.87% of its housing units in foreclosure. Is the end in sight? Yes, but not soon. Foreclosures will be a lingering problem into 2011.

Foreclosures have been occurring in waves since the housing bubble burst in 2006. First, it was flippers and speculators who discovered that the market had turned and they had a property that was worth significantly less than the debt. This group was originally intent on making a quick buck by flipping the property to someone else at a higher price. Loan files are replete with evidence that some of these borrowers lied about their intent to occupy the property or misled lenders about their financial capacity.

With no emotional attachment and with little to lose except their reputation and future credit worthiness, this group defaulted quickly—sometimes without having made a single payment. That wave has largely passed.

A second wave of defaults began in about the third quarter of 2007. This wave was led by borrowers—predominately subprime—who had purchased at the peak in 2005 and early 2006. Nearly all sub-prime loans made in that time period were "2-28 loans" meaning the interest rate was fixed for two years then reverted to an adjustable rate with adjustments tied to six month LIBOR (London Inter-bank Offered Rate). When a reset occurred, the average payment jumped about $350 to over $1,500 per month. That was enough to push some borrowers into default.

We are now in the third wave of foreclosures which is being driven by negative equity, weakening employment market and an inability to refinance at manageable rates and terms.

The third wave is expected to flood the market well into 2010. Today, an estimated 12.0 million homeowners are under-water with their mortgages. That is, they owe more than the security property is worth. Negative equity is generally not a primary default driver. Most borrowers don't have a precise idea of what their property is worth and most tend to estimate high. Nevertheless, when negative equity is combined with reduced work hours, a job loss or even an unexpected expense, default becomes much more likely.

The chart to the left is based on data from the Mortgage Bankers Association and shows second quarter 2008 delinquency and foreclosure rates for both prime and subprime loans as well as fixed and adjustable rate loans. As might be expected, traditional prime, fixed rate mortgages continue to experience the lowest delinquency and foreclosure rates. The foreclosure rate is 2.75%, which is high by long-term historical standards but pales in comparison to sub-prime adjustable rate mortgages where 35.66% are in default.

Income and house price. The long-term relationship between home prices and household income was in balance for many years. With the extraordinary run up in prices earlier this decade, prices surpassed affordability as is visually apparent on the following chart. Fearing future inability to purchase a home at rapidly escalating prices, many borrowers, who might not otherwise have done so, purchased at what was arguably an inflated price and financed with one of the more exotic mortgage loans that kept early payments low and required little or no down payment or proof they could even afford the payment when it adjusted. Prices are now moving back in line with the long term trend. Nevertheless, as loans made at the peak adjust and the underlying collateral value falls, more borrowers will default.

The chart at the bottom of the page shows foreclosure activity and composition in all counties served directly by Seacoast National Bank. Foreclosures are highest in the urban counties; a reflection of price run up, overbuilding and bust. They are lowest in the rural counties where those events did not occur.

State of the mortgage market. At the peak of the bubble in 2005, there was an estimated $920 billion in securitized sub-prime debt outstanding. New originations as late as June 2006 topped $165 billion. Today, sub- prime outstandings are about half of the peak and those balances are not being replaced. New sub-prime originations totaled only $4.0 Billion in the second quarter of 2008. Alt A originations were similarly low and Payment Option ARM new originations were virtually non-existent.

The market appears to have passed the worst of the sub-prime debacle and resulting foreclosures.

The next group of loans to reset are so-called Option Payment ARMS where borrowers could choose to pay an amount even less than the interest owed. The monthly deficiency was added to the loan balance. Total outstandings are estimated to be about $250 Billion. These loans were expected to start resetting in 2009 however falling house prices have increased loan to value ratios which, in turn, triggered contractual resets a year early. While a reset does not automatically mean a default, many will default as a result of rising payments—many of which will be very significant due to negative equity being amortized. We expect these resets to occur well into 2010.

Perhaps the most significant unknown is the effect of the *negative feedback loop* the market is experiencing today. As foreclosures occur, the security property is often put back on the market at a price less than the original debt. If a sale occurs, it is likely to affect surrounding properties driving their values down, triggering more foreclosures and thus repeating the cycle.

OCTOBER 30, 2008

THIRD QUARTER GDP NEGATIVE 0.3%

The Commerce Department reported today that the nation's Gross Domestic Product (GDP)—the broadest measure of the nation's economy—turned negative in the third quarter ended September 30th. GDP was previously negative 0.17% in the fourth quarter of 2007 but then trended positive in the first and second quarters. The return to negative growth was not quite as severe as expected however it does reinforce the view that the nation's economy is in recession. The view behind the headline number implies that the economy is weakening further and even slower growth can be anticipated for at least the next two quarters.

The decline in GDP was driven by a 3.1% decline in personal consumption—it's first decline since the 1990-1991 recession and the largest decline in 28 years. That was despite a small lingering positive effect from stimulus checks early in the quarter. There was an enormous 14% decline (annualized) in spending on durables. Non-durables fell 6.4%. That offered indisputable evidence that consumers are pulling pack sharply. Investment in residential structures fell 19% marking the 10th straight double digit decline. Investment in residential structures is now down 42% from its peak.

Trade was a large positive in Q3 with net exports adding a full 1.1% to growth. Nevertheless, growth in trade is slowing and would be expected to decline further in the next two quarters as the world economy teeters on the edge of recession or perhaps quickly falls into recession in the fourth quarter.

Government spending was also a significant contributor to Q3 growth. Real government spending rose 6% annualized adding about 1.2 percentage points to GDP growth. State and local government spending also rose but at a much slower rate.

Business investment weakened in the third quarter. This is probably a result of tighter credit conditions, softening demand and growing economic uncertainty. Fixed investment fell 1.9% annualized subtracting 0.8% from the GDP. Investment in equipment and software fell 6%. Non-residential construction has started to slow and the impact will likely be felt for the next few quarters—perhaps into 2010. Investment in non-residential structures rose 7.1% after rising 18% in the second quarter. We expect non-residential construction to continue to fall for the next few quarters as a result of rising vacancy rates, difficulty obtaining financing and lower financial returns on commercial property.

Looking Forward. The consumer continues to be about 70% of the nation's GDP so as the consumer goes so goes the economy. Looking forward, the effect of stimulus checks is no longer impacting spending in any measurable way. Business spending is slowing and exports are no longer supporting GDP to the extent they once were. While federal government spending will continue to grow, state and local government spending may retreat due to growing budget constraints. The wild card in this forecast is credit availability and how fast credit markets thaw under the Emergency Economic Stabilization Act of 2008. Given the long list of weights on the economy, we expect that Q3 GDP will show an even greater decline when preliminary and final estimates are released

30 and 60 days from now. We also expect fourth quarter 2008 and first quarter 2009 GDP to be slightly negative before returning to positive growth in mid-2009.

NOVEMBER 5, 2008

RESIDENTIAL PRICES CONTINUE TO SLIDE

The housing sector continues to send mixed signals. While existing home sales volume is up significantly year over year, it began to slow again in June. The median price continued its slide statewide. Existing condominium sale activity remained slow year over year and prices there too continued to slide. Price declines moderated nationally in September however that moderation was not felt in Central and South Florida where prices continue their steady decline. New home construction starts fell again locally with only 39 homes started in St. Lucie County; 28 in Martin and 105 in Indian River County

The housing sector continues to send mixed signals. The National Association of Realtors reported last week that sales of existing single family detached homes rose 6.2% in September (year over year) while the national median price fell 8.6% to $190,600. In Florida, results were also mixed. Volume increased 24% while median price fell 22.1% to $175,700. Falling prices in the face of rising volume implies that sales activity remains heavily skewed toward foreclosure and short sales. Indeed, public record research suggests that 50% or more of existing home sales are, in fact, foreclosure related. There is also unverified anecdotal evidence of higher rates.

Sales volume increased significantly year over year both statewide (+24%) and in most Seacoast MSAs where volume increase ranged from a low of 10.8% in Palm Beach to 51.4% in Orlando and 52.4% in Ft. Lauderdale. Year over year price declines by MSA ranged from −17.8% to −31.7%.

Volume increases have flattened significantly month over month in 2008. While Orlando and Ft. Lauderdale MSAs had large volume increases (+21.5% and +49% respectively), other MSAs were flat or negative the last six months. Similarly, price declines were negative in all Seacoast MSAs over the last six months. Declines ranged from as little as 6.9% in West Palm Beach-Boca Raton MSA to as large as 19.9% in Ft. Pierce—Port St. Lucie.

An estimated 10-12 million U.S. homeowners are "under-water" with their home mortgage meaning that they owe more than their property is worth. The number of under-water home owners in Florida is 1.2 million. While that does not suggest a default will occur in every case, there is a huge incentive for certain homeowners to simply walk away and that will clearly exacerbate housing and economic recovery.

Existing Condominium sales activity has been slow state-wide and Seacoast MSAs are no exception. Indeed, the volumes are small enough that the percentages become distorted and don't yield much meaningful trend information. Nevertheless, in all Seacoast MSAs, September prices were down significantly year over year ranging from –13.2% ($153,300) in the Melbourne, Titusville, Palm Bay MSA to as low as –37.8% in the Ft. Pierce, Port St. Lucie MSA where the median price was $140,000.

The Orlando MSA (Orange, Seminole, Lake and Osceola counties) saw its median price dip to $108,200 on only 146 sales. The median price fell 33.6% from a year earlier and is now the third lowest condominium median price in the state. Only Ocala ($57,500) and Punta Gorda ($85,000) were lower. Punta Gorda saw only 14 condominium resales year over year and the median price declined 53%.

The West Palm Beach, Boca Raton MSA fared modestly better with volume increasing 35.3% year over year although the median price fell from $180,000 to $139,800 (-22.3%).

Finished Vacant Condominiums. According to Metrostudy, there is a significant supply of newly constructed condominiums or units under construction throughout South Florida. Most of it, however, is located in the tri-county area of Palm Beach, Broward and Miami Dade counties.

Palm Beach County has an inventory of 3,152 finished but vacant condominium units. That is a 26 month supply. The inventory has been declining steadily through 2008.

Broward County has also seen its condominium inventory decline each of the last three quarters. It currently has an inventory of finished units of 2,627 for a 13.4% supply. The months of supply has been rising modestly for the last three quarters as sales slow.

Miami-Dade County is the epicenter of condominium overbuilding. While Seacoast does not have a presence there, the numbers are both interesting and startling. While the inventory has declined for five consecutive quarters, Metrostudy pegs the existing inventory at 22,522 units for a 31.9 month supply. Despite the extraordinary inventory, 1,166 additional units were started in the third quarter.

Single family detached new construction inventory is continuing its decline and is clearly moving toward equilibrium. Starts and inventory are down however sales are too thereby prolonging the time to equilibrium. Indian River County appears to be within reach of equilibrium with 713 units and a 6.5 month supply. Brevard and Palm Beach have inventory of 8.1 and 8.6 months respectively. At the opposite end of the supply range are Orange and Seminole counties in Metro Orlando that have 19.4 and 18.6 months of inventory respectively. Metro Orlando peaked later than most South Florida counties and will be slower to recover. Nevertheless, construction starts and inventory are down but sales need to rise significantly to clear the market.

NOVEMBER 7, 2008

OCTOBER JOB LOSSES SURGE

The U.S. Department of Labor reported this morning that the economy shed another 240,000 jobs in October. That is four times the average loss rate of the first seven months of 2008. Additionally, August and September job losses were revised sharply downward. August was revised down from -84,000 to –127,000 and September was revised down from –159,000 to –284,000. October job losses as well as the August and September revisions were all larger than expected. Job losses so far in 2008 total about 1.2 million and over half of the total losses have occurred in the last three months. Moreover, the revised September employment decline of 284,000 is the sharpest monthly employment decline since November 2001.

The nation's unemployment rate increased from 6.1% to 6.5% in October. That is the highest unemployment rate since March 1

March 1994. The number of unemployed persons increased by 603,000 to 10.1 million. Over the past 12 months the number of unemployed persons has increased by 2.8 million and the unemployment rate has increased by 1.7%. Among the newly unemployed were 615,000 persons who did not expect to be recalled.

Looking behind the numbers. Job losses were broad based—a clear sign that the recession is also broadening. Construction employment was down only 49,000 as most of the losses in the sector occurred in 2007 and early 2008. Goods producing industries, however, lost 132,000 job. This includes 90,000 in manufacturing led by the automakers. Retail trade cut 38,000 jobs with losses concentrated at auto dealerships and department stores. These losses are clearly the result of sharply declining retail spending. The last time the retail sector added jobs was November 2007. Losses in this sector are likely to grow in the next quarter or two.

Service-sector employment declined sharply for the second consecutive month under the weight of continued economic stress. This sector is the largest and often tends to soften downturns. Nevertheless, business and professional services lost 45,000 jobs and the finance sector shed 24,000. Leisure and hospitality businesses entered the loss column with 16,000 jobs lost. Sectors adding jobs included healthcare (+26,000) and government (+23,000).

Looking Forward. It is now clear that the economy has entered a recession that will be much more severe than anticipated as little as three months ago. The economy held its own reasonably well even after the subprime melt down in August 2007. Lingering slowness and an unprecedented financial crisis that has gripped the U.S. and the global economy since September, however, have clearly exacerbated economic performance and will continue to do so until credit begins flowing in a more normal fashion. Credit is the life blood of the economy which affects not only consumers but businesses large and small.

Employment declines will likely continue for the next couple of quarters. We expect the service and financial sectors to be the hardest hit. Retail will also decline as consumers cut back severely on their spending.

Healthcare will likely increase but at a slower pace. As employees lose jobs, they also may lose healthcare benefits and, of financial necessity, cut back on routine health care.

The outlook for federal government employment is not clear given the coming change in administration. Local government employment however, will enter the loss column though, as more counties and municipalities become starved for revenue.

DECEMBER 1, 2008

U.S. OFFICIALLY IN RECESSION

What has been painfully obvious to consumers and businesses has been officially declared by the Business Cycle Dating Committee (BCDC) of the National Bureau of Economic (NBER). The nation is in recession. It has been since December 2007 when the economy ended a 73 month expansion which began in November 2001.

The Business Cycle Dating Committee is a private non-profit group of economists based in Cambridge, MA. The committee does not forecast but rather is charged with dating the U.S. business cycle. For that reason, the announcement of a contraction often comes months after the economy has entered a recession. On the upside, the announcement may come months after the economy has begun a renewed expansion phase.

A popular rule of thumb for defining a recession is two consecutive quarters of negative Gross Domestic Product (GDP). That is largely because the GDP is a top line measure of economic growth and represents the value of all goods and services produced in the nation. The GDP contracted in Q4 2007 (-0.17%) and again in Q3 2008 (-0.5%).

A more complete definition of recession, and the one likely applied by the BCDC is a significant decline in economic activity spread across the economy, lasting for more than a few months and generally visible in employment, real income and a variety of other indicators.

The U.S. has shed jobs every month of 2008 and the total is now roughly 1.2 million. Roughly half the losses occurred in the last three months. When November numbers are released on Friday, December 5th, we expect they will show that the economy shed another 300,000 jobs.

The fourth quarter GDP is lining up for a steep decline (-3.0%-4%) as many of the supports the economy relied on through 2007 no longer exist or are weakening. Exports, consumer spending, deteriorating business earnings combined with accelerating job losses all suggest a weaker GDP and an economy that will remain in recession through at least the first half of 2009.

DECEMBER 3, 2008

KNOW YOUR ENEMY

"Know Your Enemy" was an American training film produced by director Frank Capra in 1945 at the request of Army Chief of Staff, General George C. Marshall. It was one of a series of documentary training films and was mandatory viewing for millions of soldiers. The premise was that to be successful in war, one must first know the enemy; who they are, what they do, how they act and what motivates them. From there, strategies can be formulated to conquer the enemy. Today's enemy— at least from a financial perspective—is the economy. With today's 24 hour news cycle, it is hard to avoid the negative economic news. People are often confused by what they read and hear and confusion leads to fear. While no one wants a steady barrage of bad news, understanding the economy is important for developing both business and personal strategies to successfully navigate the current crisis. Let's get to know our enemy.

The financial system is a formidable enemy of the economy. Without credit, the economy can't survive. The financial system has been in turmoil and under intense pressure for more than a year. It began with the sub-prime melt down in August 2007. That led to more mortgage loan defaults which triggered more foreclosures, greater house price declines and more personal and business bankruptcies. In turn, many financial institutions, businesses and consumers were weakened or under-mined.

The more recent turmoil began when defaulting mortgages wounded mortgage giants Fannie Mae and Freddie Mac so critically that the federal government was forced to nationalize them by placing both in conservatorship.

The extraordinary year-long turmoil led to widespread financial panic in mid-September. The series of events led to what is widely considered the worst financial crisis since the 1929 stock market crash triggered the Great Depression. Almost immediately, money market funds, commercial paper and bond issuance dried up. Credit spreads widened perilously and the stock market has been on a roller coaster ride ever since.

While the credit crisis is far from over, the damage may have been contained by swift and unprecedented government action both in the U.S. and by other global central banks. The Federal Reserve will continue to use all of its resources to stabilize the financial system. It will continue to flood the financial system with much needed liquidity.

To further force liquidity into the financial system and stimulate the economy, the Federal Open Market Committee (FOMC) of the Federal Reserve is widely expected to lower the federal funds rate to a record low of 0.5% at its December meeting. This comes after an unprecedented 0.5% cut in October that was coordinated with other central banks.

The financial panic has already done significant damage to the broader economy and despite the unprecedented actions of the Treasury and the Federal Reserve to contain the immediate damage, residual damage will be with us for several years.

One of the greater impacts and a continued enemy of the economy, is consumer confidence which, according to The Conference Board, has reached a record 40 year low. The current indicators do not bode well for short term renewed confidence.

Employment continues to be a fierce enemy of consumers and the economy. Recent national and local employment data leave no doubt that the economy has entered a recession and that it will be longer and deeper than anticipated as little as nine months ago. The national unemployment rate in October rose to 6.5% after job losses surged to -240,000 and September was revised to -284,000. That is the highest rate of decline in 14 years. So far in November nearly 100,000 additional layoffs have been announced nationally plus over 200,000 which are proposed to occur in 2009. Our view is that November payroll declines will reach somewhere near 300,000 which would put the nation's unemployment rate at about 6.8%. The nation is also on track for an unemployment rate near 8% by late 2009 or early 2010 barring any catastrophic events such as an automaker bankruptcy which could drive unemployment far higher.

Florida's unemployment rate rose to 7% in October. That is the highest since December 1993 when it was also 7.0%. Employment is down by 156,000 jobs year over year. Construction losses have been the largest at 79,800 year over year (-13.7%) however most of the losses are behind us. Professional and business services have now lost 46,900 jobs while financial services has lost 11,900. Business services is a large segment of the state's employment base and one that bears watching. Education and healthcare continue to grow as does total government. The rate of growth in local government, however, is slowing significantly as a result of severe budget pressures at all levels. We expect local government employment to move to the loss column over the next quarter. Additional cutbacks in business and professional services and finance are likely.

Weekly unemployment insurance claims (initial claims) rose to 542,000 in the week ending November 15th but fell slightly to 529,000 the week of November 22nd. Weekly initial claims of 400,000 is widely considered a threshold for recession. New jobless claims have reached a 16 year high and with no end in sight, President Bush signed a bill last Friday (11/21/08) to extend unemployment benefits.

Consumer spending fell sharply (-1.0%) in October. This was the sharpest decline since the 2001 recession. The on-going spending slump is the most severe in three decades and shows no signs of letting up. Sales fell in October as consumers cut back on almost everything with the exception of food and drugs. The steepest decline was in auto sales and at the gas pump. The latter, of course, was the result of rapidly falling gas prices. Nevertheless, consumers did not take any of that unspent money to other retailers. They appear unwilling to spend in the face of employment uncertainty, declining household wealth and sagging confidence.

On a year-over-year basis, the retail sales decline was the sharpest in decades—since the late 1960's. Housing related expenditures, such as building supplies, furniture, electronics and appliances have fallen most sharply but other retailers are not immune. Clearly, the slowdown is widespread and the recession is likely to be longer and deeper.

Gross Domestic Product. The economy, as measured by the GDP, stayed afloat reasonably well even after the subprime melt down in August 2007. It was propped up by strong exports, stronger global economy, tax rebates and strong business spending on structures. Today however, rebates are spent, we have accelerating job losses, slowing exports and a global economy either in or on the edge of recession. The third quarter GDP was negative 0.5% (revised from –0.3%) and the indicators are starting to line up for several more negative quarters, at least into mid-2009.

Foreclosures are, and will likely to remain, an enemy of both housing recovery and the broader economy. Foreclosure activity clearly dominates existing home sale activity as evidenced by rising sales volume accompanied by lower sale prices. Quarterly year over year data from the Florida Association of Realtors are presented at the bottom of this page. While sales volume rose 5% statewide in Q3, the median dropped 20%. In most Seacoast Metropolitan Statistical Areas, results were more volatile. In the Ft. Pierce, Port St. Lucie MSA, for example, volume rose 23% but the median price dropped 31%.

The huge volume in subprime foreclosures may have passed but we are now seeing foreclosures in other mortgage product segments such as Alt A, Payment Option ARMs (Adjustable Rate Mortgages) and other jumbo mortgages (loans greater than $417,000). Prime mortgage defaults are also rising as a result of job losses, declining home equity and a host of other economic factors.

A startling statistic that may keep foreclosures at an unusually high rate is that roughly 12 million homeowners currently owe more on their mortgage than the underlying property is worth. Over 1.2 million of those owners are Floridians. While being "underwater" does not automatically mean a default will occur, it is a huge incentive to walk away. With that, foreclosures will be a formidable enemy through 2011.

U.S. EMPLOYMENT PLUMMETS IN NOVEMBER

Employment declined by 533,000 jobs in November according to a report this morning by the Bureau of Labor Statistics. The loss significantly exceeded expectations of 300,000 to 350,000. The decline is the highest in 34 years and now leaves 10.3 million persons unemployed. Since the start of the recession in December 2007, a date confirmed last Monday by the National Bureau of Economic Research, the number of unemployed persons has increased by 2.7 million and the unemployment rate has risen 1.7% to its current 6.7%. The rate was 7.0% in Florida in October. November will likely be higher.

Among the newly unemployed are some 298,000 persons who lost their job and did not expect to be recalled. That group is now at 4.7 million. The size of that group has increased by 2.0 million persons over the last 12 months. The number of people who worked part time for economic reasons ("involuntary part time workers") increased by 2.8 million over the last 12 months and that group now totals 7.8 million persons. That group is significant as it is comprised of people who would like to work full time but accepted part time work as their hours had been reduced or they could not find full time employment. Another 1.9 million persons were classified as "marginally attached" to the labor force. This group has grown by 584,000 persons over the last 12 months and includes those who have looked for employment during the last 12 months but not within the last four weeks. Among this group are 608,000 "discouraged" workers, up by 259,000 over the last year. These categories suggest that many job losses are either long-term or perhaps even permanent thereby further implying structural change in employment and perhaps even the broader economy.

Job losses were broad based both by sector and geography. Losses now extend far beyond housing and construction related industries. Construction employment, however, fell by 82,000 workers. While sunbelt states, including Florida, experienced large and early construction employment contraction, those losses are now spreading to other parts of the country. The construction sector is down 780,000 over the last year of which over 10% were in Florida.

Manufacturing employment experienced 85,000 job losses in November reaching 604,000 over the year. Many of those losses are in component industries such as those who build or supply parts for primary manufacturers such as auto, electronics and others. Component industry employment changes often lag primary manufacturers.

Professional and business service employment declined by 101,000 bringing the category total to 495,000. Retail trade fell by 91,000 even after seasonal hiring is considered. Seasonal employment in November was also far lower than previous years. Job losses in financial activities have accelerated. Losses are now 142,000 year over year however we suspect the number is under-stated by the effect of severance packages in investment banking.

This employment decline will have a profoundly negative effect on the broader economy. The tentacles of employment reach nearly every sector and geographic area. The retail sales report for November released yesterday was dismal and December will likely be worse as spending will continue to slow as a result of unemployment and consumer concerns over continuing employment.

2009
RECESSION WITH A CAPITAL "R"

The recession continued with a vengeance. I described early 2009 as "Recession with a Capital "R;" a phrase which did not endear me to a few readers who were convinced that if we just stopped talking about it, the recession would go away on its own.

Nevertheless, residential values continued to slide and foreclosures rose. Commercial Real Estate would hit a low point in late 2009 when recorded prices on average were some 50% lower than their peak a mere two years earlier in late 2007.

Bailout and stimulus programs continued in early 2009. The government rolled out a huge aid package valued at $20 million in bailout money and $100 billion in guarantees to Bank of America.

In January, the U.S. had a new President. Less than a month after his inauguration, President Obama signed at $787 billion stimulus package into law. That package included money for so-called "shovel ready" projects as well as infrastructure, schools, healthcare and green energy. The program had broad emotional appeal. As recent history has shown, however, there were no shovel ready programs, green energy loans turned out to be disastrous and funds went to a wide range of costly but politically expedient ventures.

Early in the year the government began purchasing preferred shares of financial institutions under a program known as CPP or Capital Purchase Program.

On March 9th, major stock market indicators hit a 12 year low. The Dow sank to 6,547 that day but then turned around quickly in a bull run that replaced most, but not all of the wealth lost in the collapse.

In May the President signed into law major credit card reform legislation ostensibly to protect consumers. Many observers suggest however, that the opposite was true. In the nine months between enactment and its effective date, banks slashed credit limits and raised interest rates on 65% of all outstanding cards. They also found other creative ways to replace the lost fee income the law made illegal.

By July, the Administration had enacted the so-called "Cash for Clunkers" program in an effort to both jump start the economy and take gas guzzlers off the road. It did not jump start the economy and whether significant numbers of gas guzzlers were taken out of use is arguable. The final cost however, was about $24,000 for each vehicle sold, far in excess of the retail price of the average price of vehicles sold.

JANUARY 5, 2009

2009: RECESSION WITH A CAPITAL "R"

What has been painfully obvious to local businesses and consumers alike was confirmed in early December. The economy is in recession. According to the National Bureau of Economic Research, the arbiter of the nation's business cycles, the country's 73-month expansion reversed course in December 2007. At one year old, this recession has already exceeded the average duration of 10 months since World War II. Moreover, the downturn is on track to be more severe than any other recession since the 1930's.

Nearly every significant economic indicator has plummeted in the last few months. U.S. Employment posted a stunning loss of more than one-half million jobs in November alone bringing 2008 losses to nearly two-million. Additionally, consumer confidence is now the lowest on record, spending has declined to its lowest point since 1991, housing starts are at a 60-year low and the Gross Domestic Product (GDP); the total of all goods and services, has turned negative and will likely remain that way through 2009.

In September, the U.S. financial system experienced its most serious crisis since the 1929 stock market crash triggered the Great Depression.

Virtually every segment of the global financial system has been shaken and credit has become severely restricted. Unlike 1929, when government inaction and missteps contributed significantly to the Great Depression, the government acted quickly and decisively. While the potential cost of government intervention is mind-boggling, the cost of doing nothing was far greater and any repeat of the Great Depression is unlikely.

Counties served by Seacoast National Bank have not been immune. The local economy began to contract nearly two years ago reacting to the bursting local housing bubble. Today, all 16 counties served directly by Seacoast have higher unemployment rates today than they did a year ago. Rates range from a low of 6.6% in Broward County to 10.4% in St. Lucie County and as high as 11.9% in Hendry County. Unemployment is likely to increase another 1-2% in 2009 as professional, business services, financial services and local governments shed jobs.

Housing starts are near record lows, a sign the excesses created during 2002-2007 are dissipating. Nevertheless, the sales pace for newly completed homes has also declined. Housing will likely reach bottom in late 2009 barring, of course, additional unforeseen economic shock.

Existing home resale volume increased over last year but median prices have steadily declined suggesting that sales volume is heavily influenced by foreclosures.

Foreclosures have also reached record levels nationally and in most Seacoast markets. They are being driven by declining home prices, unemployment and homeowners' inability to sell their home or refinance. Moreover, some 12 million U.S. homeowners owe more on their mortgage than the underlying property is worth and over 1.2 million of those homeowners are in Florida. That is incentive for some homeowners to walk away from their mortgage. For the broader economy it suggests that foreclosures will be a fact of life for at least another two years.

Looking forward at 2009, the outlook is continued Recession... with a capital "R." Recovery will not be quick nor will it be easy. The good news is that the economy is cyclical and it will return to growth. It always does.

EMPLOYMENT PLUNGES AGAIN IN DECEMBER 2008

The U.S. economy shed 524,000 jobs in December 2008 after losing 584,000 in November. The December unemployment rate was 7.2%; the highest since January 1993. The revised November loss is the largest since 1974. December was the 12th consecutive month for job losses in the nation bringing the 2008 total to about 2.5 million. At the same time, Florida's unemployment rate climbed to 8.1%, With 752,000 Floridians unemployed out of a labor force of 9,313,000, the unemployment rate is now the highest since September 1992. There is no relief in sight as the recession continues to take its toll on employment and the broader economy.

The final employment report for 2008 showed that the economy shed an estimated 524,000 jobs, pushing the jobless rate to 7.2%—a 16 year high. The economy shed jobs in every month of 2008 with losses averaging about 68,800 through July. Losses surged by five and a half times to an average of 391,600 jobs lost each month from August through December as the force of the recession took hold. Job losses for the year totaled about 2.5 million—the most jobs shed in a single year since the end of World War II in 1945. In absolute numbers, 632,000 persons became unemployed in December bringing the total to 11.1 million out of a total workforce of 154.4 million.

The pullback in December was broad based affection most employment sectors and geographies. Construction employment declined by 101,000 jobs in December and fell 899,000 throughout the year. Construction employment peaked in September 2006. Construction layoffs began early in the sunbelt states including Florida. The losses are now moderating in the sunbelt but growing in other areas of the country.

Manufacturing employment fell by 149,000 in December. That is the largest month over month decline since 2001. Nearly one-half of the decline occurred in the fourth quarter under scoring the growing recession. Job losses in component manufacturing were widespread reflecting the slowdown in the auto and aircraft industries. Declines were greatest in fabricated metal products as well as motor vehicle components and parts.

Retail trade employment fell by 67,000 in December and by 522,000 for all of 2008. Over half the annual losses occurred in the final four months of 2008. The effect was felt the most in auto dealerships where 22,000 jobs were lost.

An additional 8,000 jobs were lost in home furnishings and 5,000 in appliances.

Wholesale trade employment fell by 30,000 jobs in December and by 164,000 in all of 2008. Reacting to several months of manufacturing downturn and wholesale trade decline, truck transportation declined by 16,000 jobs in December while air transportation declined by 4,000 jobs. The information industry lost 20,000 jobs in December as many of the nation's newspapers struggle to compete with the internet for readers.

Food services continued its downward trend reacting to declining consumer spending and a generally slowing economy. That sector peaked in June 2008 and has fallen by 104,000 jobs since. Employment in financial services declined modestly in December but fell by 148,000 during the year. The losses to date are largely concentrated geographically in the Northeast and in the investment banking sector.

Health care employment grew by 32,000 jobs in December. In all of 2008, health care added 372,000 jobs. Most of the job gains have been in ambulatory care and hospitals.

The composition of the nation's unemployment has also changed. There are now 1.9 million persons classified as "marginally attached" to the labor force. That is 564,000 more than 12 months earlier. The marginally attached category includes those who are willing and able to work and who have sought employment in the last 12 months but not in the last four weeks. Among the marginally attached are 642,000 "discouraged workers"—those who are no longer looking for work because they believe jobs are not available. That category is up 279,000 year over year.

The number of persons who worked part time in December because they could not find full time employment, hit 8.0 million in December. That category has increased by 3.4 million over the last 12 months.

Initial jobless claims for unemployment compensation rose to 589,000 the week ending January 17th from an upwardly revised 527,000 the previous week. The recent total is deep within recession territory and matches a 26 year high reached four weeks ago. The four-week average, which smooths out weekly fluctuations, was 519,250.

Looking forward, we expect nationwide employment to continue its downward trend throughout all or most of 2009. Employment indicators are lining up for another steep decline in the first half of 2009 which will likely bring 2008 and 2009 losses to about 5.0 million. That would imply an unemployment rate at or slightly greater than 9%.

While an enormous economic stimulus package ($825 + billion) is currently wending its way through Congress, it is unlikely it will produce the expected number of jobs quickly. The announced job creation components are easily 12-18 months away.

Florida Employment. Like the nation, Florida's non-agricultural employment has declined significantly and the losses are widespread both geographically and by sector. Employment declined to 7,784,000 in December and job losses have totaled 255,200 or –3.2% year over year. Declining Florida employment in December continues a trend begun in September 2007. Florida's unemployment rate is now 8.1%, its highest since September 1992 and 0.9% above the national unemployment rate.

The construction sector lost 88,200 jobs (-15.6%) year over year. While construction sector losses are moderating, the total is nearly 30% of the Florida jobs lost year over year.

The trade, transportation and utilities sector has lost 81,100 jobs (-5%) year over year. Most of the losses are in transportation as a result of a slowdown in construction and manufacturing which has led to a slowdown in trucking. The utility employment decline is a clear result of diminished construction activity.

Business services was down 53,700 jobs (-4.0%) in December year over year. While the percentage is comparatively small, the size of the sector is large and it will have a significant effect on Florida employment in 2009.

As expected, total government, which had been growing steadily, even

---

in the face of recession, entered the loss column in December when the sector experienced a loss of 4,000 jobs.

The government sector loss was expected as Florida cities and counties as well as the state itself now experience significant budget shortfalls. In fact, most states experiencing budget shortfalls which will adversely impact employment in both Florida and the nation.

Education and health services was the only sector gaining jobs among Florida's major industries.

Looking forward however, we expect that sector to soften as well. Seacoast counties as well as most counties around Florida have been experiencing declining student enrollments. This is largely in reaction to slowing population growth as families move out of Florida in search of employment.

We expect healthcare employment to continue to grow but at a slower pace as layoffs in other sectors occur and eliminate healthcare benefits for the unemployed. Indeed, in a recent survey of Florida's largest health insurers by the South Florida Business Journal, enrollment declined by 190,000 in 2008.

JANUARY 31, 2009

Q4-2008 GDP NEGATIVE 3.8%

The Commerce Department reported yesterday that the nation's GDP (Gross Domestic Product) declined at an annual rate of 3.8% in the fourth quarter of 2008. The GDP is the "top line" measure of the nation's economy and the broadest measure of goods and services produced in the nation. The growth rate was the worst since 1982 and was driven largely by declining consumer and business spending.

Consumer spending fell 3.5% overall in the fourth quarter. The decline included a 7.1% drop in spending on services; a 3.5% drop in spending on durable goods (goods expected to last at least three years) and a stunning 22.4% drop in spending on non-durable goods. The latter was the weakest showing since 1988.

Vehicle sales subtracted 2.04 percentage points from GDP after having been slightly positive through the third quarter.

On the business side, investment in equipment and software fell 27.8%, the weakest showing in 50 years. Computer and peripheral investment fell 18.9%, industrial equipment spending fell 16.6% and transportation equipment spending fell 75.7%—the steepest decline since World War II.

Business investment in structures, which had helped prop up GDP in prior quarters, fell 19.1% in the fourth quarter. That too was the weakest showing in 50 years. Most businesses worsened from the third to fourth quarter as demand slipped, consumers pulled back, businesses faced a generally tight credit market and struggled to cut costs.

Exports have been a significant support to the GDP in recent quarters. They kept the GDP in positive territory even after the subprime meltdown in August 2007. In Q4, however, exports declined 19.7% as economies around the world weakened or fell into recession. Imports, which are a subtraction from the GDP calculation, fell 15.7%.

Fourth quarter GDP included a $6.2 Billion addition to business inventories. That contributed roughly 1.32% to growth. Without the unexpectedly high inventory growth, the decline in GDP would have been about 5.12% which would have been more in line with expectations. Since inventories are high in relation to sales, the stage is set for larger GDP decline going forward as demand continues to slide and businesses struggle to work off inventories. We expect inventories to decline going forward and GDP will decline as well.

Residential investment has been a drag on the GDP for three full years. In the fourth quarter investment fell 23.6% and subtracted 0.85% from the GDP. That was the 12th consecutive decline and the third largest single quarter decline on record. Residential investment now contributes about 2.9% to GDP which is an all time low. The cycle high was 5.5%. The contribution to residential investment will remain low as long as builders are forced to cut construction starts to reduce inventories.

Yesterday's report was an "advance" report which is necessarily based on preliminary and sometimes incomplete data. The next revision will be released on February 27th and the final on March 26th. We expect a larger decline when more complete data are released.

In the same report, the U.S. Bureau of Economic Analysis reported that the price index for gross domestic purchases (prices paid by U.S. residents regardless of where goods were produced) declined 4.6%. That followed a 4.5% decline in the third quarter. That was largely driven by falling energy prices. Excluding food and energy, the price index rose 1.2%.

FEBRUARY 1, 2009

CONSUMER BALANCE SHEET AND CREDIT QUALITY RISK LOOM LARGE

Household balance sheets continue to deteriorate rapidly. Wealth declined in the third quarter at the steepest rate since 1962. At the same time, borrowing grew only 3.0% year-over-year, the slowest growth on record since 1952 when the Federal Reserve began tracking such numbers. While consumers cut borrowing they also shifted borrowing. Year over year growth in mortgage borrowing slowed to 1.5%, down from double digits less than two years ago. Growth in consumer credit slowed to 3.5% but still outpaced growth in mortgage borrowing. As cash is stretched, consumers are holding cash longer, slowing repayment and repaying less. Consumer delinquencies are steadily rising.

The aggregate net worth of U.S. households declined in the third quarter of 2008 to $56.5 Trillion. That is down from $63.6 Trillion just one year ago. The stunning $7.1 Trillion decline came largely from the declining value of assets—both home equity and securities.

Consumers' net equity in their homes has been falling for two years and so far equity has declined nearly $4.0 Trillion. That is a significant downward revision by the Federal Reserve over prior period data. The third quarter wealth decline was significant and indications are it will be just as large in the fourth quarter as both home equity and stock markets continued their unrelenting downward movement.

The financial beating consumers have endured will likely force structural changes in the way they save and spend. In the last few years the nation's savings rate was near zero and as low as negative 13% for homeowners who had home equity loans or lines of credit. Many consumers used those lines inappropriately as "de facto income." Their continued borrowing was made possible by cheap and easy credit. Consumers have now become less trusting of their wealth and have begun a swing toward savings at the expense of spending. While the long term effect will be positive, the short term effect of reduced spending will be negative and will show up in the broader economy. While the move toward saving is not unusual in a recession, it is much more evident today given the severity of the downturn.

Consumers are also reducing their borrowing. When they do borrow today, it is usually out of distress and to meet basic household needs. Household cash flow is also suffering as a result of both weakening income growth and the pronounced reduction in borrowing. The recent panic in the financial markets has served to prolong recovery or improvement in household balance sheets. When improvement does come—and it will—it is likely to be both gradual and erratic.

Consumer borrowing grew only 3% year-over-year in the third quarter. Growth in consumer liabilities also declined from $1.3 Trillion in 2006 to $425 Billion in the third quarter of 2008. That clearly underscores the significance of the consumer borrowing pull back. The data are lining up for continuing decline in the fourth quarter but the data do not yet suggest an outright decline.

Dollar borrowing has remained heavily skewed toward mortgages. Indeed, the share of household debt in mortgages was 72.5% at the end of the third quarter. That is down from 73.8% at the beginning of 2008. As consumers slow their mortgage borrowing, they are moving toward credit card borrowing. According to Moody's Investors Service, credit card balance growth is fastest in areas of the country with the largest house price declines and the weakest economies. Some of that change is a natural move from home equity borrowing as home equity dissipates. Nevertheless, a disproportionate share is distress borrowing.

Consumer borrowing will almost certainly weaken more in 2009 as labor markets weaken. That, combined with continued falling house prices, less collateral and higher debt burdens will make it more difficult to qualify for most forms of credit under what will almost certainly be stricter underwriting standards.

On the plus side, housing is now more affordable, interest rates remain at or near record lows and Fannie and Freddie will likely re-emerge later this year as viable mortgage financing sources.

Credit Quality. Household credit quality has arguably never been worse. Delinquency and default rates have risen for all types of consumer credit and, considered in aggregate, are now much higher than the 2001 recession. Credit quality deteriorated in the fourth quarter and consumer liabilities now delinquent or in default totalled $935 Billion at the end of 2008. That is approximately 8% of outstanding balances. It is also 90 basis points higher than the third quarter and three times the delinquency and default level of just three years ago.

The trend underscores the depth of the recession as credit quality erosion is clearly apparent in all credit product types and in nearly every geographical area of the country. Also noteworthy is that the quarterly delinquency increase in every bucket from 30 to 120 days was the largest on record. Moreover, defaults have also surged. They would have been higher if not for foreclosure moratoriums imposed by a number of states and financial institutions. Countrywide, for example, is offering relief to borrowers in at least 32 states as part of a settlement in connection with past lending practices. Fannie Mae and Freddie Mac began a partial moratorium in mid-December and recently extended it through January.

Credit quality is eroding almost everywhere. Mortgage credit quality is especially weak. Surprisingly, the delinquency rate for mortgage products far exceeds that of non-mortgage consumer credit products and the outlook remains grim. In 2008 the delinquency rate (30-120 days past due) for first mortgages nationwide soared past delinquencies for unsecured credit cards for the first time in history. At the end of 2008, there were roughly three million first mortgage loans in default. That is up from 1.5 Million in 2007 and less than one-million in 2006. As house prices continue to fall and more owners find themselves owing more than the property is worth some are finding it easier to default on their home mortgage while preserving unsecured credit access through credit cards. This is particularly true in 2006 and 2007 vintage high ratio loans.

The following chart shows third quarter (most recent available) delinquency and default data for Florida fixed and adjustable rate mortgage loans together with prime and sub-prime. Defaults range from 3.8% for prime fixed rate loans to a stunning 40.18% for subprime adjustable rate loans.

There are few positive signs in the housing indicators notwithstanding the fact that the National Association of Realtors reported earlier this week that sales volume was up 6.5% nationwide in December. At the same time, however, the median price was down significantly suggesting that sales are still skewed toward foreclosure and short sale transactions. With prices continuing to fall, foreclosures are likely to remain a fact of life through the remainder of this decade with significant moderation not likely until at least 2011. Even then, we expect foreclosures to remain elevated by historic standards. Many Alt A loans originated at the cycle peak in 2005 and 2006 were 5-25 adjustable rate loans (interest rates were fixed for the first five years and adjust thereafter) which will start resetting in 2010 and 2011 when rates are likely to be demonstrably higher.

The chart in the right-hand column shows new foreclosures and the ratio of foreclosures to housing units for December 2008 in all Seacoast counties. Foreclosures are up month over month and year over year. Nationally, foreclosures were up 81% in 2008 over 2007.

Non-Mortgage Consumer Credit. Credit quality has deteriorated in the bank card segment as well. Unemployment is rising which will increase delinquencies and defaults. Growth in retail sales has fallen significantly and that will put downward pressure on credit card balance growth. Additionally, tighter card lending standards are directly and negatively affecting balance growth while indirectly pushing up delinquencies.

Auto lending is exceptionally weak as rapidly declining auto sales keep the lid on borrowing. Aggregate delinquencies and defaults on both direct and indirect auto loans have reached new highs, a condition that will be exacerbated by weak vehicle sales which will limit balance growth through 2009 and into 2010.

Home equity line of credit utilization rates have risen as lenders tighten standards, reduce credit lines and homeowners fear lack of future credit availability. Delinquencies and defaults are growing in this product as well as home values continue to slide. Default rates are also being negatively impacted by rising unemployment.

Consumer Confidence once again tested new lows. Earlier this week The Conference Board reported that its consumer confidence index hit an historic low as households remained concerned about the current and future state of the economy. Confidence, by almost any measure, has been bouncing along the bottom for several months and will continue to do so.

FEBRUARY 28, 2009

Q4-2008 GDP REVISED DOWN TO NEGATIVE 6.2%—STEEPEST DECLINE SINCE Q1 1982

The Commerce Department reported Friday in its revised estimate of GDP that the nation's economy contracted in the fourth quarter much more severely than originally thought. GDP (Gross Domestic Product) declined at an annual rate of 6.2% in the fourth quarter of 2008 as compared to the advance estimate of –3.8% issued a month ago. The revised estimate is based on more complete data.

The GDP is the "top line" measure of the nation's economy and the broadest measure of goods and services produced in the nation. The negative 6.2% growth rate is the poorest showing since the first quarter of 1982 when the economy contracted at 6.4%. The current contraction is largely the product of shrinking business inventories, exports and consumer spending although most major components revealed a worse showing than originally thought.

The advance estimate last month showed that business inventories rose an estimated $6.2 Billion—a figure that surprised many economists. We opined at that time that inventories were high in relation to sales and that high inventories would set the stage for a larger GDP decline going forward. Friday's revised estimate however, shows that inventories actually shrank $19.9 Billion in the fourth quarter thereby confirming our expectation.

Exports were a significant support to the nation's GDP in 2007 and part of 2008 however real exports of goods and services decreased 23.6% in the fourth quarter. That is in stark contrast to a modest decline of 3.0% in the third quarter. The decline is a clear reaction to the softening global economy where many U.S. trading partners, such as Great Britain, the Euro Zone, Eastern Europe and the Far East are either in recession or on the edge.

Real personal consumption expenditures fell 4.3% in the fourth quarter as compared to a decrease of 3.8% in the third. At the end of the year, consumers cut back spending the most in 28 years. Durable goods (those expected to last at least three years) including cars, appliances and furniture were the hardest hit although consumers have clearly cut back on non-durable goods, especially discretionary items.

Businesses have now cut back severely as well. Nonresidential fixed investment decreased 21.1% compared to a decrease of only 1.7% a quarter earlier. Investment in non-residential structures decreased 5.9% compared to an increase of 9.7%. Equipment and software purchases decreased 28.8%—over three times the rate of the previous quarter.

Residential investment has been a drag on the GDP for three full years. In the fourth quarter investment fell 22.2% and subtracted 0.82% from the GDP. That was the 12th consecutive decline and the third largest single quarter decline on record. Residential investment now contributes about 2.9% to GDP which is an all-time low. The cycle high was 5.5%. The contribution to residential investment will remain low as long as builders are forced to cut construction starts to reduce inventories.

Looking forward, we expect the first quarter of 2009 to decline 5% with some modest improvement late in the year. When the books close on 2009 they will probably show that the economy contracted 3.5±% for the year.

MARCH 6, 2009

EMPLOYMENT DOWN AGAIN IN FEBRUARY—NATION'S UNEMPLOYMENT RATE NOW 8.1%

The U.S. Bureau of Labor Statistics reported this morning that the nation's economy lost another 651,000 jobs in February bringing the recession total to about 4.4 million. The economy has shed 2.6 million jobs in the last four months underscoring the seriousness of the current recession. January job losses were also revised from -598,000 to -655,000 and December numbers were revised from -577,000 to -681,000.

The number of unemployed persons increased by 851,000 to 12.5 million. Over the last 12 months the number of unemployed has persons has increased by 5.0 million and the unemployment rate has risen by 3.3 percentage points.

About 2.1 million persons were marginally attached to the labor force in February. This category represents those who are available, want work and had searched for employment in the preceding 12 months. The category total is up about 466,000 from 12 months earlier. These persons are not counted as unemployed because they had not sought work in the last four weeks. Among the marginally attached were 731,000 discouraged workers up 335,000 from 12 months earlier. Discouraged workers are those not currently looking for work because they believe no jobs are available for them. The number of persons working part time because full time work was not available rose by 787,000 reaching 8.6 million. The number of workers in this classification has risen by 3.7 million over the last 12 months.

Job losses in January were deep and widespread affecting most major industry types. Employment fell by 168,000 jobs in manufacturing. The majority of losses (-132,000) occurred in durable goods (consumables) manufacturing where spending was down over 22% in the fourth quarter. Employment in professional and business services fell by 180,000 in February.

The construction industry lost 104,000 more jobs in February as the industry slows nationwide and not just in the sunbelt states. Construction industry employment has fallen by 1.1 million jobs since peaking in January 2007. Roughly 40% of the losses occurred over the last four months.

Employment in truck transportation declined by 33,000 in February reacting to the widespread recession which has led to shrinking inventories (-$19.9 Billion in Q4) and declining manufacturing.

Employment in retail trade fell by 45,000 in January. Since its peak in November 2007, 592,000 jobs have been lost. Transportation and warehousing lost 44,000 jobs in January and 202,000 since the start of the recession in December 2007. Employment in financial activities declined by 42,000 in January. The total losses are about 388,000 since the peak in December 2006. By far, the greatest losses have been in the last six months since the financial crisis began in September 2008.

Health care increased by 19,000 jobs in January but even that category is down from the average of 30,000 jobs added per month in 2008.

Normally in a recession, job losses are somewhat contained by either category or geography or both. That has not happened this time. Thus far in the current recession, losses have been wide spread and virtually no sector or geography is immune. Widespread losses like this clearly under-score the breadth, depth and overall seriousness of the current recession. We expect job losses to continue to mount throughout most of 2009 with losses stabilizing late in the year or in early 2010. The nation's unemployment rate will likely reach 9.0% before stabilizing in 2010.

EMPLOYMENT CONTINUES TO DETERIORATE—U.S. UNEMPLOYMENT RATE NOW 8.1%. FLORIDA 8.6%

The U.S. economy shed 651,000 jobs in February. At the same time losses for January were revised to -655,000 from -598,000 and December was revised to -681,000 from -577,000. The nation's unemployment rate rose sharply to 8.1% with 12.5 million Americans now unemployed. At the same time, Florida's *January* unemployment rate climbed to 8.6%, With 800,000 Floridians unemployed out of a labor force of 9,256,000, the unemployment rate is now the highest since September 1992. There is no relief in sight as the recession continues to take its toll on employment and the broader economy.

The U.S. Bureau of Labor Statistics reported this morning that the nation's economy lost another 651,000 jobs in February bringing the recession total to about 4.4 million. The economy has shed 2.6 million jobs in the last four months underscoring the seriousness of the current recession. January job losses were also revised from -598,000 to -655,000 and December numbers were revised from -577,000 to -681,000. These revisions subtracted an additional 161,000 jobs from payrolls over the last two months.

The number of unemployed persons increased by 851,000 to 12.5 million. Over the last 12 months the number of unemployed has persons has increased by 5.0 million and the unemployment rate has risen by 3.3 percentage points.

About 2.1 million persons were marginally attached to the labor force in February. This category represents those who are available, want work and had searched for employment in the preceding 12 months. The category total is up about 466,000 from 12 months earlier. These persons are not counted as <u>unemployed</u> because they had not sought work in the last four weeks. Among the marginally attached were 731,000 discouraged workers up 335,000 from 12 months earlier. Discouraged workers are those not currently looking for work because they believe no jobs are available for them. The number of persons working part time because full time work was not available rose by 787,000 reaching 8.6 million. The number of workers in this classification has risen by 3.7 million over the last 12 months.

Job losses in January were deep and widespread affecting most major industry types. Employment fell by 168,000 jobs in manufacturing. The majority of losses (-132,000) occurred in durable goods (consumables) manufacturing where spending was down over 22% in the fourth quarter. Employment in professional and business services fell by 180,000 in February.

The construction industry lost 104,000 more jobs in February as the industry slows nationwide and not just in the sunbelt states. Construction industry employment has fallen by 1.1 million jobs since peaking in January 2007. Roughly 40% of the losses occurred over the last four months.

Employment in truck transportation declined by 33,000 in February reacting to the widespread recession which has led to shrinking inventories (-$19.9 Billion in Q4) and declining manufacturing.

Employment in financial activities continues to trend downward losing 44,000 jobs in February. The sector peaked in December 2006 and has lost 448,000 jobs since. Half of the losses have occurred in the last six months. The losses are concentrated in the nation's investment banking centers.

Employment in retail trade fell by 40,000 over the month and by 607,000 since its peak in December 2007. Within this sector, employment in auto dealerships declined by 9000, sporting goods by 9,000, furniture and home furnishings stores by 8,000 and garden supply stores by 7,000. Wholesale trade employment also fell by 37,000 jobs over the month.

Employment in leisure and hospitality continued its downward trend by losing 33,000 jobs in February. This is largely in reaction to declining business and personal travel as well as fewer corporate meetings being held at hotel and resort locations.

Healthcare continued to add jobs gaining 27,000 in February. Most of the increases were in ambulatory health care followed by hospitals.

Florida Employment. Florida's employment report lags the nation by a month so January employment numbers were reported today. Florida's unemployment rate rose to 8.6% which is 800,000 persons unemployed out of a labor force of 9,256,000. That is the highest rate since September 1992. It is also 0.7% higher than the national rate.

Like the nation, Florida's non-agricultural employment has declined significantly and the losses are widespread both geographically and by sector. Employment declined to 7,557,000 in January and job losses have totaled 355,700 or -4.5% year over year. Declining Florida employment in January continued a trend begun in August 2007.

The construction sector lost 100,700 jobs (-17.9%) year over year. While construction sector losses are moderating, the total is still 26% of the Florida jobs lost year over year.

The trade, transportation and utilities sector has lost 86,400 jobs (-5.3%) year over year. Most of the losses are in transportation as a result of a slowdown in construction and manufacturing which has led to a slowdown in trucking. The utility employment decline is a clear result of diminished construction activity.

Professional and business services was down 84,500 jobs (-7.2%) in January year over year. The size of the sector is large and it will have a significant effect on Florida employment throughout 2009.

As expected, total government, which had been growing steadily, even in the face of recession, entered the loss column in December but bounced back with 4,100 new jobs in January. We expect this sector to re-enter the loss column as a result of extraordinary government budget deficits at the municipal, county and state levels. Education and health services gained 23,500 jobs in January.

Looking forward, we expect nationwide employment to continue its downward trend throughout all of 2009 and into 2010. Employment indicators are lining up for additional steep declines in the first half of 2009 which will likely bring 2008 and 2009 losses to nearly 6.0 million. That would imply an unemployment rate in excess of 9.5% with significant risk to the upside.

In our view, the fundamentals for employment do not bode well going forward. The number of people working part time plus those marginally attached to the work force are growing faster than the unemployment rate itself. Secondly, the duration of unemployment has grown significantly meaning that newly unemployed are staying unemployed longer.

The underlying data also suggest a surge in unemployment may hit the service sector in the next few months. Indeed, growing layoffs in the retail sector are not yet showing up fully in the data nor are the layoffs in the financial services industry. Lengthy severance packages may help explain the delay in recognizing financial service layoffs. There is no good news in the employment numbers. Given the continuing slow-down in economic activity, we look for more of the same in the months to come.

MARCH 6, 2009

HOME SALES VOLUME AND PRICE CONTINUE TO SLIDE

Sales of existing homes nationwide sank to the lowest level in 12 years in January according to the National Association of Realtors. Sales fell 5.3% to 4.49 million units annualized. That is down from 4.74 million units annualized in December. At the same time, the median sales price declined to $170,300. That is down 3.07% from $175,700 in December and down 14.76% from a year earlier. In a separate report, the U.S. Census Bureau and the Department of Housing and Urban Development reported that sales of *new* homes declined 10.2% in January to 309,000 from a revised December total of 344,000. That is also a 48% decline from 597,000 in January 2008. The median price was $201,100 in January and there was an estimated 13.3 month supply of new homes at the current sales pace.

Compared to a year ago, January sales of existing homes were up significantly from a year earlier in every Seacoast served Metropolitan Statistical Area (MSA). In the Ft. Pierce—Port St. Lucie MSA, sales volume surged over 80% but the median price fell 34.56%. The story was similar in Brevard County (Melbourne—Titusville—Palm Bay MSA) where volume was up 46% but median price was down 32%. Buyers were clearly reacting to renewed affordability created by foreclosures and other distress transactions. The National Association of Realtors reported that 45% of transactions were foreclosure related. The local total is now about 60% in metropolitan areas and under 30% in the Heartland counties surrounding Lake Okeechobee.

There is widespread evidence of seller capitulation as well. Given the unrelenting two year decline, sellers have been more likely to accept the reality of recession pricing and, if they must sell, pricing properties to more accurately match the market.

The table at the bottom of the page shows both existing home sales volume and median prices by Seacoast served MSAs for the last six months. Notwithstanding the significant year over year volume increases evident in the January data, more recent data tell a different story. With few exceptions, median prices have been declining month over month for several quarters. While sales volume is up year over year, the increases began to flatten in June 2008 and have been erratic since. The table at the left shows net sales volume and median price change over the last six months. Sales volume decreased by as much as 30% in the Orlando MSA to as little as 4.2% in Ft. Pierce—Port St. Lucie. The statewide volume change was down 21.79% and the median price was down 32.23%. Both are net changes over the last six months.

Foreclosures continue to plague both the national and local economy. While the effect of sub-prime foreclosures is largely behind us, the protracted recession has kept foreclosures at an elevated level. Foreclosures continue to be driven by declining home prices, diminished home equity and household wealth, rising unemployment and homeowner's inability to sell or refinance. There is also a vicious cycle at play too. As foreclosed assets come back on the market, they usually do so at a lower price which forces prices lower and exacerbates recovery.

Existing single family residential home prices have now returned to "pre run-up" levels of 2003 and 2004 in most south Florida counties. St. Lucie County, which had an extraordinary and unsustainable run up in prices earlier this decade has seen prices drop precipitously. Prices have returned to 2002 levels. As a sidebar, Lee County on Florida's southwest coast and widely regarded as the nation's epicenter of housing distress has seen median prices decline to 1997 levels.

The condominium sector volumes are so small that the percentage changes are not meaningful. Median prices are also distorted by comparatively few sales—most of which were lower end product and distressed transactions. In every Seacoast served MSA and the state itself, median prices dropped to the low $100,000 range. In Ft. Pierce-Port St Lucie, Orlando and Ft. Lauderdale, the median price fell significantly below the $100,000 mark.

Looking forward, we expect more of the same for at least the next few quarters. The National association of realtors released its index of pending home sales. It too is down suggesting that closed sales will decline again over the next month or two.

New home inventories continue to decline nationally and throughout all Seacoast markets. This ongoing trend is positive as it is helping clear the excess inventory created earlier in the decade. Construction starts have also declined to record lows. Indeed, if national construction starts were to continue their current rate of decline, mathematically starts would fall to zero by year end.

Starts are now at a very low level in all Seacoast served markets as well. The bad news is that sales are down too. Despite renewed affordability and mortgage interest rates continuing to hover near record low levels, prospective buyers are not lining up to buy. Why? There appear to be several reasons. First, they don't want to catch the proverbial "falling knife." In other words, there is widespread expectation that prices will decline further. That is a high probability as foreclosed assets continue to flood the market. Second, there are widespread fears about unemployment. Third, financing is limited and often more difficult to obtain. Finally, potential buyers are waiting to see what the government will do in terms of home buyer incentives and mortgage modifications.

The oft asked question is have we hit bottom? The short answer is no. We could still find a bottom by year end but the economic headwinds are fierce and still increasing. Two things need to happen before we know we have found a bottom. First, prices must stop falling and second volumes must flatten or show some upward movement. That is not happening yet and the data continue to signal that the end is not yet in sight.

COMMERCIAL REAL ESTATE CONDITION AND OUTLOOK

The commercial real estate sector stayed afloat long after the residential sector began to sink and even as the broader economy began to weaken. Nevertheless, the commercial sector began to falter in early 2008. Today, most commercial real estate product types are under stress, values have declined and no positive change is likely in 2009.

The effects of a deteriorating economy and the worst credit crisis in six decades landed squarely in the commercial real estate sector in 2008. Going into 2008, it was apparent that the sector was softening coincident with the generally slowing economy. Retail spending was declining which quickly flowed into the real estate sector as retailers began closing underperforming stores and new development slowed to a crawl. The same was true in the office sector with declining office jobs and a diminishing need for space to support the ailing housing and allied industries.

We expected that commercial real estate values and prices would decline as a result of reduced transaction activity, rising expenses and rising capitalization and discount rates. And indeed, they did as investors abruptly shifted their analytical focus to "what is" rather than what was merely assumed to be.

Credit availability for commercial real estate was also beginning to soften in early 2008 as both investors and institutional lenders took a more cautious wait and see approach. The credit markets steadily weakened throughout year and the distress came to a head in September with the unprecedented events that led to a near collapse of the U.S. financial system. CMBS (commercial mortgage backed securities) issuance ground to a virtual halt leaving a huge void in capital for commercial real estate acquisition and finance.

With the secondary market effectively closed for business, that left commercial banks as the primary source of mortgage dollars. The timing could not have been worse as banks too struggle with capital and liquidity adequacy, limited balance sheet capacity, declining markets and regulatory pressure to shore up balance sheets and reduce troublesome loan concentrations.

Indeed, as indicated by the Federal Reserve Senior Loan Officer Survey, banks have been steadily ratcheting up underwriting standards. For most, that does not mean imposition of new and onerous standards (although some borrowers might disagree) but rather a return to fundamental credit principles, something that may have been lost in the exuberant and unsustainable run up which peaked in 2006.

According to the Federal Reserve survey, 30% to 40% of banks reported tightened credit standards in 2007. By the first quarter of 2008, the number surged to 80% and by the end of the year it was 90%.

As the curtain closed on 2008, however, commercial real estate performance was far worse than expected when the year began. Nationally, according to REIS, transaction activity (dollar volume of single property transactions) dropped 85% from its high point in the second quarter of 2007 through 2008 and 74% in just four quarters. Additionally, aggregate net operating income decreased and capitalization rates rose.

As would be expected, the combination has forced values down from their cycle highs but the decline has not yet wiped out the gains realized between 2003 and the cycle high in the third quarter of 2005 for retail and the third and fourth quarters of 2007 for office, industrial and apartment.

Mortgage performance held up reasonably well for CMBS loans in 2008. The foreclosure rate was 0.10% which was within two basis points of 2006 and 2007. Whole loans held by financial institutions did not fare as well. Net losses, according to the OCC (Office of Comptroller of the Currency), surged in 2007 and by mid-2008 reached about 0.85% for community and mid-size banks and over one-percent for large banks. The average reported by the OCC over 17 years since 1991 was 0.48% although that number is skewed by recent (2006-2008) history which reflects a clear move to riskier loan concentrations earlier in the decade.

As we look forward from the first quarter, the outlook is not good. New commercial development will be virtually non-existent. The Architectural Billing Index is one of numerous indicators leading us to that conclusion. The index is prepared by the American Institute of Architects and its premise is that architectural services precede most commercial real estate development. The index has now dropped to an all-time low as virtually nothing is on the drawing boards.

We also expect prices and values to decline further and that will trigger a rise in defaults. Over $24 Billion in CRE (commercial real estate) loans are scheduled to mature in 2009. That number rises to roughly $40 Billion by mid-2010. This is on a national basis and we believe it misses many smaller loans less than approximately $10 Million each held by community and mid-size banks.

When the loans mature, they are going to need to pay off or refinance. That will be a major crunch point as dollars are not available to refinance everything coming due. Indeed, it appears that there is about 2.5 times the loan volume coming due than there are dollars available to refinance them. For example, at the end of 2008 the syndicated loan market was virtually non-existent having experienced a cycle peak of over $80 Billion in the second quarter of 2007 and then plummeting to roughly $3.0 Billion at the end of 2008. Moreover, most commercial banks do not have balance sheet capacity to absorb what needs to be refinanced. Finally, as previously described, values are likely to deteriorate further throughout 2009 leaving many projects in high loan to value positions and not refinance-able without significant loan curtailment.

Relief could come in the form of government intervention but as of this writing (March 2009), it has not despite the billions of TARP (Troubled Asset Relief Program) and other dollars that have already been infused into the American financial system in an effort to thaw credit markets and jump start the economy.

Despite all that is being done, in our view, the over-riding question remains. What is the incentive for financial institutions of any type to loan into an already impaired market with declining collateral values—values that are almost certain to decline further in 2009?

Sector by sector. Retail real estate is clearly the weakest of the four core commercial real estate property sectors (retail, office, industrial and apartments). The sector is feeling the effects of the credit crisis and a remarkable slowdown in consumer spending. That combination is forcing structural changes in retailing. Retailers are aggressively closing under-performing aggressively closing under-performing stores, bankruptcies are surging and the effect is flowing through to retail real estate.

According to Real Capital Analytics, retail real estate transaction volume was down 60% in 2008 as compared with 2007. Capitalization rates, ("cap rates")—the ratio between net operating income and sale price—were up 60 basis points both causing and reacting to falling prices and investors sagging confidence in, and outlook for that sector.

Prices turned negative in 2008 with even the highest grade properties down 9.9% and lower end properties down as much as 25%. Prices and cap rates are now back to 2004 levels and the outlook for the remainder of 2009 is decidedly negative.

Office Real Estate. Office employment grew significantly in the middle of the decade. Much of the growth was in support of the residential real estate sector. What followed was a surge in office real estate development—especially in suburban locations. Despite a distinct and measurable increase in development, it was still more constrained than previous office development booms. That was a result of more constrained hiring practices, tenants being slower to expand into additional space, declining per capita space needs and improved technical capabilities which allowed more employees to work away from an office.

The recession hit the office sector in 2008 as office employment began to decline. Business and professional services, information technology, publishing and financial intermediation (banking and finance) all saw noteworthy declines in 2008 leading to a decline in office space needs. Additionally, corporate downsizings outpaced expansions four to one over the year.

Today, vacancy rates are surging, cap rates are rising and rent growth is flat to negative. The outlook for the remainder of 2009 is negative. Sales volume will be very low and we expect values to decline.

Industrial real estate, including warehousing, held up well while the economy was growing. Stress emerged with the housing crunch, then a pull-back in consumer spending followed by declining exports as U.S. trading partners fell into recession. To top it off manufacturing declined at home. We expect values to decline in the industrial sector for the same reasons as retail and office. The decline, however, should be more moderate.

Multifamily is perhaps the strongest sector nationwide but decidedly weak locally as a result of the "shadow market" created by an extraordinary number of condominium units and single family residences available for rent.

MARCH 18, 2009

EMERGING TRENDS IN RETAIL REAL ESTATE

Retail real estate is feeling the effects of the housing and credit crises together with a remarkable slowdown in consumer spending. That combination is forcing structural changes in retailing. Retailers are aggressively closing under-performing stores, bankruptcies are surging and the effect is flowing through to retail real estate. Rents are under pressure, vacancies are rising and investors are taking a fresh and increasingly critical look at assumptions around retail real estate investment.

Shopping centers, once naively thought to be immune from downturn as a result of the extraordinary early decade residential growth have now turned into high risk assets. No longer are there growing numbers of roof tops to justify additional retail real estate development. Instead, sagging retail spending, an unsettling jobs picture, declining household wealth and housing woes have combined to destroy any semblance of economic feasibility for new development. These same factors have put existing projects at far greater risk as retailers close under-performing stores and bankruptcies surge both locally and nationally.

The retail sector has been long overdue for correction after a decade long expansion. Too much space was constructed earlier this decade—much of it for reasons that did not include demand or economic feasibility. REITs, for example, one of the largest owners of retail assets were often pressured by shareholders to show growth. So they did, in the form of new and often unnecessary power centers and regional malls.

Retailers too were pressured by shareholders to grow. In a time of easy money, they created specialty spin offs that tended to locate in high end shopping centers and especially lifestyle centers. Today, in the age of contraction, tight money and sagging spending, these same retailers are pulling back, closing stores and consolidating in fewer locations. Every part of the sector is at risk but especially lower end unanchored malls and shopping centers. Today's centers need anchor tenants with strong credit which is getting increasingly difficult to find.

Big box retailers are not immune either. Electronics retailers are struggling along with department stores and others facing slow consumer spending. Large office supply "super-stores" are closing underperforming stores or consolidating too as businesses contract and have less need for office supplies. Others are reducing hours. REITs are selling land once intended for near term development.

What sectors will fare best? ... and worst? Grocery anchored neighborhood centers appear best positioned to withstand the recession. Consumers will continue to spend on food and essentials even as they cut back spending on discretionary purchases. Big box discounters are likely to stay afloat and deep discounters such as Wal-Mart will do well in the current economic environment.

Lifestyle centers will likely perform the worst as tenants offer products usually regarded as discretionary. These centers became overbuilt as retailers sought to expand specialty spin off stores. Early lifestyle centers were located near fortress malls and in upscale areas. The more recent development, however, occurred in lower income areas and at suburban edges and these will be most adversely affected.

What is driving retail real estate today? The current recession has landed squarely on retailing and the retail real estate sector. Indeed, rents are no longer increasing. With few exceptions today, growth is flat or declining. At the same time, vacancy rates are rising as absorption rates slow, lease renewal levels decline and tenants seek to sub lease space. Finally, capitalization rates—the ratio between a properties net operating income and its value—are rising pushing value and prices down. Consider cap rates.

For decades, capitalization rates hovered in the 10% range. Rates were often slightly lower for new, well located investment grade properties and slightly higher for older or second tier properties. The result was the lower the rate the higher the value and vice versa. In 2002, residential development began to surge and prices rose. That fuelled additional residential development and prices continued their unprecedented rise. As retail typically supports residential development, developers followed the surging residential growth with retail real estate development. Values and prices rose in the retail real estate sector as well and that fuelled yet more development. At the same time, interest rates were at historic lows as a result of monetary policy in place following the 911 terrorist attacks.

The combination of low interest rates, surging development and the apparent belief that prices would continue to rise forced capitalization rates down to levels never seen before. Rates fell below 6% and sometimes under 5%. Clearly such rates and the values they generated were unsustainable.

Today, capitalization rates are trending upward again and that is placing significant downward pressure on values. No longer are there increasing numbers of roof tops for retail real estate to follow. Moreover, investors and financial institutions alike are re-pricing risk and financing sources are extremely limited.

The CMBS (commercial mortgage backed securities) market, once the largest source of retail real estate financing is temporarily dried up and commercial banks as an industry do not have balance sheet capacity to absorb the shortfall. That has led to a record decline in transaction activity. Indeed, according to New York based Real Capital Analytics, retail real estate transaction volume fell 74% with only $19.4 billion in transaction activity nationwide in 2008 down from nearly $80 billion a year earlier.

All of those factors are putting upward pressure on capitalization rates. Indeed, rates rose an average of 60 basis points in 2008 and are lining up for a greater increase of 100–200 bps in 2009. Even the best and most desirable projects have now broken the 7.5% mark on their way back to historic norms in the mid 9% range.

Economic feasibility analysis seeks to answer the very fundamental question, *"if this project is constructed, will it be worth an amount equal to or greater than the cost to create it."* After all, there is no rational economic reason to construct something that will be worth less than it cost to build. Today, the short answer is an almost universal and resounding no. Indeed, recent transaction data are replete with evidence of retail properties selling (or being offered for sale) at prices less than the cost to build them.

Some would argue that construction costs and land costs have declined and that should justify development. While costs have indeed declined, the argument overlooks the reality of total cost of production—the so-called "all in" cost. There is a laundry list of indirect costs in any development not the least of which are the so-called carrying costs or interest and project maintenance during a prolonged absorption period. These costs are as real as bricks and mortar and need to be covered by the project. In times like these both the amount and duration of the costs are unpredictable.

All this begs the question of what needs to happen to restore economic feasibility to retail real estate. The answer is all or some combination of the following. Rents need to increase in the range of 25% to 40%. Capitalization rates need to decline to "compression era" rates in the 5% to 6.5% range. Vacancies must decline. None of these conditions is even remotely likely. Indeed, each indicator argues strongly for the continued absence of economic feasibility.

The short term outlook for retail real estate is poor and is currently being driven by recession characteristics such as a dramatic decline in consumer spending, rising unemployment, declining home equity, declining household wealth and an absence of credit. The Federal Reserve issued its latest Flow of Funds report last week and several elements were especially noteworthy. Household net worth declined $5.1 Trillion (17.9%) to $51.5 Trillion from just one year ago. Since peaking in the second quarter of 2007, household wealth is down $13 Trillion. That will likely grow to $15 Trillion by the end of the first quarter of 2009 given the rate of decline in both home and stock prices so far this year. The nation's wealth to income ratio for the household sector is now under 5%, the lowest since 1951. At the same time aggregate home equity has slipped to 43%, a postwar low and down from 58.5% just three years ago. One of the most obvious manifestations of these economic events is the significant and prolonged effect it has on consumer spending and how it negatively flows through to the retail real estate sector.

The longer term outlook for retail real estate. The previously described impairment is arguably the acute phase of the current recession. Many of these circumstances will correct themselves both naturally and perhaps with a boost from the various government economic stimulus programs. Nevertheless, we believe there are characteristics about retailing and retail real estate that are more structural and will have long-term effects on the industry and which will curtail future development.

First, many stores were opened and store concepts created merely to show growth and to feed an artificial boom created by unsustainable growth in residential real estate. Developers *"followed the roof tops"* and not the true economic demand. Many of those roof tops proved to be empty.

There are already clear signs that consumer spending habits are changing as a result of the prolonged recession and diminished credit availability. Savings is up demonstrably and discretionary purchasing is down—circumstances that seem likely to continue.

MARCH 29, 2009

FLORIDA'S UNEMPLOYMENT RATE REACHES 9.4%—HIGHEST SINCE 1976

Florida's unemployment rate rose to 9.4% in February, the highest since April 1976 and significantly higher than the nation's unemployment rate of 8.1%. Approximately 874,000 Floridians are now jobless out of a labor force of 9,252,000 according to Florida's Agency for Workforce Innovation, the state agency charged with monitoring employment.

The unemployment rate is up 0.6% from January's revised estimate of 8.8% and up 4.2% since February 2008. A total of 399,400 jobs were lost in Florida year-over-year. Florida employment has steadily declined since August 2007. Losses began in construction and have steadily grown into other employment sectors.

Construction employment, reacting to the continuing residential and now the commercial real estate downturn lost 114,600 jobs for a decline of 20.7% year-over-year. Approximately 27% of the state's total job losses have been in the construction sector. Many of the jobs originally lost in residential construction were temporarily absorbed in the commercial sector. As the commercial sector has now declined too, those jobs are likely to be long term losses and not likely to be replaced over the short term.

The Professional and Business Services sector has now lost 102,100 jobs or 8.7% year-over year. That sector bears watching as it is one of the larger sectors and as service jobs in total move in Florida so will state employment.

Leisure and hospitality lost 33,100 jobs while trade, transportation and utilities lost 86,500.

The only sector posting job gains was education and health services with an increase of 19,200 jobs or 1.6% year-over-year. Most of the increase was in nursing services and residential care facilities.

The Bureau of Labor Statistics will release national numbers for March on Friday, April 3rd. February losses totaled 651,000 jobs. The consensus for March is a loss of about 660,000. Our tally suggests job losses could total over 725,000 due to Wall Street severance packages that were likely exhausted in February plus continuing above trend declines in Professional and Business Services and Financial Intermediation.

MARCH 30, 2009

HOME SALES VOLUME UP— PRICES DOWN ... AGAIN

In a sector where good news has been scarce, new and existing home sales volume, as well as residential construction starts and permits all rose in February after dismal showings in January. Sales of new single family homes rose 4.7% according to the Commerce Department. At the same time, the National Association of Realtors reported an increase of 5.1% in existing home sales volume. Construction starts also rose 22% and permits rose 16.1%. While the positive news was welcome, the other side of the equation—median price—was less welcome. New home prices tumbled 2.85% from January to February and 18.1% year over year. The median price of a new home nationally was $200,900.

The median price for an existing home nationwide was up 0.36% to $165,400. The huge increase in construction starts was predominately in the Northeast and in the multifamily housing sector.

Existing home sales rose in Florida and all Seacoast served Metropolitan Statistical Areas (MSAs) in February and also year over year. According to the Florida Association of Realtors (FAR) volume increases were greatest in Metro Orlando at nearly +20% and slightly over +30% in Palm Beach County. Volumes in both metros fell dramatically in January but made much of it up in February.

The median price increased about 12% in the Ft. Lauderdale MSA after falling an almost equal amount a month earlier. The median price in Ft. Pierce—Port St. Lucie MSA grew 6.27% to $122,100. Changes in other Seacoast served MSAs were around two percent (plus or minus).

The table at the bottom of the page shows both existing home sales volume and median prices in Seacoast served MSAs for the last seven months while the table to the right shows the net change in both volume and price over the same time period.

The data show that the net change in both volume and median price has been generally downward over the last seven months. The most recent data, however, are erratic and still do not indicate a clear and sustainable trend. While volumes are up, the fact that median price continues to slide suggests that sales are still skewed toward foreclosures, short sales and other distressed transactions. Although there are some positive signs in the February data, it is still too early to call a bottom to the slumping housing market. We expect the current trend to continue for much of the remainder of 2009 as bloated inventories are worked down, foreclosed properties come back to market and unemployment continues to grow.

Existing single family residential home prices have now returned to "pre run-up" levels of 2003 and 2004 in most south Florida counties. St. Lucie County, however, which had an extraordinary and unsustainable run up in prices earlier this decade has seen prices drop precipitously. Prices have now returned to 2002 levels. While prices in all Seacoast markets have fallen to a level coincident with the long term level of increase, we believe there is still more room for decline. Indeed, values could fall below their level at the start of the run up earlier this decade. Inventory levels are still too high in virtually every Seacoast market. Foreclosure inventories also remain bloated and unemployment will continue to rise forcing more delinquency, default and foreclosure. These forces combine to overcome the positive effect of low interest rates and renewed affordability.

Foreclosures are still a wild card. They continue to surge and as they do, houses will come back to market at lower prices once again putting downward pressure on values and prices. Foreclosures also ebb and flow artificially as Fannie Mae, Freddie Mac, several large banks and even the judiciary impose temporary moratoria on foreclosures.

The condominium sector. as shown on the above table, volumes are so small that the percentage changes are not meaningful. Median prices are also distorted by comparatively few sales—most of which were lower end product and distressed transactions. In every Seacoast served MSA and the state itself, median prices dropped to the low $100,000 range. In Orlando and Ft. Lauderdale, the median price dipped below the $100,000 mark.

New Construction starts have been declining steadily in Seacoast served metropolitan areas for most of the last two years. Palm Beach County peaked in the second quarter of 2005 when it recorded over 9,000 new construction starts. Starts have declined every quarter since through the fourth quarter of 2008 when about 1,200 starts were recorded. Starts declined over 86% during that period. Inventory has not grown since the same time period. Supply was generally flat through 2005 and began a steady decline in early 2006. Today (Q4-2008) Palm Beach County has about an 8.5 month supply at the current rate of absorption.

At the opposite end of the performance chart is St. Lucie County where construction starts did not peak until mid 2006. It was not until early 2007 that starts began to decline in a meaningful fashion.

With everything in the pipeline it was also early 2007 before inventory began to decline. Today, inventories are down significantly but there is still an unhealthy supply at nearly 14 months.

Metro Orlando counties (Orange, Seminole, Lake and Osceola) saw inventories peak in early 2006. Osceola County, which experienced extraordinary growth earlier in the decade, much like St. Lucie County, actually peaked a year later in 2007. In fact, Osceola and St. Lucie were two of the nation's fastest growing counties in 2005. New home inventory in Metro Orlando is extraordinarily high (see table above) where Orange and Seminole counties have more than a 20 month supply.

What is a normal supply? Over the long term, three months (±) is typically considered a "normal" supply. That is roughly equivalent to what tract developers have historically budgeted for holding costs over the long term. At that level, and given a stable market, equilibrium exists. Hard and soft costs are in balance, there is reasonable profit potential, credit is reasonably available and affordable and sales prices are consistent with local household income levels. Clearly, equilibrium does not exist today.

APRIL 3, 2009

U.S. SHEDS 663,000 JOBS IN MARCH—UNEMPLOYMENT RATE GROWS TO 8.5%

Nonfarm payrolls fell in March by 663,000 jobs. At the same time, the Labor Department reported a revision to January numbers when the revised loss was 741,000 jobs. About 5.5 million jobs have been lost since the recession officially began in December 2007. Of those, 3.7 million have been in the last six months. That represents about 2.7% of the nation's labor force and is the largest loss in 50 years. The number of unemployed persons is now 13.2 million having increased by 694,000 in March. March job losses brought the U.S. unemployment rate to 8.5%, up from 8.1% a month earlier. Over the last 12 months, the nation's unemployment rate has risen 3.4%. That represents 5.3 million newly unemployed over the year. The rate is now the highest since November 1983.

March job losses were widespread across most sectors and geographies. Component industries (those producing parts for auto, computer and other industries) lost 161,000 jobs in factory employment. Factory employment has lost 1.0 million jobs over the last six months.

The construction industry lost 126,000 jobs in March as declines migrate from residential to commercial construction and also expand to geographical areas previously untouched. Construction employment has fallen by 1.3 million jobs since peaking in January 2007. Roughly half that decline has been over the last five months.

Business and professional service employment declined by 133,000 jobs in March while retail trade employment fell by 48,000. Since peaking in November 2007, retail sector employment declines have averaged 44,000 per month. Building materials, auto dealerships and appliance retailers accounted for much of the decline.

Employment in financial activities continued to decline in March. The number of jobs in that sector has declined by 495,000 since it peaked in December 2006.

The number of persons working part time for economic reasons (involuntary part time workers) grew by 423,000 to 9.0 million persons in March. At the same time, those marginally attached to the labor force is now about 2.1 million having grown by 754,000 from a year earlier. Persons in this category are ready and able to work but were not counted as unemployed because they had not searched for work in the last four weeks. Included in the marginally attached category were 685,000 discouraged workers. This is up 284,000 from a year earlier. The category includes those who do not believe there is work available for them.

Initial Claims. In a separate report, the Labor Department reported Thursday that first time claims for unemployment ("Initial Claims") rose 12,000 to 669,000 claims the week of March 28th. That is the highest level since 1982. Claims have risen 72% over the same period a year ago. The prior week (March 21st) saw claims jump to 656,750, a 96% increase from the same period a year ago.

FLORIDA'S MARCH UNEMPLOYMENT RATE REACHES 9.7%—U.S. 8.5%

Florida's unemployment rate rose to 9.7% in March, the highest since April 1976 and significantly higher than the nation's unemployment rate of 8.5%. Approximately 874,000 Floridians are now jobless out of a labor force of 9,252,000 according to Florida's Agency for Workforce Innovation, the state agency charged with monitoring employment.

The unemployment rate is up 0.6% from January's revised estimate of 8.8% and up 4.2% since February 2008. A total of 399,400 jobs were lost in Florida year-over-year. Florida employment has steadily declined since August 2007. Losses began in construction and have steadily grown into other employment sectors.

Construction employment, reacting to the continuing residential and now the commercial real estate downturn lost 114,600 jobs for a decline of 20.7% year-over-year. Approximately 27% of the state's total job losses have been in the construction sector. Many of the jobs originally lost in residential construction were temporarily absorbed in the commercial sector. As the commercial sector has now declined too, those jobs are likely to be long term losses and not likely to be replaced over the short term.

The Professional and Business Services sector has now lost 102,100 jobs or 8.7% year-over year. That sector bears watching as it is one of the larger sectors and as service jobs in total move in Florida so will state employment.

Leisure and hospitality lost 33,100 jobs while trade, transportation and utilities lost 86,500.

The only sector posting job gains was education and health services with an increase of 19,200 jobs or 1.6% year-over-year. Most of the increase was in nursing services and residential care facilities.

The Bureau of Labor Statistics will release national numbers for March on Friday, April 3rd. February losses totaled 651,000 jobs. The consensus for March is a loss of about 660,000. Our tally suggests job losses could total over 725,000 due to Wall Street severance packages that were likely exhausted in February plus continuing above trend declines in Professional and Business Services and Financial Intermediation.

MAY 4, 2009

EXISTING HOME SALES VOLUME AND PRICE SHOW FIRST SIGNS OF IMPROVEMENT

Existing home sales in Florida state-wide rose in March. Additionally, the steep decline in prices, which has gone on for 16 months nationwide and for nearly two years in Florida has slowed. While year-over-year price declines were steep at 20-30%, more recent data tell a different story. First quarter 2009 data are signaling that a housing bottom could finally be in sight and remains a possibility by late 2009. State-wide sales volume increased over 25% in the first quarter while the median price fell 8.75%. From February to March the gap narrowed further with state-wide median price flat and several markets experiencing increases. Can we now declare a bottom to this unprecedented housing crisis? No. But the signs are turning positive. Still, risk to recovery remains heavily skewed to the downside.

Existing home sales volume rose state-wide in March. Moreover, median prices began to flatten. For example, the Ft. Pierce/Port St. Lucie MSA saw median price decline 3.36% while Metro Orlando declined a modest 1.1%. Melbourne-Titusville-Palm Bay, MSA and Ft. Lauderdale MSA saw modest price increases month over month.

While monthly data have been erratic and price declines have been steep year-over-year, a trend toward price stability is emerging from first quarter data. One quarter's data is insufficient to indicate a sustainable trend and far too early to call a bottom to the housing crisis. Another two quarters, however, will add clarity.

Downside risk remains. Median price by definition means that half of the prices were lower and half were higher than the median. Looking behind the numbers, the range of sale prices was clustered fairly tightly around the median. Most sales were in the $100,000 to $200,000 price range. There were fewer in the $300,000 price range and remarkably fewer at or over $400,000.

Sales are still skewed toward foreclosures and other distress transactions. First time home buyers are the most active. Foreclosures remain the biggest obstacle to price stability. Volume remains high and when properties come back on the market, they often do so at lower prices putting additional downward pressure on values.

Housing price changes are critically linked to household income. Income and home prices virtually over-lapped each other for many years dating back to 1976. Home prices began to grow faster than household income in 2002. As prices moved higher and incomes did not keep up (and even declined) the pool of available buyers continued to shrink contributing to the housing bubble burst. Home prices nationally reached a peak in early 2006 and fell precipitously after that. Since then, home prices have become much more consistent with household income thus helping restore both affordability and market equilibrium.

Despite renewed affordability and record low mortgage interest rates, U.S. home ownership in the first quarter of 2009 fell to 67.5%—its lowest level since 2000 according to the Census Bureau. Many consumers and households who benefited from easy credit during the run up are now victims of the foreclosure crisis and the recession. Younger singles and families (under age 35) have been hurt the worst with a home ownership rate down to 39.8%.

Looking Forward, there are clearly some positive signs but the crisis is not over. We continue to believe that housing could find bottom in late 2009 or early 2010. Foreclosures and unemployment, however, will continue to put negative pressure on the housing market both locally and nationally.

IS THERE ANY GOOD NEWS OUT THERE?

The economy has officially been in recession for nearly 17 months, far exceeding the duration of all previous recessions since World War II. Indeed, this downturn is the deepest and most far reaching of any since the Great Depression over 70 years ago. With most U.S. metros and many of our global trading partners in recession, there is virtually nowhere to hide. In Florida and most Seacoast markets, evidence suggests the recession probably started 10 months before the nationwide recession was declared. Nevertheless, there are a few emerging signs of economic life. The obvious question is whether the signs are first signs of sustainable recovery or just early green shoots that will wither and die.

There has been little good economic news for much of the last two years. Consumers have grown weary in what seems like a never ending downturn. Job losses continue to mount month after month and foreclosures are at an unprecedented level and still continue to rise. Credit is impaired, household wealth has declined dramatically and both consumer and business balance sheets are in desperate need of repair. All that begs the obvious questions, when will it end? How will we know? Is there *any* good news out there?

While the worst of the recession could be behind us, as evidenced by some recent rays of hope, it is not over and recovery could still be long and painful. Nevertheless, let's look at the good, the bad and the ugly and decide whether some of the green shoots are genuine signs of recovery or whether they are destined to wither and die only to be replaced by new green shoots another day.

The economic freefall that began last fall with the near collapse of the U.S. Banking system appears to be slowing. While the recession is far from over and recovery remains a work in progress, both consumer and business sentiment appear stronger than they have been in recent months. The Conference Board's Consumer Confidence Survey, for example, surged to a seven month high in March after two of the lowest readings on record in January and February. The downside is that the level of consumer confidence is still historically low and will likely remain that way until employment improves

Equities are up over 20% in the last six weeks not only in the U.S. but also in 42 of the world's most economically influential markets. History suggests that stock market gains are often a precursor to recovery.

The rate of median house price decline has slowed and sales volumes are increasing both nationally and in most Seacoast markets. Indeed, there is evidence that existing home median prices began to stabilize in the first quarter of 2009. Pending home sales also rose and that usually bodes well for sales 30 to 60 days in the future. Finally, construction spending—both public and private—rose in March.

Mortgage interest rates remain at record lows and funds are generally available for qualified buyers. We're also witnessing renewed affordability which will lure potential buyers back to the marketplace.

Will three months of reasonably positive housing experience turn in to a sustainable trend? One would hope so but several powerful obstacles remain. Unemployment is still likely to rise throughout 2009 and into 2010. That will force more foreclosures which are already at record highs. Additional foreclosures could quickly erase the gains of the last few months and drive prices even lower. Moreover, broad and sustainable demand does not yet exist. Home sales are being driven by foreclosures and other distress transactions. The majority of buyers are first time home buyers taking advantage of government incentives and renewed affordability. Speculators have also re-entered the market and that could disrupt recovery. Move up buyers are still on the sidelines. Looking behind the numbers, there is still very little sales activity in the $350,000 and up category. Overall, there appears to be little broad and sustainable purchase demand in housing.

Consumers have gotten some much needed relief in recent months due to lower energy prices, larger tax refunds, modest payroll tax cuts and higher social security payments. Most damage to household wealth has likely already occurred. As a result, consumers look forward to rebuilding badly damaged balance sheets and perhaps restoring some of their lost wealth.

Commercial real estate began to deteriorate badly in 2008 and the worst is almost certainly yet to come. Nevertheless, the Architectural Billing Index is up. This index is based on the premise that an architect is involved in most commercial real estate projects anywhere between 18-24 months before ground is broken. As a leading indicator, the implication is that some renewed private development activity could come in the next two years or so. Nevertheless, the short term story for commercial real estate is decidedly negative. More on the commercial sector later.

Despite so-called green shoots, the outlook is not all positive. The first quarter shrinkage in gross domestic product at 6.1% exceeded most expectations. That followed a 6.3% decline in the fourth quarter of 2008. Taken together, the two month contraction was larger than any other similar period in 60 years.

If there is good news in such a contraction, it is that it resulted largely from a huge decline ($104 Billion) in business inventories. Business also stopped producing product and that also contributed to the decline in inventories. While those events intensify the current GDP slide, they also set the stage for more rapid expansion when demand stabilizes. Indeed, without the inventory component, GDP contraction would have been much smaller at about 3.5%±.

First quarter GDP was also heavily influenced negatively by business investment in plant and equipment. Indeed, non-residential fixed investment slid an astounding 38%—by far the largest decline since World War II. That alone subtracted 4.7 percentage points from first quarter growth.

The "green shoot" in this negative information is these are events that history shows typically occur *late* in a recession and the current experience is no exception. These components also tend to come back to life soon after a recession ends.

As we've written previously, consumer spending drives about 70% of economic activity. The consumer is a leading indicator in the sense that consumption tends to increase in the *later* stages of recession. In fact, in the first quarter, personal consumption grew at an annualized rate of 2.2%—the highest quarterly growth rate in two years.

Clearly, the pattern in GDP component change is consistent with post

---

WILLIAM L. PITTENGER   139

war historical experience implying that we may indeed be in the later stages of the recession at least in the context of GDP growth.

Employment is a lagging indicator in a contracting economy as the job losses usually show up after they have actually occurred and long after the slowdown that precipitated the cuts. About 5.5 million U.S. jobs have been lost since the official start of the recession in December 2007. The Labor Department will release its April advance estimate on May 8th and it is likely that an additional 650,000± jobs were lost pushing the nation's unemployment rate to about 8.7%. Unemployment tends to remain elevated even after the official end to a recession. We expect employment to bottom in early 2010 and unemployment to peak at slightly over 9% later in 2010. The green shoot in employment is that new claims for unemployment compensation have slowed recently however it is still too early to call that a trend.

Commercial real estate began to show clear signs of weakness in early 2008 and the story has gotten worse since then. Despite the rising Architectural Billing Index referred to earlier, there will be huge obstacles to private development in the interim. These include absence of renewed sustainable demand, structural changes in industry sectors—especially retail—and the relative absence of secondary market financing. The CMBS market (commercial mortgage backed securities)—the largest source of funding for commercial projects remains virtually shut down and commercial banks do not have balance sheet capacity to absorb the shortfall. That will lead to a surge in defaults, foreclosures and bankruptcies—the effects of which are likely to last into 2012.

It's about supply and demand. There will be many false dawns as the economy moves toward recovery. To have sustainable recovery, we must have real demand—not demand that is artificially stimulated or temporarily propped up. Such artificial demand will quickly dissipate when the stimulus is withdrawn or the prop removed. Real demand implies desire for a good or service backed up by purchasing power. Today, real demand does not exist in real estate as the supply and demand equation is out of balance. During the residential bubble inflation, somewhere between 25% and 40% more homes were built than there were people to occupy them either as owners or renters. Today that over-supply is being worked down but the process is slow. Commercial real estate is much the same. New shopping centers were built to follow the new housing. Warehouses and offices were built to support the needs of contractors and others serving the industry. Today, that is gone and the market struggles to absorb all forms of commercial space.

While the *green shoots* are welcome, most will not rise quickly to the level of a trend. Moreover, the current green shoots contain at least two decision traps for consumers and policy makers alike. First, confidence could be misplaced and the rays of hope are misinterpreted as the beginning of a strong recovery when all they really show is that the rate of decline has slowed and the economy is merely *"less bad."* Decisions made in the early stages of recovery are often shown to be incorrect.

The second decision trap is that policy makers see the green shoots as sustainable recovery and reduce or withdraw stimulus. During the Great Depression, the economy began to show signs of recovery in 1936. In response, the Federal Reserve began a series of rate hikes which plunged the economy into a recession (1937) within the Great Depression and the economy did not begin to accelerate again until the buildup for World War II in 1940 and 1941.

The bottom line. In my view the green shoots are real and they signal the beginning of recovery. In even the best case, however, recovery will be a long and bumpy journey.

MAY 21, 2009

AMERICA'S LOST DECADE

Volumes have been written about Japan's "lost decade"—the decade of the 1990s, when economic expansion came to a halt. How did it happen and why did it last so long? Japan's lost decade was a long time in the making. In the decades following World War II, the government implemented tariffs and policies designed to force savings. With more money in banks, credit eventually became easy to obtain and, with Japan running large trade surpluses the Japanese currency (Yen) appreciated against other world currencies. By the 1980s, with so much money available, speculation was inevitable and both real estate and stocks surged to record high levels. Housing, stocks and bonds peaked in 1989 and at one point, the government began issuing 100 year bonds. Banks also began making increasingly risky loans. At the 1989 peak of the bubble, residential real estate became extraordinarily over-valued with choice properties in Tokyo's Ginza District fetching the U.S. equivalent of $139,000 per square foot! The combination of exceptionally high values and exceptionally low interest rates fueled a massive wave of speculation.

The Japanese government recognized that such growth was unsustainable and the Finance Ministry sharply raised interest rates. This abruptly burst the bubble which led to a stock market crash, plunging real estate values, a debt crisis and a banking crisis. Prices remained low and credit became difficult to obtain—a combination of events that lasted a decade. Unemployment rose sharply but not to crisis levels. The crash led to deflation, non-performing loans and bank failures. Today, the Japanese economy has still not recovered. Economic growth is muted and the lost decade has had a profound effect on the economy, investment and everyday life.

Does the Japanese experience sound familiar?
Fast forward to the 2000s in the United States. The so-called dot-com bubble of the late 1990s burst in 2000. That led to a short recession (8 months) in 2001 that was exacerbated by the 9-11 terrorist attacks. The Federal Reserve sought to revive the shocked economy by lowering the federal funds rate. By 2003, that rate was a mere 1%. Mortgage rates dropped, home sales surged and home prices skyrocketed. That fuelled unconstrained new development. Credit was inexpensive, easy to obtain and speculation was rampant. The cycle repeated itself until the housing bubble burst in late 2007.

The bursting of the housing bubble severely weakened the broader economy and The Great Recession emerged. That recession turned out to be the worst since the Great Depression of the 1930s. But is there more to the story? Does the entire decade of the 2000s have characteristics of an American lost decade? Look at the charts to the left.

Employment in the United States was a lost decade in the 2000s. Employment grew by only 400,000 jobs even though the population grew by 30 million. On a percentage basis, employment fell by 0.8%. Compare that with an average growth of 27% per decade from 1940 through 1999. Today, the nation has over 15 million people unemployed and 45% of them have been unemployed long term (defined as for 27 weeks or more).

The nation's Gross Domestic Product (GDP) may also have experienced a lost decade. Real GDP grew by an average of 1.9% per year for the full decade. That is the worst economic performance in six decades. Only the Great Depression decade of the 1930s was worse. The same story is true for consumption and income. Both grew slower than any other decade since the 1930's. As a sidebar, note that consumption grew much faster than income—a likely by-product of easy and inexpensive credit.

MAY 25, 2009

FLORIDA'S UNEMPLOYMENT RATE DECLINES TO 9.6%

Florida's unemployment rate declined to 9.6% in April. That is 0.2% lower than the revised March rate of 9.8% but up 4.0% since April 2008. Before April, unemployment had risen every month since March 2006 when the rate was 3.3%. Unemployment in most Seacoast served counties also declined slightly in April although St. Lucie and Indian River counties remain among the highest in the state at 12.7 and 11.9% respectively. Florida's unemployment rate remains 0.7% higher than the nation which was 8.9% in April. Despite the modest decline, Florida's jobless rate is still the highest since December 1975 when it was 10.0%.

The April unemployment rate represents 885,000 jobless Floridians out of a labor force of 9,239,000. Despite Florida's employment volatility and slowing population growth, the labor force has grown steadily. In January 1999 the labor force was 7,652,019. In January 2006 when construction employment began to weaken, it was 8,766,882. It grew from there to 9,342,600 in December 2008. So far in 2009, the labor force has declined steadily but modestly to its April level of 9,239,000.

All of Florida's metro areas lost jobs year over year. The largest annual decline was in the Miami-Ft. Lauderdale-Pompano Beach metro which lost 97,100 jobs (4.1%) followed by Orlando-Kissimmee metro which lost 54,600 jobs (5.0%). The largest decline was in Cape Coral-Ft. Myers where the rate of job loss was 8.8% year over year.

By sector, construction job losses have totaled 105,200 for a 19.8% decline year over year. Although Florida's job losses have increased in most sectors, construction losses still account for about 26% of the state's job losses year over year. While construction losses began to slow in recent months, they resumed their increase in April as a result of the steadily softening commercial real estate market.

Other large sectors losing jobs in April included trade, transportation and utilities (down 79,700 or 5.0%); professional and business services. (down 77,900 or 6.7%) and manufacturing (down 39,400 or 10.4%). Education and health services grew by 17,000 jobs (1.6%) as a result of growth in nursing and residential care facilities.

Florida's employment situation remains volatile and it is too early to discern an improving trend.

JUNE 5, 2009

U.S. JOB LOSSES SLOW IN MAY 345,000 JOBS LOST— UNEMPLOYMENT RATE HITS 9.4%

Nonfarm payrolls fell in March by 345,000 jobs in May That is the smallest decline since September 2008. The economy has shed an average of 643,000 jobs in each of the last six months. At the same time, March and April job loss numbers were revised to show 82,000 more lost jobs each month than previously estimated. The number of unemployed persons increased by 787,000 in May bringing the total unemployed to 14.5 million. Since the official start of the recession in December 2007, employers have shed 6.0 million jobs and the unemployment rate has risen by 4.5 percentage points. Unemployment in May was pegged at 9.4% which is the highest in 26 years.

While decelerating job losses were welcome, unemployment is still at near record high and the losses have been widespread geographically, by industry type and by population segment. Steep job losses continued in manufacturing where 156,000 jobs were shed. Losses occurred in most component industries—those which produce parts for automotive and other industries. Motor vehicles, machinery and fabricated metal products accounted for about half of the overall decline in factory employment. Motor vehicles and parts employment has fallen for most of the decade. The decline has been about 50% since its last peak in February 2000.

The rate of decline moderated slightly in construction. In May, job losses totaled 56,000 as compared to an average of 117,000 construction jobs lost each of the previous six months. The rate of decline also slowed in retail trade as well as in business and professional services.

The number of persons working part time for economic reasons (involuntary part time workers) was essentially flat in May at about 9.1 million workers. The number of workers in this sector has grown by 4.4 million since the recession officially began. About 2.2 million persons were also "marginally attached" to the workforce. That is 794,000 more than a year earlier. This group of workers had searched for employment sometime in the last 12 months but not in the four weeks prior to the most recent survey. Included in the marginally attached category are 792,000 discouraged workers. That is up 392,000 from a year earlier. This category includes people who are no longer searching for work because they don't believe a job is available for them.

Involuntary part time and marginally attached are perhaps the most concerning indicators as their rate of growth is exceeding unemployment as a whole. The implication is that unemployment could grow for a longer period of time than currently expected and workers may stay under-employed for a longer period of time.

Initial Claims. In a separate report, the Labor Department reported that there were 496,822 new claims (not seasonally adjusted) for unemployment insurance the week ending May 30th. That is down 41,577 from the prior week. At the same time, Continuing Claims are up suggesting that fewer people are applying for benefits while the unemployed are staying unemployed longer.

Outlook. Employment always lags the business cycle. As a result, we expect employment to decline throughout 2009 and unemployment to rise into at least the second quarter of 2010 even with improvement in the broader economy.

JUNE 8, 2009

CREDIT QUALITY SLIDES—
FORECLOSURES RISE

Mortgage foreclosures are no longer limited to sub-prime and exotic loan products. The problem has now reached into the prime sector with a vengeance due largely to unemployment and declining home values. According to the Mortgage Bankers Association (MBA), nearly 13% of all U.S mortgage loans were delinquent or in foreclosure in the first quarter. That is the worst performance on record. Not surprisingly, the bubble states of California, Arizona, Nevada, and yes, Florida were the hardest hit. High end product is now the most difficult to sell with inventory exceeding lower end product four to one. According to the National Association of Realtors, the median time necessary to sell a house at $750,000 or more is 40 months. Foreclosures are surging and the effects are likely to be felt well into 2011.

Mortgage loan delinquencies and foreclosures are rising at a rate not seen in the 37 years the Mortgage Bankers Association has been tracking the data. Prime fixed rate loans have now surpassed sub-prime loans and have become the largest share of loans moving into foreclosure. The biggest problems facing defaulting homeowners today are unemployment and an inability to sell property and pay off debt. Last year, it was resetting interest rates on sub-prime and payment option ARM loans that were pushing homeowners over the edge.

At the end of the first quarter, states with the highest overall mortgage delinquency rates were Nevada at 11.75%; Mississippi at 11.7% and Florida at 10.56%. Based on new foreclosure starts, Nevada saw 3.35% of its mortgages start foreclosure followed by Florida at 2.79% and Arizona at 2.52%.

The rate of foreclosure increase was predictable. Foreclosure starts had been artificially constrained over much of the past year by moratoria imposed by Fannie Mae, Freddie Mac, several large servicers and even by several states and municipalities. Judicial intervention has also slowed the pace of foreclosures. As moratoria were lifted, foreclosures surged.

Today, Florida is second in the nation for foreclosures with one in every 135 housing units in some stage of foreclosure as compared to one in every 374 for the nation.

Underwater homeowners. Approximately 24% of American homeowners with a mortgage owed more than the home was worth at the end of the first quarter of 2009. That number has steadily risen from 4% at the end of 2006; 6% in 2007 and 20% in 2008. Two Seacoast served metropolitan areas are among the top 10 underwater metros in the U.S.—Port St. Lucie in St. Lucie County and Orlando in Orange County.

By loan type, approximately 25% of prime loans are underwater as compared to 45% of Alt-A loans. Approximately 50% of subprime loans are underwater as are 73% of Option Payment ARM loans.

Rising unemployment is now the leading cause of new foreclosures. Today, the nation's unemployment rate is 9.4% and the Florida rate is 9.6%. In absolute numbers, approximately 14.5 million American's are jobless including 885,000 Floridians. Both Florida and the U.S. unemployment rates are expected to approach or possibly exceed 10% in the next few months.

Mortgage modifications are also off to a painfully slow start and it is apparent that modifications limited to only interest rate reductions are not working. More aggressive modification including principal reduction will be required if the current tact is to work.

Reform legislation had been introduced in the U.S. Senate which, among other things, would have allowed bankruptcy judges to reduce or "cram down" principal. The administration argued that this would give financial institutions more incentive to modify loans. The industry argued that it resulted in judicial modification of contracts and gave judges too much power. The bill was defeated on April 30th. Additional legislation will almost certainly be proposed.

As an aside, the Office of Comptroller of the Currency and the Office of Thrift Supervision, in a joint study, discovered that 43% of modified loans were delinquent again within eight months.

Looking Forward. Despite some promising signs in the broader economy, credit quality is still growing steadily and uniformly worse and foreclosures are showing no signs of abating. In fact, mortgage loan defaults are on track to reach an astounding four million this year representing nearly one in 12 first mortgage loans. As moratoria on foreclosures have now expired, it seems certain that foreclosures will rise well into the summer. As most victims of foreclosure will lose their homes, these properties will be put back on the market at a steep discount negatively affecting surrounding home prices and homeowner wealth. Indeed some six trillion dollars in home equity has vanished since house prices peaked three years ago and less wealthy home owners make for very reluctant spenders.

Foreclosures also create extraordinary pressure for the financial institutions that own them. Losses on all subprime, alt-A and jumbo loans made during the housing boom will easily top one trillion dollars—an amount nearly equal to the total capital underpinning the entire U.S. banking system. Until these extraordinary losses abate, even the healthiest and best capitalized financial institutions will be reluctant to lend to even the most credit-worthy borrowers and that, by itself, could easily de-rail recovery of the broader economy.

JUNE 24, 2009

FLORIDA'S UNEMPLOYMENT RATE RISES TO 10.2%

After dipping modestly in April, Florida's unemployment rate surged to 10.2% in May turning in the worst performance in 30 years. Florida employers shed another 26,000 jobs in May leaving 943,000 Floridians jobless out of a labor force of 9,232,090. Florida has lost 417,500 jobs year over year. Nationally, non-farm payrolls declined by 345,000 jobs swelling the ranks of unemployed by 787,000 and bringing total unemployed to 14.5 million and an unemployment rate of 9.4%. The number of unemployed persons nationally has increased by 7.0 million since the recession officially began in December 2007 and the nation's unemployment rate has risen by 4.5 percentage points.

Eighteen months into the recession, payroll employment continues to fall, unemployment continues to rise and there is almost certainly more to come. Employment is unlikely to find bottom until late 2009 or perhaps into 2010. The unemployment rate is not likely to stop climbing until mid-2010. This is characteristic of virtually every recession since World War. II as employment tends to lag recovery of the broader economy. Indeed, the recovery from the current recession may be a jobless recovery just like it was early in the decade after the dot com | 911 recession. At that time job losses continued even as the broader economy began to show robust growth.

As the economy recovers from the current recession, employers will almost surely be slow to rehire. As a result, it may be several years before there is full recovery in the labor market.

Looking behind the numbers. Professional and business services lost the most jobs year over year at 92,600 (8.0%). The sector has been trending down steadily since the real estate bubble burst nearly three years ago. The construction sector also continued to lose jobs. May 2008 to May 2009, the sector lost 90,800 jobs (17.4%). The industry was propped up temporarily as workers took their skills from the residential to the commercial real estate sector. Now that the commercial sector is also in decline, construction is losing more jobs.

Trade, transportation and utilities lost 82,200 jobs (5.2%). That too is largely a result of the real estate decline where fewer goods are transported and there is reduced demand for utility services.

Leisure and hospitality employment increased long after the housing bubble burst. Today, however, the industry is feeling the full force of the recession as consumers cut back on both business and personal travel. In May, the sector lost 55,100 jobs (5.8%) year over year.

Similarly, local government increased employment even as other sectors shed jobs. Today, however, local government has entered the loss column with a loss of 12,500 jobs. Given severe budget constraints at all levels of government from municipal to expect the local government sector to shed jobs for the next year. The wild card is, of course, the impact of federal stimulus spending which could temporarily reverse the downward trend.

Other sectors losing jobs include financial services—another victim of the housing crisis which began with residential and moved into commercial real estate. A total of 23,500 jobs were lost in May year over year.

The only major sector experiencing employment growth was education and health care. Most of the 5,000 job increase was in nursing and residential care facilities. Both public and private education payrolls are shrinking as a result of declining school enrollment around the state and particularly in the areas most affected by construction job losses.

JULY 5, 2009

U.S. JOB LOSSES RISE SLIGHTLY IN JUNE. UNEMPLOYMENT RATE NOW 9.5%

The U.S. economy shed another 467,000 jobs in June according to an advance estimate by the U.S. Department of Labor. That is higher than the 322,000 (adjusted) job losses recorded in May but lower than the 670,000 average recorded between November 2008 and March 2009. There are now 14.7 million persons unemployed resulting in an unemployment rate of 9.5%—the highest in a generation but only modestly higher than 9.4% recorded in May. Since the recession began in December 2007, 7.2 million people have lost jobs and the unemployment rate has risen by 4.6 percentage points. In Florida, 943,000 persons are jobless resulting in a 10.2% unemployment rate. Despite some positive economic signs such as a near bottom in housing and easing of the economic free fall that began last fall, employment is a lagging indicator and losses will likely rise well into 2010.

The current recession has now plagued the U.S. Economy for 18 months. It has become the longest, broadest and deepest since World War II and arguably the most severe since the early days of the Great Depression nearly 75 years ago.

Unemployment in every metro area in the country is now higher than it was a year ago. Nearly a third of the nation's 370 metro areas have jobless rates in excess of 10% and 15 cities now have unemployment rates over 15%. Most Seacoast served counties are now in double digits with Indian River and St. Lucie counties leading the way down with 13% and 13.3% unemployment rates respectively.

By sector, manufacturing cut 136,000 jobs in June compared with an average for the prior three months of 159,000. On par with previous months, job losses in motor vehicles and parts totaled 26,500. The full impact of auto industry layoffs at Chrysler and General Motors and their dealerships has not been fully reflected in the numbers and probably won't be until late this year as buy out and severance packages burn off.

Employment in professional and business services declined by 118,000 in June. The industry has shed 1.5 million jobs since its peak in December 2007. Financial activities declined by 27,000 jobs. Since the recession began, this industry has lost 489,000 jobs, far less than expected given the extraordinary credit services melt down in late 2008.

Retail trade lost 21,000 jobs in June. Losses in the sector have been moderating for the last three months even as the industry has deteriorated.

The information industry lost 21,000 jobs in June, a number very consistent with the last three months. Roughly half the decline was in publishing as the print media continues to struggle with reduced advertising sales and competition from the internet.

Construction lost 79,000 jobs. That is more than in May (-48,000) but it is the first back to back losses of *less than* 100,000 since last October. Losses in residential and commercial construction were about equally balanced.

The surprise sector was federal government where there was a loss of 49,000 jobs. Much of this was in temporary jobs added in March and April to do preparatory work leading up to the 2010 census. The loss trend should reverse course in the second half as the federal government aggressively begins hiring longer term employees for the census. Additionally, the FDIC is hiring aggressively to liquidate the assets of failed banks and thrifts. Most of the census and FDIC jobs are, however, temporary and intended to last only one to three years.

Local government employment continues to decline due to well publicized budget shortfalls. The number of local government job losses in the second half will likely rise as many municipalities begin a new fiscal year with fewer employees. Now that local government has entered the loss column, we expect sector losses to grow and remain elevated for at least 6-8 quarters as there are no apparent long term funding sources available to make up budget shortfalls.

Healthcare employment was the only major sector to grow in June with 21,000 new jobs. Despite the gain, that is down from an average of 30,000 jobs per month in 2008.

Economic stimulus related jobs in both public and private sectors have not materialized nearly as fast as hoped. An interesting sidebar is that lawyers are reportedly challenging nearly every major project on behalf of environmental groups, states, municipalities and others. As a result, implementation of many so called *shovel ready* projects is not likely to occur until late 2009 at the earliest. Neither public nor private job additions are likely to show up in the numbers until 2010.

Behind the numbers. The employment to population ratio continued to trend down finishing June at 59.2%. The ratio is down 3.2 percentage points since the recession began.

About 2.2 million persons were marginally attached to the labor force in June. That is 618,000 more than a year earlier. This category of persons includes those who are willing and able to work; have searched for a job in the last 12 months, but had not searched in the four weeks preceding the survey. Among the marginally attached workers are an estimated 793,000 discouraged workers. Discouraged workers are those who are not currently looking for work because they believe there are no jobs available for them. That is up 373,000 from a year earlier. This number has steadily risen and suggests that more job losses in this recession may be more permanent than cyclical.

The number of persons working part time for economic reasons has also risen significantly since the recession began but it was relatively unchanged from May to June. About 9.0 million workers fall into this category. That number has risen by 4.4 million—nearly double—since the recession began.

Wages are falling. The average work week declined to 33 hours in June—the lowest on record. While average hourly earnings were flat, nominal wages still continue to decline as many workers are taking pay cuts, unpaid leave or fewer hours. Those who are employed are seeing raises, bonuses and other forms of compensation evaporate. Unpaid furloughs for state and local government workers are also becoming increasingly common.

In the current recession, those who become unemployed are staying unemployed longer. The percentage of people who have been unemployed 27 weeks or longer has risen to 29%. Fifteen percent of idled workers have been out of work for more than a year. Thirty three states (including Florida) plus the District of Columbia have established extended benefit programs. The amount of benefit both initially or in extended benefits varies widely by state.

The unemployment rate is now the highest in a generation. Additionally changes in the nation's employment profile appears more structural than cyclical. In previous recessions, workers who lost jobs were later called back or found similar work with other companies when the economy began to recover. This time is different. More job losses are permanent. They have affected every educational, age, gender and racial segment of the population. In this recession, many professionals and skilled workers have been terminated making this recession much different than others in recent years.

The largest population sector to have been displaced in this recession is men over 45 years old who have lost construction or manufacturing jobs. The total since 2006 is over 3.5 million and will certainly grow as auto industry workers are displaced in coming months. Many of the displaced workers will not find work at comparable wages. This structural dislocation will almost certainly slow recovery of the broader economy. Unlike younger workers, many in this age group own houses, have families, may be supporting children in college and perhaps even be caring for elderly parents. In addition to human tragedy, these workers are in their prime producing and innovating years and as the group is so large, their loss will impair productivity, innovation and raise social costs in the broader economy.

Looking forward. Employment is a lagging indicator in a down economy and in the recovery phase. Nevertheless, recent employment reports have provided numerous insights into the future. For example, the permanent nature of recent job losses and structural changes to the economy are especially revealing.

After the last severe recession in the early 1980's, many displaced workers were able to return to their previous employment. Even so, the nation's unemployment rate did not return to pre-recession levels for five years after the peak.

The last two recessions of the early 1990's and early 2000's were followed by jobless recoveries. That was driven largely by the permanent nature of job losses during each recession. The scale of job losses in the current recession and especially their permanent nature is much greater than the most recent recessions. Additionally, the two hardest hit industries in this recession—construction and manufacturing—are not likely to bounce back any time soon.

Job losses will likely continue throughout 2009 and very likely into 2010. We continue to expect unemployment to peak in 2010 and remain elevated into the foreseeable future. Recovery will be a long and bumpy road.

JULY 25, 2009

HOUSING BOTTOM FORMS— WHAT COMES NEXT?

After nearly three years of gut wrenching house price declines, clear signs of stabilization have emerged. Over the last six months, sales volumes have increased significantly and free falling prices have leveled off in Florida and nearly all Seacoast markets. Nationally, sales of single family detached homes rose 2.4% to about 4.3 million transactions in June while the median price rose to $181,600. Median price is down 15.4% in June year over year but up 4.01% month over month. Median price nationally has been rising modestly each month since the beginning of the year. The story is similar in Florida albeit more volatile. Sales are up 28% but median price is down 28% year over year. Both numbers are up month over month and Florida's median price in June was $148,000.

Transaction volumes are up year over year in all Seacoast served Metropolitan Statistical Areas (MSA). Month over month, all but one Seacoast served MSA (Melbourne I Palm Bay) had an increase in volume and all showed an increase in median price. The table at the bottom of this page shows existing home volume and median price for the last 11 months. The graphs on the next page show the long term trend in home prices since 1994. The bottom line in each graph is the trend line or natural level of long term growth. After adjusting out major peaks and valleys, the rate of increase in the state and Treasure Coast has steadily increased about 3% annually not including the effect of inflation. In Palm Beach County and Metro Orlando, it has been about 4%.

The performance line is unadjusted and shows the run up, peak and collapse of housing prices. The currently important story is that the freefall has stopped as evidenced by the last six months' performance. Most Seacoast markets over-shot the trend line on the downside. Most however, are stabilizing or showing modest price increases. Barring additional unforeseen economic shock, we expect that trend to continue. While there will not be measurable price increases prices will bounce along the bottom and return to trend over the next 12-24 months.

Looking Forward. Prices have fallen over 40% from their late 2007 peak. While there is no good news in that statistic for consumers who purchased homes at or near peak, the good news for the broader market is that there is renewed affordability as prices have returned to a level consistent with local income levels. We do not, however, expect prices to increase appreciably for the next few years. If history is a guide, it took single family housing about seven years to return to robust growth from the downturn of the late 1980s and early 1990s. It took the condominium market some 13 years.

In spite of the recent good news about housing, inventories of both new and existing homes remain too high and it is likely to be another year before inventories return to a more normal level. For existing housing "normal" means 90 to 180 days. For new housing it generally means 60 to 120 days. Currently, Palm Beach County has about a six month supply of new homes while Port St. Lucie is about 12 months and Metro Orlando much longer. Inventory alone will keep a lid on price increases for the foreseeable future.

The Census Bureau estimates that roughly 2.6% of the homeowner housing stock nationwide was vacant at the end of the first quarter. That rate was 1.8% in the first quarter of 2005 and has steadily increased since. This is a clear effect of the unsustainable overbuilding that occurred when the nation and especially sun belt states like Florida built far more homes than there were people to occupy them.

Employment will also be an issue. Florida's unemployment rate is now 10.6% with nearly one-million Floridians out of work. That alone, plus the fear of losing a job by those who are employed today, are likely to slow house purchases. Clearly it is taking its toll on potential move up buyers as well. Income too is constrained. The average paid work week has declined to 33 hours and more people than ever are working part time for economic reasons.

Finally, foreclosures continue to rise and will be a fact of life through 2011. In June, 12,087 homeowners in Seacoast markets entered foreclosure and that rate is not likely to decline soon. All these factors will combine to limit price increases for the next few years as the market bounces along the bottom in search of stability.

AUGUST 3, 2009

GROSS DOMESTIC PRODUCT LESS BAD IN Q2

The nation's Gross Domestic Product (GDP) contracted at a less severe rate of 1.0% in the second quarter a decline much shallower than the 6.4% decline experienced in the first quarter. The GDP is the top line measure of the nation's economy as it represents the total of all goods and services produced. The numbers underlying the headline GDP are significant, not only for what they tell us about the second quarter but also for the clues they offer about what the short term economic outlook could be. The Commerce Department's Bureau of Economic Analysis makes a comprehensive revision to the accounts underlying GDP each July and this year's revisions are both significant and revealing.

The GDP decline of 1.0% in the second quarter of 2009 was better than the consensus estimate of about 2.0% going in to the quarter. This is an "advance" estimate and will be refined over the next two months as more data become available. The "preliminary" estimate will be released at the end of August and the "final" estimate in late September.

The second quarter data are consistent with an economy still on track to bottom out late in the second half of 2009 and perhaps squeeze out some anemic growth by the first quarter of 2010. Any growth, however, will not be enough to prevent employment from continuing its decline although employment decline will be less severe than experienced earlier in 2009.

Key components of the GDP which contributed measurably to change included domestic spending which fell less rapidly in the second quarter although consumer spending was a big disappointment falling 1.2% compared to modest growth (0.6%) in the first quarter. Consumers continued to save more and spend less.

Saving was up 5.2% in the second quarter. Savings had been running near zero and as low as negative 13% during the housing boom as many consumers spent more than they made with home equity lines of credit. Higher savings may be a long term positive for the economy but it is currently a short term negative for GDP growth as consumers and the broader economy go through significant structural and what we believe will be long term change in spending and credit use habits.

Spending on durable goods (those expected to last three years or more) declined 19.7% while spending on nondurables (consumables) fell 13.1%. Spending on services rose 1.3%.

On the business side, fixed investment spending by businesses continued its downward slide by declining 60% quarter over quarter and 21% year over year. The quarterly decline was made up of a decline of 30.6% in fixed asset spending; 20.6% decline in equipment spending and a 9.6% decline in spending on structures.

Inventories also weighed heavily negative on the GDP declining 27.2%. Inventories have declined significantly for several quarters. The positive news in declining inventory level is that some manufacturers may need to ramp up production again in the not too distant future even in the face of recession level demand. This is, of course, an industry specific issue. Today, inventory to sales ratios remain elevated however that could change quickly given the speed at which inventories are declining.

The need to ramp up production is quickly becoming apparent in the auto and light truck sector. The recent *cash for clunkers* program has been remarkably successful. Originally a $1.0 Billion program, the House recently (July 31st) approved another $2.0 Billion for the program. At this writing, the Senate has not yet acted. It remains to be seen whether this program will prove to be a sustainable boost to auto sales or merely a temporary blip on the radar screen. Our view is the latter.

The initial $1.0 Billion allocated for *cash for clunkers* could result in 225,000 sales however it is unclear how many of those were a direct result of the program. There were roughly 9.7 million auto sales recorded in June and we expect to see about 10.5 million recorded for July when the numbers are released this week.

Our view of manufacturing in general is that, while inventories are being slashed, sales remain at remarkably low recessionary level and even when restocking of inventories occurs, it is likely to be transitory and not sustainable long term. The bottom line, in our view, is that the fundamentals for sustainable manufacturing recovery are not yet in place. Consumer spending will need to increase and that will be driven by employment, wage growth and improvement in household balance sheets. Significant headwinds remain.

The nation's exports declined 25.6%. Imports declined by 72.8%. The result is a net positive for the GDP.

Government spending rose in the second quarter. Part of the increase was probably due to the economic stimulus program (American Recovery and Reinvestment Act) but most was not. Non-defense spending rose 4.7% which, at 0.1% eased the severity of the contraction. Defense spending, however, rose 21.3%. Part of that growth was likely a rebound from first quarter contraction.

Finally, inflation was virtually non-existent in the second quarter, rising only 0.2%

Benchmark revisions. The Bureau of Labor Statistics of the Commerce Department continually revises the GDP as more data become available. The estimates are probably never really final but evolve over time. Each July the Commerce Department releases annual revisions that could date back several years. Additionally, a significant revision occurs every five years. That significant revision occurred last month.

This cycle, there were modest revisions to economic growth as far back as 1929. They were not especially significant however revisions in the current decade were.

Revised data show that the economy contracted—as evidenced by real GDP decline—at 3.9% over the last four quarters. That is the steepest peak to trough decline in post-World War II history.

The revisions to the *National Income and Product Accounts* (NIPA) show that the economy grew long term at an average annual rate of 3.4%. That is 0.1% higher than previously estimated. From 1997 through 2008, the economy grew at a slightly slower rate of 2.8% which is also 0.1% above previously published estimates.

Significantly, the revisions clearly show that the current recession is now the worst since the Great Depression. It has now passed the early 1980s and the late 1950s in terms of its severity. The revisions also show that the inflation adjusted GDP rose just 0.4% for all of 2008 as compared to the original published estimates of 1.1%.

Revisions also show that the 2001 recession that plagued the job market for years now hardly measures as a sustained contraction. According to the BEA, earlier contractions showed little or no change.

Looking Forward. While a less severe contraction in the GDP is welcome news, it does not signal the end of the recession and a return to robust growth. We continue to believe that the recession will still come to an end, as measured by GDP, later this year or perhaps early 2010. It seems highly possible—perhaps even probable—that the National Bureau of Economic Research, Business Cycle Dating Committee, the official arbiter of the nation's business cycle, could declare a turnaround during that time. That will not, however, signal a return to robust growth given the headwinds that remain.

The consumer will continue to face enormous difficulty even after the GDP turns positive. Employment is still likely to decline into 2010 and unemployment will remain elevated for quite some time. As we've written previously (see Economic Perspectives, July 5, 2009), many job losses in this recession, unlike others, have been permanent rather than cyclical. Many of the hardest hit employment sectors such as construction, business and professional services are not likely to bounce back quickly.

The consumer has lost significant wealth as a result of the housing and stock market downturns. It is unlikely we will see more than renewed stability in the housing market until 2012 and perhaps only sluggish growth for as long as a decade.

Florida will have an even tougher road to recovery. The Gross State Product (GSP) declined 1.6% in 2008. While GSP will likely turn positive in 2010, robust growth is highly unlikely. It will take the state several years to shake off the effects of the housing implosion. Significant housing growth is not likely before 2012 given the severity of the slump.

Tourism and retail trade in Florida will also take several years to bounce back given the significant decline in consumer spending. Florida tourism has experienced a 2.3% decline in the number of visitors since the second half of 2008. That was driven by weak domestic and foreign economies which forced many domestic and international visitors to curtail vacation and travel plans.

AUGUST 8, 2009

JOB LOSSES SLOW IN JULY— UNEMPLOYMENT 9.4%

U.S. non-farm payrolls declined by 247,000 jobs in July causing the unemployment to fall fractionally from 9.5% to 9.4%. That is the first decline since April 2008. The job loss number was lower than expected and a significant improvement over the June revised loss of 443,000 jobs. At the same time, May and June job loss numbers were revised down (made less severe) by a combined 43,000 jobs. The average monthly job loss for the May through July time period was—331,000. That is about half of the –645,000 average decline experienced monthly between November 2008 and April 2009. In July, roughly 14.5 million persons were unemployed. While the economy is still shedding jobs, the pace of decline is slowing and appears consistent with an economy where output has hit bottom and growth is set to resume in the not too distant future.

The number of long term unemployed and the number of under-employed is still worrisome. The number of long term unemployed, which is defined as those jobless for 27 weeks or more, rose by 584,000 to 5.0 million in July. The number of people working part time for economic reasons was little changed at about 8.8 million. Additionally, about 2.3 million persons were marginally attached to the labor force. These are people who want to work, are available and who had searched for work in the preceding 12 months but not within four weeks prior to the survey. The marginally attached category is about 709,000 higher than a year ago. Among the marginally attached are 796,000 discouraged workers, up 335,000 in the last 12 months. Discouraged workers are those not currently looking for work because they believe there is not a job for them.

The Bureau of Labor Statistics (BLS) also produces six alternative measures of employment under-utilization. The "U-6" measure includes marginally attached workers as well as discouraged and those working part time for economic reasons. If those persons were counted as unemployed, the U.S. unemployment rate would be over 16%—nearly double the U-6 rate in July 2007. The Florida rate on the same basis would be 15.6%.

Most major employment sectors shed jobs in July. Construction declined by 76,000 jobs which is in line with monthly average decline of 73,000 for the last three months. That is still down from the monthly average loss of 117,000 jobs from November through April. Most of the jobs lost were in commercial construction and more specifically in the multi-family housing sector. The numbers are not surprising. Residential construction has probably hit bottom but commercial has a ways to fall and the job losses will show up over the next two quarters.

Manufacturing cut 52,000 jobs in July as compared with 131,000 in June. The big change was in motor vehicles where employment rose by 28,000 jobs. Even if motor vehicles and parts are excluded, manufacturing job losses still slowed to 80,000 from 109,000 the prior month. Moreover, the work week jumped from 39.4 to 39.8 hours, led by motor vehicles at 40.5 hours. This is all welcome news.

While the unemployment rate declined slightly, we do not interpret the prior month as a peak. The rate declined, not because employment grew, but because the size of the labor force declined. The data showed employment down 155,000 jobs and the labor force down

422,000. Unemployment therefore fell by 267,000 jobs. Over the last 12 months, there has been no increase in the size of the labor force and that has served to cushion the unemployment rate.

AUGUST 12, 2009

HOW BIG IS THE NEXT SHOE?

Commercial real estate is widely believed to be the next shoe to drop in the nation's economic crisis. The only question is, "how big is the shoe?" Today, most commercial real estate product types are under stress. Commercial real estate fundamentals are weakening dramatically due largely to declining employment, which is now taking a toll on spending and office jobs and thus adversely impacting all major commercial real estate sectors (office, retail, industrial and multifamily). By most accounts, the next shoe to drop is huge and the primary drivers are falling prices combined with an inability to refinance the commercial real estate debt scheduled to mature this year and next.

The demand for housing is referred to as primary demand as everyone needs a place to live. The demand for commercial real estate is therefore secondary demand as not everyone needs office, retail or warehouse-industrial space. Commercial development under normal conditions tends to follow housing. As the housing bubble began to inflate earlier this decade, commercial developers were quick to start commercial projects. After all, residential builders were assumed to need space to store construction materials, equipment, appliances and furniture. Real estate support services such as agents, financial services, title companies and others would need new office space to support all the anticipated new residential development. And, of course, the anticipated thousands of new residents would need places to shop thereby fuelling development of new shopping centers, big box retailers and more.

Just like house prices, which, in some areas more than doubled during the *bubble inflation stage,* commercial real estate too saw huge price and value increases. Rents increased but not as fast as sale prices. That had the effect of forcing capitalization rates ("cap rate") down. A capitalization rate is the ratio between a property's net operating income and its value or price. The lower the rate, the higher the value. Whereas capitalization rates had been 8-10% for decades, the early 2000s became an era of *"cap rate compression"* when capitalization rates dropped into the 4-6% range and occasionally even lower. That had the effect of pushing prices and values to unsustainably high levels. Investors who purchased at such low rates, often did so with the expectation that prices and values would continue to rise and—just like the housing assumption—they believed they could sell at a profit or easily refinance.

Reality set in when the housing market began to implode in 2007. It became apparent that an extraordinary number of home purchases were made by "flippers" who had no intention of actually living in the home but planned to re-sell (flip) it quickly to someone else who *also* expected to make a profit. For the first time, it became apparent that Florida builders had constructed somewhere between 25% and 40% more homes than there were people to occupy them either by purchase or rental. That touched off a wave of residential foreclosures that continues largely unabated to this day. It also contributed to the deepest and broadest recession since World War II—a recession which also continues to linger.

Despite the imploding residential market, commercial real estate held its own into 2008. Then consumer and retail spending began to decline concurrent with the deepening recession. Fewer real estate transactions meant fewer office jobs and slower development meant less need for warehousing. Slower spending and development as well as fewer occupied homes (than assumed a year or two earlier) meant trouble in the retail sector. Finally, the U.S. financial markets came close to collapse in mid-September when the fall of Lehman Brothers capped a nearly year-long series of unprecedented events in the U.S. financial system. All of these events converged to create a "perfect storm" in the commercial real estate sector. Indeed, no commercial product type has been spared from the storm and values are declining even at this writing.

Where are we today? Commercial real estate has now passed residential in terms of its rapid and unprecedented value and price decline. Indeed, according to Chicago based RERC, a commercial real estate research firm, values declined 20-25% recently in just two quarters as compared to 30-35% in five years during the downturn of the late 1980's and early 1990's.

We expect commercial real estate values, as an asset class, to decline 15% to 20% during 2009. Another similar decline is possible in 2010 without dramatic improvement in both the CMBS (commercial mortgage backed securities) market and the broader economy. Neither seem poised for significant improvement at this time.

Capitalization rates have already risen about 200 basis points off their compression era lows. Properties which were purchased on very low cap rates as little as three years ago are now likely to see capitalization rates in the 8.0 to 10.0 range leading to a much lower value which could lead to a loss on resale or an inability to re-finance without significant curtailments.

RERC also reported renewal probability is now about 64% and the time necessary to re-lease vacated space is about 7.4 months. Space offered for sublease is being leased at an average discount of 13.85% off its original rate. Our local research suggests that subleases have been at least 20% less than original lease rates given the severity of the overall decline.

All this suggests that available inventory in virtually every commercial real estate product sector will continue to grow over the short term (12 to 24 months). When it does lease again, or when new space is leased, it will almost certainly do so at rates much lower than the original lease rate or the rate anticipated at the time the project was developed. Additionally, there will likely be significant concessions in the form of so-called "free rent" and tenant improvement allowances.

The debt bubble is rapidly inflating. Today, there are currently about 2.5 times the commercial real estate loan dollars needing to be refinanced than there are dollars available to refinance them. Typically, loans are intended to finance demand and turn that demand into reality. Today, however, there is virtually no commercial real estate loan demand. Loans are being requested today to re-finance five year old demand. Moreover, many projects financed during the run up were highly leveraged and non-recourse meaning that loans were high loan to value and the lender could only look to the property and not the guarantor(s) in the event of default. Today, many of the properties securing those loans are worth much less than when the loans were made. That, combined with the CMBS market being virtually closed for business and banks not having balance sheet capacity to absorb the shortfall is creating an enormous debt bubble which will almost certainly burst in the next 12 months or so.

According to New York based Real Capital Analytics (RCA), a firm engaged exclusively in commercial real estate research, approximately $2.2 Trillion in commercial real estate projects acquired or refinanced between 2004 and 2008 have lost value. Indeed, some $1.3 Trillion in equity has been wiped out or remains at risk. The dollar value of distressed properties has risen $67 Billion to a total of $115 Billion.

RCA also reports that the aggregate value of office, retail and industrial properties has fallen 34.8% since their October 2007 peak.

Commercial real estate delinquencies are now near seven-percent, exceeding even the early 1990's when delinquencies hit six-percent.

The bubble continues to grow bigger as only about 10% of troubled assets have been cleared and that has been largely in one-off transactions. Many investors appear to be waiting for the bubble to burst when they can acquire assets for mere pennies on the dollar. Government programs intended to clear large numbers of assets have been largely unsuccessful. The Troubled Asset Relief Program (TARP), morphed into something much different than originally intended. The Public Private Investment Partnership (PPIP) has yet to gain traction as a result of its perceived onerous terms and investor's fears that the federal government could change the rules as it has done in other programs.

When can we expect a commercial real estate rebound? The sector will continue to weaken and values will decline throughout this year and next. Recovery is unlikely before mid-2012.

AUGUST 17, 2009

FLORIDA POPULATION DECLINES—FIRST SINCE 1946

Demographers from the University of Florida's Bureau of Economic and Business Research (BEBR) reported last Friday that Florida's population declined by about 50,000 residents between April 2008 and April

2009. That is the first decline since hundreds of thousands of military personnel stationed in Florida were demobilized in 1946 following World War II. Not even during the Great Depression did population decline. During that time, new residents arrived in search of work. The recession has slowed migration across the country but Florida, a destination for seniors and retirees, has been particularly hard hit. Prices began to rise in 2002 and eventually rose to the point that both retirees and families were priced out of the market and Florida lost its long time image of affordability. Many families left Florida in search of more affordable housing. Many others, who might have come to Florida, did not.

When the housing market began its long and painful slide in 2007, construction throughout most of Florida came to a halt. As is did, many construction workers—especially migrant construction workers—left the state in search of work elsewhere. That included thousands of Mexican workers who left the state as well as Columbians who had fled violence in their country in the 1980s and 1990s. Many returned to South America. Now that affordability has returned to Florida housing, many residents of other states who might wish to migrate to Florida find they can't. Some are unable to sell their homes. Others have seen their household wealth deteriorate and are now financially unable to relocate.

Finally, Florida's job creation engine has stalled. Florida once had unemployment as low as 3.3%. Today, it is 10.6% and likely to increase modestly before improving late next year or in 2011. Even as unemployment improves, however, the rate is likely to remain elevated (7-8%) offering little employment incentive to move to Florida.

Is Florida's first population loss in more than six decades a trend or demographic anomaly? While much will be made of the loss, 50,000 against a total state population of over 18.7 Million is statistically insignificant. In our view, the declining population will be a short lived anomaly. While Florida has temporarily lost its image of affordability and its job creation engine has temporarily stalled, the fundamentals that have attracted people to Florida for decades have not been lost. Florida's population will return to growth mode, albeit slow growth for the next few years. The widely touted statistic that 1,000 people move to Florida every day is not likely to resume anytime soon, but modest growth will.

WHY UNEMPLOYMENT WILL REMAIN ELEVATED

As previously reported (Economic Perspectives—August 8, 2009) the nation's unemployment rate declined marginally to 9.4% in July. The decline itself, however, does not mean it is time to celebrate. The data behind the headline number tell a different story. Indeed, last month's modest decline was not because employment increased but rather because the labor force shrunk. The ranks of those marginally attached to the labor force (2.3 Million), discouraged workers (796,000) and those working part time because full time employment was not available (8.8 Million) have risen sharply thereby reducing the number of full time non-farm payroll employees. The nation's unemployment rate is likely to top 10% in the next few months. The rate may start trending down modestly in 2010 but will still not return to its pre-recession level for several years.

Once recession is over, the nation will need strong hiring to cause a meaningful change in the unemployment rate. Over 7.0 Million jobs will have been lost through 2009 in the recession. The economy will need to recover those plus roughly 100,000 more each month just to compensate for the increased size of the labor force that will likely result when currently discouraged and part time workers return to the labor force. There is nothing currently known or in the data that suggest such growth is even possible.

Unlike previous recessions, many of today's job losses are permanent rather than cyclical. In most previous recessions, workers who were laid off were often called back when their industry or the economy recovered. This time, many of those workers will not be called back especially those in manufacturing, financial and business/professional services. Many of those jobs were created during the housing and construction boom and they won't be replaced at anything near the prerecession rate.

For years, demographers and economists assumed that workers older

---

than 55 would slowly leave the work force. Instead, the labor force participation rate of the 55-64 age group has been rising. The increase is largely a result of wealth destruction caused in the recession. Many workers are forced to work longer. Labor force participation in the 55-64 age group is expected to be about 64.4% by the end of this decade and 65% by 2020. More older workers in the workforce longer combined with moderate employment growth and a larger labor force may translate into higher long term unemployment.

Finally, productivity has improved in the last two years. Companies are generally being forced to do more with a leaner workforce. According to the Bureau of Labor Statistics productivity increased in the second quarter of 2009 to 6.3% in the business sector and 6.4% in the non-farm business sector. Manufacturing productivity increased 5.3% which was 3.9% in durable goods manufacturing and 2.0% in non-durables (consumables). The reason for increased productivity was working hours falling faster than output. Business productivity peaked in the second quarter of 2003. It reached its cycle low of about 1% in the first quarter of 2009.

Unemployment will likely hover in the 9% range in 2011; the 6.5% range in 2013 and perhaps settle in at around 5% in 2014 where it is likely to remain for several years. The days of 4% unemployment are gone for at least a decade or more.

AUGUST 22, 2009

987,000 FLORIDIANS JOBLESS IN JULY—UNEMPLOYMENT RATE NOW 10.7%

Florida employers shed another 17,000 jobs in July leaving approximately 987,000 Floridians jobless out of a workforce of 9,193,000. The state's unemployment rate is now 10.7%—the highest since October 1975 when it was 11.0%. The July rate is unchanged from the June revised rate of 10.7% but it is 4.4 percentage points higher than a year earlier. An estimated 401,100 jobs have been lost year over year. This is steeper than the national rate of decline and continues a long series of job losses which began in August 2007. The decline started with construction jobs and has now spread to nearly every employment sector. Florida's historic low for unemployment was 3.3% in July 2006.

Florida's labor force has always been volatile due to its large share of real estate and construction employment together with its tourist and agriculture oriented activities. These sectors are usually among the first to be adversely affected in a recession and the current economic downturn is no exception.

Florida's job losses began in the construction sector following the housing down turn. Many of those displaced construction workers migrated to the commercial sector; a move that cushioned total job losses in the broader construction sector for at least a year. By mid-2008 however, many of the commercial construction jobs were lost too. Between July 2008 and July 2009, the construction sector lost 78,900 jobs or 15.6% of the sector total.

In July 2009, by far the most jobs were lost in the trade, transportation and utilities sector. Approximately 99,100 jobs were lost year over year with most of them (-69,700) attributable to the recession driven decline in retail trade. We expect the retail component to continue to lose jobs and not reverse course until employment rebounds.

Financial activities lost 23,200 jobs year over year. That is 4.4% of the sector work force. Sector losses were divided between finance and insurance (-16,300) and real estate (-6,900).

Professional and business services, another large sector, lost 90,600 jobs or 7.9% of the sector work force year over year. Most of those jobs can be traced back to the decline that began in the housing sector. That clearly illustrates the huge effect housing has, both directly and indirectly, on the broader economy. An important take away here is that the broader economy cannot improve significantly until housing improves.

Leisure and hospitality lost 40,400 jobs year over year. That is about 4.3% of the sector workforce. Within the sector, arts, entertainment and recreation lost 13,100 jobs while the accommodation sector, which includes hotels, motels and restaurants, lost 27,300 jobs. The latter is a clear reaction to the recessionary slowdown in leisure and business travel as well as meals away from home.

Government lost 9,900 jobs. Within the sector, local government lost 10,200 jobs while federal government in Florida had a small gain.

Education and health services gained 5,400 jobs year over year. That is the only sector to add jobs. Behind the numbers though, education lost 4,000 jobs while health services added 9,400 jobs.

AUGUST 22, 2009

OFFICE VACANCIES SURGE

Office vacancy rates are rising in nearly all metropolitan areas across the country. Increases have been most pronounced in Florida and other sunbelt states that had the greatest run up during the housing boom years and which are now experiencing the most severe corrections. Office vacancies rose in 66 of the nation's 79 primary metros. At the same time effective rents declined in 72 of those 79 areas as a result of extensive concessions. Of the ten metros with the largest vacancy increase, six are in California and four are in Florida.

Huge office job growth in housing, construction and allied industries together with easy credit fuelled an extraordinary amount of office development, especially in suburban locations, between 2003 and 2007. When the speculative housing bubble burst, office employment soon followed and the demand for office space declined dramatically. In addition, aggressive corporate cost cutting contributed to diminished demand for office space. Most companies are not expanding and many are cutting back bringing large amounts of sub lease space to market.

The West Palm Beach | Boca Raton metro has the highest office vacancy in the nation at 25.3%. That is according to a recent report by CBRE. The metro saw extraordinary employment growth between 2003 and 2005 together with an extraordinary amount of new office development. The metro has now lost 3.7% of its office jobs in the last two years. The office job loss actually began in 2005 and has been steady and steep since then. Today nearly 500,000 square feet of space is available for sub-lease and is likely to be on the market for 6-12 months and command about 15–20% less than the original lease amount.

Metro Ft. Lauderdale has a 16.7% office vacancy rate and has lost 7.1%

of its office jobs in the last two years. It has nearly 600,000 square feet available for sub lease.

Metro Orlando has a 17.2% vacancy and has lost 3.3% of its office jobs over the last two years. Space available for sublease is approaching 1.0 million square feet—nearly double the South Florida availability.

All Florida metros experienced negative net absorption meaning that new space started several years ago is still in the lease-up stage plus additional space is coming back to market for sublease.

Looking forward, local office markets will get worse before they get better. We expect unemployment to continue to rise well into 2010. That will soften demand for office space even more. The current economic environment has curtailed new office construction and is weighing heavily on rents. Given the breadth of the recession, office markets locally will continue to struggle for the next few years. New development is not likely to be economically feasible until 2012.

Office Vacancies in Key Florida Metros—June 2009

Florida Metro	Q2 2007	Q2 2008	Q2 2009	% Chg Office Jobs 2007–2009
West Palm Bch Boca Raton	11.3	18.1	25.3	-3.7
Ft. Lauderdale	7.2	12.6	16.7	-7.1
Miami	7.2	9.2	12.4	-6.4
Orlando	9.0	12.1	17.2	-3.3
Tampa | St Pete Clearwater	12.3	15.0	20.7	-7.4
Jacksonville	14.3	22.7	19.9	-7.4

SOURCE: Reis, CoStar, BPRE Research

NEW HOME EQUILIBRIUM COMING INTO VIEW

New home sales rose 9.6% nationally in July. The Census Bureau and the Department of Housing and Urban Development jointly reported that July sales rose to 433,000 units at a seasonally adjusted annual rate. That follows an upwardly revised June rate of 395,000 sales. Sales for April, May and June were all revised up. July's increase was the fourth consecutive monthly increase and the strongest showing since September 2008. The last time monthly sales rose so significantly was in February 2005. Sales are now up 32% since their January trough but down 69% from their bubble peak of nearly 1.4 million units nearly four years ago. Looking forward, we expect sales to decline again temporarily after the $8,000 tax credit available to some first time home buyers expires in November. From there, pent up demand, renewed affordability and historic low interest rates will fuel modest volume increases. Nevertheless, sales volume is likely to remain under 900,000 units for several years even after recovery.

The new home report follows other housing reports including the National and Florida Associations of Realtors, Federal Housing Finance Agency and S&P Case Shiller—all of which were more positive than they have been for nearly three years.

The number of new homes for sale declined to 271,000 units in July. That is the 27th consecutive month of decline and the lowest level since March 1993. During more normal times, when supply and demand are in balance, inventory hovers near the 300,000 mark. This inventory decline is a fundamental reason why housing permits and construction starts are beginning to rise (see Economic Perspectives, August 25, 2009).

At the same time, the number *of finished* new homes is declining. Finished home inventory dropped to 120,000 units in July. Inventory remains slightly bloated. In a normal market, that figure would be below 100,000. The record high was 199,000 units in January 2008. Inventory has steadily fallen since then.

Months of supply of new homes fell from 8.5 to 7.5 months. The noteworthy bad news in the report is that the time to sell a new home rose from 0.6 months to an all-time high (since 1963) of 12.4 months despite the strong uptick in demand.

The median new home price was $210,100 in July. That compares to $181,600 for an existing home. The price difference between a new home and an existing one has narrowed but existing homes continue to outsell new homes by a huge (and growing) margin.

The story is similar in Seacoast core markets. In Indian River County, new home inventory has declined for 11 consecutive quarters, from a peak of nearly 2,000 units to only 500 at the end of the second quarter of 2009. That is still a 10.7 month supply at the current sales pace. New construction starts also declined from a peak near 2,000 in the second quarter of 2005 to only 250 today—an approximate 88% decline.

St. Lucie County built longer into the downturn reaching a peak of 2,500 units in late 2006. Inventory currently stands at about 800 units which is still a 17 month supply at the currently slow sales pace. There were only 112 new construction starts in the second quarter—down 96% from its 2006 peak.

Martin County inventory has only 225 finished units, down 76% from its late 2006 peak. Current supply is about 10 months at the current sales pace. There were only 60 new starts in the second quarter, down 96% from the early 2006 peak.

Palm Beach County inventory has declined every quarter since the second quarter of 2005 to about 1,200 units representing an approximate 8.5 month supply. Starts are down 92% since the peak in 2005 to only 758 starts in the second quarter of 2009.

U.S. ECONOMY SHED MORE JOBS IN AUGUST

The U.S. economy shed another 216,000 jobs in August pushing the unemployment rate to 9.7%—a 26 year high. The loss was the smallest since August 2008. At the same time, July's job loss rate was revised to negative 276,000 which was more severe than previously reported. Most of the bad news in the revisions came from the state and local government sector where 54,000 more jobs were lost than were shown in the advance estimate. That sector has lost jobs all year.

The most notable change was in the private services sector where job losses totaled 62,000, the smallest decline since April 2008. During the first quarter of this year, the sector was shedding jobs at the extraordinary average rate of 358,000 per month. The manufacturing sector also continued to shed jobs at a pace slightly greater than in July. While virtually no manufacturing sector added jobs, the pace of decline has slowed over the last few months. The same pattern holds in construction where the sector lost 65,000 jobs in August, down from 73,000 in July. Predictably, the majority of losses were in commercial which was down 35,000 jobs while residential was down 23,000.

Employment in financial activities declined by 28,000 jobs in August. The sector has lost 537,000 jobs since the start of the recession in December 2007 but the rate of decline has slowed significantly in recent months.

Employment in a wide variety of sectors such as retail, professional and business services, warehousing and others have slowed their precipitous rate of decline over the last few months. That is a significant improvement from the November 2008 through April 2009 time period.

Health care employment rose by 28,000 jobs in August. The sector has added 544,000 jobs since the recession began. There was also a 200,000 job increase in social services that was not fully anticipated.

While private sector payrolls are improving, the government sector continues to worsen as state and local governments remain cash strapped. That sector lost 79,000 jobs in the last three months. Most of the cuts were in education.

Underemployment is pervasive. Persons working part time for economic reasons was little changed in August at about $9.1 million. These persons are working part time because their hours had been cut or they were unable to find full time employment. About 2.3 million workers are marginally attached to the workforce. That is an increase of 660,000 year over year. Finally, there were about 758,000 discouraged workers—those who would like to have a job but feel none is available for them. The Bureau of Labor Statistics tracks these categories in several alternative measures of employment. If the three categories were added to the unemployed, the nation's unemployment rate ("U6 measure") would be 16.8% rather than 9.7%.

Total hours worked in the private sector declined 0.3% in August after a 0.1% increase in July. That is bad news for household incomes which have been under pressure for most of the last year. There was some modest offset as average hourly earnings rose 0.3% for the second straight month. Hours worked have been running about 2-3% lower than in the second quarter. That is much milder than the 7.8% decline in the first quarter.

There is widespread evidence that the decline in employment is slowing and will continue to do so into 2010 before finding bottom. No leading indicator has emerged to suggest employment will start growing anytime soon. Moreover unemployment has not yet peaked. Until we start seeing sustained employment gains, unemployment will rise. We will still likely see 10% unemployment by early 2010 before it changes course.

SEPTEMBER 21, 2009

ONE MILLION FLORIDIANS JOBLESS IN AUGUST

Florida employers shed another 15,000 jobs in August leaving 984,000 jobless out of a civilian labor force of 9,194,000. The state's unemployment rate is now 10.7%— the highest since October 1975 when it was 11.0%. The August rate is only fractionally changed from the revised July rate of 10.8% but 4.2 percentage points higher than August 2008

---

when statewide unemployment was 6.5%. Florida's civilian labor force declined slightly (-0.64%) year over year. The state's headline rates are seasonally adjusted which smooths out some peaks and valleys in the data. Not seasonally adjusted, there were 1,013,000 jobless Floridians translating to an unemployment rate of 10.9%.

Florida employers have shed 372,700 jobs since August 2008. The August job numbers continue a downward trend begun two years ago in August 2007 when the housing market began to collapse and construction came to a halt. In recent months however, job losses have been moderating but stabilization appears unlikely before late 2010 with robust growth not returning until at least 2014.

The downturn in Florida employment began in the construction industry with residential construction the hardest hit. The impact was cushioned when many of the lost residential construction jobs were absorbed in the commercial sector. Today, commercial construction has reached a record low and job losses continue to mount. Year over year in August, Florida lost 62,700 construction jobs.

In August, the business and professional services sector lost the most jobs. Losses totaled 93,300 jobs or 8.2% of the sector work force year over year. Similarly, financial activities lost 28,900 jobs which is 5.5% of its work force. State and local governments also shed 8,900 jobs in August year over year.

Many of these losses can be traced to the crash of the state's housing industry. An extraordinary number of jobs were created in both the private and public sectors to service what was then expected to be continued growth in housing. That demand began to disappear in 2007 and today, there is no leading indicator to suggest jobs will return to their pre-boom level any time soon. Like the nation, many of Florida's job losses in this recession are permanent rather than cyclical and the loss is rippling through the broader economy, including commercial real estate where the demand for office space, for example, has diminished dramatically.

In other Florida employment sectors, manufacturing lost 45,000 jobs (12.2%), trade, transportation and utilities lost 85,100 jobs (5.4%) and leisure and hospitality lost 35,200 jobs (3.7%). All are year over year losses.

The only industry to gain jobs was the private education and health care sector. All of the gain was in healthcare and social services which grew by 9,100 jobs. Private education declined by 4,200 jobs year over year in August.

There are approximately 366,768 unemployed persons in Seacoast markets. That is 36% of the state total. Approximately one-third of the Seacoast market unemployed are in the four county Metro Orlando area.

The three Treasure Coast counties have a combined 34,970 unemployed persons.

SEPTEMBER 28, 2009

SALES VOLUME DECLINES BUT LOCAL EXISTING HOME PRICES STABLE IN AUGUST

Existing single family home sale volume slipped both nationally and in most Seacoast markets in August from volumes reported in July. Sales volumes had been rising steadily for most of the last 12 months. Prices were stable or up fractionally. The volume decline was widespread and although there is no readily apparent cause, we do not consider a one month decline in volume to be a reversal of trend. The national median price for an existing single family home was $178,300 in August. That was down 1.8% from July when it was $181,600. Median existing home prices in Seacoast served Metropolitan Statistical Areas (MSA) are generally lower ranging $113,000 in the Ft. Pierce Port St. Lucie MSA to $144,200 in Orlando. Palm Beach and Broward counties are higher at $245,700 and $217,000 respectively.

Florida and Seacoast served metros continued a trend begun about eight months ago when existing home prices began to stabilize after an extraordinary fall that began in 2007. Historically low interest rates, a tax credit and renewed affordability have drawn buyers off the sidelines. In Florida, 13,850 existing homes traded in August. That was 28% more than a year earlier but down nearly 13% from July. The decline breaks a nearly year-long trend of increase. There is no truly plausible explanation for the decline—only speculative assumptions. A one month volume decline however, is not particularly worrisome. All the widely watched indices such as Case-Shiller, FHFA (Federal Housing Finance Agency, and Realtor associations tell a similar story—that is that housing has reached bottom and is now exhibiting clear signs of stability.

Median price nationally was down slightly in August, declining from $181,600 to $178,300. The median price in Florida was $147,400 which was virtually unchanged from a month earlier but down 22% from a year earlier when it was $188,500. Median prices in Seacoast markets were lower except for Palm Beach and Broward counties which have historically been, and continue to be higher. A 13 month history of both volume and price trends for each Seacoast served MSA appears at the bottom of the previous page.

New home sales volume, nationally, inched up a modest 0.7% in August to a 429,000 seasonally adjusted annual rate. The rate of change was statistically insignificant in every region of the country. The number of unsold new homes fell to 262,000 units marking the 28th straight monthly decline. The months of supply at the current sales pace fell from 7.6 to 7.3 months. At the same time, the median time period to sell a new home rose to 12.9 months. That is the longest time period recorded since tracking began in 1963.

Construction starts and permits. Housing starts nationally increased 1.5% in August from an all-time reported in July. Tracking that data series began in 1960. Starts totaled 598,000 units annualized. Of the total, 479,000 were single family starts and 119,000 were multifamily. Both figures are annualized. On a percentage basis, single family starts declined 3.0% while multifamily surged upward 25.3%. The multifamily surge is deceiving as it was based on a record low of only 95,000 units in July. The multifamily sector remains in a deep slump and the short term outlook is grim.

Building permits were up 2.7% nationally. Single family permits were flat and most of the increase was attributable to the multifamily sector. Permits are an important metric as they tell a story of expected construction starts in the short term future. Permits in August imply lackluster performance in September and October. Nevertheless, both starts and permits are consistent with a housing market that is beginning to turn positive but is still remarkably fragile and could turn negative again with even modest economic shock.

Starts and permits are at exceptionally low levels in all Seacoast served markets as well. According to Metrostudy, annualized construction starts as of the second quarter of 2009 totaled 254 in Indian River County; 112 in St. Lucie County; 60 in Martin County and 758 in Palm Beach County. The volume of construction starts is not likely to improve as long as prices remain below the cost to build. Most permits issued in Seacoast markets recently have been for remodeling or new construction on behalf of owners. There has been virtually no proposed speculative construction by builders.

New home inventory also remains high locally. By Metrostudy's second quarter census, Indian River County still had 501 new homes for a 10.7 month supply while St. Lucie County had 830 for a significantly elevated 16.9 month supply. Martin County had 225 homes available for a 9.9 month supply and Palm Beach County had 1,188 new homes available for an 8.5 month supply. All months of supply are based on the current rate of absorption.

The median price of a new home is roughly 20% higher than the median price of an existing home and existing homes are now outselling new homes at a rate of roughly nine-to-one both nationally and locally.

Tax Credit. The $8,000 tax credit available to some first time home buyers clearly boosted sales. While the final number will not be known for some time, the credit was probably responsible for 350,000 to 400,000 sales that might not otherwise have occurred. To receive the credit, purchases must be closed by the end of November. Due to the successful and significant stimulative effect, Congress is being lobbied hard to renew the credit and possibly increase it to $15,000. An increase is unlikely due to its cost. At this writing, it is unclear if the credit will be renewed at $8,000. If it is not, sales volume will almost certainly decline by early 2010. In our view, the credit did not create or stimulate new demand. Rather it shifted future demand earlier in the recovery.

The tax credit is expensive and will probably subtract upwards of $4.0 Billion from tax revenue at a time when revenues are already down and spending is up due to stimulus spending.

WILLIAM L. PITTENGER   179

Median price trends. Existing home prices statewide have stabilized after a dramatic rise and an equally dramatic fall. While relative stability and renewed affordability both exist, prices are skewed to the downside as a result of foreclosure and short sales and fear in the marketplace built on employment concerns and still low, but modestly rising, consumer confidence. The overwhelming number of transactions in recent months have been in the low to mid $100,000 price range with comparatively few over $400,000.

The outlook. While relative stability has returned to the existing home market, it remains fragile. In our view the best that can be expected over the next two to three years is for home prices and volumes to bounce along the bottom with little or no change. There is no leading indicator to suggest that housing will return to robust growth anytime soon. Foreclosures are still problematic and are likely to remain that way well into 2011. Employment is a deep concern and will affect home purchases and foreclosures over the short term. New construction is not economically feasible and will not likely become feasible until the sales pace pick up and prices rise enough to justify new construction. These factors, together with a broader economy that is likely to recover very slowly, will keep a lid on home sales and curtail price increases in the foreseeable future.

After the last major downturn in the early 1990's, it took the single family housing market about seven years to return to robust growth. It took the condominium market 13 years. Recovery from "The Great Recession" will likely be similar.

OCTOBER 2, 2009

U.S. JOB LOSSES ACCELERATE AGAIN IN SEPTEMBER— UNEMPLOYMENT RATE RISES TO 9.8%

The U.S. economy shed another 263,000 jobs in September. The reading was worse than widely expected and worse than the August revised loss of 201,000 jobs. Nevertheless, the rate of decline in private employment is slowing. The rate of state and local government job losses, however, accelerated as severe budget constraints grip nearly every level of government including public education. That sector took a big job hit in September at the beginning of the new school year.

Since the official start of the recession in December 2007, 7.6 million jobs have been lost bringing the ranks of the currently unemployed to 15.1 million. In a side note, the Bureau of Labor Statistics announced its intent to revise March 2009 payroll employment down by 824,000 jobs based on a full employment count of unemployment insurance records. This implies that total job losses since the beginning of the recession may be over 8.0 million.

Among the unemployed are 603,000 persons who became newly unemployed or who completed temporary jobs. The number of long term unemployed (defined as those unemployed for 27 weeks or more) rose by 450,000 to 5.4 million persons. A full 35.6% of unemployed workers have now been unemployed for 27 weeks or more. It has become painfully clear that once a person becomes unemployed, they are likely to remain unemployed for an extended period of time. Moreover, the statistics suggest too that the longer a person is unemployed, the longer it takes to find a job.

In September, the number of persons working part time for economic reasons (involuntary part time workers) was nearly the same as August at 9.2 million. Those marginally attached to the workforce total about 2.2 million; some 615,000 more than a year earlier. Among the marginally attached were 706,000 discouraged workers. Persons in that group are no longer searching for work as they don't believe there is a job available for them. That group has increased by 239,000 persons over the last year.

Private employment fell by 210,000 jobs in September, much worse than the 182,000 decline in August. In the private services sector, the number of job losses widened to 94,000 from 50,000 in August. Retail was down 39,000 as compared to 9,000 a month earlier. Private education service jobs declined by 17,000 as compared to just 4,000 in August. Auto dealers lost 5,000 jobs after adding 4,000 jobs a month earlier. The change is not surprising since the sales surge from cash for clunkers disappeared. Construction payrolls declined by 64,000 jobs after a 60,000 loss in August. Manufacturing jobs declined less sharply in September (51,000) as compared to August (66,000).

The government sector continues to deteriorate. State and local governments have now lost 160,000 jobs over the last four months. In September, the sector lost 47,000 jobs of which 29,000 came from education. The education sector as a whole (public and private) lost 46,000 jobs in September.

The unemployment rate is now 9.8%, up from 9.7% a month earlier and nearly double the rate a year ago. There was nothing in the employment situation report that would suggest the economy would add jobs anytime soon. Instead we see a re-affirmation of our view that unemployment will hit 10% in the fourth quarter and peak slightly higher than 10% in early to mid-2010.

The most comprehensive measure of unemployment known as the "U-6" rose from 16.8% to 17% in September. This alternative measure includes involuntary part time and marginally attached workers referred to previously. An equivalent measure is not tracked on the Treasure Coast but if it were, equivalent unemployment would be about 25%.

OCTOBER 29, 2009

HOUSING REDUX—A SUMMARY OF HOUSING REPORTS

Housing starts nationally inched up 0.5% in September to 590,000 units (annualized). Digging deeper into the data, single family starts increased 3.9% while multifamily starts fell a staggering 15.2% to 89,000 units. That is the second lowest multifamily reading since the data series began in 1959. These results come after a flat August reading.

According to Metrostudy, third quarter construction starts were almost non-existent in Seacoast core markets. Indian River County recorded only 46 starts in the quarter. St. Lucie and Martin Counties recorded just 15 and 11 respectively while Palm Beach County recorded 297 quarterly starts.

At the same time, building permits, a leading indicator of construction starts in the short term future, declined nationally 1.2% with single family permits declining 3.0% and multifamily permits rising 6.0%. August and September permit data point to flat or small declines in single family construction starts the remainder of 2009. The results will be similar locally.

New home sales nationally fell 3.6% in September to a seasonally adjusted 402,000 annual rate. The estimates for June, July and August were also revised down. The number of unsold new homes fell to 251,000. That is the 29th straight monthly decline. The months of supply for finished vacant homes was unchanged in September at about 7.5 months. The median time for sale of a new home was also unchanged over August at about 13 months—its highest reading since the data series began in 1963. Finally, the number of completed new homes offered for sale fell to 109,000. It peaked in January 2008 at 199,000 units.

While the national numbers are less than stellar, local numbers are worse. According to Metrostudy, Indian River County has a total inventory of 471 new homes. At the current rate of absorption, that is a 12.3 month supply. St. Lucie County has 727 homes available for a 16.6 month supply. Martin County has 184 homes available for a 9.5 month supply while Palm Beach County has 1,175 new homes available for a 9.9 month supply.

Existing home sales. Sales of both existing single family homes and condominiums surged in September. Sales of single family homes rose 9.4% nationally while condo and co-op sales rose 9.7%. Sales were up in all four census regions of the country. The national inventory fell to 3.63 million units from its July 2008 peak of 4.57 million units. The inventory numbers do not include the so-called shadow inventory of foreclosed homes which are still owned by banks. The National Association of Realtors Pending Home Sales Index has risen about 10% more than the existing home sales activity since January. This implies that there is a significant pipeline of homes pending closing. The sales should show up in October and November sales numbers.

S&P/Case Shiller, produces 10 and 20 city indices of home prices. The indices are highly regarded and perhaps the most widely watched nationally. Only Tampa and Miami are surveyed in Florida. Seasonally adjusted prices increased for the third straight month and are another indicator that the market is slowly recovering.

The market for single family housing continues on a slow track to recovery. Multifamily remains in a deep slump and recovery is several years away. While some analysts forecast additional declines in 2010 they are modest by almost any measure (2.5%–4.5% in Florida). In our opinion, prices will fluctuate within a narrow range throughout 2010.

NOVEMBER 6, 2009

ECONOMY RETURNS TO GROWTH IN Q3

The first estimate of third quarter Gross Domestic Product (GDP) grew at an annualized rate of 3.5% after declining for four consecutive quarters and five quarters total since late 2007. Clearly that is good news. But should we interpret the news to mean the recession has ended? Will the good times roll? No. The GDP is the top line measure of the nation's economy and the broadest measure of goods and services produced in the nation. Because it is such a broad indicator, it is widely used to gauge the general health of the economy but it is not the sole indicator of whether the nation is or is not in recession. The GDP is comprised of hundreds of components.

The good news in the report is that the economy is growing again. It also underscores the belief that the recession may have *technically* ended sometime between June and August of this year. The Business Cycle Dating Committee (BCDC) of the National Bureau of Economic Research (NBER) is a committee of academic economists headquartered at Princeton University. The committee is the official arbiter of the nation's business cycle. It does not forecast the timing of peaks and troughs but rather dates them after the fact. Indeed, the current recession officially began in December 2007 but the BCDC did not call that date until 12 months later.

The BCDC does not rely solely on the GDP to date the business cycle but rather uses a wide range of indicators over a lengthy period of time. In this case growth in the 3% range was anticipated however the BCDC

---

made it clear in public comments that it was struggling to reconcile growing GDP against an unemployment rate that was also rising. The message is that the committee is unlikely to officially declare an end of the recession until well into 2010.

The current estimate is an "advance" estimate based upon what are admittedly incomplete data. The estimate is subject to further revision. A "preliminary" estimate will be released a month from now and a "final" estimate two months from now. Each estimate is subject to change as more information becomes available.

Looking behind the numbers that comprise the GDP, consumer spending rose 3.4% after falling 0.9% in the second quarter. Spending on durable goods (defined as those expected to last three years or more) rose 22.3% in contrast to a decrease of 5.6% a quarter earlier. Durable spending was led by spending on motor vehicles and parts which rose at a 56.3% annual rate due largely to the "cash for clunkers" program. Even so, motor vehicles contributed less than half of the overall consumer spending increase. At the same time, spending on non-durables (consumable items) increased 2.0% after falling a nearly identical amount a quarter earlier.

There was widespread improvement across all major consumption categories. Business equipment, software spending and residential fixed investment all returned to growth in the third quarter. Residential fixed investment turned in an impressive performance by growing 23.4% in the third quarter after falling a nearly identical amount a quarter earlier. The increase is a clear reaction to improving residential real estate activity. Non-residential fixed investment, however, fell 9.0% after falling 17.3% in the second quarter. The decline is more evidence of continuing weakness in the non-residential real estate sector.

Both exports and imports returned to growth as well. Exports were up 14.7% while imports were up 16.4%. While the net result was a 0.5% drag on GDP growth, the fact that both increased is a clear sign that global trade is improving.

Inventories added 0.9% to growth simply because they were falling less sharply.

U.S. JOB LOSSES SLOW BUT RATE RISES

Nonfarm payrolls fell by another 190,000 jobs nationally in October according to an advance estimate by the Bureau of Labor Statistics (BLS). That brings the ranks of the unemployed to 15.7 million. Slightly over 8.0 million jobs have now been lost since the start of the recession in December 2007. In a separate survey, the nation's unemployment rate rose to 10.2% (from 9.8%), its highest since April 1983. The unemployment rate has grown by 5.3 percentage points since the start of the recession. October was the first time unemployment has crossed the 10% mark since 1983.

While employment continues to decline, there were a few distant glimmers of positive news. The rate of decline has slowed significantly from earlier this year when job losses were over 700,000 per month. Additionally, August and September losses were revised to show 91,000 fewer jobs lost than originally reported and the three month moving average of monthly jobs lost is now about 178,000.

The number of temporary jobs increased by 34,000 plus the number of overtime hours worked rose. Both are leading indicators that point toward modest improvement in the labor market. The growth in overtime hours implies that factory orders are increasing. Similarly, employers frequently test the waters with temporary help before making a commitment to new hiring.

Despite the distant glimmer of positive news, job losses continue. Manufacturing lost 61,000 jobs in October which is the largest loss since June. Manufacturing job losses combined with an increase in overtime hours clearly shows both the depth of the recession and the uneven nature of the recovery.

Construction payrolls also fell by 62,000. There was a stark contrast between employment in the residential and commercial sectors. The residential construction sector is beginning to stabilize, albeit at a very low level, after huge losses the last two years. The sector lost 15,000 jobs in October. Contrast that with the non-residential sector where

33,000 jobs were lost. The implication is that residential is leveling off while nonresidential construction still has a long way to fall.

Retail shed another 40,000 jobs as employers remain cautious in the face of sagging consumer confidence, unemployment and absence of income growth. Transportation and warehousing also lost another 18,000 jobs. State and local governments have been shedding jobs since mid-2009 and shed another 16,000 in October. The decline is clearly due to widespread budget cuts. As state and local governments lose jobs, the federal government added 16,000 jobs in October. Much of it was probably stimulus related. Some of it was likely FDIC hiring. The agency is staffing up around the country to manage the expected wave of bank failures in 2010 and beyond.

The only key sector to add jobs was healthcare. The sector added 29,000 jobs in October and has now added 597,000 jobs since the December 2007 start of the recession.

Those who are working part time for economic reasons totaled about 9.3 million in October. That total was little changed month over month but it has steadily grown faster than the rate of joblessness. Similarly, those marginally attached to the work force now totals about 2.4 million, having grown 736,000 year over year. The "U-6" measure of unemployment, which includes part time and marginally attached workers was 17.5% in October.

We expect job losses to continue to ease but not enough to reduce the 10.2% October unemployment rate. Instead,

NOVEMBER 18, 2009

WHAT'S NEXT? A CONCISE LOOK AT ECONOMIC RECOVERY AND BEYOND

As economic recovery begins to take shape at virtually every level from local to global it seems appropriate to take a look at what the economy might look like during an after recovery. This is not a look into the crystal ball but rather a forecast of things most likely—though not

---

guaranteed—to happen using the best currently available information. Just like the economy signaled its probable downturn three years ago, it is now sending off signals of a probable upturn. Those signals can be measured and used to make inferences about the short term future. With the exception of the commercial real estate sector which continues to weaken, both housing and the broader economy are likely to end 2009 in much better condition than they began the year. The local and U.S. economies will still face significant challenges. Unemployment is much higher than it would be in a healthy economy. Credit and the demand for credit remain in a synchronized decline. Economic activity remains weak and economic growth, though measurable, won't be strong enough to achieve robust growth anytime soon. With that backdrop, let's look at several key factors driving recovery and shaping what happens next.

The nation's economy endured 10 recessions between the end of World War II and the beginning of the current recession in late 2007. Those recessions lasted between six and sixteen months with an average duration of 10 months. Real GDP declined 0.4% to 3.8% with an average decline of 2.0%. Nonfarm employment declined an average of 2.7% and the average unemployment rate grew by 3.2% during each of the 10 recessions.

The 10 previous recessions were caused by a variety of factors such as shifts in monetary policy, withdrawal of government spending after war time, dramatic rise in oil prices, the Iranian revolution and more.

The current recession is like none of the previous 10. Indeed the cause was the product of interest rates which were too low, too long which led to excess liquidity which helped inflate the housing bubble. When the bubble collapsed, the effect was felt globally and eventually landed squarely in the broader economy. The current recession will have lasted 23 months if an official end is declared in October. Employment is down over 5% and unemployment is up over 5%. Real GDP has declined 3.8%. By almost any measure, the current recession has been broader and deeper than any of the previous 10. At its deepest point in late 2008, this recession was perhaps most similar to the Great Depression of the 1930's. In fact, with the near collapse of the U.S. banking system in September 2008, there was widespread concern that that "The

Great Recession" could fall into the second Great Depression.

Unlike the 10 previous recessions, the severity of this one led to structural changes in the broader economy. The current recession is a true balance sheet recession much like the Great Depression and the more recent Japanese experience. We have, and will continue to see, massive deleveraging where virtually everyone has had to get their balance sheet in order by purging debt and, perhaps more importantly, recognizing the asset deflation that has occurred almost universally. Let's look at some reasons for structural change. We'll then explore the expected result.

The shrinking boomer economy. The baby boom generation refers to those born between 1946 and 1964. Roughly 77 million babies were born during those years as military service people came back from World War II and started families. The peak birth rate was reached in 1957 when 4.3 million babies were born—a number not equaled before or since. The boomer generation is the largest demographic cohort ever and historically, as the baby boom generation moved, so moved the economy. For example when boomers began buying homes, sales of starter homes surged. When they began moving up, sales of move up homes surged. Today, this generation represents 28% of the American population. Deaths have steadily been replaced by immigrants and the Census Bureau expects the baby boom generation to be about 57.8 million strong through at least 2030. That year, boomers will be between the ages of 66 and 84 and will still far outnumber any generation before or since. As a result boomers will continue to have a profound effect on the economy for many years to come.

One of the most significant effects will be savings. Boomers, as a group, were historically free spenders. They had faith in rising markets and this decade was no exception. Today, however, boomers have moved from spending to savings which has helped propel a national savings rate from zero to about 5%. If the emerging savings trend holds, about $400 Billion will come out of annual consumption. That is more than enough to move the nation's GDP downward. The economy has grown at an average annual rate of 3.5% since 1965. During the recent bubble decade (1995-2005) the boomer share of GDP growth was about 78%. Going forward, GDP is more likely to average near 2.4% due to declining consumption.

The "paradox of thrift, popularized by economist John Maynard Keynes in his 1930 book, Treatise on Money" asserts that individual savings is a virtue but if it spreads to the entire economy, it can curtail spending and output thereby dampening prospects for recovery and growth. The paradox is alive and well in the current economy.

The loss of $15 Trillion in household wealth during the recession triggered a profound adjustment in consumer attitudes about spending and saving. In fact, a recent survey commissioned by CitiGroup suggests strongly that the return to thrift may be a permanent lifestyle change for all consumers regardless of age or ethnicity. This is just one more piece of evidence that the nation's economic model may no longer be structured as heavily around spending going forward. Among other key findings, the survey found that 63% of U.S. of consumers thought the change in the way they spend and save was permanent. Only 29% said they would go back to pre-recession spending. This attitude shift has also caused retailers to rethink the value proposition.

The baby boom generational shift that was widely expected to occur as boomers retired and passed the baton to the next generation has not yet begun. It was widely expected that boomers would begin to retire early given the general prosperity of their lifetime.

Then came the crash and today 69% of boomers (age 54-63) are not financially prepared for retirement. As a result they are staying in the work force longer, spending less, more likely to value shop, buying fewer luxury cars and more.

Employment has seen unprecedented structural change. Employment increased dramatically between 2002 and 2006. Much of it in response to an extraordinary increase in residential real estate development. Employment in construction and allied services rose. Office jobs increased significantly in real estate construction, sales, lending, closing and more. Architects, engineers, designers, real estate attorneys and others flourished. Locally, where the economy was heavily real estate and construction driven, unemployment declined to a cycle low of about 3.3%. Nationally, unemployment sunk to under 5%. What was almost universally overlooked was that much of the employment growth was artificial. It was being created by a housing bubble where both sales volume and prices were increasing at double digit rates over a very short time period. Worse, many players caught up in the "irrational exuberance" of the day implicitly assumed that the growth would continue unabated.

The employment sector came crashing down soon after the subprime mortgage melt down in August 2007. Today, nearly 36,000 people are unemployed on the Treasure Coast; over 1.0 million in Florida and nearly 16 million in the U.S.

Looking forward, a large number of job losses in this recession are permanent rather than cyclical. Many of the construction, sales, financial and business service jobs created during the "bubble era" will not be replaced. Moreover, since real estate development—especially housing—will not likely return to its pre-run up rate for perhaps as much as a decade, post recovery employment will likely be much lower than pre run up employment.

Today, job losses are slowing (-190,000 in October) and initial claims for unemployment have fallen into the low 500,000 range. What is not happening though, is job creation. The Labor Department reported in its September (most recent report) Job Openings and Labor Turnover Survey (JOLTS), that job openings in September were up only fractionally from their August historic low which was down 48% from its June 2007 peak.

Looking forward, it is likely that the nation's unemployment rate will grow to the high 10% range by year end 2010 and remain higher than normal through 2013. Return to robust growth is unlikely before late 2014 or 2015. Clearly the days of 4% unemployment are gone for a decade or more.

Housing is where it all began and it too has experienced profound structural change. The collapse of the subprime mortgage market in August 2007 was quickly followed by the collapse of the U.S. housing market. Only recently has it begun to show signs of stability and early signs of new life.

During the run up that began in earnest in 2002, prices and sales volumes doubled in some areas. Nationally, sales volume rose from 5.25 million homes in 2001 to 8.36 million in 2005. For perspective, annualized sales were 4.89 million in September 2009. The run up was followed by an equally severe downturn. In fact all of the price gains and more during the run up were erased between late 2007 and mid-2009. In Florida, the peak to trough decline over that time period was 43%. In St. Lucie County, one of the hardest hit areas in the country, the peak to trough decline was nearly 60%.

Foreclosures also continue unabated. While the subprime foreclosure debacle is behind us, Payment Option ARMs are resetting now and will continue to do so through 2011. Foreclosures are also moving into the prime sector. Foreclosures will keep a lid on price increases at least into 2011.

In previous recessions, housing demand fell as a result of weak income and declining employment. The recession led to pent up demand that was naturally unleashed when the economy recovered. This recession is different. Future demand was satisfied before its time during the bubble years. Those who bought too early and later lost their homes to foreclosure are unlikely to get a new mortgage anytime soon. The result is that the current downturn is not building unsatisfied demand for new homes. At best it is only helping to restore equilibrium to the supply and demand relationship.

During the last major real estate downturn of the late 1980's and early 1990's it took a full seven years for single family housing to return to robust growth. It took condominiums 13 years. Moody's Economy. Com has forecast 14 years peak to peak for housing to return to robust growth.

Combine excessive inventory and the effect of foreclosures with curtailed spending, reduced household wealth, potentially difficult financing and a paltry appetite for risk and we have a housing market that will do well to catch up to the natural rate of growth. The end result is that housing will not be a significant builder of wealth for individual homeowners nor a strong contributor to GDP growth in the broader economy.

Credit will be constrained for several years largely because of a synchronized decline in both credit supply and demand. The popular refrain that if banks started lending again, the economy would improve, is grossly incorrect. On the demand side, the need for credit is to refinance five year old demand; much of which was artificial and bubble driven. There is virtually no new demand today. On the supply side, commercial banks were only 30% players during the run up. Over 70% of financing was securitized. Today, the CMBS market is non-existent. Indeed there have been no new issuances in the last five quarters. Commercial banks do not have balance sheet capacity to absorb refinance demand. They also struggle with capital, liquidity and unhealthy concentration issues.

NOVEMBER 23, 2009

FLORIDA EMPLOYERS CONTINUE TO SHED JOBS

Florida employers shed another 25,000 jobs in October bringing the total jobs lost since last October to 339,600. Florida now has 1,027,000 persons unemployed out of a labor force of 9,175,000 for an unemployment rate of 11.2%—only fractionally higher than the revised September rate of 11.1% and one-percent higher than the nation's unemployment rate. The October unemployment rate is 4.3 percentage points higher than it was one year ago and the highest since June 1975 when it was also 11.2% The last time Florida unemployment was higher was over 34 years ago in May 1975 when it hit 11.9%.

While Florida's total employment is about 9,175,000, its non-agricultural employment is 7,340,000. Over 1.8 million persons are employed in agricultural pursuits primarily in central and south Florida including the heartland counties surrounding Lake Okeechobee. Agricultural employment is usually volatile due to its seasonality. Moreover, total employment does not include hundreds of workers who work in agriculture on a contract, seasonal or day labor basis making a true count of agricultural workers very difficult.

Considering only the non-agricultural sector, which is 80% of Florida's total work labor force, job losses have totaled 339,600

Since October 2008. That is a decline of 4.4% which is steeper than the nation's 4.0% rate of job decline. Florida's job losses continue a trend begun in August 2007. Nevertheless, the rate of decline has moderated over the last few months. The rate of year over year decline was 5.4%

---

in March as compared to 4.4% in October.

Florida's unemployment rate is now being negatively influenced by the so-called "denominator effect." Florida's total labor force has been shrinking recently. In October the total labor force was 9,175,000. In September it was 9,200,000 and in October 2008 it was 9,317,000. With employers still shedding jobs—albeit at a slower rate—the unemployment rate mathematically increases and will continue to do so until employment begins to rise, the labor force stops declining or a combination of both. We don't expect that to happen before mid-2010 at the earliest. We expect Florida unemployment to be well above 10% into 2011. Moreover, Florida employment is not likely to return to robust pre run up growth until 2014 or 2015. Even then it is likely to remain much higher than the cycle low of 3.3% for a fairly lengthy period of time due to structural changes in employment and the broader economy (see Economic Perspectives, November 18, 2009.)

The October employment report continues to show how dependent upon real estate and construction the state and the Treasure Coast really are. While construction losses are slowing the sector is still losing jobs. Indeed, transportation and utilities, professional and business services and construction are the biggest job losers. These three sectors account for about two-thirds of the job losses state wide. Financial activities, leisure and hospitality as well as local government also reported losses.

Health care and social assistance were the only sectors to gain jobs. While the gains were modest, the trend should continue.

NOVEMBER 25, 2009

GDP ADJUSTED DOWN IN SECOND ESTIMATE

As we wrote in the November 6th issue of *Economic Perspectives,* there are three estimates of Gross Domestic Product (GDP) each quarter plus an annual revision each July. Each revision is based on more complete information. The advance estimate, which we wrote about on November 6th, was the first estimate for the third quarter. At 3.5% growth, it showed the economy coming back to life. That advance estimate, however, was revised down to 2.8% today in the *preliminary* (second) estimate. While the economy is still growing at 2.8%, the growth is not quite as robust as first thought. The revised estimate, however, is more in line with expectations.

The current revision showed that consumer spending rose 2.9% rather than 3.4% as first estimated. Business spending on structures also fell 15.1% rather than 9.0% as first thought. Both imports and exports were revised up but the import number was bigger. Since imports are a deduction from GDP, foreign trade subtracted 0.8% from the total GDP. Inventory decline was larger than first thought however its overall effect on GDP was negligible.

There was also new information in the second GDP estimate including the first estimate of corporate profits for the third quarter. Profits rose 10.6% over the second quarter but are still down about 6.7% year over year. Profits did best in the financial sector (primarily investment banking) where they benefited from very low cost of funds. The increase in profits is more likely the effect of cost cutting rather than a significant rise in sales. Net corporate profits rose to 10.7% of GDP, a rate just shy of the all-time high of 10.8% reached in the second quarter of 2005. Record corporate profits bode well for future hiring.

Wage and salary incomes were revised up sharply (+$82.2 billion at an annual rate) for the second quarter as more complete information became available about supervisors pay, bonuses and stock options. The higher level of wages and salaries carried through to the third quarter. As a result, personal savings was revised up to 4.5% from a previously reported 3.4%.

A lack of capital spending, continuing high unemployment and reduced consumption are the primary components constraining GDP growth. We expect capital spending to turn positive in early 2010 and job growth to inch up later in the year. In neither case, however do we anticipate dramatic improvement in GDP.

Looking forward, we see little to change our forecast of GDP. It will probably lose a little momentum in the fourth quarter and come in between 2.0% and 2.5% due mainly to sluggish consumer consumption, housing construction starts and industrial production. A rate near 2.5% is likely for 2010.

FLORIDA EXISTING HOME SALES VOLUMES AND PRICES DEFY U.S. UPWARD TREND

Sales of existing homes surged 7.4% nationally in November—the last surge driven by the first tax credit for first time home buyers. The tax credit has now been both extended and expanded to include other than first time buyers. At the same time, the Mortgage Bankers Association "Purchases Index" fell to its lowest level since 1997 suggesting that existing home sales are likely to plunge in December and stay low well into the first quarter of 2010 until the effect of the new tax credit is felt. In Florida, existing home sales were down 7.48% and median price was down 0.93%. In most Seacoast served markets, volume and price declined modestly.

Existing home sales rose nationally in November as the original first time home buyer tax credit came to an end. That surge had the effect of reducing the existing home inventory to 3.51 million units from its July 2008 peak of 4.57 million units. Nationally, the inventory stands at 6.5 months and indicates that inventories are steadily clearing. These inventory numbers do not include the so-called *shadow inventory* of homes which are held by banks and not yet listed for sale. The Census Bureau measures the "Homeowner Vacancy Rate" each quarter. In the third quarter, the rate stood at 2.6%—far greater than its normal rate of 1.7%. While that does not tell us the precise size of the shadow inventory, it does suggest it remains quite large with a significant supply of foreclosed homes still in the pipeline.

Florida's existing home sales volume defied the national trend and fell 7.48%. The median price fell modestly by 0.93%. Locally, Ft. Pierce, Port St. Lucie Metropolitan Statistical Area (MSA) squeezed out a slight increase in both volume and price while all other Seacoast markets declined. The Melbourne, Titusville, Palm Bay MSA was the big loser with a 27% decline in volume and 9.33% decline in median price.

The median price of an existing home nationally in November was $171,900, unchanged from October but down 4.4% year over year.

Price decline is clearly slowing. As recently as July, the year-over- year decline was -13%. Nevertheless, the median price nationally is still higher than Florida where it is $139,000. The median price is lower in all Seacoast served counties with the exception of Palm Beach County where it was $227,900 and Broward County where it was $182,900. Prices in these two counties have historically run higher than the state or nation.

In Florida volumes and prices have been relatively flat since early 2009. The fluctuation has generally been within five-percent up or down suggesting relative stability, albeit at a relatively low level.

House prices have now returned to 2001 and 2002 levels in most markets. Property owners have generally given up all gains experienced between about 2003 and 2007. Owners who bought homes earlier, however, are still ahead.

According to S&P / Case-Shiller, the third quarter national home price index is down 8.9% year over year; down 27.1% over three years and down 13.5% over five years. The index is up 41.4% over 10 years and up 75.4% over 15 years.

Foreclosures remain elevated in Florida and in most Seacoast served counties. In Orange County (Orlando) one in every 106 housing units was in some state of foreclosure in November. In Osceola County (south of Orlando) the ratio was a stunning one in every 78 households. In St. Lucie County on the Treasure Coast, the ratio was one in 135. In 2005, Osceola and St. Lucie were two of the nation's fastest growing counties. By 2007, they had two of the nation's largest inventory hangovers and foreclosures have grown since then to the point that they remain among the highest foreclosure counties in the nation.

Subprime mortgages dominated foreclosure activity until recently. Today, foreclosures have moved into the prime sector. Payment Option Adjustable Rate Mortgages (ARMs) will likely peak in late 2011 and that will keep foreclosures high into 2012. Additionally, the primary drivers of foreclosures today are employment issues such as unemployment, reduced hours or wages, etc.

Another emerging driver of foreclosures is so-called *strategic default* where property owners who can afford to pay determine they are too far under water to recover and they intentionally walk away. Researchers at the University of Chicago, Northwestern University and the European University Institute estimated that 26% of today's foreclosures are strategic as social and moral barriers to foreclosure have fallen.

As foreclosures move into the prime sector, they also move to higher loan amounts where buyers bought *too much house* or did so with Payment Option ARMS. The next wave of foreclosures (mid 2010) will likely be in the $400-$600,000 range.

The foreclosure outlook is not good. According to First American Core Logic, one in four homeowners owe more on their home mortgage than the underlying property is worth. Moreover, delinquency rates hit an all-time high at the end of the third quarter. Delinquency, combined with the elevated shadow inventory (see page one) suggests that foreclosures will continue at high levels into the foreseeable future.

Homeownership rate will slip. Homeownership in the U.S. peaked in March 2006 at about 69%. The *Great Recession* punctuated by a foreclosure epidemic drove house prices down an estimated $5.9 Trillion in aggregate. The homeownership rate is now 67.3% and likely to decline further as foreclosures rage on and owners once again become renters. Former homeowners will rent as they struggle to rebuild their balance sheets the next few years.

Looking Forward, we expect sales to decline modestly in December. The first tax credit shifted some 2010 sales into 2009 and the second shifted late 2010 sales into early 2010. Additionally, the Mortgage Bankers Association reported that its purchase only index had fallen to its lowest level in 12 years. It is fast becoming clear that the tax credit is not stimulating or increasing demand but rather just shifting it to earlier time periods at significant cost to the U.S. Treasury. Bottom line: 2010 sales volume will be about the same as 2009. Moreover, prices are likely to remain flat throughout 2010. We do however, acknowledge that at least two prominent and well-respected sources are forecasting another 5-10% price decline nationwide in 2010.

2010
RECOVERY BEGINS

On September 20, 2010 the Business Cycle Dating Committee (BCDC) of the National Bureau of Economic Research (NBER) declared that, what had come to be widely known as The Great Recession, ended at the end of June 2009, some 15 months earlier. Another way of looking at that same conclusion is that the economy had reached its cyclical low and could only rebound from here.

Despite the recession having been declared ended, many consumers and businesses did not see it that way. Employment continued to be erratic in 2010 fluctuating between job gains and losses. Nationally, losses began to moderate. In Florida, however, unemployment rose to 12.2% which was the highest in the previous 35 years.

It would take another three years for housing to find a definitive bottom. At the same time foreclosures continued largely unabated and continued to be the largest threat to broader economic recovery. Speculation about whether the nation was likely to experience a "double dip" recession.

Commercial real estate reached its cyclical low point in December 2009. Values were a full 50% lower that their peak just two years earlier in December 2007. That led to commercial real estate being the leading cause of distress for community banks and the FDIC insurance fund. Large banks usually had sufficient capital to absorb losses in commercial real estate. Community banks did not. In fact, community bank loan concentration of commercial real estate soared dramatically, often to over 500% (or more) of capital. The banking regulatory agencies issued guidelines with respect to commercial real estate loan concentrations in December 2010. The agencies warned that institutions with over 300% of capital concentrated in commercial real estate would be subject to enhanced scrutiny.

The Dodd-Frank Wall Street Reform and Consumer Protection Act was signed into law by the President on July 21, 2010. The Act is the most sweeping piece of banking legislation to be enacted in the previous 50 years. The Act contains some 2,000 pages of text and 16 titles. It requires agencies to conduct as many as 67 studies to determine how to put flesh on the legislative bones. Finally it requires agencies to promulgate 243 new regulations. At this writing (Summer 2014) roughly half of the deadlines have reportedly been missed.

Overall, 2010 was a year of modest recovery but it was agonizingly slow with numerous false starts and setbacks.

JANUARY 9, 2010

U.S. JOB LOSSES SLOW— UNEMPLOYMENT RATE 10%

Nonfarm payrolls fell by 85,000 jobs nationally in December according to an advance estimate by the Bureau of Labor Statistics (BLS). That brings the ranks of the unemployed to 15.3 million. Over 7.7 million jobs have now been lost since the start of the recession in December 2007. That number has declined by about 300,000 jobs. The decline, however, is not the product of new jobs being added but rather more persons leaving the work force, becoming marginally attached or working involuntarily part time for economic reasons. Indeed, the size of the labor force fell sharply in December suggesting that households do not yet perceive a positive change in the job market.

The loss of 85,000 jobs in December was more than expected however the November numbers were revised to show a gain of 4,000 jobs—the first gain in two years. October was revised to show a loss of 127,000 jobs as compared to the original loss estimate of 111,000 jobs. Job losses averaged 691,000 each month in the first quarter of 2009 compared to an average loss of 69,000 per month in the fourth quarter. The fact that they have declined so sharply is good news for the economy. The bad news, however, is that employers are not yet adding jobs in any significant numbers. The nation's unemployment rate remains at 10.0%. It has doubled from 5.0% at the start of the recession in December 2007 and is still the highest in 26 years.

The number of long term unemployed (defined as 27 weeks or longer) continues to trend up. In December, total long term unemployed reached 6.1 million persons with four out of 10 jobless workers having been unemployed for 27 weeks or more.

The number of persons working part time for economic reasons (sometimes called involuntary part time workers) remained steady at about 9.2 million workers. That number has changed little since March 2009.

About 2.5 million workers were marginally attached to the workforce in December. That number is 578,000 higher than it was a year earlier. Among the marginally attached were 929,000 discouraged workers. That number is up from 642,000 a year earlier. This group represents those not currently looking for work because they believe there is no job available for them.

The most comprehensive measure of underemployment (U-6) which includes headline unemployment plus marginally attached, discouraged and part time rose fractionally to 17.3% in December.

The civilian labor force participation rate fell to 64.6% in December. That ratio has remained relatively constant for over a year. The employment population ratio declined to 58.2% in December. That ratio is down slightly as a result of the growing number of discouraged workers and others leaving the work force.

By sector, another 53,000 construction jobs were lost in December. The losses were spread throughout the sector which has lost some 1.6 million jobs since the recession began. Manufacturing lost 27,000 jobs over the month and over 2.1 million since the recession began. Roughly three quarters of the manufacturing losses were in the durable goods component (goods expected to last more than three years).

The number of temporary jobs increased by 47,000 jobs. Factory overtime hours remained flat at 3.4 hours. Both are leading indicators and both suggest modest improvement in labor conditions. The growth in overtime hours implies that factory orders are increasing. Similarly, employers frequently test the waters with temporary help before making a commitment to new hiring.

PAYBACK, DOUBLE DIP OR SEASONALITY?

The National Association of Realtors reported that its Pending Home Sales Index declined 16% in November. The index was down in all regions of the country after having risen for nine consecutive months. Pending home sales are a leading indicator of closings 30-60 days in the future. A 16% decline is large and suggests that sales will be down significantly in December and January when those numbers are released. As we reported previously (Economic Perspectives—December 30, 2009) sales of existing homes in Florida 7.48% in November. Several Seacoast counties experienced greater declines in both volume and price. National volume, however, was up 7.5% in November.

New home sales also tumbled 11.3% in November and estimates for August, September and November were all revised down. The number of unsold new homes declined to 235,000—the 31st consecutive monthly decline and the lowest inventory since 1971. At the same time the months supply of new homes rose from 7.2 to 7.9 months and the months necessary to sell a new home remained constant at 13.6 months. The number of new homes offered for sale peaked in January 2008 at 199,000 units and has fallen steadily to the November low of 101,000 units.

According to Metrostudy, new home inventories have declined significantly in all Seacoast markets but the months of supply remain elevated by historical standards. This is due to paltry absorption—not large numbers of finished homes. Indian River and St. Lucie Counties have 12.3 and 16.6 months of supply respectively while Palm Beach County has 7.5 months.

Mortgage loan applications are also down. According to the Mortgage Bankers Association, application volume declined 22.8% in the week ended December 25th and volume was flat the following week. Looking behind the numbers, a 30.5% plunge in refinance volume the week of December 25th followed by a 1.6% decline the following week drove the overall decline in application volume. The purchase only index declined by 4% the week of December 25th but rose an almost equal amount the following week. Much of the volatility is seasonal and the next few weeks reveal more.

Finally, S&P / Case Shiller, perhaps the most widely watched of the national indices, reported that prices were flat in both their 10 and 20 city surveys. Prices have risen in 18 of the 20 cities since hitting bottom several months ago. Nevertheless, Case Case Shiller expects another 5-10% price decline during 2010.

The obvious question is why are prices and volumes suddenly declining after several months of increase? Are we facing a "payback" for the first tax credit which shifted sales from 2010 into 2009? Are the declines merely seasonal? Or, is something more systemic happening such as a "double dip" for housing meaning that conditions could get worse before real sustained improvement occurs. Let's look at several trends.

The weakness in new construction stems from the absence of demand, declining values and the fact that new projects are not economically feasible. Most proposed projects if constructed today would be worth less than their cost to create. While we acknowledge that the cost of land and materials have declined, there is no demonstrable demand for new space and absorption periods are prolonged. As a result, the cost of managing, maintaining and funding the cost of capital during what is likely to be a lengthy absorption period renders most projects not feasible. In our view, it will likely be 2012 or beyond before wide scale residential or commercial development becomes feasible again.

Second, consumer confidence is off its low point but consumers are still concerned about employment and the future of the economy. They are therefore deferring purchases.

Third, there is another wave of foreclosures about to hit the market. Payment option ARMs were popular mid-decade and defaults are now beginning to occur and will continue through 2011. As foreclosed properties come back to market, price increases will be even less likely.

The bigger issue in our view is "payback" for the first time home buyer tax credit that expired at the end of November. It did not create new demand but rather it shifted demand (sales) from 2010 into 2009. As a result, recent sales numbers became inflated as buyers rushed to close before the deadline. The tax credit was little more than a "transfer payment" in the sense that it did not create any new value for the economy. The tax credit has now been renewed and expanded. Since there is still no apparent new demand, the credit will likely move late 2010 purchases to early 2010 at significant cost to the Treasury.

In our view, the conditions driving recent volatility are explainable and do not point to a double dip housing recession. Given current and expected low demand, local sale volumes and prices in 2010 will be consistent with 2009 levels.

JANUARY 27, 2010

FLORIDA EXISTING HOME SALES RISE IN DECEMBER BUT DECLINE NATIONALLY

Sales of existing homes in Florida rose 4.31% in December, regaining part of what was lost the previous month and resuming a trend begun in early 2009. Sales volume increased most months throughout 2009. Median price stabilized in early 2009 and has since bounced up and down within a narrow range. November's data were a little inconsistent but that appears to be an aberration rather than a reversal of trend. While Florida's sales volume increased in December, sales nationally fell 16.7%. The decline appears to have been "payback" for the first tax credit that ended at the end of $8,000. The decline was not a surprise.

Existing home sales in Florida rose 4.31% in December month over month and nearly 33% year over year. At the same time, the median price remained essentially flat at $140,400 in December as compared to November but down 9.71% compared to a year earlier. Sales rose for the last few months of the year in anticipation of the first time home buyer tax credit expiring at the end of November. As expected, sales volume fell in November but rebounded in December.

Local performance was similar. The Ft. Pierce, Port St. Lucie MSA which also includes Martin County, was essentially flat. Palm Beach County, however, surged with a 16% increase in volume and a **9%** increase in median price. Metro Orlando, which includes Orange, Seminole, Lake and Osceola counties remained essentially flat while

Brevard volume rose 11% after a 27% decline a month earlier.

At the national level, sales volume declined 16.7% to 5.45 million units. Sales are up significantly from the 4.74 million units a year earlier but far short of the bubble era peak of over 7 million units in December 2005.

The months of supply remains at about 7.2 months, significantly less than a year earlier when it was 9.4 months.

The median price of an existing home nationally in December $177,500—up from $175,000 a year earlier and significantly higher than Florida's December median of $140,400.

December's national decline in volume was expected. The National Association of Realtors, Pending Home Sales Index fell 16% in November. The index is a leading indicator of sales 30-60 days in the future. The 16.7% decline in December was consistent. We also expect to see another, but more modest, decline a month from now when January sales figures are released.

We believe the decline is largely payback for the first tax credit which moved sales likely to have occurred in 2010 into 2009. That tax credit has been renewed and expanded to include some existing homeowners. The key question is whether the new credit will jump start sales. At this time, the second tax credit appears to be off to a slow start and may very well simply time shift sales from the second half of 2010 into the first half. Nevertheless, we continue to forecast sales volume declining modestly throughout the remainder of the first quarter and again in the third quarter due to timing of the tax credit. Indeed, there are no leading indicators to suggest that there is any new demand to jump start sales.

Data are not yet available to show how broadly the first tax credit was used. The IRS will capture the data from 2009 tax returns. Based on Realtor surveys and anecdotal evidence, however, the credit was not as widely used in Florida as it was in other parts of the country. There could be several reasons for that including high unemployment which continues to rise as well as a pending wave of Payment Option ARM foreclosures which will eventually increase existing home inventory from its already bloated level and put even more downward measure on prices.

While the worst is over for single family detached housing at the lower end price points, the stress is now clearly evident in upper end housing. With greater financial resources, high end homeowners were able to wait out the market and postpone realization of price declines that were occurring in the lower end. As more and more high end owners are now being forced to sell, they too are experiencing significant price declines. That emerging trend is apparent in the S&P Case / Shiller data for the last few months. The highest tier in the Case / Shiller data is performing much worse than the lowest tier in 12 of 16 metro areas where data are available.

Negative equity is growing at the high end where prices nationally have fallen about 27% from their peak. The decline is significantly less than the decline at the low end but is likely to rise as more homeowners are forced to sell and accrued declines are realized.

The trend toward defaults in the higher tiers is also apparent in third quarter Mortgage Bankers Association delinquency data. The 30 day delinquency rate among prime borrowers rose by more than 33 basis points compared with a decline of 42 basis points in the subprime sector. While subprime foreclosures still remain high, credit quality is deteriorating more quickly in the prime sector.

The Mortgage Bankers Association purchase only index which tracks applications for financing for home purchases is currently at its lowest level since 1997 which does not bode well for late first quarter sales. Mortgage interest rates are also likely to rise in the second quarter after the Federal Reserve stops buying mortgage booked securities at the end of March. Clearly, the housing market is fragile.

JANUARY 29, 2010

ECONOMY EXPANDED AT 5.7% IN 4TH QUARTER

In a clear sign *The Great Recession* is moderating, the nation's Gross Domestic Product increased at a 5.7% seasonally adjusted annual rate in the fourth quarter of 2009. That is the fastest pace of growth in the last six years. GDP is the broadest measure of the economy and represents the total of all goods and services produced in the nation. This estimate by the Commerce Department is an advance estimate based on information currently available. A second estimate will be released in about 30 days and a third in 60 days.

The economy has now expanded for two consecutive quarters after having contracted for a full year before that. The third quarter of 2009 showed 2.2% expansion. Despite the fourth quarter surge and assuming 5.7% holds after revision (admittedly a bold and improbable assumption), GDP will have declined 2.4% for the full year of 2009. That is the largest full year decline since the economy contracted by 10.9% in 1946 at the end of World War II.

The GDP news, however, is mixed. Much of the Q4 increase was driven by U.S. businesses shedding excess inventory—a total of about $33.5 Billion worth. For perspective, businesses reduced excess inventory $139 Billion in the third quarter and $160 billion in the second. Inventories accumulated through 2008 as sales dried up, manufacturing declined and businesses were left with significant amounts of unsold inventory. The inventory contribution to GDP in Q4 was huge at about 3.4 percentage points. While there will be more inventory reduction to come, such a lofty 3.4% contribution is not sustainable and we fully expect GDP growth to be slower throughout 2010.

At the same time, final sales (GDP less inventories) improved from 1.5% to 2.2%. Residential fixed investment rose 5.7% after an 18% upward surge last quarter. Foreign trade was also a plus as exports surged higher, far outpacing imports.

Consumer spending, the largest component of GDP at about 70%, rose only 1.44 percentage points. Growth in spending has been modest and has been constrained by a weak labor market, modest income growth, low consumer confidence, severely diminished household wealth, tight credit and a general movement from spending to savings. We expect that trend to continue at least through 2010.

The weakest sector was spending on business structures, which fell 15.4%, the fourth-consecutive double digit decline. The decline is continuing evidence of the huge negative effect of the commercial real estate crisis which began in 2008 and continues unabated.

There is a lot of uncertainty in today's GDP numbers and they do not fully reconcile with other economic indicators, especially rising unemployment. The unemployed spend little, they don't buy houses, they don't buy cars and, for the most part, unemployment is a huge drag on the broader economy.

We expect the 5.7% GDP estimate to be revised down in subsequent estimates. We also continue to expect 2010 GDP to hover in the 2.5% to 3.0% range—far lower than today's Q4 estimate but still positive. The 3.4% contribution of inventories and increased exports are not sustainable. The economy also needs time to re-balance itself and re-gain stability. To borrow from the Broadway Musical, "A Funny Thing Happened on the Way to the Forum"—*"A Funny Thing Happened on the Way to Economic Recovery—Everything Changed."*

FEBRUARY 1, 2010

NEW HOME SALES DECLINE IN DECEMBER

Sales of new single family homes nationally fell 7.6% in December to 342,000 units at a seasonally adjusted annual rate. According to the Census Bureau which tracks and reports new home data, sales volume increased in the Northeast and Western United States but declined in the South and Midwest. At the same time, sales volumes for both October and November were revised up.

The December inventory of unsold new homes stands at 231,000 units after having fallen for 32 consecutive months. That is the smallest inventory since April 1971. The number of *completed* new homes for sale stands at 99,000 units which is down from its peak of 199,000 units in January 2008. The months of supply of new homes at the current absorption rate rose from 7.6 to 8.1 months. New home sales totaled 374,000 units in all of 2009. That is 22.9% below 2008 performance. Moreover, there were only 23,000 sales in December. Both annual and monthly numbers represent all time low readings.

The median time necessary to sell a new home rose to 13.9 months— the longest time period on record since data collection began in 1963—

some 46 years ago. If there is any good news in an otherwise dismal report, it is that builders will soon need to ramp up construction or face not having product to sell. The problem with that is that most new construction today is not economically feasible. While land, material and labor costs have all declined during *The Great Recession,* absorption period costs, especially the cost of capital, render most development projects not feasible. To paraphrase "High Rise" author Steven Adler, the interest clock doesn't stop ticking just because sales are slow.

The median price of a new home in December was $221,300 compared to an existing (resale) home at $177,500. That $43,800 price difference may also be slowing new home sales as purchasers opt for lower priced existing homes. Indeed lower priced houses have been the best sellers for a year or more.

Housing construction starts nationally fell four percent in December. Single family starts fell 6.9% while multi-family starts rose 12.2%. Permits, however, rose 8.3% in December after a 4.5% increase in November. Additionally, after hitting an all-time low and bouncing along bottom for months, multifamily permits posted a solid increase from 120,000 to 145,000. Overall, permits were up10.9%.

Locally, new home inventories (supply) are no longer the problem. Demand is the problem. Metrostudy Chief Economist, Brad Hunter, recently described the current problem as potential buyers' fear for their livelihood (employment), difficulty with financing, concern that home prices will fall further and an inability to sell the "other house." New home supply in Seacoast core markets is shown on the chart to the left.

Since hitting bottom in May and June last year, prices have ticked up and volumes have risen from their recession lows. Nevertheless, the recovery is fragile and continues to face strong headwinds such as growing unemployment and foreclosures. Moreover, the Federal Reserve, through its purchases of mortgage backed securities and the federal government's support of Fannie Mae and Freddie Mac have helped keep credit flowing and mortgage interest rates low. The bulk of the support, through mortgage backed securities though, is scheduled to cease in March and that could raise rates and slow sales. In all likelihood, however, we do not expect a new and steep decline. Just more of the same.

MORTGAGE WOES CONTINUE TO THREATEN RECOVERY

According to the Mortgage Bankers Association (MBA), the delinquency rate on 1-4 family residential mortgages rose to 9.64% of all loans outstanding in the third quarter of 2009. That is up 40 basis points from the second quarter and up 265 basis points year over year. This is the highest delinquency rate since the MBA began tracking and publishing the data in 1972. By definition, the delinquency rate includes loans at least one payment past due but not in foreclosure. The combined percentage of all loans delinquent and in foreclosure is now 14.41%—the highest ever recorded. The percentage of loans 90 or more days past due as well as those in foreclosure or where foreclosure has started all set new record highs in the third quarter.

Increases in delinquencies, defaults and ultimately foreclosures originally driven by subprime loans. Origination volume had grown to $625 Billion in 2006 and outstandings totaled $1.24 Trillion by the end of 2006. When these loans began to reset in an environment of declining values it is easy to understand how the subprime collapse wreaked so much financial and economic havoc at all levels of the economy from local to global.

Today, however, the problem has landed squarely in the prime sector and is less mortgage product driven than it is employment driven. The nation's unemployment rate has roughly doubled since the economy officially fell into recession in December 2007. Moreover, some 8.0 Million people have lost jobs during that time. About 5.5 million of those job losses were in the last year alone. Indeed, the nation's current employment situation is the worst since the Great Depression and it is having a profoundly negative effect on credit quality as well as the broader economy.

The volume of subprime delinquencies remains high. As the chart at the bottom of the page indicates, 45.37% of subprime loans in Florida are seriously delinquent. This breaks down to 30.65% of fixed rate subprime loans and 58.61% of adjustable rate subprime loans. Despite these extraordinarily high percentages, subprime is no longer the biggest problem.

The conventional wisdom has been that prime fixed rate loans were generally the safest and least likely to default. Nevertheless, they are now the largest share of loans entering foreclosure. The MBA reported that 33% of foreclosures started in the third quarter were prime fixed rate loans and that the category made up 44% of the quarterly increase in foreclosures.

FHA loans, sometimes pejoratively referred to as the "new subprime," have increased rapidly since the collapse of the subprime market. Indeed, there were 1.1 million new originations year over year at the end of the third quarter. There is too little default history to draw meaningful conclusions at this time.

Florida's third quarter delinquency is summarized by loan type on the table at the bottom of this page. Approximately 18.81% of serviced loans were seriously delinquent at the end of the third quarter. About 28.93% of prime ARM loans were seriously delinquent.

A record 3.8 million foreclosure actions were filed against 2.8 million housing units in 2009. Filings include lis pendens, auction notices and bank repossession notices. The 2.8 million housing units is up 21% from 2008 and up 120% from 2007. Foreclosures peaked in July with over 361,000 filings nationally. The volume then declined for four straight months. The decline, however, may be deceiving as it was being driven by short term factors such as trial .loan modifications, state legislation extending the foreclosure process and most of all a seriously clogged foreclosure pipeline.

A record 349,519 housing units received foreclosure notices in December. That is up 14% month over month.

Nevada, Arizona and Florida posted the three highest foreclosure rates in 2009. California, Florida, Arizona and Illinois accounted for over 50% of all of the nation's foreclosures in 2009 according to Realtytrac.

The highest rate of foreclosure was in Nevada where 10% of housing units received at least one foreclosure notice. Arizona was second at six percent and Florida third at 5.93%.

Florida had 516,711 properties receiving foreclosure notices. That is an astounding one in every seventeen housing units. Filings in Florida are up 34% over 2008 and up 212% over 2007.

With so many loans delinquent, in default or entering foreclosure (see chart on page one), it is clear that foreclosures will continue to increase well in to the foreseeable future. We have reported for the last 18 months that foreclosure abatement would not occur before 2011 at the earliest and there is no current leading indicator to suggest otherwise. In fact, there is a new wave of Payment Option ARM mortgage defaults and foreclosures wending its way through the system now. The sheer volume virtually guarantees no abatement before 2011 and perhaps much longer.

Payment Option ARMs grew wildly popular in the middle of the decade. Nationwide, originations grew from $150 Billion in 2004 to a peak of $250 Billion in 2006 to only $20 billion by 2009. Approximately 10% of these loans were originated in Florida and 74% in the sunbelt states of Florida, California, Nevada and Arizona. Most were originated with little or no cash down; most were stated income loans, and some had 40 year amortization periods. By contract, these loans would reset when or if the loan to value ratio rose to 110% to 125% (depending on what was specified in the loan documents). Most borrowers paid the minimum possible and the outstanding balance grew. That, plus the collapse in values, caused loans to reset much earlier than expected. As a result, the delinquency rate soared from a fraction of one-percent in 2005 to 32% in 2009.

MARCH 3, 2010

FEWER FORECLOSURES OR CALM BEFORE THE STORM?

Foreclosure filings including default and auction notices as well as bank repossessions declined to about 315,716 nationally in January 2010. That is 10% fewer than a month earlier and 12.5% fewer than the peak of 361,000 set in July 2009. Nevertheless, foreclosures remain high; more are coming and they remain a threat to the nation's economic recovery.

The trend was similar in 2008. Foreclosure filings built to a crescendo in the second half of the year. They declined in early 2009 and increased again throughout the year. Given that pattern plus rising defaults, still deteriorating mortgage credit quality (see page 2), underwater home-owners, foreclosures moving into the prime sector and a likely wave of Payment Option ARM defaults, we expect foreclosures to peak again in late 2010. Indeed, foreclosures, short sales and deed in lieu transactions appear likely to peak this year at about 2.5 million before beginning to abate modestly in 2011 and beyond. That statistic refers to "lost homes," not just foreclosure action notices.

Not surprisingly, the sunbelt states including Florida, California, Arizona and Nevada lead the way with the highest number of foreclosures. Nevada remained the highest foreclosure state for the 37th consecutive month. One in every 95 housing units in Nevada received some sort of foreclosure notice. That compares to one in every 409 housing units nationally; one in every 187 in Florida and one in every 152 housing units in Seacoast served markets. Arizona foreclosure action notices rose four-percent over the month making it the second highest state for fore-closures with one in every 129 housing units receiving a notice. California ranks number three, Florida number four and Utah number five.

According to a report released recently by First American CoreLogic, a record 24% of residential properties were "underwater" at the end of 2009. In other words, these homeowners owed more on their mort-gages than the underlying collateral property was worth. That represents about 11.3 million homes. About 620,000 properties fell into a negative equity position in the fourth quarter alone. California had the largest number of negative equity mortgages at about 2.4 million, followed by Florida with 2.2 million. Underwater mortgages are largely concentrated in five states. About 70% of Nevada home mortgages are underwater followed by Arizona at 51%, Florida at 48%, Michigan at 39% and California at 35%. States with lowest percentage of under-water homeowners include New York at 6.3% and Oklahoma at 6.0%.

According to the Federal Reserve, mortgage credit quality is continuing to weaken—a trend begun in late 2006. Credit cards and total con-sumer loans, however, are showing early signs of improvement although it is far too early to call that a trend. We suspect that still weakening mortgage credit quality is being driven by the growing number of underwater homeowners who are giving up in record numbers. Strategic default is a growing phenomenon where homeowners who can afford to pay, choose not to because they believe they are so far underwater they will never recover. Indeed, a 2009 study by Northwestern and Chicago University economists estimates that about 26% of foreclosures today are strategic and usually when the homeowner is more than 10% underwater.

Addressing our headline rhetorical question, there is no apparent trend in the recent downward change in foreclosures. It is more likely the calm before the next storm.

MARCH 9, 2010

U.S. JOB LOSSES MODERATE

February non-farm payrolls declined by 36,000 jobs according to an advance estimate by the U.S. Bureau of Labor Statistics. While that is twice the decline experienced in January, it is a fraction of the 750,000+ average job losses experienced at the depth of the Great Recession in late 2008 and the average monthly loss of 690,000 in the first quarter of 2009.

Despite the job losses, there are several kernels of good news in the estimate which together suggest that payrolls could begin to grow modestly or at least stop declining later in 2010. First, temporary help grew by 48,000 jobs. Employers often test the waters with temporary help before committing to new permanent hiring. Manufacturing was also fractionally higher with an increase of 1,000 jobs on the heels of a 20,000 job gain in January.

Second, productivity surged and has probably reached its limit Employees have been doing more with fewer staff for several years which has driven up productivity. It is doubtful that productivity can rise much higher. Fourth quarter productivity growth was up 6.9% and output was up 7.6%. Year over year productivity growth in the fourth quarter was climbing at 5.8%—a rate nearly triple that of the last 50 years. At the same time, hourly compensation was down 2.8% after adjusting for inflation. Nevertheless, it is virtually impossible to separate productivity gains which are cyclical and driven by recessionary cut backs from gains driven by companies using new technology and finding better ways to produce products and services. As software and technology purchases have been soft the last three years, we suspect that most of the recent productivity increase has been recession driven. With that, it is reasonable to expect productivity to start declining this year and that will cause hiring to increase modestly.

Third, inventories have been declining dramatically (see Economic Perspectives—January 29, 2010) to the point that manufacturers will need to ramp up production and begin hiring again.

Looking behind the headline numbers in the Employment Situation Report, construction employment fell by 65,000 jobs after falling 77,000 a month earlier. Most of the loss was in non-residential construction (45,000 jobs lost) followed by residential with 11,000 jobs lost and civil engineering projects (infrastructure) accounting for the remaining 9,000.

State and local governments continued to feel the squeeze of declining tax revenues and together lost about 25,000 jobs. Most of the losses were in education. The federal government had a net gain of 7,000 jobs and added another 15,000 temporary workers for the census. March should show a large gain in temporary employment as the Census Bureau is expected to add another 100,000 jobs. Nevertheless, temporary census hiring has been slower thus far this year than it was in previous decades. There is no apparent reason for the delay.

Retail jobs were flat in February while healthcare continued to trend upward. The report did not show as severe an impact from weather as anticipated. That could be a data collection problem that will be corrected in subsequent releases. The winter storms in the Northeast, Midwest and Mid-Atlantic states should have affected employment more than the numbers seem to show.

The unemployment rate remained steady at 9.7% which is a positive sign. The underemployment rate (U6 measure) which includes the marginally attached, involuntary part time workers and discouraged workers rose modestly to 16.8%.

MARCH 13, 2010

FLORIDA'S UNEMPLOYMENT RATE NOW HIGHEST IN 35 YEARS

Florida's unemployment rate surged to 12.2% in January 2010. The headline "seasonally adjusted" rate was 11.9%. Florida's unemployment rate is now equivalent to May 1975—some 35 years ago—and is now the highest in the history of this data series. Florida, as well as the nation and all states also released revised historical data. That process is known as "benchmarking" and is done every March. Florida's unemployment rate remains significantly higher than the nation's 9.7% rate (10.6% not seasonally adjusted). The nation's rate has been stable for the last two months. Florida's unemployment rate a year ago in Florida was 8.7%.

Florida's non-agricultural employment stood at 7,144,300 in January after a month over month decline of 6,100 jobs. Florida has lost 303,200 jobs year over year—a workforce decline of 4.1%. Florida's total employment including agricultural is 8,131,000 indicating that nearly 1.0 million persons (986,700) are employed in agriculture.

The 12.2% unemployment rate does not represent the total count of the Florida's unemployment stress as it does not include persons working part time as they can't find full time employment. It also does not include those who are marginally attached to the work force or have given up looking for a job because they have come to believe there is not a job available for them. The national rate of *under* employment including those groups is about 16.8%. We suspect it is substantially higher in Florida but data are not available for a reliable estimate. The payroll numbers also do not include independent contractors such as many real estate sales people who are not eligible for unemployment compensation.

Looking behind the numbers, the usual suspects continue to dominate the job losses. The construction sector continued to lose the most jobs at 90,700 year over year. Over the year, construction has lost 20.4% of its sector jobs.

Transportation and utilities lost 56,600 jobs year over year or 3.7% of its work force. That sector is closely allied to construction and housing and is likely to continue to lose jobs or at least see its employment remain at a low level. Similarly, professional and business services lost 44,900 jobs year Seacoast Counties in Red over year or another 4.2% of its workforce. Manufacturing was down 42,200 jobs; leisure and hospitality was down 39,700 jobs and financial activities lost 27,800 jobs. Local and state government lost 2,500 jobs.

Private education and health services added jobs. Together they added 23,600 jobs. Health services was the big winner once again with a gain of 19,500 jobs—primarily in ambulatory health care services. Private education gained 4,100 jobs after having lost jobs for several months.

The U.S. Census Bureau is currently hiring about 63,700 Floridians. Most will be temporary jobs paying $9 to $16 per hour.

Manufacturing has been declining in the U.S. for decades. While Florida never had a large manufacturing share, it did have a high level of construction for most of the last four or five decades. Construction became, in essence, the new manufacturing. Indeed, it was the leading employment sector for men in the 19-45 age group who had been displaced from manufacturing jobs in other states or who naturally migrated into Florida construction jobs. Today, the high level of construction jobs or even opportunities no longer exist in Florida and are not likely to exist at previous levels well into the foreseeable future. That will likely curtail employment growth for much of the current decade. Moreover, the hardest hit employment group is that same group (men, 19-45) who are not college educated—so-called blue collar workers. With what will very likely be fewer construction and trade jobs in the foreseeable future, unemployment in this sector will likely remain elevated.

APRIL 12, 2010

U.S. GAINS JOBS IN MARCH— UNEMPLOYMENT 9.7%

Payroll employment grew by 162,000 jobs in March. That is the largest gain in three years. At the same time, however, February numbers were revised down by 14,000 jobs. The average gain for the first quarter was positive at 54,000 jobs per month—a significant improvement over the monthly losses of 700,000+ jobs between late 2008 and early 2009. While the headline job gain is good news, the economy has a very long way to go to recover from The Great Recession and so far job growth remains rather modest.

The important number in the March job report is not the 162,000 gain but rather the mix of jobs and the events which drove the gain. First, there was a significant bounce back from the February numbers which were negatively affected by the winter storms that plagued the northeast, middle Atlantic states and parts of the Midwest.

The federal government also added 48,000 temporary census workers and will continue to do so throughout at least the second quarter. That is a small fraction of the nearly one-million workers expected to be hired for the census. Additionally, census hiring is lagging behind that of previous census years. So far, 72,000 census workers have been added as compared to 139,000 in the comparable period of 2000. Using previous census years as a guide, specifically 1990 and 2000, hiring will likely peak in the second quarter and be gone in the fourth quarter. In May 2000 for example, 348,000 workers were hired but 225,000 were shed in June. The wild card this year that was not present in previous census years is the extraordinary number of vacant homes that will be difficult and time consuming to factor into the census.

Given the weather bounce back which is certainly positive but difficult to reliably measure, plus temporary census hiring, we should not read too much into the March headline number of 162,000 jobs. What is clear though, is that we will likely see significant volatility in the payroll employment numbers for most of the year.

Looking behind the headlines, the private services sector added 82,000 jobs as compared to an increase of 55,000 in February. About half the March increase was in temporary employment not including census. That bodes well for future hiring as employers often test the waters with temporary help before committing to permanent employment. Gains also included about 27,000 new jobs in healthcare, 15,000 in retail, 17,000 in manufacturing, 22,000 in leisure and hospitality and even 15,000 in construction. The construction gain was the first since June 2007. Construction lost 59,000 jobs a month earlier probably due to weather. We believe it would premature to suggest that construction has turned the corner. There is still a lot of pain in Florida and other sunbelt and rustbelt states. Each sector gain, though small, is welcome. Considered together, the gains clearly indicate modest labor market improvement.

Financial services shed 21,000 jobs in March. Professional and technical jobs were down by 13,000 and information sector was down 12,000. Government added 39,000 jobs. At the federal level, all of the gain was temporary census workers. At the state and local levels, 9,000 jobs were lost. While federal employment will continue to grow, state and local government will continue to decline at ever growing numbers. State and local governments across the country are plagued by declining revenues as a result of depressed real estate values providing fewer ad valorem tax dollars and unemployment which is curtailing spending and sales tax dollars.

The nation's unemployment rate remained steady at 9.7% ink (9.749%). The household survey from which the unemployment rate is derived showed an increase of 264,000 jobs however the labor force rose by 398,000 so the total number of unemployed rose by 134,000 persons. The increase in the size of the labor force is primarily the result of marginally attached and discouraged workers who may have dropped out last year coming back to the labor force will slow the pace of unemployment rate decline due to the "denominator effect" of a larger labor force.

The most comprehensive measure of *under*employment (called the U-6) takes into account the basic measure (U-3) at 9.7% and adds those marginally attached to the work force, discouraged workers and those working part time for economic reasons. The rate of underemployment edged up slightly to 17.9% in March. That same measure on Florida's Treasure Coast is between 22% and 25%. As more information becomes available, we peg it at nearer the 25% mark.

About 2 3 million persons were marginally attached to the work force in March compared to about 2.1 million a year earlier. The number of persons working part time for economic reasons rose to 9.1 million in March and discouraged worker count increased to about 1.0 million, up 309,000 from a year earlier.

The most recent report (April 8th) of Initial Claims, that is first time claims for unemployment insurance, rose by 18,000 to about 460,000. While that number is down from its peak, it remains solidly in recession territory. The number of workers continuing to receive benefits (continuing claims) declined by 131,000 to 4.55 million. That is the lowest level since December 2008. MP The number of long term unemployed (defined as 27 weeks or more) increased by 414,000 over the month to 6.5 million. Today 40% (44.1%) of the unemployed have been unemployed over weeks.

A disappointing component of the jobs report was a decline in average hourly earnings (0.1%). Nevertheless, it is more important that hiring is increasing as wages will soon follow.

The Bureau of Labor Statistics also reported a decline in job openings. At the end of February, there were 2.723 million job openings across the nation. That is a decline of 131,000 job openings from January but still 385,000 above last July's low.

With job openings totaling 2.723 million and 14.871 million persons unemployed, there are now 5.46 job seekers for every available position. That is an improvement over year end 2009 when there were over six job seekers per position. It is significantly worse than the 2007 pre-recession level of 1.55 job seekers per available position. We expect competition for available positions to remain fierce as improving conditions draw more job seekers back to the labor force.

As shown in the bottom chart in the left hand column of this page, the hires and separations rates are converging. They both eased lower to about 3.1%. Early last year, separations significantly exceeded hirings. The last time hiring exceeded separations was in November 2007. With the expected high level of census hiring, we expect hirings to surpass separations over the next few months. While that is positive, hirings may retreat again this year.

Much of the information we are now seeing—at least from a macro perspective—is beginning to suggest that the recession is easing. Manufacturing inventories have bottomed and payrolls have increased. Hours worked and the work week itself have increased, temporary hiring has increased and productivity has almost certainly peaked. These are all signs that hiring may soon pick up.

Nevertheless, over 8.0 Million people have lost jobs since the official start of the recession in December 2007. If the labor market is to recover in 2013 and 2014, the economy needs to create well over 200,000 jobs each month just to recover the losses. Over 300,000 jobs each month would be necessary to experience meaningful growth. From today's perspective, that does not seem reasonable given the current slow pace of job creation. While the economy is clearly gaining strength, job growth is still insufficient to reduce the slack in the labor market. Until that happens, full recovery of the broader economy is by no means assured.

MAY 2010

LOOKING FORWARD FROM MID 2010—WHAT COMES NEXT?

As economic recovery continues to take shape at virtually every level from local to global it seems appropriate to take a look at what the economy might look like during and after recovery. This is not a look into the crystal ball but rather a forecast of things most likely—though not guaranteed—to happen using the best currently available information. Just like the economy signaled its probable downturn three years ago, it is now signaling recovery. Those signals can be measured and used to make inferences about the short term future. With the exception of the commercial real estate sector which remains weak, both housing and the broader economy are likely to end 2010 in much better condition than they began the year. The local and U.S. economies will still face significant challenges. Unemployment is much higher than it would be in a healthy economy. Credit and the demand for credit remain in a synchronized decline. Economic activity remains weak and economic growth, though measurable, won't be strong enough to achieve robust growth anytime soon. With that backdrop, let's look at several key factors driving recovery and shaping what happens next.

The nation's economy endured 10 recessions between the end of World War II and the beginning of the current recession in December 2007. Those recessions lasted between six and sixteen months with an average duration of 10 months. Real GDP declined 0.4% to 3.8% with an average decline of 2.0%. Non-farm employment declined an average of 2.7% and the average unemployment rate grew by 3.2% during each of the 10 recessions.

The 10 previous recessions were caused by a variety of factors such as shifts in monetary policy, withdrawal of government spending after war time, dramatic rise in oil prices, the Iranian revolution and more.

The current recession is like none of the previous 10. Indeed the cause was the product of interest rates which were too low, too long which led to excess liquidity which helped inflate the housing bubble. When the bubble collapsed, the effect was felt globally and eventually landed squarely in the broader economy.

The current recession has now gone on for over 30 months. Many economists believe it may have technically ended in the third quarter of last year but the Business Cycle Dating Committee, the official arbiter of such matters, has not yet called its end.

Nevertheless, employment is down over 5% and unemployment is up over 5%. Real GDP declined 3.8% at it's trough. By almost any measure, the current recession has been broader and deeper than any of the previous 10. At its deepest point in late 2008, this recession was perhaps most similar to the Great Depression of the 1930's. In fact, with the near collapse of the U.S. banking system in September 2008, there was widespread concern that that "The Great Recession" could fall into the second Great Depression.

Unlike the 10 previous recessions, the severity of this one led to structural changes in the broader economy. The current recession is a true balance sheet recession much like the Great Depression and the more recent Japanese experience. We have, and will continue to see, massive deleveraging where virtually everyone has had to get their balance sheet in order by purging debt and, perhaps more importantly, recognizing the asset deflation that has occurred almost universally.

Spending and the shrinking boomer economy. The baby boom generation refers to those born between 1946 and 1964. Roughly 77 million babies were born during those years as military service people came back from World War II and started families. The peak birth rate was reached in 1957 when 4.3 million babies were born—a number not equaled before or since. The boomer generation is the largest demographic cohort ever and historically, as the baby boom generation moved, so moved the economy. For example when boomers began buying homes, sales of starter homes surged. When they began moving up, sales of move up homes surged. Today, this generation still represents 28% of the U.S. population. Deaths have steadily been replaced by immigrants and the Census Bureau expects the baby boom generation to be about 57.8 million strong through at least 2030. That year, boomers will be between the ages of 66 and 84 and will still far outnumber any generation before or since. As a result boomers will continue to have a profound effect on the economy for many years to come.

One of the most significant effects will be savings. Boomers, as a group, were historically free spenders. They had faith in rising markets and this past decade was no exception. Today, however, boomers have moved from spending to savings which has helped propel a national savings rate from zero to about 5%. If the emerging savings trend holds, about $400 Billion will come out of annual consumption. That is more than enough to move the nation's GDP downward or at least curtail its growth. The economy has grown at an average annual rate of 3.5% since 1965. During the recent bubble decade (1995-2005) the boomer share of GDP growth was about 78%. Going forward, GDP is more likely to average near 2.4% due to declining consumption.

The "paradox of thrift, popularized by economist John Maynard Keynes in his 1930 book, "Treatise on Money" asserts that individual savings is a virtue but if it spreads to the entire economy, it can curtail spending and output thereby dampening prospects for recovery and growth.

We don't expect that to occur. We do expect consumers to remain more conservative, spend less and shed debt. Consumer spending will likely become a smaller part of GDP.

The loss of $15 Trillion in household wealth during the recession triggered a profound adjustment in consumer attitudes about spending and saving. In fact, a late 2009 survey commissioned by CitiGroup suggests strongly that the return to thrift may be a permanent lifestyle change for all consumers regardless of age or ethnicity. This is just one more piece of evidence that the nation's economic model may no longer be structured as heavily around spending going forward. Among other key findings, the survey found that 63% of U.S. of consumers thought the change in the way they spend and save was permanent. Only 29% said they would go back to pre-recession spending. This attitude shift has also caused retailers to rethink the value proposition.

The baby boom generational shift that was widely expected to occur as boomers retired and passed the baton to the next generation has not yet begun. It was widely expected that boomers would begin to retire early given the general prosperity of their lifetime. Then came the crash and today 69% of boomers (age 54-63) are not financially prepared for retirement. As a result they are staying in the work force longer, spending less, more likely to value shop, buying fewer luxury cars and more.

Employment has seen unprecedented structural change. Employment increased dramatically between 2002 and 2006. Much of it in response to an extraordinary increase in residential real estate development. Employment in construction and allied services rose. Office jobs increased significantly in real estate construction, sales, lending, closing and more. Architects, engineers, designers, real estate attorneys and others flourished. Locally, where the economy was heavily real estate and construction driven, unemployment declined to a cycle low of about 3.3%. Nationally, unemployment sunk to under 5%. What was almost universally overlooked was that much of the employment growth was artificial. It was being created by a housing bubble where both sales volume and prices were increasing at double digit rates over a very short time period. Worse, many players caught up in the "irrational exuberance" of the day implicitly assumed that the growth would continue unabated oblivious to the fact that the growth could not be sustained.

The employment sector came crashing down soon after the subprime mortgage melt down in August 2007. Today, over 312,000 people are unemployed in South Florida (Palm Beach, Broward and Miami-Dade counties). That is 28% of the Florida total of 1,113,000. Over 15.3 million persons are unemployed nationally.

Looking forward, a large number of job losses in this recession were permanent rather than cyclical. Many of the construction, sales, financial and business service jobs created during the "bubble era" will not be replaced. Moreover, since real estate development—especially housing—will not likely return to its pre -run up rate for perhaps as much as a decade, post recovery employment will likely be much lower too.

Today, job losses are slowing and initial claims for unemployment have fallen into the mid-400,000 range (still recessionary). What is not happening though is job creation. The Labor Department reported in its March (most recent) Quarterly Job Openings and Labor Turnover Survey (JOLTS), that job openings were little changed at about 2.7 million—far below their 3.5 million peak in June 2007. Looking forward, it is likely that the nation's unemployment rate will continue to hover near 10% and remain higher than normal through 2013. Return to robust growth is unlikely before late 2014 or 2015. Clearly the days of 4% unemployment are gone for a decade or more.

Housing is where it all began and it too has experienced profound structural change. The collapse of the subprime mortgage market in August 2007 was quickly followed by the collapse of the U.S. housing market. Only recently has it begun to show signs of stability and early signs of new life.

During the run up that began in earnest in 2002, prices and sales volumes doubled in some areas. Nationally, sales volume rose from 5.25 million homes in 2001 to 8.36 million in 2005. For perspective, annualized sales were 5.77 million in April. The run up was followed by an equally severe downturn. In fact all of the price gains and more during the run up were erased between late 2007 and late 2009. In Florida, the peak to trough decline over that time period was nearly 50%. In South Florida it was well over 50% and over 60% on the Treasure Coast.

Foreclosures also continue unabated and have now moved solidly into the prime sector. Strategic Foreclosure is a new phenomenon plaguing the market. These are represented by people who can afford to pay but won't believing they are so far under water they will never recover and that any equity they might have had is permanently gone. Some studies show that over 25% of recent foreclosures were strategic. We do not expect foreclosures to abate until late 2011 at the earliest and that will keep a lid on meaningful price increases for the foreseeable future.

In previous recessions, housing demand fell as a result of weak income and declining employment. The recession led to pent up demand that was naturally unleashed when the economy recovered. This recession is different. Future demand was satisfied before its time during the bubble years. Those who bought too early and later lost their homes to foreclosure are unlikely to get a new mortgage anytime soon. The result is that the current downturn is not building unsatisfied demand for new homes. At best it is only helping to restore equilibrium to the supply and demand relationship. During the last major real estate downturn of the late 1980's and early 1990's it took a full seven years for single family housing to return to robust growth. It took condominiums 13 years. Moody's Economy.Com has forecast 14 years peak to peak for housing to return to robust growth.

Combine excessive inventory and the effect of foreclosures with curtailed spending, reduced household wealth, potentially difficult financing and a paltry appetite for risk and we have a housing market that will do well to catch up to the natural rate of growth. The end result is that housing will not be a significant builder of wealth for individual homeowners nor a strong contributor to GDP growth in the broader economy.

Credit will be constrained for several years largely because of a synchronized decline in both credit supply and demand. The popular refrain that if banks started lending again, the economy would improve, is grossly incorrect. On the demand side, much of the need for credit is to refinance five year old demand; much of which was artificial and bubble driven. There is very little new demand today. On the supply side, commercial banks were only 30% players during the run up. Over 70% of financing was securitized. Commercial banks do not have balance sheet capacity to absorb refinance demand. Most struggle with capital; some with liquidity. Almost all small banks struggle with unhealthy commercial real estate loan concentrations.

There have been 78 bank failures thus far in 2010. That follows 140 in 2009. The number of FDIC insured banks has now dipped under 8,000 and the agency has over 700 banks on its problem list.

FORECLOSURES: A DETOUR ON THE ROAD TO HOUSING AND ECONOMIC RECOVERY

Foreclosures remain at historically high levels with no short term end in sight. The extraordinary rise in foreclosures began with the collapse of the subprime sector in August 2007. Foreclosures at that time and through 2008 were largely product driven. That is, they were caused in large part by exotic mortgage types, low teaser interest rates which began adjusting upward to unaffordable levels, mortgages made to those who were clearly unqualified and even fraud, which is now showing itself to have been remarkably widespread.

The collapse led to dramatically rising unemployment, especially in construction and housing related finance and business sectors. The result? More foreclosures. The real estate market as a whole has been trapped in a vicious downward spiral ever since.

Today, the foreclosure crisis is no longer subprime driven. With the exception of cleaning up the subprime remains, foreclosures have moved aggressively into the prime sector and perhaps more than ever are being driven by declining or lost home equity. Indeed, foreclosures still pose a major threat to the housing market to the point housing remains a drag on the broader economy.

According to Moody's Economy.com, nearly 15 million homeowners are underwater nationwide. That is, these homeowners owe more on their mortgage than the underlying collateral is worth. These home owners represent about one-third of all mortgage borrowers. Not surprisingly underwater homeowners are concentrated in the states which experienced the largest boom followed by the largest bust. In Nevada, for example, 80% of mortgage loans were underwater at the end of last year. In Florida, 50% were underwater. Nevada and Florida were followed by Arizona and California.

An estimated 9.0 million homeowners had loan to value ratios higher than 120% at the end of last year. In California, roughly 1.6 million homeowners had loan to value ratios greater than 120%. California was followed by Florida with 1.1 million homeowners. having loan to value ratios higher than 120%. Such extraordinarily high loan to value ratios account for about $2.5 Trillion in outstanding mortgage dollars nationwide. In other words, more than one-quarter of mortgage dollars outstanding could be at risk of default with negative equity playing a role. The total amount of negative equity at the end of last year is estimated to have been about $900 Billion nationwide. Negative equity homeowners in California owe $254 Billion more than their homes are worth followed by Florida at $88 Billion.

Many struggling homeowners have tried to rent their homes to avoid foreclosure only to find that market rental rates have also declined by about half as a result of the shadow market of foreclosed properties coming back to market as rentals at rates far less than is necessary to cover their higher outstanding payments, taxes, insurance and home-owner fees.

All this sets the stage for a continuing high level of foreclosures. It also sets the stage for a high level of "strategic default" where home owners who can afford to pay choose not to as they believe their equity is gone and it will be a very long time before values rise and they are able to recover any of their equity. Most "strategic defaulters" believe that they will never recover and that default and its consequences are preferable to what they believe to be throwing good money after bad. Studies suggest that 20-25% of recent defaults may be strategic.

Nationwide, there was one foreclosure for every 400 housing units. In Florida, the ratio was one in 174 meaning that the foreclosure rate was over twice the rate of the nation. Even though there are positive signs of economic recovery, the short and medium term outlook for housing is still a material threat to recovery of the broader economy.

CRE PRICE DECLINE NOW STEEPER AND DEEPER THAN RESIDENTIAL—MAY TAKE A DECADE TO REBOUND

When the housing market began its downward spiral in 2006, many observers expected the damage to be contained within the residential sector and not expand into the commercial sector. That observation was naive at best. While that could have been accurate if the housing crisis was short lived, the evidence at the time suggested otherwise. By early 2007 it was clear that Florida had an extraordinary inventory of unsold new homes. In fact, at peak, Florida had some 25% to 40% more homes than there were persons to occupy them. The same was true in other sunbelt states including Nevada, California and Arizona. The demand—and I use the term loosely—was bubble inflated and not real or sustainable demand at all.

What does this have to do with commercial real estate? The demand for commercial real estate such as office and retail space is known as "secondary demand." Not everyone needs that type of space. It is therefore secondary to housing which is primary. Nevertheless, an enormous amount of office space was created to support the expanding housing industry. Office occupying jobs were growing dramatically and the widespread assumption—which was not supported by fact—was that more office space was necessary to accommodate more builders, developers, sales and title agents as well as lenders and others in support of housing. More retail space was also created to support new residents assumed to be coming to occupying the new homes. Once the housing market collapsed, the commercial real estate market was not far behind. When the music stopped, communities were left with huge inventories of unsold homes as well as office, retail and warehouse space that was no longer needed. In our view, most of it was never needed as the perceived demand was only an illusion.

Office employment rose dramatically from 2004 through 2007 and fell in an even more dramatic fashion beginning in 2008. The performance can be seen in the top chart at the left. As a sidebar, the lower peak in years 2000 and 2001 was the effect of the rise and fall of the dot com bubble.

The Great Recession, as it has come to be known, exacerbated the commercial real estate down turn. Simple downsizings, takeovers and a tsunami of corporate bankruptcies reduced the demand for office space in an already bloated market. Similarly, consumer spending together with low consumer confidence and record unemployment reduced the demand for retail space in a sector that was already bloated.

The middle chart at the left is a comparison of housing and commercial rise and fall since 2000. Both sectors experienced the same fate and the graph lines are similar in shape. Commercial prices continued to rise for two full years after the residential sector peaked. The commercial real estate collapse also followed residential by about two years. Once it collapsed, however, the commercial price decline was both steeper and deeper than residential. Nationwide the price decline was about 35% in 2009 alone. Peak to mid-2010 decline has been nearly 40% since prices peaked in late 2007 and early 2008. At this time it is still too early to call the bottom in commercial real estate values. Financing is still the wild card. The absence of a commercial mortgage backed securities (CMBS) market and the inability for owners to refinance will drive more properties into foreclosure. As those properties come back to market, they will almost certainly do so at even lower prices thus continuing the vicious downward price spiral.

In Central and South Florida, the story is nearly identical. Our analysis of local price trends has shown decline consistent with the nation at roughly 35% to 40%. It also shows that smaller "Mom and Pop" properties have experienced decline in the 50% range. Without financing and re-financing ability, further decline of 10% to 15% is not out of the question in the second half of 2010.

CRE values are now at a level last seen in 2002 after the collapse of the dot com bubble and before the extraordinary run up that led to The Great Recession. Without question, commercial real estate is now the weak link in economic recovery and will likely remain that way for several years. As far as a return to prices of 2007? That may take a decade or more. The market will first need to purge its bloated inventory. That will be a long term challenge. There is a record amount of excess inventory and relatively few companies are relocating or expanding. Moreover, much of the mid-decade value increase was the result of "cap rate compression." That is, capitalization rates declined to unsustainably low levels (often as low as 4.5— 6.0%) after having been in the 8-10% range for decades. Low rates (which result in higher prices and values) were a dangerous bet on prices continuing to rise. Organic growth through rental rate increase was never sufficient to drive prices or value to the extraordinary levels they actually reached. The decades long range of 8-10% is indicative of a balanced market. At this level, values grow organically. They change (up or down) by natural changes in the supply and demand relationship. We see nothing in the near or medium term which would cause rates to return to those compression era levels and resultant high values and prices. Indeed, we are more likely to see the opposite for a prolonged period of time.

Non-residential construction also peaked in 2007. The decline since then has been precipitous and, according to The Bureau of Economic Analysis, the decline has been the steepest in 50 years. There is no rebound in sight.

The banking and finance sector now bears the load of the egregious over building and doing so on foundation they should have known was crumbling. Many banks made some or their largest and worst loans between 2004 and 2008. Indeed, CRE loans outstanding increased nationwide by more than $1 trillion during that five year period. The lending mentality was *damn the torpedoes, let's grow.* The biggest players were CMBS investors and commercial banks—especially small banks— who now hold a disproportionate share of troubled CRE loans. Thrifts and life insurance companies were largely sidelined this time having taken their lumps in the last major downturn. Delinquencies began to surge in 2009. Delinquencies have continued to grow in 2010 with CMBS delinquencies at the end of May some 25 times higher than at the end of 2007 (see table to the right).

According to data from the FDIC, smaller banks are perhaps at the greatest risk. Many perceived a growth opportunity late in the expansion and the seized it. Today, the day of reckoning is here. Bloated inventories still exist, rents are down, vacancies are up, capitalization rates are up and banks are left holding the bag with unhealthy CRE loan concentrations and a disproportionate amount of capital devoted to CRE.

Banks will continue to fail. There were 140 failures in 2009 and 86 in the first half of 2010. Failures are on track to surpass the number in 2009.

Looking Forward. Demand for office space will remain suppressed for a long time given the extent of overbuilding, falling rents, rising vacancies and capitalization rates returning to pre-compression levels. Likewise, industrial and warehouse occupancy experienced a deep decline during The Great Recession. Two industries that generate the most demand for warehousing—housing and automotive—were the most impaired. Retail was negatively affected by a deep recessionary decline in spending as well as low consumer confidence and high unemployment. The sector will take several years to recover. Moreover there have been structural changes that will cause retail to look much different than it did in 2007. Banks will remain troubled for the next few years. The chart at the bottom left shows bank CRE assets as a percent of total assets by bank size. Nearly one-third of assets for some banks are in the troubled CRE sector and recovery remains several years off.

JULY 30, 2010

BANKING TURMOIL LINGERS— SMALL BANKS NOW AT GREATEST RISK

Small banks are facing a perfect economic storm much like big banks did nearly two years ago. Unlike 2008, when the subprime mortgage meltdown drove big banks into crisis, today's problem for smaller banks is both recessions driven and self-inflicted. Today, loan demand and corresponding revenues are down, economic recovery is taking a breather, commercial real estate credit quality has seriously eroded and commercial foreclosures are very likely to be the next foreclosure crisis. Some small banks also remain plagued by capital and liquidity constraints together with unhealthy commercial real estate loan concentrations and rising loan losses. Moreover, some small banks made serious strategic blunders in last decade's bubble era when they stepped out of their community bank mold and ventured into unfamiliar loan territory with unusually large loans, capital markets participation, out of market loans, land loans with no short term development plan, loans secured by unfamiliar product types but most of all, loans made late in the growth cycle and even after the market had already begun its downward spiral. Indeed, FDIC data suggest that most current delinquencies are dominated by CRE loans originated between 2005 and 2008.

Clearly, many of the lessons learned two decades earlier during the thrift crisis were forgotten or ignored under the misguided belief that this time would be different. As history has shown time and again, it never is. Indeed, in their 2009 book called "*This Time Is Different, Eight Centuries of Financial Folly,*" *Reinhart and Rogoff* show how rich and poor countries alike have been lending, borrowing, crashing and recovering for centuries; each time asserting that the old rules no longer apply and *this time is different.*

Commercial real estate credit quality has eroded significantly and quickly. As the top left chart shows, delinquencies in both bank portfolios and in commercial mortgage back securities (CMBS) began increasing in 2008 and surged dramatically in 2009. At the end of May 2010, CMBS delinquencies had increased to a level over 25 times their level at the end of 2007 when "The Great Recession began.

As the bottom chart indicates, delinquencies are out pacing reserve growth and the reserve coverage ratio has slipped significantly. While some of the slippage is likely the product of reserves being released due to asset sales and charge offs, the trend, in our view, is not healthy at a time when evidence suggests the next wave of foreclosures will be in the commercial sector. Harvard law professor, Elizabeth Warren, who also chairs the TARP oversight panel, shares that view of commercial foreclosures.

In addition to credit quality deterioration, banks are struggling with revenue production as there is a synchronized decline in both supply and demand for credit. The popular refrain chanted endlessly by bank critics goes something like this. "*If banks would only start lending and stop hoarding the money they received from the government, the economy would recover.*" That assertion is grossly inaccurate and adds nothing to

---

explaining the complexity of the problems in today's economy in general and the financial sector in particular. The credit crunch that followed the near collapse of the financial system in late 2008 has eased. Credit is flowing, but not at the extraordinary and, in our view, irresponsible and uncontrolled rate seen during last decade's bubble inflation period. According to the Federal Reserve Board's Senior Loan Officer Survey, credit has been curtailed as financial institutions return to more responsible, prudent and tried and true underwriting standards. Additionally, consumers are shedding debt, not taking on more. Unemployment is at near record levels and consumer confidence remains low.

In addition, fewer consumers are able to obtain credit today after having experienced delinquencies, defaults, foreclosure and more.

The reality is that both supply of, and demand for, credit have declined. According to the Federal Reserve Board's Flow of Funds Report shows that consumer credit outstanding has declined for 18 out of the last 20 months. The cumulative decline has been about $167 billion. Credit declined $9.1 Billion in May alone and that followed a decline of $14.9 Billion in April.

The Mortgage Bankers Association tracks both purchase and re-finance mortgage loan applications weekly and reports findings in the form of an index. The MBA "Purchase Only Index peaked at 529.3 in June 2005 near the peak of the housing bubble. Just last week, it was 168.9—a 68% decline, despite record low interest rates and existing home prices which have fallen nearly 50% from peak in Florida and 55% to 65% in much of Central and South Florida.

While some assert there is huge demand for commercial real estate credit, the reality is that the demand for credit is only to refinance five year old bubble driven demand which was not real economic demand at all. Today, occupancy and rents are down and capitalization rates are up—all contributing to astounding 40-50% decline in value.

The end result is that significant growth in both real estate and consumer credit is still several years off., A return to credit levels of the bubble era may be a decade or more off even as the economy improves.

The Troubled Asset Relief Program (TARP) program could have some unintended consequences for small banks. TARP was created in October 2008 following the near meltdown of the U.S. banking system. It allowed the U.S. Treasury to purchase up to $700 Billion in illiquid or difficult to value assets from banks and other financial institutions. The program went through a series of iterations which included the creation of a Capital Purchase Program (CPP). Through preferred stock purchases from banks, the Treasury infused $205 Billion into more than 700 banks. Most of the money went to 17 of the nation's 19 largest banks; each having assets in excess of $100 Billion. The program requires payment of a five-percent annual dividend to the Treasury. That dividend payment will rise to nine-percent after five years if the funds are not repaid by then. Repayment of the government CPP investments were expected to come from private equity capital and bank revenues as they returned to profitability. Most of the large banks receiving CPP dollars have already repaid the investment and have returned to profitability—some earning record profits in recent quarters.

The story is much different among smaller banks. Approximately 690 smaller banks received CPP dollars and are now struggling to repay the funds and redeem their preferred stock. According to a recent report from the panel overseeing the TARP program, fewer than 10 percent of small bank CPP recipients have repaid the funds. Moreover one in seven smaller banks have already missed a dividend payment. Since the funds represent a Treasury investment in preferred bank stock and are not a loan, banks can legally defer the dividend payment. The problem however, is that the dividends accrue and then increase to nine-percent in 2013 which means that financial stress is constantly rising. Many small banks have been unable to raise private equity capital. Even worse, some who have successfully raised capital have seen much of it quickly dissipate through loan losses. The obvious unintended consequence is that some small banks will continue to weaken and become vulnerable to takeover or, at worst, failure.

Concentration Risk. Smaller banks are also at greater risk due to larger and unhealthy concentrations in commercial real estate. The chart at the top left shows that banks with less than $100 million in assets have nearly 20% of those assets in commercial real estate. The ratio exceeds 30% for banks with $100 million to $1 billion and also $1 billion to $10 billion. The ratio drops to less than 10% for institutions with total assets over $10 billion. That is largely due to size and portfolio diversity.

From a capital perspective, Florida banks had 392% of their Total Risk Based Capital (calculated by the FDIC as the median percent of Total Risk Based Capital) in commercial real estate at the end of the first quarter of 2010. That is down from about 407% a year ago. The Florida ratio is among the highest in the nation including other so-called *sand states*. Nevada had a ratio of 252% while California reached 380% and Arizona 387%.

AUGUST 7, 2010

WEAK EMPLOYMENT REPORT ADDS UNCERTAINTY TO RECOVERY

The nation's Employment Situation report for July was disappointing. It follows a similarly disappointing report in June. Combined with recent declines in GDP growth, retail sales, new home sales, single family residential construction, durable goods orders, consumer confidence and more, the indicators lead to concern that the economy could be in for another recession—a so-called double dip. While economic recovery has clearly slowed in recent months, economists remain divided about whether the recent change of direction is just the recovery taking a breather or whether it is a much more sinister negative change of direction. What is clear though is that many economists are lowering their forecasts and extending the expected time frame for recovery.

Yesterday's jobs report showed that payroll employment declined by another 131,000 jobs. That followed a revised loss of 221,000 jobs in June. Private sector employment *increased* by about 71,000 jobs. Private sector employment has increased by 630,000 jobs this year with about two-thirds of that total occurring in March and April. The number of unemployed persons nationwide remains at about 14.6 million and the unemployment rate remained steady in July at 9.5%. The number of involuntary part time workers—those who want to work full time but can't find a full time job—totaled about 8.5 million. That category has declined by 623,000 since April. At the same time, about 2.6 million persons remain marginally attached to the work force and 1.2 million of those are classified as discouraged workers. That figure is up 389,000

RECESSION CHRONICLES

year over year. Discouraged workers are those not currently looking for work as they believe no job is available for them.

Once unemployed, the duration of unemployment is lengthening. Long term unemployment is defined as 27 weeks or more and the average is now slightly over 35 weeks with 6.6 million persons or 45% of the unemployed falling into the long term category.

While payroll employment declined by 131,000 jobs, much of the decline was in government sector. Federal government employment declined by 143,000 jobs due mainly to the expected termination of temporary census workers. According to the Census Bureau, 167,157 temporary workers are still on the payroll. The government sector surprise, however, was in state and local government where employment declined by 48,000 jobs. That is twice the change for the last three months and is a product of deteriorating state and local government fiscal conditions created by declining tax revenues and budget shortfalls. There is no leading indicator to suggest conditions for state and local governments will improve anytime soon. Recessions weigh heavily on municipal governments as tax receipts are slow to trickle in even after the private sector has recovered.

Manufacturing added about 36,000 jobs over the month while health care added 27,000. Financial activities declined by 17,000 jobs while business and professional services declined by 13,000 jobs. After several months of gains, temporary employment fell by 6,000 jobs which is statistically insignificant.

At this stage of the cycle, we would expect roughly 100,000 net nonfarm payroll jobs to be created each month. Even that would indicate painfully slow recovery considering the depth of this recession. Growth, however, is much weaker, jobs are not being created as needed and private hiring is not rebounding at a rate anywhere near previous and much milder recessions. According to the JOLTS report (Job Opening and Labor Turnover Survey), there are still about eight candidates for every job opening even though people are leaving the labor force in high numbers.

Looking forward, we do not expect job growth to be strong enough to create any improvement in the unemployment rate for another year. Indeed, we expect it to top 10% again by year end due mainly to continuing machinations in the size of the labor force and only modest job growth.

CRE DRIVES SMALL BANK AND FDIC DISTRESS

The aggregate value of the U.S. commercial real estate market in late 2007 was estimated to be about $6.5 Trillion and loans outstanding totaled about $3.5 Trillion—a comfortable margin. Today, as values have declined upwards of 50%, collateral values are roughly equal to outstanding loan balances and, as the economy shows renewed signs of weakness, there are many reasons to suspect that values may deteriorate further. In recent weeks we've witnessed renewed declines in retail sales, new home sales, residential construction, durable goods orders, consumer confidence, business confidence and especially two consecutive problem ridden employment reports. All of these reports imply at least a renewed slowdown in the broader economy if not an outright retreat into recession—a so-called "double dip." Moreover, none of these indicators bode well for the commercial real estate sector where properties already experience high vacancies, sagging rents and significantly reduced cash flow—cash flow vital to repay the debt.

Even more daunting is that commercial loans made at the peak or late in the cycle, even as the market was turning, are now maturing. According to new data from the Federal Reserve, Mortgage Bankers Association and research by Deutsche Bank, about $250 billion in commercial real estate debt will mature this year followed by $300 billion in 2011 before peaking at nearly $350 billion in 2012. Most of that debt is now held by commercial banks and thrifts. Indeed, $200 billion of the $250 billion scheduled to mature this year is held by banks and thrifts. Additionally, about two-thirds of the loans scheduled to mature are currently underwater. That is, the collateral is worth less than the outstanding loan balance. According to the research firm Foresight Analytics, banks currently hold about $176 billion in *identified* problem real estate loans.

Most ominous of all, there is no place to refinance commercial real estate debt given depressed values and sagging property cash flows combined with high risk of further deterioration.

One solution: restructure loans. Give borrowers more time, extend maturities, reduce interest rates and *hope* conditions will improve in the future allowing borrowers to recover and repay. The federal banking agencies also issued guidance last October intended to offer banks ways to restructure problem loans. They also allowed banks to record loans as "performing" when they are still doing so under the original loan terms even if the collateral value has fallen below the loan amount. That allows the bank to record a smaller reserve for loan loss even as the risks are increasing. Supporters call this prudent and necessary relief. Critics call it *"extend and pretend."*

While regulators still expect banks and thrifts to act prudently, some have taken the new guidance as license to do otherwise and not recognize losses as quickly as necessary. Nearly $24 billion in nonresidential loans had been restructured by the end of the first quarter—over three times the dollar amount a year earlier. At the same time, problem loan growth outpaced loan loss reserves which are shrinking. (See our July 30th commentary). Modifications have clearly slowed the surge in defaults but are they also "kicking the can down the road" to a potentially bigger problem?

Here's the issue with not dealing with collateral deterioration quickly as extend and pretend is doing. Capital is defined as assets minus liabilities. If a bank continues to carry a real estate secured loan on its books with the collateral at an unrealistically high value even as its value, in reality, is declining, the bank could theoretically find itself insolvent but still have lots of capital—at least on paper. This, of course, assumes large numbers of loans are treated in this fashion and the bank is not

Modification can be prudent in an isolated number of cases and that decision should be made on a case by case basis. Widespread or imprudent *extend and pretend*, which the surge in modifications and the decline in reserves implies, is an inflating bubble waiting to burst when underlying.

AUGUST 31, 2010

HOUSING MARKET ON THE EDGE AS SALES PLUNGE

Housing is both a cause and effect of current economic pain. It is causal in the sense that it is typically a big contributor to GDP and has a huge and positive multiplier effect on allied industries (building materials, appliances, furniture and more). For the last few years, however, it has been a drag, contributing little or nothing to economic growth. It has also led to a profoundly negative decline in employment as comparatively few homes are being built, sold, financed, closed and more. Indeed, the decline in housing is also a leading contributor to the decline in commercial real estate activity. Many office, retail and industrial projects built to serve the *perceived* housing demand (which was artificial and not real demand anyway) are now virtually vacant and have lost much of their value. On the other side of the equation, housing is "effect" in the recession in the sense that weakness in the broader economy leads to a lack of confidence and consumers fear purchasing right now. The tentacles of housing reach deep into the broader economy and the broader economy cannot return to robust growth without a much stronger housing market.

July data just released (August 24th) by the National Association of Realtors (NAR) show that existing home sales declined 27.2% to their lowest level in 15 years. That, despite record low interest rates and renewed affordability. In Florida, for example, median prices have returned to levels not seen since early last decade.

Sales declined to 3.83 million units nationwide from a downwardly adjusted 5.26 million sales in June and 5.14 million units in July 2009. Those figures include single family detached homes, town homes, condominium units and co-ops and are seasonally adjusted annual rates. The single family component was 3.37 million units, down from 4.62 million in June and down 25.6% from the 4.53 million level in July 2009. For perspective, annual sales have averaged 4.9 million over the past 20 years and 4.4 million over 30 years. The median single family home price was $183,400 in July which is a slight increase over a year earlier.

Inventories also continued to climb. The current inventory is about 3.98 million homes for sale. At the current sales pace, that is a 12.5 month supply, the highest since October 1982 when inventory stood at 13.8 months. Inventory also broke through the cycle high of 11.3 months established in April 2008 near the worst of the recession. Inventory has averaged 6.2 months for the last decade. Inventory of six months is typically regarded as the long end of the normal range.

Distress sales accounted for about 32% of all existing home sales in July. Foreclosures continue unabated and banks currently hold a huge shadow inventory of homes. That will keep the lid on price increases firmly in place for the foreseeable future.

On the heels of the National Association of Realtors existing home sales report, the Commerce Department reported even worse news in the new home sector. Sales fell 12.4% to a mere 276,000 annualized rate from a downwardly revised rate of 315,000 sales in June. Those are nationwide numbers. Sales are down 32.4% over the past year and down 80% from their 2007 peak. New home inventories remained flat at about 210,000 units in July. This equals the lowest level since 1968 and represents a 9.1 month supply as compared to 8.0 months in June. The number of new homes under construction fell 0.9% to 209,000 in July. That is the smallest number of new homes on the market since February 1970—some 40 years ago. The supply of unsold new homes has fallen 23% over the year and the median price has fallen 4.8% over the year to $204,000.

The gap between new and existing homes is widening both in terms of sale volume and price. The national median price of a new home in July was $204,000 as compared to an existing home at $183,400. Builders are still having difficulty competing with the rising tide of foreclosures coming back to market. The statistics are also skewed as most of the existing home sales have been smaller homes in the lower price ranges while new home prices reflect larger and higher priced homes—most left over from the trend to larger, higher priced homes in the latter part of last decade as prices surged out of control and so-called "McMansions" were a large part of construction activity. New home construction will remain muted for the foreseeable future as new home construction in most areas is not economically feasible. That is, it costs more to build than the finished product will be worth. There is evidence—at least anecdotally—that large and financially sound builders are once again acquiring finished lots that have come back to market at very low prices as a result of foreclosure, bankruptcy or banks purging non-performing assets. Nevertheless, don't look for a surge in construction anytime soon. There is still inventory to clear. Equally important, unemployment will likely worsen before it gets better and there is still enormous economic and fiscal policy uncertainty. Consumers are experiencing angst over what comes next for the economy. Is it more of the same, a double dip recession, deflation, or even a plunge into depression? Consumers are also clearly concerned about the threat of increased taxes at the worst possible time, the ultimate cost of healthcare, the value of the dollar and overall uncertainty around the direction of an out of touch administration.

The $8,000 first time home buyer tax credit has had a significant effect on the timing of sales but not the number of sales. While the intent was to stimulate sales its net effect was to move sales from one period to another. The first tax credit expired in November 2009. Before it did, sales surged to 6.49 million units annualized and fell steadily for three months thereafter. Sales recovered in March and April as buyers rushed to meet the new April 30th deadline for expiration of the second tax credit. Today, we are witnessing a huge payback for the second credit.

The credit was expensive. The most recent hard data available from the Treasury was just before eligibility for the credit expired at the end of April. As of then, some 2.2 million people had filed for the credit at a cost to the Treasury of $16 billion. That is up from 1.8 filers at a $12.6 billion cost to tax payers only a month earlier. April was an exceptionally active month as potential buyers rushed to meet the deadline. Time will tell what the ultimate cost was however we expect it to be north of $20 billion.

As we've seen time and again the last couple of years, stimulus without underlying demand is worthless. The homebuyer tax credit is but one case in point. It moved very few buyers into the market who weren't there anyway. An estimated three out of five buyers reportedly expected to buy within two years anyway. Take away the artificial and temporary support the tax credit offered and the result is still an extraordinarily weak market where the risks remain heavily skewed to the downside. The recent downturn in home sales will likely put pressure on Congress to once again extend the credit. In our view, that would be ill advised since each iteration of the tax credit has resulted in diminished results as compared to the one before it. Many of those likely to use the tax credit have probably already done so. Moreover, trade up homeowners would have to sell in a very depressed market and repurchase in a fairly short time. A $6,500 tax credit (assuming any extension would be at that level) for trade up buyers would not appear to adequately price the risk one would take in doing so.

Is renting the new American dream? Probably not but a disproportionate number of respondents expressed favorable views about renting in a May 2010 Harris Interactive Poll. Seventy six percent of respondents said that renting is a better option than buying a home in the current real estate market. Seventy eight percent of those responding said they were current homeowners. With unemployment frozen near ten percent, people are cautious about committing to a long term mortgage.

With prices soaring last decade, housing became a means of financing a lifestyle—usually far beyond the homeowners' means. Today, reality has returned. A house is once again a place to live. Nevertheless, the housing crisis has changed the way many look at housing. For decades, homeownership was an absolute good thing which provided personal and family stability. Today, homeownership, for many, is a burden and a source of instability.

Foreclosures continue largely unabated. RealtyTrac reported there were over 325,000 foreclosure notices filed in July. That is a four-percent increase over the previous month but a 10% decrease year over year. Total notices equates to one in every 397 households receiving some sort of foreclosure filing. Total foreclosure filings have been over 300,000 for 17 consecutive months. Of the total 325,000 filings in July, 97,123 were new filings.

Nevada, Arizona and Florida continue to dominate the foreclosure news. One in every 82 housing units is in some stage of foreclosure in Nevada; one in 167 in Arizona and one in 171 in Florida.

There has been a lot of speculation about the possibility of a so-called

---

double dip recession recently. That assumes, of course, that the economy actually emerged from recession last year as many thought. Not wanting to parse words, let's assume double dip recession is a possibility. Moody's Economy.Com puts that possibility at about one in four or 25%. If a double dip occurs, house prices could fall another 20% making the road to recovery even longer and more difficult with housing not recovering again until 2012.

SEPTEMBER 6, 2010

AUGUST EMPLOYMENT LESS BAD—STILL NO REASON TO CELEBRATE

There were no surprises in the August Employment Situation Report released Friday by the Bureau of Labor Statistics. Nonfarm payrolls declined by 54,000 jobs as 114,000 more temporary census jobs were eliminated. Private sector payroll employment rose by 67,000 jobs. The July report was also revised to show a gain of 107,000 jobs—positive news but far too few jobs. So far this year, the economy has added about 95,000 jobs per month on average. The largest gains were during the first quarter. At the current average pace, it would take about seven years to regain the private sector jobs lost during the recession. Recovery from The Great Recession will be another jobless recovery much as it was following the relatively minor recession in 2001.

The number of unemployed persons was little changed at about 14.9 million and the unemployment rate inched up fractionally to 9.6%. The number of jobless persons increased by 261,000 but the labor force also increased by 550,000 jobs. The unemployment rate has hovered in a narrow range of 9.5% to 9.7% throughout all of 2010. It was about 10% during the fourth quarter of 2009.

While economic recovery has clearly slowed in recent months, economists remain divided about whether the recent change of direction is just the recovery taking a breather or whether it is a much more sinister negative change of direction. While there are conflicting data, what is clear, is that economists have lowered their forecasts and have extended the expected time frame for recovery.

Looking behind the headline numbers, the number of persons employed but working part time for economic reasons rose by 331,000 over the month to 8.9 million. These people represent those whose hours had been reduced or they are unable to find a full time job.

About 2.4 million persons remain marginally attached to the work force. That is about 200,000 fewer than a month earlier. Among the marginally attached workers are about 1.1 million discouraged workers. That is an increase of 352,000 year over year. These persons are not currently looking for work as they do not believe a job is available for them.

The number of long term unemployed (defined as unemployed for 27 weeks or more) declined over the month to 6.2 million. In August, 42% of the unemployed had been jobless for 27 weeks or more. Despite the decline the number of long term unemployed continues to be a disturbing statistic. The duration of unemployment has surged dramatically during The Great Recession. The trend has been, once unemployed, people are staying unemployed longer. Among other things, that trend lends credence to our previously expressed view that more job losses during this recession are permanent rather than cyclical and the job market is undergoing significant structural change. To put long term unemployment in perspective, the current total is roughly three times what it was in the recessions of the early 1990s and 2001 and twice what it was in the more severe recession of the early 1980s.

We expect long term unemployment to be a drag on recovery and the broader economy for years to come given the permanent nature of so many of the losses.

The August winners and losers by sector. Healthcare employment increased by 28,000 jobs in August with most of the growth in ambulatory health care services. So far in 2010, and in most of 2009, the health care industry has averaged about 20,000 new jobs per month. Manufacturing, however, declined by 27,000 jobs over the month.

In the professional and business services category, temporary help services bounced back by 17,000 jobs in August. This sector has added 392,000 jobs since its employment low in September 2009. Temporary help is an important sector to watch as employers often times use temporary help before committing to permanent employment.

Employment in other sectors such as wholesale trade, transportation, warehousing, information and financial activities changed little in August.

State and municipal government budgets are hemorrhaging due largely to declining tax revenues—another unintended consequence of the housing boom and bust. 49 states are required by their state constitutions to run balanced budgets. Most have been slicing and dicing budgets and programs for the last 18 months and have nowhere else to go except to continue or begin cutting jobs. State and municipal government jobs make up about 15% of U.S. jobs. Given the depth of budget deficits, it is likely that as many as 2.0 million jobs may need to be cut to meet state constitutional budget mandates for balanced budgets. Clearly that will cripple thousands of state and local programs.

The Florida Employment Situation. Florida releases employment data several weeks after the U.S. Department of Labor's Bureau of Labor Statistics. The following information is from July 2010 data released by Florida's Agency for Workforce Innovation on August 20, 2010. August data will be released on September 17th. Florida's seasonally adjusted unemployment rate for July was 11.5% up fractionally from June and significantly higher than the nation's 9.6% rate. Florida's total workforce in July was 9,214,000. It's non-agricultural work force was 7,238,000 which was a 5,700 job increase over the previous month. Year over year, that is a net increase of about 2,700 jobs. That was the first annual increase in jobs since June 2007.

Sectors gaining jobs year over year in July included health services and private education (+36,700), professional and business services (+8,000) and total government (+8,800). Sectors losing jobs year over year in July included construction (-27,500), financial activities (-18,600) and information (-9,400).

Rural Hendry County, west of Palm Beach County and south of Lake Okeechobee had the highest unemployment rate in the state at 19.7%.

IN MEMORY OF THE GREEN SHOOTS

Last year at this time, many were heralding the early signs of recovery—the so-called green shoots. Several important indicators had become "less bad." The nation had been losing 600,000 to 700,000 or more jobs per month. By August 2009, losses moderated to only (and we use the term loosely) 216,000 jobs although the jobless rate remained at a 26 year high. The freefall in housing prices had slowed and there was widespread evidence that a trough had been reached. The nation's gross domestic product turned positive in the third quarter and has remained positive ever since.

While some economists declared the recession over in the third quarter of last year, the Business Cycle Dating Committee (BCDC) of the National Bureau of Economic Research (NBER) did not. That body is the official arbiter of the nation's business cycle. The committee does not forecast but rather it dates peaks and troughs in the nation's business cycle by using a wide variety of economic indicators over an extended period of time. Indeed there is no single indicator nor rule of thumb (such as the widely touted two quarters of GDP decline is a recession) to declare the beginning or the end of a recession and the start of renewed expansion. As recently as its April 2010 meeting, the committee had not declared an end to this recession and there is no evidence to expect it will soon.

In May of last year (Economic Perspectives, May 6, 2009) we acknowledged the green shoots, but also asked the question *"are they sustainable or will they wither and die."* We opined that the recession was far from over; recovery remained a work in progress and it would be a long, rocky and sometimes painful journey back. We concluded that … *"it will almost certainly be years before we see the robust growth of the not too distant past."* That was then—16 months ago.

Now is now. Over the last three months, the economy has weakened at virtually every level. GDP growth (Q2-2010) slowed and will likely be flat or only slightly positive by the end of 2010. Hiring is weak and will likely get weaker. The commercial real estate sector has lost half its value and is still deteriorating. Bank credit quality is deteriorating and pushing many to insolvency. The FDIC is broke (except for a $500 billion lifeline from the U.S. Treasury) and can't take over failing banks fast enough. Housing has taken another dip with existing home sales plunging some 27% in July to the lowest level in 15 years and the largest monthly decline based on records dating back to 1968. New home sales also plunged 12.4% to a new record low in July.

The retreating economy has caused widespread speculation that the U.S. is headed for a double dip recession or worse. Indeed, even "depression" has been uttered by several prominent economists and law makers. A double dip implies that the economy actually came out of recession. More likely, the economy never emerged from recession last year as some opined and what we are seeing today is more of the same with conditions retreating to those experienced earlier, but not at the depth of the recession. Indeed, talk of depression is overblown. Lingering recession is perhaps more descriptive.

False recovery starts are not unusual during recessions. Even during The Great Depression of the 1930's, the economy witnessed countless *green shoots* and a few false recovery starts. Indeed, there were six quarterly upticks in the GDP averaging about eight-percent—far higher than the three percent average uptick in 2009. Each time, many wanted desperately to believe the worst was over only to be disappointed time and again.

In fact, the economy experienced a deep recession within the depression in 1937. In the spring of that year, wages, production and corporate profits returned to their pre-crash levels of 1929. Unemployment was still high at over 14% but far below its 1933 peak of 25%. The Roosevelt administration, at the urging of the Treasury, took these *green shoots* as a signal that the worst was over and spending should be cut and taxes raised to begin balancing the budget. The Works Progress Administration (WPA) which employed millions at it peak, slashed its payroll. The Public Works Administration (PWA) projects were brought to a halt. At the same time the Federal Reserve began tightening the money supply.

These policy blunders plunged the economy back into deep recession. Unemployment surged to 19% while manufacturing output fell by

37% to a level equivalent to the depths of the depression in 1933. The Great Depression came to an end only as the U.S. began its buildup for World War II. Employment, manufacturing and government spending all rose dramatically in response to the war effort.

Over the last three months, the economy has showed renewed and significant signs of weakness. Let's look at several key economic components and what they might portend for the short term future of the broader economy.

The Gross Domestic Product is the top line measure of the nation's economy. It is the total of all goods and services produced. After four consecutive negative growth quarters, real GDP turned positive in the third quarter of 2009 and has stayed positive ever since (4 quarters). After 3.7% growth in the first quarter of 2010, GDP growth slipped to 1.6% in the second quarter and is lining up for sub-par growth of well under 2.0% in the third quarter. The slowing growth came from stronger imports and a smaller improvement in business inventories. The trade deficit also widened and subtracted 2.8 percentage points from growth in the quarter. Personal consumption expenditures and consumer spending both rose, but did so at a very slow pace of 1.6% and 1.9% respectively—both annualized. Spending will remain at these levels until employment improves. The downside risk is that employment turns significantly worse. Housing also continues to be a drag on GDP growth as it has for three years. It will likely remain a drag until employment improves, foreclosures abate and remaining housing inventories reach equilibrium.

Spending on non-residential structures increased in the second quarter for reasons that are not readily apparent given the inventory overhang. We suspect the increase will be adjusted out in future revisions or spending will naturally return to a more normal level in the next quarter or two.

Federal government spending has been a positive for GDP growth but stimulus spending is quickly waning and state and local governments are aggressively cutting spending. Government spending is likely to become a negative for economic growth throughout the rest of 2010.

Business inventories account for a large share of growth. Indeed, it is the change in inventory levels that affect GDP growth on a quarter over

---

quarter basis. Inventory growth will likely be smaller in the next few quarters as businesses remain cautious about holding too much inventory. The Bureau of Economic Analysis released GDP revisions with the Q2 results. Revisions are an annual process. This year, revisions were made to GDP estimates for 2007, 2008 and 2009. The downward revisions showed that the recession was actually much deeper than originally reported and the economy has a much deeper hole to climb out of. Revisions showed that real GDP fell 4.1% from peak in the fourth quarter of 2007 to trough in the second quarter of 2009.

Looking forward, the risks are to the downside. Having dug deeply behind the headline numbers, we now expect third quarter GDP growth to be at or very near 1.5% and fourth quarter growth to be in the one percent range. There are no current leading indicators to suggest growth *greater than* two-percent for at least the next two or three quarters.

The employment situation is decidedly negative and the U.S. economy finds itself in uncharted territory. Severe recessions, are typically followed by strong labor market recoveries. The U.S. has experienced recessions this severe and recoveries this jobless but never on top of one another. That argues strongly for three points we've made before. First, this recession has been like no other and recovery too, will be like none other. The technology boom a decade ago has rendered many jobs obsolete and retraining will be necessary to replace them. Second, the recession did not actually end in mid 2009 as so many want to believe. Third, this recession has driven structural change deep into the heart of the employment sector specifically and more generally into the broader economy.

Productivity rose for five consecutive quarters. Part of that can be explained by technological advances but most is simply workers producing more. Productivity peaked in the first quarter. The strategy of more with less ran out of road in the second quarter when hours worked increased sharply. That is often prelude to renewed hiring. Nevertheless with 8.9 million jobs having been lost during The Great Recession, there is a lot road to make up.

The nation's unemployment rate (August) remains unacceptably high at 9.6% and leading indicators point to unemployment topping 10% again before the end of 2010. While layoffs have slowed, new jobs are not yet being created in numbers anywhere near sufficient to drive down the unemployment rate.

While corporate profits have risen significantly in recent months, employers still face uncertainty and fear about the direction of taxes, health care cost, regulation and many other impediments that are causing them to delay hiring.

The housing sector saw existing single family home sales decline to 3.37 million units in July. That is down 25.6% from a year earlier. The entire existing home sector, which includes condos, coops and townhomes, in addition to single family detached was down 27.2%—the largest decline in 15 years. New home sales also declined 12.4% to a mere 276,000 units annualized. Sales are down 32.4% year over year and 80% from the 2007 peak.

Prices and values have declined dramatically making homes more affordable. Prices are down 30% or more nationally and 50% to 65% in most of Florida and other bubble states.

Nevertheless, housing demand is also at a very low level. Potential homebuyers wrestle with unemployment or fear of unemployment. They fear that home prices will decline further given the very high level of foreclosures with no end in sight. Many face significantly reduced household wealth and a disproportionate number are experiencing impaired credit. That combined with tighter credit standards make home purchases impossible for many.

The second home buyer tax credit which expired in April created no new demand. It merely moved sales that would likely have occurred anyway to an earlier time at very great cost to tax payers (see *Real Estate and Economic Commentary* dated August 31, 2010). Part of what we are witnessing today is payback for the tax credit. Without another renewal of the tax credit, we can expect sales to rebound very modestly in coming months. Nevertheless, weak demand is the more important underlying issue and that is not likely to improve anytime soon.

The economy is undeniably in bad shape and has worsened in recent months. Still, it is not as bad as it was during the depths of the recession and concerns that it will be are over blown. Nevertheless, it will be a long, slow and painful crawl back to robust growth.

FLORIDA SECOND TO NEVADA IN FORECLOSURES

Even though Florida foreclosures have declined for five consecutive months, the state remains second in the nation for foreclosures. Only Nevada has more. Approximately 17% of U.S. foreclosures are in Florida where one in 155 housing units received some sort of foreclosure legal filing in August. That compares to one in 381 housing units nationwide. Florida's foreclosure filings are up 10% from July but down 9% year over year. Pre-foreclosures (lis pendens), the first legal filing in a foreclosure action, fell about 46% year over year but rose fractionally over July thereby ending five straight months of declining initial actions. The median existing single family home price has fallen about 32% peak to trough nationwide. In the so-called "sand states" of Florida, Arizona, California, Nevada and even Hawaii, the decline has been in excess of 50% with additional declines still likely due to the fundamentally weak housing market where demand is minimal and sales activity has been propped up with government incentives.

In Florida, an estimated 46% of mortgages are underwater meaning more is owed on the mortgage than the underlying collateral is worth. Underwater mortgages are about 68% in Nevada, 50% in Arizona and over 30% in California. In states such as Michigan that are economically depressed for reasons other than overbuilding last decade, 38% of mortgages are underwater.

Approximately 10% of Florida and Arizona mortgages are currently in foreclosure. That rate soars to about 14% in Nevada. In California, the rate is 7.5% and nationwide it is about 1.2%.

The pipeline of foreclosures, as represented by mortgage delinquencies, continues to build. At the end of August, approximately 5.8% of all Florida residential mortgages were 90 days or more delinquent. In Nevada, the ratio was 7.3% and in California about 5.6%. Those figures compare with the national rate of 1.2%.

The chart at the left shows all Central and South Florida counties. Each column shows new filings against total housing units in some stage of foreclosure. The number in parentheses is the ratio of new filings to total foreclosures for the month. The general trend shows that new filings are generally declining as a ratio to total foreclosures. That would suggest that foreclosures are now moving through the court system in a somewhat orderly fashion. Nevertheless, there are notable exceptions. St. Lucie County foreclosure new filings still remain high as a percent of total but the numbers are declining.

A two-tiered market for sales of foreclosed vs. non-foreclosed homes has clearly emerged both nationally and in Florida. Across the nation, foreclosure sales accounted for 31% of all residential sales in the first quarter of 2010 according to Realtytrac. The average sale price of a property in some stage of foreclosure was about 27% less than the average price of a property not in foreclosure. The average discount for a property sold while in the pre-foreclosure stage was 14.7%. That discount increased to 34% for properties sold as REO (real estate owned by banks and other institutional lenders).

Foreclosures will continue to be a scourge on the housing market for several years into the future as the housing market struggles to regain equilibrium.

SEPTEMBER 21, 2010

RECESSION OVER SAYS BUSINESS CYCLE DATING COMMITTEE

The Business Cycle Dating Committee (BCDC) of the National Bureau of Economic Research (NBER), the official arbiter of the nation's business cycle, today (September 20, 2010) declared that the recession reached a trough and therefore ended in June 2009. The BCDC is a group of academic economists based in Cambridge, MA which has responsibility for dating peaks and troughs in the nation's business cycle.

The Great Recession, as it has come to be known, therefore officially lasted 18 months and was the longest since The Great Depression of the 1930's. The peak of the last business cycle and therefore the start of the recession was in December 2007 although the BCDC made that declaration a full 12 months later in December 2008. The end is being announced some 17 months after the presumed end. Such lengthy delays are not unusual as the committee is charged with *dating* peaks and troughs—not forecasting them.

The committee makes its decisions based on a wide variety of macroeconomic indicators over a fairly lengthy period of time and over a broad geography. They rely heavily on the two broadest indicators of economic performance, the Gross Domestic Product (GDP) and Gross Domestic Income (GDI). Both are subject to annual revision and were in fact revised in July and August by the Bureau of Economic Analysis. The BCDC waited until those revisions were made to decide the recession had technically ended. The average of GDP and GDI was 3.1% above its low in the second quarter of 2009 but remained 1.3% below the previous peak in December 2007 which, in large part, contributed to the reasoning behind the June 2009 trough date.

There are no fixed rules about what weights the committee applies to any particular indicator or what other measures are used in the process. The widely touted rule of thumb that two quarters of GDP decline equals a recession or two quarters of rising GDP equals recovery is just that—a simplistic rule of thumb which is not a measure the BCDC relies on.

Many observers have been debating the possibility of a "double dip" recession. Indeed, much of the debate centered around whether The Great Recession had ended and a "double dip" was likely or whether the renewed weakness in the economy that began in about June 2010 was just more of the same. The Business Cycle Dating Committee has now taken the position that The Great Recession has ended and if a double dip occurs, it will be a new recession and dated separately. The committee made no assertion that the economy is strong, robust or is performing anywhere near its potential. Indeed, it is very clear that The Great Recession was extraordinarily broad, deep and created profound structural change. Even though the recession has been officially declared over, nearly 15 million Americans remain unemployed. The nation's unemployment rate is hovering just under 10%, long term unemployment is at a record high, homes have lost nearly 40% of their value and commercial real estate has too. Nearly 340,000 households (one in 381) received some sort of foreclosure notice in August. Finally, banks are failing in near record numbers and many more will certainly follow. The story is worse in Florida, Nevada, Arizona and California where both the rise and fall of housing was the greatest.

What are the odds of a double dip? No one knows for sure but the *doom and gloomers* put the odds at nearly 100%. A few prominent economists and lawmakers have even uttered the word "depression." Those extreme views seem hard to rationalize. As we wrote a few weeks ago in a commentary called "In Memory of the Green Shoots," those views are way over blown. In our view, the odds of another recession—a double dip—are more likely 25% to 35%. The economy is undeniably in bad shape and has worsened in recent months. Still, it is not as bad as it was at the mid 2009 trough. Nevertheless, it will be a long, slow and oftentimes painful crawl back to robust growth.

SEPTEMBER 28, 2010

EXISTING AND NEW HOME SALES STILL NEAR RECORD LOWS

August existing home sales nationally rose 7.6% to 4.13 million units from an upwardly revised 3.84 million units (an additional 10,000 sales) in July. Both figures are seasonally adjusted annual rates and include single family detached residences, condominium and townhouse units as well as co-op units. In July, sales plunged to their lowest level in 15 years following the end of the home buyer tax credit program. Despite 290,000 more sales over the month, August was not much better than July and sales remain at their second lowest level. August sales remained about 19% below their August 2009 level with 970,000 fewer sales in August 2010 than there were a year earlier. For perspective, annual sales have averaged 4.9 million over the past 20 years and 4.4 million over 30 years. The median existing home price for all types of housing units was $178,600, up fractionally from a year ago.

Total housing inventory declined about 0.6% to 3.98 million existing homes of all types offered for sale. That is an approximate 11.6 month supply at the current sales pace—down from 12.5 months of supply in July. It is also the highest inventory since October 1982 when inventory stood at 13.8 months.

In another survey issued concurrently by the National Association of Realtors, an estimated 31% of sales were to first time home buyers. That is down from 38% a month earlier. Investors are again playing a bigger part in market activity representing some 21% of sales as compared to 19% in July. All cash sales slipped to 28% in August from 30% in July. Finally, distressed sales accounted for about 34% of all sales in August. That is up from 32% in July and 31% a year earlier.

The single family detached sector saw sales increase 7.4% to 3.62 million units on an annualized seasonally adjusted basis. Here too, sales volume is over 19% less than a year ago. The median existing single family detached home price was $179,300 which was down from $183,400 a month ago but up fractionally year over year.

On the heels of the National Association of Realtors existing home sales report, the Commerce Department reported dismal news in the new home sector. Sales were little changed from July and remain at a mere 288,000 sales *nationwide*. August sales were down 29% year over year. The median new home price in August was $204,700—essentially unchanged over July but the difference between prices of existing and new homes continued to widen. The August median price was also the lowest in over six years and the number of new homes offered for sale fell to 206,000—the lowest level since 1968. The supply of new homes was about 8.6 months, down only fractionally from a month earlier but up from 7.8 months a year earlier. New home inventory fell 1.4% over the month but 21.4% over the year.

Sales of existing homes in Florida rose three -percent in August over July and one-percent—a mere 90 units—year over year. Prices declined in August as compared to July at nearly every level from national through Florida and to the Central and South Florida county level. The exceptions were Palm Beach County in South Florida and Brevard County— the nation's Space Coast—in Central Florida. The increase in Palm Beach County was statistically insignificant while Brevard County moved off its new cycle low of $99,400 reached in July. The Space Shuttle program has only two flights left before the program is terminated next year. Approximately 900 employees will be terminated at the end of September and the total will be about 7,000 direct job losses. With the multiplier effect, well over 20,000 jobs are expected to be lost in Brevard County.

Housing inventories remain stubbornly high at almost every level despite renewed affordability which has come back in line with income levels and interest rates which are at record lows. At peak, there were an estimated 25-40% more homes than there were persons to occupy them either as owner or renter. Since the recession began, immigration has slowed and there has been a sharp drop in new household formation. Combined with record unemployment, inventories will be slow to decline.

SEPTEMBER 29, 2010

FLORIDA EMPLOYMENT WEAKENS AGAIN

August data from Florida's Agency for Workforce Innovation (AWI) show that employment worsened again at both the state level and in every central and south Florida county. While Florida has 29,800 more jobs than it did a year ago, it also has 119,000 more unemployed persons. That is attributable to the fluctuating size of the total labor force and the distribution between agricultural and non-agricultural employment. Approximately 1,084,000 Floridians were jobless at the end of August out of a total labor force of 9,229,000. Florida's non-agricultural labor force totaled 7,227,900 after a loss of 16,000 jobs.

Florida's unemployment rate also rose to a seasonally adjusted 11.7%. Not seasonally adjusted, it was 12.4%. The process of seasonal adjustment removes some of the peaks and valleys which are known to occur at or about the same time every year. The difference in the state level rate in August was largely linked to the seasonal change in agriculture and crop production. Hendry County, which is heavily agricultural, had the highest unemployment rate in the state at 20.6% (not seasonally adjusted). That rate should decline over the next few months although the rate does tend to consistently run higher than other nearby agricultural counties.

The industry gaining the most jobs year over year in August was private education and health care which grew 3.2% or 33,500 jobs over the year. Most of the gain was on the health care side and predominately in ambulatory health care services. Professional and business services gained 11,000 jobs while leisure and hospitality added 9,300.

Construction was again the loser of the most jobs over the year at about 17,800. Financial activities was a close second losing 15,100 jobs. The two sectors are closely allied and as construction activity has declined so have financial activities. Manufacturing lost 6,000 jobs. Total government lost 1,114 jobs which was fewer than expected. The local government sector continues to be propped up by federal stimulus dollars which will run out soon. At that point, we expect the local government component of employment to lose jobs in growing numbers.

Indian River and St. Lucie counties on Florida's Treasure Coast experienced a surge in unemployment. Indian River topped 16% however that may be artificially inflated by Vero Beach based Piper Aircraft putting approximately 700 employees on a one week furlough. Without that event, Indian River County's unemployment rate would have been closer to St. Lucie County at slightly over 15%.

Florida International University's annual Labor Day look at Florida employment revealed there were growing gaps between employment for the rich and the poor and by race and ethnicity. African-American unemployment stands at 15.5%; Hispanic was 11.6% and White was 8.9%.

NOVEMBER 29, 2010

HOUSING MARKET IN DISARRAY. OUTLOOK STILL BLEAK

Existing home sales volume declined nationally and in Florida in October. Total home sales, including single family detached, townhomes, condominium units and co-ops declined to a seasonally adjusted annual rate of 4.43 million units in October. That is down from 4.53 million in September and down 25.9% from the 5.98 million sales reached in October 2009 at the time sales were surging prior to expiration of the first time home buyer tax credit.

Single family detached home volume, the largest component of the total, fell 2.0% to a seasonally adjusted annual rate of 3.89 million units in October. That too is down from 3.97 units on an equivalent basis in September and 25.6% below the 5.23 million level reached a year earlier. For perspective, annual sales have averaged 4.9 million units annually over the last 20 years and 4.4 million over 30 years. Sales are now at their second lowest level in the last 15 years.

Total existing housing inventory declined 3.4% to 3.86 million homes available for sale at the end of October. That represents a 10.5 month supply at the current sales pace. Inventory was fractionally higher at 10.6 months in September. That is the highest since October 1982 when there were 13 months of inventory. For comparison, inventory averaged 8.8 months throughout 2009; 10.4 in 2008 and 8.9 in 2007.

First time home buyers accounted for 32% of existing home sales. That is unchanged from September but down from 50% a year earlier. The October 2009 figure is skewed upward due to the home buyer tax credit. Investors purchased 19% of existing homes in October. That was up fractionally from 18% in September and 14% % a year earlier. Rather than severely restricting financing to investors, agencies are now allowing it in an effort to help clear excessive inventories. Indeed, the FHA has loosened its "anti-flipping" rule expressly for that purpose.

The existing home median price was $171,100 in October substantially unchanged from $171,500 recorded in September and down slightly from $172,000 recorded a year earlier.

The National Association of Realtors (NAR) Pending Home Sales Index (PHSI) slipped slightly in September (most recent release).

The PHSI is a widely watched indicator of future (1-2 months) sales as it is based on executed contracts. Its reliability, how-ever, has been diminished in the last year or so due to continuing house price declines, foreclosures, credit impairment and uncertainty—all of which have contributed to greater than usual con-tract cancellation.

New home sales volume declined 8.1% in October to a seasonally adjusted annual rate of 283,000 units. Sales have declined nearly 80% from their 2007 peak. Prices have fallen too and the median price gap between new and existing homes is narrowing. The median new home price was $194,000 in October, the lowest in seven years, compared to an existing home median price of $171,100. While new homes would logically be expected to cost more than an existing or "used" home, the simple affordability difference has moved more buyers toward lower priced existing homes.

According to a joint release by the U.S. Census Bureau and the U.S. Department of Housing and Urban Development, there were an estimated 550,000 residential building permits issued nationally in October. That is fractionally above the number in September but 4.5% below a year earlier. Carving out the single family detached sector, there were 406,000 permits issued.

While permits theoretically portend short term future construction, in the last few years, builders and developers have often obtained permits to preserve their ability to do so with no short term intended construction. That has reduced the number of permits that evolve into short term housing starts.

At the same time, estimated housing starts were at a seasonally adjusted annual rate of 519,000 units, 11.6% below the revised September estimate of 588,000 and 1.9% below the October 2009 estimate of 529,000 units.

In Florida, 11,888 existing single family residences and 5,147 condominium units changed hands in October. Single family sales declined 21% over the year while condo units declined five-percent. The median single family home price state wide was $136,600, down three-percent from a year earlier. The median condo unit price was $82,400, a decline of 22% from October 2009.

Median prices declined in all Central and South Florida counties with the exception of Miami-Dade and Broward (Fort Lauderdale) where median prices were up 12% and three-percent respectively. Brevard County (Kennedy Space Center area) experienced a new cycle low of $97,600. That is over 60% less than the cycle high of $248,700 in August 2005. The nation's space shuttle pro-gram is scheduled to end in 2011. About 7,000 relatively high paying jobs are expected to be lost. With the multiplier effect, job losses are likely to be three to four times that number.

Elsewhere in Florida, the median price of an existing home in Ft.

Myers–Cape Coral MSA fell to $90,000 while Punta Gorda fell to $96,200. Both MSAs are on Florida's southwest coast. Inland along the Interstate 4 corridor between Orlando and Tampa, Lake-land fell to $94,200 while Ocala, on the Interstate 75 corridor north of Orlando and south of Gainesville, fell to a record low of $79,600.

The effect of Florida's housing crisis has landed squarely in the banking and finance sector. The Mortgage Bankers Association reported that at the end of the third quarter of 2010, 11.02% of the 3.2 million mortgages serviced in Florida were delinquent at least 30 days. The MBA's breakdown was 3.55% were 30 days late; 1.63% were 60 days past due and 5.84% were 90 days or more past due. Most of the latter category will likely result in foreclosure. Nationwide, the percentage of mortgages past due at least 30 days stood at 13.52% in the third quarter. That is higher than Florida but a decline from its peak of 14.42% in early 2009.

Florida continues to lead the nation in foreclosures with 13.68% of mortgages in some state of foreclosure. Florida is followed by Nevada at 9.72%. Nationwide, foreclosures are rapidly moving inland from both coasts as well as from the sunbelt states of Florida, California, Arizona and Nevada and a few Midwest "rustbelt" states. Rampant over-building was experienced in nearly every state with very few exceptions. Clearly, however, the sunbelt states experienced the most over-building and have suffered the most.

The table at the left shows foreclosure activity in most central and south Florida counties. Note that new filings are still running at high levels of 30% to over 50% of total foreclosures. While not all new filings will result in foreclosure, the high level is still worry-some.

DECEMBER 8, 2010

WHY HOUSING WON'T IMPROVE ANYTIME SOON

Despite record low interest rates, renewed affordability and other seemingly positive factors, the housing market still faces unprecedented headwinds that will prolong its recovery. An expression frequently used to explain the problem is the "fundamentals are not there." But what are the fundamentals implied by that rather non-descript and over used phrase? Do they include a couple of readily identifiable and measurable characteristics that are holding the housing market back or are the so called fundamentals a series or combination of characteristics that make measurement more complex. Our view is the latter. While one or two characteristics may not have a profound effect on the broader housing market, considered together, the fundamentals add up to a serious impact. Here is our view of what those fundamentals are and how they are impacting housing recovery.

Inventories are too high and are likely to remain that way for the foreseeable future. There are two types of inventory which impact or are at least destined to affect housing. They include both the visible inventory of homes which are capable of being identified and the so called "shadow inventory" which is inventory held by banks and loan servicers which is not yet offered for sale.

The biggest component of visible inventory is existing homes offered for sale by members of the National Association of Realtors. At the end of October, that inventory stood 3.86 million homes. That was down fractionally from a month earlier but still a 10.5 month supply at the current sales pace. Add to that about 242,000 new homes offered for sale by builders plus those offered for sale by owners and the visible inventory total grows to about 4.2 million homes. That is roughly where it has been for several months. Note that the inventory of new homes for sale is exceptionally small. Nevertheless, it still represents an 8.6 month supply at the current sales pace. Builders continue to have difficulty competing with exceptionally low priced existing homes.

CoreLogic, a business analytics firm, reported in late November that the shadow inventory of homes increased from 1.9 million to 2.1 million units in August, the most recent month for which data are available. CoreLogic measures shadow inventory as loans where payments are 90 or more days past due; plus those in foreclosure plus those which have been foreclosed upon but are not yet offered for sale. That puts visible and shadow inventory together at about 6.3 million units which is well over a year's supply and perhaps as much as two years depending upon how shadow inventory moves through the system. Shadow inventory is volatile and the forecasting risk inherent in both measuring it and tracking its movement is huge. For example, the volume of assets moving from foreclosure to bank owned status declined 35% in October. That is a direct result of well publicized foreclosure processing problems. These and previous moratoria have lengthened the timeline and have introduced even more uncertainty into the process.

In our view, the shadow inventory may be the biggest single threat to housing recovery. If banks quickly return large numbers of houses to an already over-supplied and fragile market, prices will al-most certainly decline further resulting in even more foreclosures and the cycle repeats itself.

House prices remain unstable. While the free fall has ended (barring additional unforeseen economic shock) prices are still fluctuating within a narrow range. Nationally, the median existing home price in October was $171,100 little changed from both a month and a year earlier ($171,500 and $172,000 respectively).

The S&P/Case-Shiller Index for the third quarter of 2010 was released on November 30th. Composite indices for both 10 and 20 cities are published quarterly. The 20 city index showed prices down 1.5% from the third quarter of 2009 and down 2.0% from last quarter. An important conclusion from the index is that U.S. house prices have generally returned to 2003 levels.

Foreclosures continue largely unabated and the pipeline continues to grow. The Federal Reserve's forecast of foreclosures remains grim for the next few years. They expect about 2.25 mil-lion foreclosures both this year and next plus another 2.0 million in 2012. Foreclosures soared from about 1.0 million in 2006, the year home prices peaked, to about 2.8 million in 2009 when prices likely hit a cycle trough. Foreclosure inventories are now over seven times higher than long term historical averages and are continuing to rise. Moreover, as foreclosure activity increases, more six and 12 month delinquent loans are moving into foreclosure and the extremely delinquent category of more than 12 months continues to both grow and age. Payments have not been made in more than a year on one-third of all loans 90 or more days delinquent. Moreover, of loans that are more than two years delinquent, 18% have still not entered foreclosure. The reasons for such delays are not totally clear.

The continuing pace of new foreclosure filings is also alarming. According to Realtytrac data, about 17% of filings in October were new filings as opposed to subsequent filings such as auction notices, etc. New filings surge to over one-third in Florida statewide and over 50% by the hardest hit Florida counties.

Foreclosure Crisis extends the timeline and introduces even more uncertainty into the housing market at a time when uncertainty is least needed. The crisis involves signing documents electronically (robo-signing) or without proper oversight or diligence, improper or no verification of who actually owns the property and who has the right to foreclose and much more. There is more than mere anecdotal evidence of fraudulent paperwork and improper activities but it remains to be seen how big the problem really is. Some view it as little more than a paperwork problem confined to a small number of banks, servicers and law firms. Others see it as a far more systemic problem that could derail or at least slow housing recovery and perhaps even upend recovery of the broader economy. Some also view it as a political grand-standing opportunity.

The Congressional Oversight Panel that monitors the government's bailout program issued a warning not to underestimate the reach of the foreclosure crisis. The panel also echoed the pre-dominant view that the true extent of the problem remains to be seen.

There is widespread concern that Congress could enact more legislation that may seem consumer-friendly on the surface but could have a profoundly negative effect on the mortgage industry and therefore consumers as a whole. For example, some lawmakers are attempting to resurrect so-called "cram down" legislation that would give bankruptcy judges the power to reduce mortgage amounts. Others are pushing for some big banks to spin off their mortgage servicing functions alleging conflict of interest. Still others advocate even more aggressive mortgage regulation at the federal level in addition to what is already being created under the Dodd Frank and SAFE Acts. Whatever the depth or the out-come of the problem, the result is clearly a blow to a fragile housing market.

Strategic Foreclosures continue to mount as a growing number of homeowners discover they are so far underwater on their home loans that they believe they will never recover. Strategic defaulters, as they've come to be known, may have the capacity to repay but choose not to. Some studies suggest that strategic defaults may account for as many as 25% to 35% of all defaults with no end in sight. They are driven by a very large percentage of underwater home loans.

Employment is a fundamental which is currently negative for housing and recovery of the broader economy. The Bureau of Labor Statistics (BLS) announced last Friday that the economy created a mere 50,000 private sector jobs and lost 11,000 local government jobs for a net gain of 39,000 jobs and an unemployment rate that now hovers just under 10% at 9.8%. The cycle peak was 10.1% in April. Currently the ranks of the unemployed number 15.1 million, a number equal to the recession peak. More disturbing is that fully 6.3 million people have been unemployed long-term which is defined by the BLS as 27 weeks or more. Additionally, most of the Great Recession job losses have been permanent rather than cyclical and are therefore not likely to be replaced.

The hardest hit sector has been construction. Manufacturing employment growth has been flat for decades and construction be-came, in a sense, the new manufacturing. It was employment for a very large number of both skilled and unskilled workers in their prime working years of 18-43. Now the construction sector has col-lapsed and nearly one million jobs have been lost. The outlook for a rebound is not good. Construction jobs were, in large part, driven by the housing bubble. As much of the housing growth was artificial and resulted in widespread overbuilding, much of the construction employment too was bubble driven and jobs won't be replaced.

The U.S. had a lost decade for jobs in the 2000s. Following the relatively minor recession in 2001, it took over four years to regain lost jobs. During that time, wages stagnated and The Great Recession struck. Wage growth remains flat and the period following The Great Recession is shaping up to be a jobless recovery as well.

Job growth is not keeping pace with a growing labor force or a rising population. Indeed, there were only 400,000 Americans employed at the end of 2009 than were employed a decade early in 1999. Nevertheless, population grew by 30 million during the decade. The U.S. economy actually lost jobs on a percentage basis during the 2000s after having gained jobs every decade since the Great Depression of the 1930s.

Roughly eight million jobs were lost during the recent recession. That left a very deep hole for the economy to climb out of and jobs are not being created anywhere near fast enough to even begin the long climb.

The nation's unemployment rate has averaged 5.7% since 1948—some 62 years. Given the structural employment changes that have occurred in the last three years, it is likely that the "new nor-mal" will be higher in the range of 6.5%–7.5% after recovery.

Unemployment, the fear of unemployment, the structural changes in employment, slow growth prospects and the likelihood of continuing stagnant wage growth combine to create a huge obstacle for potential home purchasers. These fundamentals combined will not support growth of housing either in terms of volume of home purchases and price increases r several years.

Underwriting standards are frequently cited as a reason for impaired housing growth. The reality is that underwriting standards have returned to those prevalent in an earlier time when there were no exotic mortgage instruments, cash down payments were required and a clear and convincing assessment of a borrower's ability and willingness to repay the loan were underwriting norms. Today, more borrowers are credit impaired than ever before and household wealth has declined dramatically from the heady days of the middle of last decade when people saw themselves as rock stars or oligarchs able to afford their every wish—at least on paper.

These are a few of the fundamentals we often allude to. When combined, they paint a short and mid-term housing picture that looks bleak.

FLORIDA EMPLOYMENT REMAINS WEAK. JOB LOSSES CONTINUE TO RISE

First the good news. Total employment rose in most Central and South Florida counties in November as compared to a year earlier. The sector gaining the most jobs year over year was private education and healthcare which grew by 28,900 jobs or 2.7%. Leisure and hospitality gained 21,400 jobs (+2.4%). The service sector saw job increases too with professional and business services growing by 10,100 jobs (+ 2.7%) and other services which gained 13,600 jobs (+4.4%).

Now the bad news. Florida lost 55,000 jobs over the year. Moreover, most Central and South Florida counties also lost jobs in November when compared with the previous month. The sectors losing the most jobs included the *usual suspects*. Construction lost 12,900 jobs (-3.6%) while manufacturing was down 9,200 jobs or about 3.0%. Financial activities declined 8,100 jobs (3.0%) while total government declined by 7,900 jobs and information services was down 5,500 jobs. Government and information job losses were less than one-percent each.

While most Central and South Florida counties experienced an increase in jobs year over year, three did not. Broward County was the biggest loser with a loss of 12,381 jobs. Brevard County in Central Florida (the nation's Space Coast) lost 4,890 jobs while Martin County on the state's Treasure Coast lost 568 jobs.

Florida's unemployment rate rose to12.2% in November (12.0% seasonally adjusted). All Central and South Florida counties remain solidly in double digits with St. Lucie County leading the way at 15.2%; Indian River at 14.5% and, Miami-Dade at 13%.

2011
RECOVERY AT GLACIAL SPEED

The year 2011 was remarkable by extraordinary uncertainty and inactivity in many sectors of the economy. Banks and other financial institutions spent the year cleaning up the mess left by the recession as well as extraordinary numbers of problem loans and foreclosures. Lending activity was nil. Businesses worried about the onslaught of new regulation, specifically the Dodd-Frank Act which was signed into law in mid-2010. It required some 243 new regulations. Critics (including the author) asserted the Act was designed to cure the problem just passed

Consumers and businesses worried about the possibility of a second recession as U.S. incomes fell, consumer sentiment declined and consumers were generally pessimistic about the economy. Consumers also feared for their jobs as they watched the extraordinary number of job losses accompanied by slow recovery.

Housing markets were still in disarray and struggled to find equilibrium. While prices rose and fell intermittently, foreclosures were still exerting a dampening effect on the housing market. Inventories of existing homes for sale remained low as sellers were still reluctant to enter the market. At the same time, investors were the largest cash purchasers. They were purchasing at the low end of the range with the expectation of flipping houses for a profit as prices rose. By doing so, they siphoned off market share from potential first time home buyers.

Commercial real estate markets were still reeling from the recession. Banks were still resolving countless problem commercial real estate assets; something they would continue to do for another year. Opportunities for new loans were virtually non-existent due to a fundamental absence of demand. The only apparent loan demand was to refinance five year old faux demand which had already led to extraordinary loan losses. Moreover, new projects were not yet economically feasible. That is, they would cost more to create than they would be worth when finished.

While the recession was officially over, the economy still appeared locked in a downturn with recovery advancing, then retreating; all at glacial speed.

JUNE 23, 2011

HOUSING MARKET STILL IN DISARRAY

Slowing economic recovery is weighing heavily on housing. According to the National Association of Realtors, sales of existing single family homes declined 3.2% to 4.24 million units in May on an annualized basis. That is 15.4% below sales volume a year earlier. The comparison, however, is flawed as sales surged a year ago as purchasers were rushing to complete sales under the federal government's second home buyer tax credit program. After expiration of the tax credit programs, sales collapsed again and have been subdued ever since.

The median existing single family home price was $166,700 in May. That is down 4.5% from a year earlier but up slightly from a month earlier when it was $161,100. Sales of all housing types (single family, condominium and co-op) declined 3.8% to 4.81 million units from a downwardly revised 5.0 million units in April. The median existing home price was $166,500 and it too was down 4.6% from a year earlier.

Distressed sales accounted for about 37% of all sales. That is up from 31% a year earlier. On average distressed homes typically sold for at least 20% less than an otherwise comparable non-distressed transaction. The gap is clearly narrowing as more distressed properties come to market. Buyers are migrating toward the distressed transactions due to markedly lower prices. As little as 12-18 months ago, however, buyers were faced with the decision of paying more in a near immediate non-distressed transaction or paying less but perhaps waiting weeks or months for a short sale to be approved by a financial institution or clear the legal hurdles of foreclosure.

All cash transactions accounted for about 31% of existing home sales in May. Most purchases were made by investors (20%). First time home buyers purchased 35% of the existing homes in May.

Due to significantly reduced prices and continuing record low interest rates, affordability is at a 40 year high. That, in itself, would be expected to pull prospective buyers into the market, however, weak employment, continuing foreclosures with a fear prices may decline further and low consumer confidence are keeping many buyers firmly anchored on the sidelines.

Declining sales were geographically broad based in May. Sales in the Northeast fared the best with only a 2.5% decline year over year and a median price of $241,500 which was up 6.1% from a year ago. Sales in the Midwest declined 6.4% and realized a median price of $136,400 which was 8.5% less than a year ago. The South fell 5.1% and witnessed a median price of $149,200 which was 3.1% less than a year ago.

Total existing home inventory fell fractionally in May to 3.72 million units which, at the current sales pace is an approximate 9.3 month supply. Inventory has remained relatively constant in the mid three million unit range since 2008. Suggesting not much progress is being made clearing inventory.

Similar to the Realtor data, S&P Case-Shiller 10 and 20 city existing home price indices showed that prices declined nationwide by 4.2% in the first quarter. This follows a decline of 3.6% in the fourth quarter of 2010. The current reading represents an annual decline of 5.1% and represents a new recession low. Twelve of the 20 cities surveyed and the composite index posted new lows in March. Those cities were Atlanta, Charlotte, Chicago, Cleveland, Detroit, Las Vegas, Miami, Minneapolis, New York, Portland (Oregon) and Tampa. Eleven of the 20 cities have now recorded eight or more months of steady price decline. These data confirm that the nation is, indeed, in the throes of a double dip housing recession with median existing home prices down 33% nationally from their peak in 2007. Median prices are now back to their 2002 levels essentially wiping out a decade's worth of gains. A troubling comparison is that the house price decline has now exceeded that experienced during the Great Depression of the 1930s when the decline was 31%. After the depression, it took median home prices 19 years to recover.

New Home Sales data issued jointly by the Census Bureau and U.S. Department of Housing and Urban Development show new home sales (sales by builders) in May at a seasonally adjusted annual rate of 319,000 units. That is down from the revised April rate of 326,000 units but above the year ago total of 281,000 units. The median price of homes sold was $222,600, down three percent from a year ago but substantially above the median existing home price of $166,700. Existing homes have, of course, been battered by the foreclosure crisis. There are also an estimated 166,000 new homes offered for sale nationally which, at the current sales pace, is an approximate 6.2 month supply. The median time necessary to sell a new home at the end of May was 9.2 months. That is down from 14 months in 2009 but up from 7.9 months in 2010.

Builders continue to have difficulty competing with much lower priced existing homes especially as prices continue to decline and may continue to do so into the short term future. The pace of builder sales is at a near record slow rate.

The National Association of Home Builders (NAHB) publishes an index which contains three components: single family sales; single family sales expected within six months and prospective buyer traffic. All three components declined in the most recent survey. The composite index declined by three percentage points from June 2010. The component for single family sales expected in six months fell the most at four points. That component is down seven points year over year. Geographical sub-indices were mixed. The index for the Northeast U.S. rose by two points while the three other sub-indices (South, West and Midwest) all declined modestly.

The composite index has now fallen to its recent low point reached last September and is only slightly above its all-time low reached in January 2009 when the nation's economy was near its worst. House prices, both new and existing, have been declining for more than three years and many U.S. metros have seen prices fall below their natural rate of growth. In other words, median prices are currently below what they might have been had the bubble and its subsequent burst not occurred and wreaked so much economic havoc.

Improvement in housing fundamentals will likely not be enough to restore confidence in the housing market. Full recovery will also require improvement in consumer credit worthiness which deteriorated dramatically during The Great Recession. Renewed credit worthiness will also require significant labor market improvement which has been modest to date.

Foreclosures. New foreclosure filings fell nine-percent in April after rising significantly in March. According to Realty-Trac, there were 214,927 notices filed in May. This includes initial notice of default, auction and bank repossessions. New filings have steadily fallen for the last 16 months. The May figure is down 33% from a year earlier and shows that one in every 605 U.S. properties received some sort of foreclosure filing in May.

The declining number of foreclosures is not the result of a reversal of fortune in the marketplace but rather a slowdown across all stages of the foreclosure process. There continue to be serious procedural bottlenecks at nearly every step. These hurdles have nearly doubled the time necessary to move a foreclosure from the initial notice of default to REO.

Currently the time period is around 400 days. A year ago it was 340 days and four years ago it was 151 days. Even with fewer foreclosures, the new supply of real estate owned (REO) is greater than the number of units being sold each month and REO remains at a near record high level. Foreclosures at all stages are likely to rise again as the hurdles created by last year's robo-signing fiasco are cleared and foreclosures once again move through the system in a more orderly and timely fashion.

The Mortgage Bankers Association weekly survey showed its three indices (composite, purchase and refinance) down for the week and continuing what has been an erratic pattern of loan applications. The composite index, which covers both purchase and refinance volume, was down 5.9% over the week but more significantly, down 11.5% from a year ago. The refinance index was down 7.2% over the week but down 16.6% year over year. The purchase index was down 2.3% for the week but up 4.3% from a year ago.

The Federal Housing Administration (FHA) reported that it too is feeling the pain of the housing crisis and recession. The number of FHA-backed loans declined 27% in February as compared to January. Newly originated FHA loans totaled roughly $16.8 billion during February continuing a downward trend that has been apparent since late last year. The agency guaranteed $8.3 billion in purchase money loans in February, down from $11.4 billion the previous month.

Housing Outlook. The housing outlook remains bleak for several fundamental reasons. First, inventories are too high. The visible existing home inventory, as estimated by the National Association of Realtors, stood at 3.72 million units which is an approximate 9.3 month supply. Add to that, 166,000 new homes for sale by builders for a 6.2 month supply and visible inventory totals some 3.88 million units.

Business analytics firm CoreLogic tracks shadow inventory which the firm defines as the total number of distressed properties not currently listed for sale plus those seriously delinquent (90+ days) plus those in foreclosure or REO. According to CoreLogic's June 2011 report, that total is about 1.7 million units. While the total has declined, it is still an estimated five month supply. While shadow inventory can be difficult to measure and is arguably the riskiest forecast component, it is probable that visible plus shadow inventories could total at least 12 months.

Second, prices continue to decline and there is no leading indicator to suggest that trend will change over the short term. In our view, an additional five to 10 percent declines is probable and an even greater decline remains a possibility.

CoreLogic estimates that there are some two-million loans that ae negative by at least 50% or $150,000. That number will almost certainly grow as prices continue to fall.

Third, REO inventory is at near record high levels and is growing faster than sales from inventory are occurring. Additionally, current hurdles in foreclosure processing will prolong housing recovery for another year.

Fourth, the employment situation is not good and unemployment remains high by historical levels. Given all the headwind, housing recovery is not likely before 2014 or 2015.

WHAT HAPPENED? THE SAD STATE OF HOUSING

Housing remains seriously impaired. Indeed, it has been for five years now. Today, it is the epicenter of U.S. economic woes and remains a serious drag on recovery of the broader economy. Moreover, the collateral damage from the housing collapse has been enormous and widespread. Its affects are being felt far beyond just housing and allied industries such as construction and finance. Its tentacles reach wide and deep into numerous employment sectors as well as into state and municipal government. The following is a by the numbers look at what has happened over the last few years. We'll also look at how deep the hole is and how long it might take to climb out.

Most recessions begin with some sort of economic shock such as monetary policy gone awry, oil crises, the 9-11 terrorist attacks and more. Over time recessions tend to migrate to the housing sector. This time was different in the sense that The Great Recession began with a housing crisis and the contagion spread from there to numerous other sectors. It's effect was amplified by unintended consequences of innovation in mortgage finance and securitization which outpaced both regulation and risk management and to cause what began as over building in the U.S. to spin out of control and become a global housing and financial crisis without precedent. Recovery will also be long and difficult. As centuries of economic history have shown, recessions that include both housing and financial crises tend to be more severe and have both longer and more erratic recoveries.

Not in recent history has our nation experienced a housing recession as broad, deep and severe as the one we've experienced for the last five years. On a national level, median existing home prices have declined 33% from their 2006 peak. That is a steeper decline than the 31% experienced over 70 years ago during The Great Depression of the 1930s. Following that decline, it took housing some 19 years—nearly two decades—to recover. The story is worse in Florida and other states (Nevada, Arizona, California) where new construction was unconstrained for half a decade and defied the basic economic principal of supply and demand. Since then, prices in Florida, for example, have declined nearly 53% from peak to trough (2006 through February 2011). Several Metropolitan Statistical Areas in Florida, such as Miami-Dade, Ft. Pierce-Port St. Lucie and Melbourne-Titusville-Palm Bay have experienced declines from 62% to 65% and there is likely more decline to come.

Looking back at the heady days of the 2000s, existing home sales rose to 5.25 million in 2001; 6.175 million in 2003 and a record 8.357 in 2005. By May 2011, however, sales volume had slipped to 4.24 million units at a seasonally adjusted annual rate. That's a decline of just under 50%. Similarly, there were 908,000 new homes sold in 2001; 1.086 million in 2003 and 1.283 million in 2005 By the end of 2010, new home sales volume had plunged to a mere 323,000 units; a decline of nearly 75% from the 2005 peak.

During the bubble years, real estate related employment flourished. Builders, sales agents, mortgage brokers, architects, engineers, designers, title agents, real estate attorneys and real estate appraisers were making extraordinary amounts of money, far beyond what they had ever made before and far in excess of what was typical from an historic perspective. It was a product of supply and demand. As we now know, however, much of the demand was not real but rather bubble inflated and destined to lose air. Take the appraisal industry, for example. During the run up in house prices and volumes, appraisal fees rose and turnaround times were extended. Perceiving an opportunity, many persons migrated to the industry and met the relatively modest licensing requirements. The economic principal that *excess profit breeds ruinous competition* showed itself throughout the housing industry and the appraisal industry was not immune.

In August 2007, the sub-prime bubble imploded. Sub-prime lending volume grew from $160 billion in 2001 to $310 billion in 2003 and peaked at $625 billion in 2005. After the collapse, volume declined 70% to $191 billion in 2007 and to around $20 billion in 2008. The subprime collapse was soon followed by the housing crash. The nation's economy limped along for a year before the near collapse of the U.S. financial system in September 2008. Global recession quickly followed.

Fast forward to mid 2011. The Great Recession technically ended in mid-2009 according to the Business Cycle Dating Committee (BCDC) of the National Bureau of Economic Research (NBER). Perhaps a more practical way of looking at the mid 2009 recession end is that is when the broader economy hit its cyclical rock bottom. There has been modest but erratic improvement since then but improvement has been painfully slow and it is still not certain whether the broader economy will slip back into a new recession or not.

What has not improved, however, is the housing sector. Housing has entered a *double dip* downturn. Home prices continue to fall, albeit more modestly, but there are no leading indicators to suggest short term improvement.

The continued housing downturn has had a profoundly negative effect on sector related employment. For example, Bureau of Labor Statistics data show that construction employment peaked in April 2006 at around 3.5 million jobs following five years of rapid growth. The trend was downward from there falling by 1.22 million jobs or 65% through mid-2009. The contagion spread to non-residential construction then on to the remodeling sector as well and employment continues to decline but at a slower rate than at the depth of the recession.

The Mortgage Bankers Association (MBA) reported that mortgage industry employment declined by about 257,000 jobs between February 2006 and February 2011. Peak employment was 505,000 in February 2006. That is a decline of 51%. Employment is also 5.9% lower than it was a year ago with just 248,000 workers in the mortgage origination workforce. That is the lowest level since 1997. Indeed, employment declined by 12,000 jobs in just January and February of this year according to the Bureau of Labor Statistics.

Importantly, the MBA also released its revised mortgage volume forecast in May. The organization now expects new origination loan volume to reach about $1.07 trillion this year with refinance volume making up $511 billion, or roughly half the total. Next year, however, the MBA origination volume is forecast to decline to around $966 billion including just $236 billion in refinance volume. The 50% ratio of refinance volume therefore falls to only 25% of the total.

Appraiser employment is more difficult to gauge. While some appraiser job losses were accounted for in the mortgage sector, many appraisers are self-employed or independent contractors. They are not tracked in payroll employment numbers by the Bureau of Labor Statistics. The number of appraiser licensees can be used as a proxy. According to the Federal Registry of appraisers maintained by the Appraisal Sub Committee (ASC) of the Federal Financial Institutions Examination Council (FFIEC) there were 121,000 active licenses and certifications held by 98,500 individuals. By the end of 2010, the numbers had declined to 110,000 licenses and certificates held by some 90,500 individuals. We suspect that the federal registry numbers may understate the number of appraisers who have left the industry. Many continue to renew their licenses while not practicing, perhaps looking forward to a renewal of the heady days of the mid-2000s.

Today the appraisal industry, like all housing affiliated industries, is undergoing a cleansing process. These industries will look a lot different and the ranks of practitioners will be a lot thinner post-recession than they did pre-recession or even today.

To summarize, existing home sales volume is down roughly 50% from its peak. Prices are down nationally 33%. New home sales volume is down 75%. Construction employment is down 65% and mortgage industry employment is down 51% with short term future loan volume expected to decline even more. House prices have fallen to 2003 levels (Case-Shiller 20 City Index). House prices in Florida are at 2002 levels. In Phoenix they are at 2000 levels and Las Vegas is revisiting 1999 levels.

The current situation. The housing crisis has left a very deep hole to crawl out of. Despite near record low interest rates and affordability at a 40 year high, buyers are not moving off the sidelines in any significant numbers—at least not in the numbers necessary to achieve short term recovery. The problem is largely supply-side in nature. Simply stated there are too many homes at unusually low prices. That number is not decreasing. Instead it is increasing. By some accounts, there may be as many as 1.6 million too many homes. Additionally, homeownership is down to near 64% from its 69% peak; household formation is down; mortgage credit is not available to a large segment of the population and foreclosures continue largely unabated.

Negative equity is the leading cause of foreclosure. Today 22% of homeowners are in negative equity positions. That figure grows to 40% in the so-called sand states. Moreover, 37% of all recent existing home sales have been distressed sales and around 30% of all recent home sales occurred at a loss compared to the previous sale.

Looking forward at housing recovery. The current housing decline appears to be tracking the pattern witnessed in previous asset bubbles, their collapse and subsequent recovery. First comes a steep decline for several years. A brief but usually tenuous rally tends to follow. The rally is usually followed by several years of volume and price stagnation. The current downturn began in earnest in 2007. By 2010, there was modest rally and this year both volume and price were again in decline. We appear to be in that period of stagnation which will likely last at least through the current decade. Looking at historical asset bubbles, this pattern was evident in the DJIA (Dow Jones Industrial Average during and after The Great Depression when it took 35 years to recover. As previously described, it also took house prices 19 years to rebound after the Great Depression. In Japan, the Nikkei trades at less than a third of what it did 22 years ago.

What we are experiencing is clearly systemic in nature. It will change the way we look at real estate. It has changed the way we buy, sell and finance real estate. We are in a period of wide spread stagnation in both income and house prices as well as and sales volumes. That stagnation is likely to impact the real estate industry for years to come.

AUGUST 9, 2011

THE PROBABILITY OF SECOND DIP RECESSION

Questions many business people and professionals have about the probability of recession are first, whether it will happen and second, how do we estimate the probability before it occurs. Is the forecast just a wild guess, an educated guess or is there really some science behind it. The answer is the latter. While we never know precisely and we always face the possibility of unforeseen economic shock, there is a little science underlying the opinion. The following is a brief, but high level, explanation of both recession risk and forecasting methodology as well as how the Business Cycle Dating Committee (BCDC), the official arbiter of the nation's business cycle, works.

By definition, a forecast is a judgment about the probability of a future event happening or not happening based on currently known or reasonably knowable information. It is not an exercise in crystal ball gazing nor is it an absolute guarantee that the forecast will materialize. That is why most forecasts are expressed in probabilities.

The nation's business cycle (contraction versus expansion) is dated by the Business Cycle Dating Committee (BCDC) of the National Bureau of Economic Research (NBER). The committee is comprised of a group of academic economists at Princeton University. When dating the business cycle, the committee considers a wide variety of economic indicators over a reasonable period of time and from a broad geographical area. It is not as simple as often depicted such as a recession is measured by two quarters of negative GDP (Gross Domestic Product) or expansion by two quarters of growing GDP. While GDP is considered, so are financial market indicators, labor market conditions, housing, manufacturing, imports v. exports, confidence and much more. When the BCDC declared *The Great Recession* had ended in June 2009, they relied heavily on GDP and GDI (Gross Domestic Income). At that time, the average of GDP and GDI was 3.1% above its low in the second quarter of 2009 but 1.3% below its previous peak in December 2007 when the recession officially began.

Note too that the announcements were made a year or more after the recession began or ended. The beginning of *The Great Recession* was declared to be December 2007, however, the announcement came a year later in December 2008. Similarly, the recession technically ended in June 2009 but the announcement was not made until September 2010. The committee is not in the business of forecasting. Rather its sole responsibility is dating the business cycle and it would rather be right than fast. Economic data are also revised frequently and the committee will usually wait for revisions as it did before declaring the recession had ended in mid-2009.

In forecasting a change of direction in the business cycle before the BCDC acts, we too consider a wide variety of indicators and evaluate them individually. We also weigh each factor's relevance and potential impact. We then assign a probability weight to each indicator. Since a

---

WILLIAM L. PITTENGER   279

wide variety of indicators are considered, some tend to wash out others. We understand that any forecast can be rendered moot if unexpected or economic shock occurs. We saw that with the 9-11 terrorist attacks, the Japanese earthquake and tsunami earlier this year as well as other catastrophic events over the years. Sans unknown or unknowable events, however, it is possible to get reasonably close to a supportable and defensible forecast of change of direction in the business cycle including the probability of a short term dip into a new recession.

While the economy is very weak and perilously close to falling back into recession, our analysis suggests the probability is still less than one in two. Our probability judgment is around 35% to 40%. Nevertheless, only time—and the BCDC—will tell for sure.

SEPTEMBER 29, 2011

RECESSION RISK STILL RISING

A few weeks ago we wrote that the nation's economy had slowed to stall speed and was inching perilously close to another recession. At the time we forecast the probability of another recession at 35% to 40%; double our forecast six months earlier. Data released in late August and throughout September suggest that the probability has now risen to over 50%.

Recall that *The Great Recession* was officially declared over by the Business Cycle Dating Committee (BCDC) of the National Bureau of Economic Research (NBER) in June 2009. Perhaps a better description might be, that the second quarter of 2009 marked the lowest point in the cycle. Following that, there was modest expansion. Throughout the second half of 2009 and well into 2010 we witnessed modest growth in some sectors. In the first half of 2011, however, we saw softening in just about every sector of the economy and economic growth has been at stall speed ever since.

What we have seen appears consistent with the historical pattern witnessed during and after other severe asset bubbles such as we experienced with housing the middle of last decade. When the bubble bursts, as the housing bubble did in 2007, there are steep and broad based price declines. We saw that in housing from 2007 through 2009. Then comes a brief but tenuous rally. Again, we saw that too in 2010. Finally, there is more volume and price stagnation; something we experienced in the first half of 2011 and are likely to continue to experience going forward.

While the housing market has clearly fallen into a double dip recession, the broader economy has avoided that fate—at least for now. Nevertheless, the signs of recession are everywhere and the third quarter could very well mark the tipping point. There is little doubt that the nation remains locked in a deep and long downturn much like the U.S. experienced in the 1870s and 1930s; periods of deep recession following major asset bubbles.

The Bureau of Economic Analysis issued its third estimate of second quarter Gross Domestic Product (GDP) this morning. The report showed that the output of goods and services in the U.S. rose by 1.3% in the second quarter on an annualized basis. In the first quarter, real GDP increased by a mere 0.4%.

Looking behind the numbers, employment turned in a dismal performance in August with a zero net gain. Job growth has weakened significantly in recent months with payrolls expanding by an average of only 35,000 jobs per month over the last three months. That is far short of the number of new jobs needed for either a sustained recovery or to recover the millions of jobs lost during The Great Recession. Payrolls remain stagnant and continued weakness in employment is enough in itself to tip the scales toward recession.

Consumer and business confidence both remain low and pose a significant recession risk. Consumers consistently report that they fear for their jobs and they have little confidence in the economic future, As a result, they are reluctant to spend. At the same time, businesses remain reluctant to hire for fear they may need to lay off again in short order. Both consumer and business confidence is being negatively impacted by political wrangling, the inability of the government to come together, the debt crisis and more.

It all comes back to jobs. Personal consumption expenditures by consumers make up 70% of the economy. If consumers don't have jobs, they can't spend. Even if they are employed but fear for their jobs, they don't spend. That will trigger a slowdown in manufacturing and other key sectors. Recession looms large and, when the data are in, this quarter may tell the story.

2012
MORE GLACIAL SPEED RECOVERY

The year 2012 was widely regarded as a "growth recession." That is, GDP had turned positive yet economic recovery was still painfully slow and erratic.

The nation was dominated by the presidential election campaign throughout most of 2012; a campaign which ended with the re-election of President Obama to a second term.

There was a familiar theme throughout housing reports most of the year. That is, prices and volume had both contracted but the contraction was moderating. By the end of the year, however, it became clear that housing recovery was solidly in place.

APRIL 1, 2012

RESIDENTIAL SALES VOLUME AND PRICES DIP

Despite widespread wishful thinking about housing having reached a bottom, most recent housing reports suggest otherwise. Even as some broader economic indicators look modestly stronger, house prices have continued to decline and sales volumes have remained flat for the last few months. That apparent inconsistency speaks volumes about the severity of last decade's housing collapse and the length of time it is likely to take to reach bottom and begin a sustainable recovery. While we may be closing in on a bottom, it is still too early to call.

According to the highly regarded and widely watched **S&P Case-Shiller Home Price Indices**, existing home prices declined again in the three months ending in January 2012 as compared to the same period last year. The 10 city composite index declined 3.9% and the 20 city composite dropped 3.8%, not seasonally adjusted. On a seasonally adjusted basis, the decline in both indices was about 0.8% and represents the fifth consecutive month of decline. Home prices fell in eight of the 10 cities measured in the 10 city composite and 17 of 20 cities in the 20 city composite. Indeed, prices reached new post-crash lows in January. Atlanta, Chicago, Cleveland, Las Vegas, New York, Portland, Seattle and Tampa all tested new lows. Only three cities registered gains. Phoenix inched up 0.9% while Washington climbed 0.7% and Miami rose 0.6%.

Existing home prices, as measured in the 10 city composite, have now fallen to May 2003 levels and the 20 city composite has fallen to a level last seen in December 2002. From the 2006 peak, prices have fallen on average around 35% throughout the U.S. Peak to trough declines were much more severe in sunbelt areas such as Las Vegas which has declined 61%. Miami has declined 50.7% and San Diego has fallen 40.6%.

While Case-Shiller tracks repeat sales, the **Federal Housing Finance Agency (FHFA)**, tracks purchases and refinance data from Fannie Mae and Freddie Mac; the two government sponsored enterprises it regulates. The index therefore tracks only a portion of the housing market and is not nearly as broad as others such as Case-Shiller and the National Association of Realtors. Nevertheless, the FHFA purchase only index lends support to the Case-Shiller findings. The index was virtually unchanged in January as compared to December and down 0.8% year over year. The index has gained no appreciable ground since hitting its bottom in March 2011.

The **National Association of Realtors (NAR)**, whose data are relied upon heavily as a measure of existing home sales volume reported that existing home sales volume slipped modestly (0.9% month over month) to 4.59 million (annualized) units. Investors purchased about 23% of the homes in February, mostly for cash. All told, cash sales represented about 33% of February's sale volume. Foreclosures accounted for about 20% of February sales while short sales accounted for 14%. Investors and first time purchasers are competing aggressively at the lower price points in the market. The U.S. median home price, according to NAR, was $156,600; fractionally higher than a month ago; equal to a year ago but significantly less than 2009, 2010 and 2011.

Sales are running about four percent faster in the three months ending in February than the previous three months ending last November. Inventory increased again to a 6.4 month supply (from 6.0) although new listings appear to have driven part of that gain. Realtors and their customers generally anticipate an improved spring selling season.

The last few seasons have been remarkably disappointing. The pace of sales, averaged over the last three months remains about 36% below the historically fast pace registered in 2005 and is about on par with the pace registered in 1997.

The National Association of Realtors also publishes a **Pending Home Sales Index (PHS)**. The PHS index is based on a large national sample of contract signings reported by local and state Realtor associations. Since it is based on contracts and not yet closed transactions, it is forward looking and is reasonably representative of closed existing home sales one to three months into the future. An index of 100 is equal to the average level of contract activity in 2001; the first year of the survey.

The index was down in February, retreating 0.5% to 96.5. Nevertheless, it is still significantly higher than a year ago when it was 88.4, some 8.4% lower. The South and West United States delivered the highest readings (at or near 100) although both were down from year ago levels. The Northeast U.S. slipped fractionally but is still 18% higher than a year ago. Similarly, the Midwest regional index climbed modestly and is about 19% higher than a year ago. While the PHS index has been erratic, the general pattern is up. The PHS index together with other leading indicators seem to suggest that existing home sales volume is likely to remain flat for the next few months and very likely throughout the year.

The mediocre news in the existing housing sector was followed by similarly mediocre news in the new home sector. According to a joint report by the U.S. Census Bureau and the Department of Housing and Urban Development, new home sales were at a seasonally adjusted annual rate of just 313,000. This is marginally less than the revised January level but is significantly (11.4%) above the year ago level.

The median price at the end of February was $233,700 and the inventory of new homes offered for sale was about 150,000 for a 5.8 month supply at the current sales pace. Builders continue to have a difficult time competing with much lower priced existing homes where the median price was $156,600. New housing development is generally not economically feasible today meaning that sales prices are often less that the cost to build. Until that metric changes and development becomes economically feasible, new home development and sales will bounce along at near record low rates.

Foreclosures continue to play adversely into housing recovery. According to real estate analytics firm, **CoreLogic**, 22.8% of all residential properties encumbered by a mortgage were worth less than the mortgage amount. That is fourth quarter 2011 (most recent) data and represents some 11.1 million properties. That number is up from 10.7 million a quarter earlier. Another 2.5 million properties are at what CoreLogic refers to as near negative equity.

These borrowers have less than five percent equity and it would take very little to push them into negative territory. All told, negative and near negative equity totals some 27.8% of all mortgages for a dollar total of $2.8 trillion. That figure is alarming as it is back to the same level as it was in the third quarter of 2009.

At the state level, Nevada posted the worst negative equity rate at 61% followed by Arizona at 48% and Florida at 44%. Low end homes in all areas fared the worst. The 10 states with the most underwater mortgages (ranked worst to best) are: Nevada, Arizona, Florida, Michigan, Georgia, California, Idaho, Maryland, Ohio and Virginia.

The Office of Comptroller of the Currency (OCC) issues a quarterly Mortgage Metrics Report which describes the performance of residential first mortgages serviced by large national and federal savings banks. The fourth quarter 2011 survey covers 31.4 million first lien loans worth $5.4 trillion. That is about 60% of all U.S. first lien loans. The fourth quarter report was issued in late March and showed that overall mortgage performance remained relatively stable. There was also measurable improvement on a year ago basis. Still, there is a very large number of residential loans wending their way through the loss mitigation process. At year end 2011, nearly 27.6 million mortgages or almost

88% of the loans covered by the survey were current and performing.

Outlook. At a time when many broader economic indicators are improving modestly, it is unusual to see housing struggling so severely. Robert Shiller, of Case-Shiller fame recently opined that the U.S. could experience a Japanese-style housing slump that could last for years. *"I'm worried that home prices have been declining now for about five years. There's a lot of downward momentum"* with year over year and even month over month declines.

APRIL 25, 2012

CMBS DELINQUENCIES

Commercial mortgage backed securities are the product of commercial real estate loans which are bundled into securities and sold to investors. Like residential mortgage backed securities, they have proven to be a double edged sword. While they made the commercial mortgage market more liquid, like their residential siblings, many were packaged, sold in whole or in tranches—some with questionable ratings and due diligence. Unlike most of their residential siblings, however, most loans originated for sale were done so on a non-recourse basis meaning that in the event of default one could only look to the property for repayment and not the borrowing entity. Given that characteristic, commercial mortgage backed securities have typically experienced a higher default rate than loans secured by comparable properties that were intended to be held by banks and not sliced, diced and sold far and wide in the form of securities.

Delinquencies have historically been very low hovering around one-percent or less since this financing vehicle became popular in the 1990s. Indeed, delinquencies were exceedingly low most of last decade before beginning to surge with the collapse of the commercial real estate market coincident with The Great Recession in mid 2008. Note that CRE prices peaked in December 2007.

At the end of February 2012 (most recent data available, the 60 day plus delinquency rate for CMBS loans was 9.39% according to Moody's Investor Services. That rate is up fractionally from 9.3% in January. As of February, the 60 day plus delinquency rate has been above 9%

for 14 consecutive months and has hovered in the same approximate range since mid 2011. Outstanding delinquent loans increased about $0.2 Billion to $53.8 Billion. Newly delinquent loans increased $2.9 Billion over the month, exceeding the $2.7 Billion that were resolved. Outstandings have been declining for eight consecutive months. In terms of vintage (year of origination), delinquencies for CMBS issued in 2003, 2005 and 2008 fell with 2008 falling some 10 basis points. All other vintage years experienced higher delinquencies led by 2002 with more than a 100 basis point increase. Until recently. "late cycle" loans originated in 2007 as the market was already crashing led the way.

MAY 5, 2012

A FAMILIAR REFRAIN. HOUSE PRICES DECLINE ... BUT

It's been a data rich couple of weeks for the housing sector with monthly reports on existing housing from Case-Shiller, the National Association of Realtors, the Federal Housing Finance Agency, HUD, Census Bureau and more. Most of the reports had an all too familiar theme: house prices and volumes declined again compared to year ago levels but the rate of decline has moderated over the last few months.

Case-Shiller survey results for the three months ending in February 2012 showed that on a year ago basis (that is, February 2012 compared to February 2011), median existing home prices continued their modest decline. The 10 city composite decline was 3.6% while the 20 city composite decline was 3.5% over the same period. In both cases, declines have moderated, albeit fractionally. The cities (metros) included in each index are shown at the left. Results are not seasonally adjusted. The Case-Shiller indices are unique in that they are based on repeat sales.

Though house prices are still well-below year-ago levels, the rate of decline is slowing. Price declines for the three month period ending in February were generally milder than they were over the three month period ending in January. Similarly, month-to-month changes are improving, posting gains in the 10 and 20-city composites for the first time in almost a year. Indeed, home sales have been trending higher

---

since the middle of 2011 although the gains have been modest and not widespread.

Although conditions may be improving, the outlook still remains bleak. For example, Miami, has been showing significant monthly gains since October. Nevertheless, house prices remain at just half of their previous peak. Thus, even if prices surge upward (and there is no leading indicator to suggest that is likely) it will take years or even decades for home prices values to pass their pre-bust levels. Remember that after The Great Depression of the 1930s, the event that was arguably the most similar to the recent recession, it took 19 years for house prices to recover.

The current outlook is for more but relatively modest price declines. The recent settlement by the states attorneys general with mortgage servicers will likely lead to a reacceleration in foreclosure processing. Even though the foreclosure inventory contracted over the past year, according to RealtyTrac, it is likely to rise again before it heads down for good. Prices will therefore dip through the end of the year and more widespread price appreciation is still not likely before 2013.

On the heels of the Case-Shiller report, the **National Association of Realtors** released its survey of existing home sales volume and median price for March. Sales of all types of residential property single family, condo, cooperatives and townhouses) declined 2.6% to a seasonally adjusted annual level of 4.48 million units. That is down from an upwardly revised 4.60 million units in February but still 5.2% above the year ago level of 4.26 million units. Prices have now shown nine months of modest year over year sales volume increases.

Total housing inventory declined 1.3% to 2.37 million units which is a 6.3 month supply at the current sales pace. Listing inventory is 21.8% less than a year ago and substantially below the 4.04 million listings at the peak in July 2007. Anecdotal evidence from the western United States and to a lesser extent in South Florida suggests there may actually be too few available properties as compared to the level of buyer interest. How wide spread that might be and whether diminished sales volume is a product of too little supply or too little demand or both remains to be seen. The answer should come into sharper focus over the next few months. What is clear, however, is that a fully self-sustaining and widespread housing recovery is still a long way off.

The national median home price for all housing types according to NAR was $163,800 in March. That is up 2.5% from a year ago. Distressed properties, primarily foreclosed properties or short sales accounted for 29% of all March transactions. The breakdown was 18% foreclosure and 11% short sales.

Foreclosures sold at a calculated "discount" of about 19% while the discount for short sales was 11%. The gap has narrowed substantially from a year ago when it was about 40%. The term "discount" may be a misnomer. As we wrote nearly two years ago, the difference between foreclosure or short sale prices and otherwise similar but non-distressed properties appeared linked to two fundamental factors. First distressed assets typically had some degree of deferred maintenance. Second, the time necessary for these assets to work their way through servicer approval process was extraordinarily long. Buyers were faced with the delay plus deferred maintenance or seemingly paying more to avoid the time, risk, cost and aggravation. Today, as properties are wending their way through the system much more quickly and efficiently, the gap is narrowing. Combined with continuing declines, prices are migrating to the lower end of the range.

All cash purchases accounted for about 32% of all existing home transactions; down from 35% a year ago. Cash purchases were dominated by investors at about 21% of the transactions. Again, that is down fractionally from a year ago when it was 22%.

In the single family detached sector sales declined by 2.5% to a seasonally adjusted annual rate (SAAR) of 3.97 million units. Single family detached homes accounted for nearly 90% of all existing residential transactions. The median price was $163,600 which was up 1.9% from year ago levels. Condo and co-op sales fell 3.8% to 510,000 units (SAAR). The median condo price was $165,200 which was 7.1% above a year ago.

The National Association of Realtors also publishes a **Pending Home Sales Index (PHS)**. The PHS index is based on a large national sample of contract signings reported by local and state Realtor associations. Since it is based on contracts and not yet closed transactions, it is forward looking and is reasonably representative of what might be closed existing home sales one to three months in the future. An index of 100 is equal to the average level of contract activity in 2001; the first year of the survey.

The index rose 4.1% in March. The decline reported a month earlier was revised to a 0.4% increase. The pending home sale index is now 12.8% above the March 2011 level which bodes well for the number of future closed sales in May and June. Nevertheless, it is important to remember that these results may overstate housing performance. Still tight credit and lingering low credit scores will create some degree of contract failure which is difficult to gauge.

The Federal Housing Finance Agency (FHFA) released its purchase only index results for February and exceeded expectations on the up side. The index increased 0.3% in February and is now up 0.4% year over year.

The index is now down 19.4% from its April 2007 and is roughly equivalent to its level in January 2004.

The FHFA is the regulator and conservator for mortgage giants Fannie Mae and Freddie Mac. While the results are encouraging, as they show the first increase since 2007, they may also overstate the health of the broader U.S. residential real estate market. Unlike Case-Shiller, National Association of Realtors and other broader indices, the FHFA lacks complete coverage. Notably missing are data on cash transactions, jumbo loans and agency loans such as FHA ands VA. Cash transactions tend to put downward pressure on prices especially in high foreclosure states.

Following the somewhat mediocre existing housing reports, **HUD and the Census Bureau** delivered an equally mediocre report on new home sales for the month of March. Sales of new homes fell 7.1% from the February level to an *annual level* of 328,000 units. At the same time the Census Bureau revised February sales up significantly. February sales were revised up 13% while January sales rose three percent. As a result of the revisions first quarter new home sales advanced by an annualized 17% from the fourth quarter. At the same time months of supply ticked up to 5.3. Despite the increases, the pace of new home sales at 328,000 annualized is only slightly above its record low. The median price was $237,600 which is making it difficult for builders to compete with significantly lower priced existing homes, particularly those that have been foreclosed upon.

Despite mixed reports as well as some improvement in the broader economy, **The Outlook** for housing is still not good. The hole created by extraordinary overbuilding and the subsequent housing collapse is simply too deep to climb out of quickly. Yale economics professor, Robert Shiller, co-creator of the survey that bears his name told Reuters News Service recently that housing may take a generation to rebound given the weak labor market and consumer unease which are outweighing record low interest rates and record high affordability. The Wall Street Journal also reported that a *"full-fledged recovery is still years off for many markets."*

MAY 17, 2012

ARE WE THERE YET? HAVE WE REACHED A DEFINITIVE HOUSING BOTTOM?

Opinions are mixed about whether or not the housing market has found a definitive bottom. Buyers, sellers, agents and builders anxiously await some sort of "all clear" signal to be sounded before they jump back into the market. News stories are replete with wishful thinking and hopes that the bottom is here and the housing market will soon change direction; pent up demand will be unleashed and both sales volume and prices will surge upward. Whether the market has reached a definitive bottom is still arguable. While a bottom would lead to more consumer confidence and move some off the sidelines, the bigger story is what happens next and what the short and mid term future might hold for housing.

After five years of unprecedented housing distress, affordability is now at an historic high due to record low mortgage interest rates and existing home prices that have retreated to levels last seen early last decade. In many areas, inventories too have fallen as much as 40% to roughly 2005 levels. In some areas that has actually led to shortages which have even pushed prices up and generated multiple offers on a single property, something we have not seen since before the housing collapse. This is especially true in California in the under $500,000 category although there are similar anecdotes from South Florida and other areas.

The arguments for and against a bottom are both predictable and as different as night and day. Brokers, builders and lenders are warming up and poised at the starting gate as if waiting for the bell. Consumers aren't so sure and many, but surely not all, economists are doubtful. Yale University Professor and Economist, Robert Shiller, who is also co-creator of the Case-Shiller Home Price Indices, which bear his name recently commented that the U.S. could face a Japanese-style housing slump that could last for years. *"I'm worried that home prices have been declining now for about five years. There's a lot of downward momentum with year over year and even month over month declines."* Economist Gary Shilling added in the Wall Street Journal that house prices could still decline by 20% or more. He offered that it would take another 22% decline to return median home prices to the trend identified by Robert Shiller which stretched back to 1890 and which prevailed until last decade's housing bubble. Shilling points out that the problem is inventory driven and it will likely take four years to work off the excess, during which time home price growth will be constrained.

The housing market faces some remarkably strong headwinds in the form of foreclosures, shadow inventory, diminished home equity, employment, stagnating wages, financing availability and more. Although some positive things have happened and while the broader economy has shown modest signs of recovery, the negatives affecting short term housing recovery outweigh the positives.

Consider foreclosures and shadow inventory. While foreclosures were down 17% year over year in March (according to RealtyTrac), they still total nearly 200,000 loans across the nation. Additionally, nearly 65,000 new actions were filed in March. One in every 662 housing units nationally received some sort of foreclosure notice. That ratio is roughly double in Florida (1/336), Georgia (1/361),Arizona (1/300), Nevada (1/301 and elsewhere.

Much of the contraction in the number of foreclosures over the last year was caused by last year's "robo-signing scandal." Following that, many large banks and servicers were reluctant to move forward with foreclosure filings. Now, however, most have settled with both regulators and State Attorneys General. That will likely mean re-acceleration of fore-closure activity before the rate trends down for good. This is likely to cause home prices to dip modestly through at least the end of this year and constrain prices longer term.

CoreLogic, a leading provider of information and analytics, reported recently that for every two homes offered for sale, there was one in the "shadow." In other words, roughly half the shadow inventory has not yet entered the foreclosure process. By definition, *shadow inventory* means homes in foreclosure or where loans are at least 90 days delinquent. The shadow inventory stands at about 1.6 million units compared to a year earlier when it was 1.8 million. It is also about four times higher than it was at its low point (380,000) which was also the peak of the housing bubble in 2006. Moreover, shadow inventory appears to be concentrated in the states with the largest price decline thus adding more credence to the notion that the leading cause of foreclosure is negative equity. In addition, the shadow is largely comprised of assets in the lower price ranges. As the shadow moves to foreclosure, then on to REO (Real Estate Owned) at banks, there will continue to be down-ward pressure on prices.

Employment has improved but job growth is still too slow to restore jobs lost during the Great Recession. While the economy has gained 3.745 million jobs since the declared end of the recession in June 2009, the economy still needs another 5.0 million to return to the pre-recession peak.

In April there were 12.9 million Americans unemployed. That is 8.1% of the labor force and the economy created only 115,000 new payroll jobs. While the nation's unemployment rate has hovered above eight-percent for 39 consecutive months, recent declines in the unemploy-ment rate have not been the product of significantly more jobs but rather a contracting labor force. Indeed, more workers have simply dropped out. Some have retired. Others have become discouraged and have just given up looking for employment. Indeed, the labor force participation rate has dropped to 63.6% (April 2012) which is the lowest since 1981.

Looking behind the numbers, some 5.1 million of the total 12.9 million unemployed or 41.3%, have been unemployed long term. By Bureau of Labor Statistics definition that is 27 weeks or longer. An additional 7.9 million workers were employed part time for economic reasons meaning they would prefer to work full time but could not find full time employment. Still another 2.4 million workers were "marginally attached" to the work force and 968,000 were discouraged and had given up. All that brings the underemployment rate (BLS alternative measure U-6) to 14.5%.

In addition to unemployment, there is evidence that wages are stagnating. In a study by Pew Research, it was revealed that workers who lost a job between 2007 and 2009 and who subsequently became re-employed, earned, on average 20% less than they did at the job they lost. Additionally, a large share of the jobs being created currently are lower pay.

During previous recessions, including the 10 since World War II (not including the most recent) most unemployment was cyclical and workers were called back to the same or similar jobs. Today's unemployment is more structural in that more losses are permanent and won't come back. Technology has been chipping away at employment for several decades and the need for retraining is perhaps greater than ever.

Finally, the nation's unemployment rate has averaged 5.7% for nearly 64 years. Looking forward, we can expect the average rate to be higher, perhaps in the 6.5% to 7.5% range due largely to structural changes and the lasting impact of technology.

Employment, including a lingering higher average unemployment rate, stagnating wages, longer term unemployment, uncertainty and other structural changes will continue to weigh heavily on housing. After all, the unemployed or underemployed and those with stagnating wages can't or won't buy or they buy less.

Diminished home equity is an issue that has received comparatively little attention since the housing bust but one that will weigh heavily long term. Intuitively, one might expect that as house prices rose, so would equity. Instead the opposite occurred as consumers withdrew equity on a regular basis to make other purchases. In 2006 for example, homeowners extracted $500 Billion of home equity; an amount equal to roughly 3.8% of GDP. The collapse in home prices which began in 2007 destroyed much of the remaining equity. Since equity was extracted for new home purchases, investment, entrepreneurial endeavors, education and financing or refinancing small business, the ultimate effect of diminished equity is likely to impede economic growth over at least the next decade.

Diminished home equity will weigh on housing and the broader economy in numerous ways. It will constrain move up buyers, lead to an absence of mobility to accept better job opportunities, lead to an inability to fund small business and even lead to an inability to obtain higher education thus possibly constraining wages for the next generation of consumers.

Conclusions. The implicit assumption that reaching a definitive housing bottom will result in a new round of rising home prices is wrong. A definitive bottom may, however, enhance potential home buyer confidence. What happens next is the more important story.

Foreclosures and the shadow inventory will continue to keep a lid on home prices for several years as the market works through the excess of distressed inventory. That is likely a two to four year process. Employment too will constrain home purchases as a result of a new normal in unemployment, stagnating wages or slow wage growth and a reduced rate of household formation. Reduced home equity will constrain move up buyers and limit other buyers ability to relocate and perhaps accept better employment.

In our view, the housing market has hit a bottom in the broad sense that the free fall in prices is over; barring, of course, some currently unforeseen economic shock. Nevertheless, it will still be several years before we see a full, self-sustaining recovery and a robust market. Prices are still likely to fluctuate, both up and down, within a fairly narrow range of two to five percent for at least the next 18 months. Price growth will remain generally flat with no truly discernible and predictable upward movement.

RECESSION RISK RISING AS ECONOMY LOSES MOMENTUM

Questions many business people and professionals have about the probability of recession are first, whether it will happen and second, how does one estimate the probability before it occurs. They wonder too if a forecast is just a wild guess, an educated guess or whether there is actually some science behind it. The answer is the latter. While we never know precisely and we always face the possibility of unforeseen economic shock, there is a little science underlying the opinion. The following is a brief, but high level, explanation of both recession risk and forecasting methodology as well as how the Business Cycle Dating Committee (BCDC), the official arbiter of the nation's business cycle, works.

By definition, a forecast is a judgment about the probability of a future event happening or not happening based on currently known or reasonably knowable information. It is not an exercise in crystal ball gazing nor is it an absolute guarantee that the forecast will materialize. That is why most forecasts, including this one, are expressed in probabilities.

The nation's business cycle (contraction versus expansion) is dated by the Business Cycle Dating Committee (BCDC) of the National Bureau of Economic Research (NBER). The committee is comprised of a group of academic economists at Princeton University. When dating the business cycle, the committee considers a wide variety of economic indicators over a reasonable period of time and from a broad geographical area. It is not as simple as often depicted such as a recession is measured by two quarters of negative GDP (Gross Domestic Product) or expansion by two quarters of growing GDP. While GDP is considered, so are financial market indicators, labor market conditions, housing, manufacturing, imports v. exports, confidence and much more. When the BCDC declared *The Great Recession* had ended in June 2009, they relied heavily on GDP and GDI (Gross Domestic Income). At that time, the average of GDP and GDI was 3.1% above its low in the second quarter of 2009 but 1.3% below its previous peak in December 2007 when the recession officially began.

Note too that the announcements were made a year or more after the recession began or ended. The beginning of *The Great Recession* was determined to be December 2007, however, the announcement came a full year later in December 2008. Similarly, the recession technically ended in June 2009 but the announcement was not made until September 2010. The committee is not in the business of forecasting. Rather its sole responsibility is dating the business cycle and it would rather be right than fast. Economic data are also revised frequently and the committee will usually wait for revisions as it did before declaring the recession had ended in mid-2009.

In forecasting a change of direction in the business cycle before the BCDC acts, we too consider a wide variety of indicators and evaluate them individually and collectively. We attempt to mimic what the BCDC is most likely to do. We also weigh each factor's relevance and potential impact. We then assign a probability weight to each indicator. Since a wide variety of indicators are considered, some tend to wash out others. We understand that any forecast can be rendered moot if unexpected economic shock occurs. We saw that with the 9-11 terrorist attacks, the Japanese earthquake and tsunami last year as well as other catastrophic events over the years. Sans unknown or unknowable events, however, it is possible to get reasonably close to a supportable and defensible forecast of change of direction in the business cycle including the probability of a short term dip into a new recession.

Economic recovery has lost the momentum it had only a few short months ago. Financial markets are not conducive to robust growth and all told, employment is weak, adding only 115,000 payroll jobs in April. Both business and consumer confidence are low, GDP is weak at 2.2% annualized and housing continues to struggle. Weaknesses could grow as European economies and U.S. trading partners slip into recession. Combined, we estimate the probability of recession within six months to be about 30%.

U.S. JOB CREATION TOOK A BIG STEP BACK IN MAY—ECONOMIC RECOVERY FALTERS

The U.S. labor market disappointed in May when payroll employment increased by only 69,000 jobs. The previous two months were also revised downward by a net total of 49,000 jobs. That leaves total job creation for the last three months at: March +143,000; April +77,000; and, May +69,000 for an average of just over 96,000 new jobs per month. Of the total 69,000 jobs added in May, 82,000 were private sector jobs. Government lost about 13,000.

The unemployment rate rose fractionally to 8.2%. Approximately 12.7 million Americans are unemployed and 5.4 million have been unemployed long term, which the Bureau of Labor Statistics (BLS) defines as 27 weeks or longer. Long term unemployed account for about 42.8% of the total and is clearly one of the more disconcerting indicators. Unlike previous recessions, where most job losses were cyclical and workers were called back to the same or similar jobs, today's losses are more permanent as a result of structural changes in both labor dynamics and in the broader economy. Clearly more Americans unemployed today are staying unemployed longer than ever before.

In addition to the 12.7 million unemployed, another 8.1 million Americans were employed part time for economic reasons meaning that they were unable to find full time employment or their hours had been reduced. In addition, 2.2 million workers were considered marginally attached to the work force. This group is in the labor force; wants full time work, had searched within the last 12 months but had not searched in the four weeks leading up to the May survey. Included among the marginally attached are 830,000 workers who are considered "discouraged" workers. These former workers are not currently looking for work because they do not believe a job is available for them.

The rise in the unemployment rate from 8.1% in April to 8.2% in May was largely the result of more people (642,000) moving back into the workforce in search of work. The labor force participation rate dropped to 63.6% in April, its lowest reading since 1981. In May, it increased a statistically insignificant 0.2% to 63.8%, still historically low. In our view, the decline is being driven by two fundamental factors. First is cyclical due to the recession and its aftermath. The second is demographic as a result of an aging population, many of whom are retiring and dropping out of the work force. Another important demographic and labor statistic is the employment to population ratio for the 25 to 54 age group. This cohort is the primary working group in the U.S. The ratio was 75.7% in May and has generally been moving sideways for more than a decade.

The Bureau of Labor Statistics calculates "Alternative Measures of Labor Underutilization." While the so-called headline unemployment may be 8.2%, the under-employment rate is nearly double that at 14.8% when marginally attached workers and those working part time for economic reasons are considered.

In other labor market indicators, the average work week declined to 34.4 hours while average hourly earnings increased slightly to $23.41 per hour. Over the last 12 months, average hourly earnings have increased 1.7 percent.

On average, the economy added 96,000 jobs per month during the three month period ending in May. During the previous three month period—December through February—an average of 252,000 jobs were added each month. A longer-term look back shows that the economy added about 164,600 jobs monthly over the previous six months. Private sector job growth was about 169,400 per month while the government sector lost jobs. The total is far too few jobs to make the economy self-sustaining or bring the economy back to pre-recession employment levels. Another five-million jobs are needed to accomplish that. At 200,000 jobs per month, that implies another 25 months to revisit pre-precession levels. That would be mid-2014. At 125,000 per month, employment recovery would stretch into late 2015. Employment change, however, is never precisely linear. Our outlook is for employment to regain some momentum but a return to pre-recession levels is still likely to be a 2015 event. More likely, however, there will be a new and higher stabilized unemployment rate.

JULY 25, 2012

UNDERSTANDING THE FISCAL CLIFF—WHAT IS IT? POSSIBLE EFFECTS? OPTIONS AND OUTLOOK?

The "Fiscal Cliff" is a popular term used to describe the financial conundrum the federal government will face beginning at year end. The situation was created by law in the summer of 2011 following the failure of the presidentially appointed bi-partisan *Super Committee* to agree on a deficit reduction plan. Republicans wanted to cut spending and not raise taxes. Democrats wanted a combination of spending cuts and increased taxes. In what was thought to be an unlikely scenario at the time, a variety of automatic tax increases and spending cuts were agreed upon in case the Super Committee failed. The automatic measures included enough pain for both parties so that incentive would be created to reach agreement. Nevertheless, it failed.

The Super Committee failure meant that the automatic deficit reduction measures would kick in beginning at the end of 2012. None of them are politically popular and all of them, if implemented as scheduled, will be like falling off a (fiscal) cliff into recession. Hence the term.

The concept is simple yet even deciding on the potential impact is not. Some of the impact numbers being touted refer to the impact in 2013 and others take into account the impact for a decade. There is little agreement on precisely what the numbers are nor their full impact. A one year estimate may not include everything and a lot can happen to change or derail the plan over 10 years rendering both estimates suspect.

On the tax side, the Bush era tax cuts are scheduled to expire on January 1st. An estimated $340 billion would be pulled out of the economy in 2013 and 2014 after the tax cuts sunset. The effect between 2013 and 2022 is estimated to be $2.8 trillion. Another $90 billion would come out of the economy in 2012 with the December 31, 2012 expiration of the Obama era payroll tax holiday and $25 billion more from expiration of emergency unemployment benefits. The Alternative Minimum Tax (AMT) so-called "patch" will increase taxes $90 billion in 2013 and $805 billion between 2013 and 2022. Other effective tax increases will occur by raising the capital gains tax to 20%; eliminating the 10% bracket; cutting the child care credit in half and much more. Moreover, tax increases driven by the new healthcare law will begin to take effect in 2013 and for years thereafter.

On the spending side, defense spending would be reduced 10% or $30 billion in 2013 and as much as $510 billion over time. Medicare providers would take a two-percent reduction (about $11 billion) and there would be an eight percent reduction in non-defense discretionary spending. These examples are by no means a complete list. Percentage reductions in spending are nearly impossible to implement especially in defense spending. As Pentagon observers point out, "you can't cut two thirds of an aircraft carrier."

Given the complexities of federal budgeting and spending, it is unclear what the precise fiscal impact will be either in 2013 or over time. What is clear however is that the impact will result in a huge economic impact for the U.S. The Congressional Budget Office (CBO) estimates that if the combination of higher taxes and spending cuts as currently proposed are enacted, they would reduce the federal deficit by as much as $560 billion. At the same time, however, the plan would reduce the Gross Domestic Product (GDP) by four percentage points in just 2013. As first quarter annualized GDP was 1.9% and the GDP is tracking at or around 1.3% annualized for the second quarter, the result could be economically catastrophic.

The options for dealing with the problem range from doing nothing to falling off the fiscal cliff into recession. Doing nothing would be like punting the problem to a potentially new President and Congress when they take office in 2013. It obviously does nothing to solve the problem. Similarly, neither party wants to take responsibility for a devastating fall over the fiscal cliff. Additionally, striking a meaningful compromise before or after the election but before tax increases and spending cuts take effect seems equally implausible. The most plausible measure, in our view, would be modest compromise on tax increases and spending cuts.

The cost of indecision is already weighing heavily on the economy. The uncertainty is likely to shave at least 0.5% off GDP growth for the year as consumers cut spending and businesses slow manufacturing and defer hiring.

JULY 28, 2012

HOME SALES RESULTS MIXED IN JUNE—EXISTING AND NEW HOME SALES DECLINE

According to the National Association of Realtors, **existing home sales** in June fell 5.4 % to a seasonally adjusted annual rate of 4.37 million units. That is down from an upwardly revised total of 4.62 million a month earlier but still 4.5% higher than the year ago level of 4.18 million units. Total sales include all residential property types including single family detached, town house, condominium unit and co-op. The median existing home price for all property types was $189,400 which is an increase of 7.9% from a year ago. The increase marks the fourth consecutive monthly price increase and the strongest price gain since the median rose 8.7% year over year in February 2006; a month which marked the beginning of the end of the housing bubble.

Distressed sales (foreclosures and short sales) accounted for 25% of all June sales. Foreclosures sold at an average calculated discount of 18% and short sales at a 15% discount. That is according to the National Association of Realtors (NAR) and is in comparison with transactions that did not have similar elements of distress. NAR also reported strong potential buyer interest in comparison to prior periods but activity may be constrained by declining inventories. In June, total unsold inventory declined 3.2% to 2.39 million units. That represents a 6.6 month supply at the current sales pace and is up from 6.4 months a month earlier. Last year at this time, inventory stood at 9.1 months.

First time homebuyers accounted for 32% of all purchases while all cash sales, driven by investors, edged up to 29%. The investor component was 19%. Investors appear to be purchasing a large share of moderately priced homes for cash thus edging out first time home buyers and creating the tight inventory in the lower price ranges.

Single family detached residences dominated residential sales activity although the sector declined 5.1% to a seasonally adjusted annual rate of 3.90 million units. The median price was $190,100.

Regionally, sales activity was mixed. Total sales in the Northeast declined11.5% on a median price of $253,700. That is down 1.8% from a year ago. In the Midwest, sales slipped 1.9% but the median price rose14.6% to $157,600. In the South, sales declined 4.4% but the median price rose 6.6% to $165,000 year over year. Finally, sales fell 6.9% in the West but the median price was a strong $233,300.

New Home Sales. The Census Bureau and Commerce Department jointly reported new home sales figures for June. Sales declined 8.4% to 350,000 annualized units month over month. That is a five month low. At the same time, the May total was revised up to 382,000. On a quarterly basis, sales were up 13%.

Although 350,000 sales is paltry compared to more robust economic times, it is the strongest performance since April 2010. New home sales are still near their historic low of 250,000 in late 2011. Sales double the current month's annualized performance, or say, 700,000, would be at or near the long term average. The peak was set in November 2006 with nearly 1.4 million annualized sales.

Inventories have been declining for both new and existing homes and that has been pushing both price and volume up. There are currently about 144,000 new homes for sale suggesting a 4.9 month supply at the current sales pace. Inventories are generally tight especially in the lower price range.

The median single family home sales price was $234,500 in June. Pricing is weak and the median price is down 3.3% year over year. Given the lower priced existing home competition, it remains difficult for builders to compete.

The price gap between a new single family home ($234,500) and an existing home ($190,100) is significant and is driven by several factors such as depreciation and distress characteristics in the existing home sector but also by economic feasibility. One can still buy an existing home for less than it would cost to build one (replacement cost) and that fact too is helping keep a lid on new home price increases. It is likely to continue to do so for the foreseeable future.

CASE-SHILLER: HOME PRICES FIRMING?

Median existing home prices reported by S&P Case-Shiller were mixed this month and suggest different directions depending on whether one looks at month over month numbers or year over year and whether one seasonally adjusts the numbers or does not. On a year ago basis, the 10 city composite index declined one-percent from last year compared to a 2.2% decline reported last month. The 20 city composite index also declined 0.7% year over year compared to the 1.9% drop experienced last month. On a month to month basis, not seasonally adjusted, however, both the 10 and 20 city indices rose 2.2% On a seasonally adjusted basis, the gains were slightly weaker on a month to month basis registering just 0.9%. The results this month are more than a little confusing and beg the question, which figures should we rely upon?

In our view all of them. There is a time to look at annual numbers and a time to consider monthly changes. Both are valid and tell a slightly different story. Similarly, there is a time to seasonally adjust and a time not to adjust. What we are seeing this month is some recent upward price movement over the three month period ending in May. The movement was downward for a several previous months over the last year therefore skewing the annual numbers to the negative. Similarly, the process of seasonal adjustment is also breaking down. Seasonal adjustment is a statistical adjustment made to accommodate fluctuations based on predictable and normal seasonal changes. In the case of housing, history consistently tells us that spring and summer are peak seasons and sales slow in the fall and winter. School openings and closings also affect seasonality. As the changes are predictable, the peaks and valleys can be statistically smoothed.

Recently however, the seasonal adjustment process has been affected by distress transactions which have tended to remain relatively constant throughout the year and not seasonally dependent. Regardless of the statistical anomaly, prices rose modestly (+2%) short term as revealed by the month over month numbers but declined modestly (1.0%) on an annual basis. As that is a current phenomenon, we interpret it to suggest that prices are showing early signs of at least firming. A single quarter is too early to declare a trend however the recent movement is both measurable and meaningful. The next few months will tell for sure.

Another positive sign is that an increasing number of metros covered by this release experienced May prices above year ago levels. For example, once seriously impaired, Phoenix leads the way with prices up 11.5% year over year. On the down side, prices declined modestly (0.1%) in Cleveland and Boston. Prices declined a whopping 14.5% in Atlanta year over year. Atlanta continues to be the only metro experiencing double digit declines.

Downward price pressure from foreclosures and distress transactions is moderating but not by much. The foreclosure pipeline is still sizeable but the process is moving much faster now that agreements between state attorneys general and large banks have been reached. At the same time, demand, particularly at lower price points, is being supported by investor purchasers even to the point of causing inventory shortages in some areas of the country, particularly California and to some lesser extent in South Florida.

Despite recent evidence of firming prices, the outlook for housing remains somewhat dreary. The jobs outlook is not conducive to home purchases. There is still a sizeable foreclosure backlog and shadow inventories are substantial; all signs that housing demand will bounce along the bottom well into 2013.

AUGUST 3, 2012

CMBS DELINQUENCIES RISE AGAIN IN JUNE

The 60 day delinquency rate for commercial mortgage backed securities moved up fractionally to 9.93% in June from 9.83% a month earlier. At the end of 2011, delinquencies stood at 9.32% overall. Delinquencies were relatively flat in 2011 but began inching up again in early 2012 with renewed weakening of the broader economy and brisk European headwinds. In June, delinquency rates increased for office, retail and hotel but declined for industrial and multifamily. The rates for each property class are shown in the table at the bottom of this page.

The total volume of CMBS loans outstanding decreased in June to $557.6 billion from $560.5 billion the previous month. Outstanding balances have steadily been declining in both the CMBS sector and in bank portfolios as few new loans are made and most construction is still not economically feasible. June was the 12th consecutive month of declining balances in the CMBS sector. Since early 2010, balances have declined 25%.

The year 2007 was the largest vintage year for new CMBS originations. It was also one of the poorest performing vintages. December 2007 was the peak value month for most commercial real estate assets. The trough occurred two years later in December 2009 and by that time the sector had lost 50% of its value.

The overall CMBS delinquency rate is nearing 10% after hovering around 9% since early 2010. As of June roughly 85% of five year CMBS loans originated in 2007 had already matured leaving just 15% to come due before year end.

The total outstanding balance of delinquent CMBS loans rose $300 million in June to a total of $55.4 billion. While $3.8 billion in loans were newly delinquent, $3.4 billion were resolved.

Delinquencies have historically been very low hovering around one-percent or less since this financing vehicle (CMBS) became popular in the 1990s. Indeed, delinquencies were exceedingly low most of last decade (around 1%) before surging with the collapse of the commercial real estate market coincident with The Great Recession in mid-2008.

AUGUST 8, 2012

REAL ESTATE AND ECONOMIC ROUNDUP

Bankruptcy Filings Down Year Over Year. According to the U.S. Bankruptcy Courts, personal bankruptcies rose 1.1% from the first quarter to the second quarter of 2012 but declined in the second quarter as measured year over year. There were 1.3 million petitions (down

14.2%) in the second quarter as compared to the same period last year. There have been year over year declines now for seven consecutive quarters. The overall decline in personal filings has slowed but they remain significantly lower than their 2010 peak. Personal Chapter 7 petitions fell the most (15.9%) since June a year ago. Business filings have now declined for 12 consecutive quarters. The quarter over quarter decline was 5.7%. While the number of filings is still elevated the trend is moving in the right direction.

The Federal Reserve Senior Loan Officer Opinion Survey showed that about 9.5% of reporting banks eased standards for commercial and industrial loans for medium and large businesses in the second quarter. The other 90.5% reported that standards were unchanged. About 4.9% of reporting banks eased standards for small business with the largest share of banks unchanged. In the residential mortgage sector, standards for prime mortgages were unchanged but standards tightened for non-traditional mortgage products. About 25% of banks reported slightly stronger demand while 16% reported modestly weaker demand. For consumer lines of business, 23% of reporting banks reported easing standards for auto loans to individuals but only 11% reported easing credit card standards. Consumer loan demand reportedly increased modestly for all types of consumer loan products in the second quarter. There has been very little easing of standards in the commercial real estate sector as banks continue to work though recession driven loan losses and face little discernible demand for new CRE product.

Is an FHA Bailout in our nation's future? The Federal Housing Administration (FHA) was created during The Great Depression of the 1930s. Today it guarantees loans to borrowers with spotty credit and low down payments of as little as 3.5%. In return, it charges 1.75% of the principal up front plus a modest annual premium to help insure against loss. The FHA lost market share in the early 2000s as subprime lenders offered even easier terms. By 2007, however, the subprime sector had collapsed leaving the FHA as the only game in town. The FHA almost singlehandedly kept the housing market functioning during the credit crunch that began in 2008. In 2006, the FHA insured loans worth about $52 billion. By 2009 that number was $330 billion. Today, about 700,000 of those loans, worth some $100 billion are viewed as questionable. Buried deep in the projections of the Office of Management and Budget (OMB), is a line item of $668 million for a potential bailout of the FHA. While the FHA appears reasonably sound today, the large number of questionable loans suggests it may not stay that way. Recently, the FHA has taken aggressive steps to improve its fiscal health. It has tightened lending standards and has become much more aggressive with lenders who commit fraud or even cut corners. Nevertheless, just the risky nature of the business model is such that a downturn in the economy could necessitate a bailout.

Hotel Occupancy Rose in the week ending July 28, 2012. According to Smith Travel Research (STR), hotel occupancy jumped 3.3% to 75.1% putting broad based occupancy at its highest level since 2007. At the same time, the average daily rate (ADR) rose 4.8% to $108.95 while revenue per available room (REVPAR) rose to $81.95. Overall occupancy is back to pre-recession "normal" and will likely move higher due to a dearth of new construction.

AUGUST 20, 2012

BUDGET DEFICIT IMPROVES BUT FEDERAL SPENDING STILL OUT OF CONTROL

The Federal Budget Deficit for July, the tenth month of the fiscal year was about $70 billion, down from $129 billion a year ago. This was roughly one-billion less than the Congressional Budget Office projected deficit for the month. The July improvement however, may be a bit deceiving as a $36 billion payment was shifted from July to June due to July 1st falling on a Sunday. Nevertheless, the deficit for the first 10 months declined by $126 billion. That is a reduction of 11.5% compared to last fiscal year.

While some of the improvement was calendar driven, there was noticeable improvement in receipts which were up 6.1% in the first 10 months. Fiscal year to date income tax receipts were up 4.2% year over year. Corporate tax receipts surged 29.8% while year to date payroll tax collections rose 3.8%. The budget deficit will decline in fiscal 2012 as a result of strong corporate profits and the tax receipts they generate.

An end to 2009 era stimulus spending and modestly increased personal tax receipt revenue will also contribute positively.

On the expense side, fiscal year to date spending was about $10 billion less in July than the same period last year. The decline was largely the result of less military, Medicaid, unemployment insurance and education spending as well as the expiration of certain stimulus tax credits. Nevertheless, spending on Social Security, Medicare and contributions to the GSEs (Fannie Mae and Freddie Mac) rose as did the interest on the federal debt.

Despite some improvement in the budget deficit, federal spending remains out of control at unsustainable levels as the government spends about $1 trillion more than it brings in. The U.S. is currently about $400 billion away from the negotiated $16.39 trillion debt ceiling limit. Nevertheless, the federal government has already spent $700 billion it doesn't have so the debt limit is likely to be reached sooner rather than later and well before calendar 2013. The Federal Reserve prepared chart (FRED = Federal Reserve Economic Data) at the left shows the exceptionally wide gap between income (blue line) and expenditures (red line).

Where does the government spend money?
The largest federal expenditures, as a percent of revenues, are 19% each for Social Security and National Defense. That is followed by other social type expenditures such as Medicare at 13%, Health at 10% and Income Security at 16%. All the other expense categories are much smaller percentages but huge real numbers. Interest accounts for 5%, Veteran affairs accounts for 4% and Education accounts for 3%. Education, Training, employment and Social Services account for 3%. Other categories such as Energy, Natural Resources, Agriculture, Community and Regional Development Justice and General Government each account for around 1% of federal expenditures.

With less than two months left in the federal fiscal year, interest on the federal debt for fiscal 2012 is projected by the U.S. Treasury to be $323,050,646,977.43. Now that's real money!

APARTMENT SECTOR SOARS— BANKS MANAGE EXPENSES

The rental apartment market has roared back to life despite wide spread weakness in the broader economy. Indeed, the sector has become the post-crash darling as fundamentals strengthen. According to commercial real estate analytics firm Reis, the national vacancy rate is now at its lowest point in a decade having fallen 20 basis points in the second quarter to a current 4.7%. The market has tightened significantly and developers have moved off the sidelines. As might be expected, new development has also surged. Reis reported 10,000 new units came on line in just the second quarter. Their 2012 forecast is for 70,000 units followed by 150,000 new units in 2013. Demand will likely remain high for the next year or two. The greatest current demand appears to be in tech concentrated metros. (San Francisco, Denver, Sacramento)

So far, new development has been constrained only by the availability of financing. Banks remain skittish as well they should be. The 60 day delinquency rate for commercial mortgage backed securities (CMBS) rose fractionally to 9.93% as $3.8 billion in newly delinquent CMBS loans entered special servicing. Despite a tight apartment market and strong fundamentals, the apartment sector still leads the way with a 14.09% delinquency rate. That is down from 15.13% a year ago but still higher than all other CRE sectors including hotel. Overall capitalization rates ("cap rates") for top tier space are once again showing signs of compression as they drop to 2006 levels in the five and six percent range. As more and more units come on line, fundamentals could, once again, become stressed.

Are we seeing an apartment bubble in the making? Not yet but time will tell. Builders are anxious to build and there is little demand to do so in any other CRE product sector. Migration to the apartment construction sector is inevitable. It is times like these in the apartment sector when circumstances become ripe for bubble inflation. So stay tuned and watch carefully for turning points. FOCUS continually monitors supply and demand relationships and turning points so check back frequently.

Bank Efficiency Ratios. All regulated financial institutions in the U.S. must file a Report of Condition and Income, known less formally as a "Call Report." The reports must be filed within 30 days of the end of a quarter. The information becomes public information and they yield a wealth of financial information about banks individually and collectively.

One indicator is the expense ratio, sometimes referred to as a bank's efficiency ratio. As might be expected, ratios vary significantly by bank size. Larger banks tend to be (but certainly not always) the most efficient. In the second quarter of 2012, the largest banks (those over $50 billion in assets experienced an average expense ratio of 59.8% while the smallest with less than $250 million in assets experienced the highest expense ratios at slightly over 70%. Other banks experienced expense ratios in between. As a percent of assets banks of most sizes, including the largest, experienced ratios in a tight percentage range of 2.5% to 2.9%. The smallest banks, (under $150 million in assets saw a higher ratio of 3.5% on average.

Smaller banks generally lack financial size, diversity and infrastructure to contain their expense ratio in the same way large banks can. Nevertheless, a bank's expense ratio should never be regarded as the sole indicator of its health. The old adage, "it costs money to make money" is true in banking. Often money must be spent even to exit unprofitable branches or lines of business. It is therefore prudent to evaluate expense ratios on a longer term stabilized basis.

AUGUST 27, 2012

RESIDENTIAL SALES VOLUME UP BUT PRICES DOWN— HOUSING RECOVERY INTACT BUT STILL FRAGILE

Existing home sales volume increased 2.3% in July as compared to June according to the National Association of Realtors (NAR). Total volume at a seasonally adjusted annual rate (SAAR) was 4.47 million units. The gain was anticipated but it was not enough to make up for the decline a month earlier when sales declined 5.4%. Sales still remain below April and May levels but are up 10.4% from volume (4.05 million) reported a year ago.

At the same time, the **median price** for all housing types (single family, condo, co-op and townhouse) was $187,300. That is down fractionally from $188,000 in June but still solidly above (+9.4%) the $171,200 recorded 12 months ago. The July year over year gain was the strongest since January 2006 at the peak of the market. That gain is signaling more confidence in the housing markets. The median single family detached home price was slightly higher at $188,100 which was 9.6% higher than a year earlier. The detached sector accounted for 3.98 million transactions which was about 2.1% higher than in June and 9.9% higher than a year ago.

Geographically by census region, the Northeast performed the best with 7.4% (+580,000) more sales than a year ago and a 3.5% higher median price of $254,200. The Midwest gained 2.0% more sales in July (1.04 million units) and a $154,100 median price which was 5.8% higher than a year earlier. In the South, existing home sales rose 2.3% to 1.77 million units on a 6.6% increased median price of $162,000. Finally, volume in the West was essentially unchanged at about 1.08 million units however the median price soared upward 24.6% year over year to a median price of $238,600. All volumes cited are seasonally adjusted annual rates (SAAR).

First time buyers accounted for 34% of all July transactions and all **cash purchases** were 27% of the total, down from 29% in June. **Investors** accounted for 16% of the all cash purchases.

Months of inventory were essentially unchanged at 6.4 months which is reasonable and consistent with long term historical levels in the existing home sector. Inventory levels have largely been stable for the last six months. Last year at this time, months of inventory stood at 9.1 months. Total inventory in July stood at 2.4 million units. Sales also appear to be occurring faster. Around 33% of sold homes had been on the market for 30 days or less and 21% for six months or longer.

There appears to be a **shortage of inventory** in the lower price ranges and that may be pushing the median price up. That will correct itself, in part, as new distress properties hit the market later in the year. Most distressed properties (but certainly not all) tend to be concentrated in the lower price ranges. Nevertheless, tight inventories in a generally underperforming market is unusual and is likely driven by several factors. One is foreclosure timing followed by investors who are quick to purchase lower priced assets as they come to market. In our view, underwater mortgages probably play a significant role. Nationwide, over 22% of homeowners are underwater. That figure rises dramatically in at least 10 states including Nevada at 61.2%; Florida at 45.1%; Arizona at 43.4% and the list goes on. Move up buyers who might be logical purchasers have been sidelined due to inability to sell their existing homes as a result of owing more on their existing mortgage than the home is worth. Additionally, even if they could sell, there is often not enough equity to provide cash for a new down payment. This latter constraint has no easy fix.

In July, **distressed properties**, generally foreclosures and short sales, accounted for around 24% of sales. They were divided equally between foreclosures and short sales at 12% each. Additionally, foreclosures sold at prices which, on average, were 17% less than otherwise similar but non-distressed properties. Short sales sold on average for 15% less. The gap between distressed and non-distressed transactions is narrowing as lenders and servicers become more efficient at moving transactions through the pipeline.

Listings were up 1.3% in July over June but are down almost 24% year over year. The decline is probably the result of fewer distress transactions *currently* entering the pipeline. This appears to be a matter of timing and not a trend as servicers are working through the backlog that occurred before settlements were reached with state attorneys general and federal regulators. The anticipated foreclosure volume has just not yet hit the market.

The timing issue implies that sales volumes will increase but the distress nature of the transactions may again put downward pressure on prices. The good news is that mortgage delinquencies are abating and the anticipated foreclosure surge later this year appears to be the last major wave barring, of course, currently unforeseen economic shock.

New Home Sales. Fast on the heels of the NAR existing home sales report came the Census Bureau reports on new home sales and new residential construction for July. New home sales rose 3.6% to 372,000 units on a seasonally adjusted <u>annual</u> basis (SAAR) in July as compared to a month earlier. The volume soared 25.3% higher than a year ago. The originally reported June annualized total of 350,000 units was also revised upward to 359,000. New home sales volume hit a bottom in late 2011 and sales have been trending modestly upward ever since.

Months of supply stood at 4.6 in July. That is down from 6.7 months a year ago and 8.5 months in mid 2009 at technical start of economic recovery. New home supply remains historically tight as inventories are 31.3% lower than a year ago.

At the same time, the **median price of a newly constructed home** declined to $224,600 from $227,000 a month earlier. The median price is down about 2.4% over the year. Pricing in general remains weak. As we reported earlier, the median price of an existing home in July was $187,300 ($188,100 for single family detached). It too was down fractionally on rising volume. Builders continue to struggle to compete with lower priced existing homes and especially distressed homes where the prices are very significantly lower. Builders are also wrestling with an absence of economic feasibility meaning that most homes constructed today are actually worth less upon completion than their cost to construct. Nevertheless, new home sales are trending in the right direction but they are starting from a very low level.

Housing starts declined to 746,000 units (annualized) in July. That is down from 754,000 units a month earlier but up 22% over the year. Starts have been averaging about 697,000 annualized units for the last 12 months. Moreover, the 12 month average has increased every month since August 2011. Single family detached construction starts declined by 6.5% in July while multifamily starts increased by 12.4%. Geographically, housing starts declined in three of the four census regions. Only the Midwest saw an increase month to month (+17%). The regions with the largest housing markets (South and West) saw the largest declines.

Building permits increased 6.8% over the month to 812,000 with both single and multifamily permit levels rising. Permitting is tracking at its strongest pace August 2008. July year to year comparison was strong rising some 30%. Since July 2010, permit volume has risen 51%.

Housing completions increased 7.1% over the month and 5% over the year. Completions have increased in five of the last six months with the multifamily sector driving most of the improvement (see August 22nd FOCUS Commentary). The single family sector remains relatively stable.

The National Association of Home **Builders Housing Market Index** is showing improvement. It has done so for four consecutive months. The index measures present sales; expected sales in the next six months and traffic from potential buyers. While all three components are near five year highs, most of the improvement was driven by the present sales index reading followed by the potential buyer traffic reading. The expected sales reading hovered around neutral.

Builder confidence is improving but more homebuilders report conditions as poor than report them as good. Home building conditions remain sluggish. As an aside, The Conference Board recently reported that the share of consumers planning to buy a home had dropped to its lowest level in six months.

Rental housing is playing a significant role in the housing market as recession driven home buyer impairment as well as government policy moves push more consumers to rental housing. First, many new households are headed by young adults which is the demographic least likely to pursue homeownership. Second, many former homeowners, some of whom (perhaps arguably) should not have been owners and were subsequently foreclosed upon, have necessarily returned to rentals. Third, slow income growth of the last few years means many potential homeowners do not have the financial capacity to purchase or perhaps to operate and maintain a residence. Indeed, from 2000 to 2008 real per capita income grew at an annualized rate of 2%. During 2010 and 2011, the rate was less than half that at 0.8%. Finally, there is a stunning lack of confidence among consumers as revealed by nearly every key consumer sentiment or confidence survey.

Outlook. The housing sector as a whole is clearly improving and showing much needed signs of life. Nevertheless, the sector is climbing out of a very deep hole and the climb is still likely to be long, slow and torturous. While the freefall certainly appears over, barring, of course, unforeseen economic shock, the damage was significant and recovery will take time.

CONFIDENCE WEIGHS ON BROADER ECONOMY

According to the **Conference Board (August 28th), consumer confidence** took an unexpected and large dip in August. The index measures both present and expected conditions around employment, income, purchasing plans and inflation expectations. The index has now declined for five of the last six months and is at its lowest level since November 2011. The unexpectedly large decline was driven by the expectations component of the survey and suggests that consumers are considerably more downbeat about where the economy is heading. When reviewing survey responses by age group, all three surveyed groups saw declines. The under 35 age cohort had the smallest decline while the oldest (over 55) had the largest decline.

Expectations of future income prospects were discouraging and expectations for inflation rose. These changes in consumer sentiment are not welcome news in an already weak economy. It also does not bode well for consumer spending over the short term especially when considered with weak job and income growth and currently rising gasoline prices.

In a separate report, the three major components of the **Bloomberg Consumer Comfort Index** which include state of the economy, personal finances and buying climate, all deteriorated in the most recent survey (August 23rd). Sentiment was consistently weak among geographic regions of the country and among income groups. The indicators are generally indicative of an economy in the throes of recession rather than one that has technically been recovering for three years. The Bloomberg index has now slipped for six consecutive weeks.

Rising prices seem to be the recurring theme in the key confidence reports. Gas prices hit $3.80 per gallon nationally last week. That is the highest in three months. Moreover, crop prices have risen sharply in recent weeks as a result of drought conditions. That has sparked fears of rising food prices.

Small business confidence remains soft according the National Federation of Independent Business (NFIB). Small business survey respondents generally reported that sales and profits are weaker than last quarter and they are being adversely affected by deteriorating consumer spending. Rising food and gasoline prices are still taking a bite out of consumers' ability and willingness to spend and that is translating to impairment in small business confidence. Business generally are unwilling to grow inventories or make significant capital expenditures. The NFIB index is at its lowest level this year but is still slightly higher than a year ago.

Manufacturing, which has supported the modest economic recovery, is also currently showing signs of fatigue as demand wanes both domestically and internationally. The Bureau of Labor Statistics Mass Layoff Report for July showed manufacturing payrolls declined significantly. Mass layoff events (more than 50 people at a time) rose by one third and affected some 15,827 employees: a 50% increase. Additionally, core capital goods orders have declined measurably over recent months. That supports the observation that business investment is slowing.

Continuing uncertainty over the possible year end fiscal cliff is weighing heavily on both consumer and business confidence. Indeed, the non-partisan Congressional Budget Office (CBO) opined (August 23rd) that a recession lies at the bottom of the fiscal cliff if the currently scheduled federal tax increases (expiration of tax cuts) and spending cuts are allowed to occur at year end.

AUGUST 30, 2012

CMBS 60 DAY PLUS DELINQUENCIES RISE ACCORDING TO MOODY'S INVESTOR SERVICES

The 60 day delinquency rate for commercial mortgage backed securities moved up to 10.06% in July from 9.93% a month earlier. At the end of 2011, delinquencies stood at 9.32% overall. Delinquencies were relatively flat in 2011 but began inching up again in early 2012 with renewed weakening of the broader economy and brisk European headwinds. In July, delinquency rates increased for office, retail, multifamily and hotel but declined fractionally for industrial. The rates for each property class are shown in the table at the bottom of this page.

The total volume of CMBS loans outstanding decreased in July to $553.6 billion from $557.6 billion in June. Outstanding balances have steadily declined in both the CMBS sector and in bank portfolios as few new loans are being made, resolutions are increasing and most new construction today is still not economically feasible; meaning its value when complete is often less than the cost to create it. Over the last year, shrinking outstanding balances have been largely the result of pay downs outpacing new originations. We expect that trend to continue at least into 2013. Outstanding balances have declined for 49 of the last 54 months after peaking at $793.5 billion in December 2007. That month was also the value peak for commercial real estate loans; the starting point from which CRE as a sector lost 50% of its value. The current delinquency rate is now over 10% for the first time on record. Since early 2010 it has hovered just over 9% and has increased 0.76% since the beginning of 2012. That is more than double the full year 2011 increase.

The total outstanding balance of delinquent CMBS loans rose $300 million in July to a $55.7 billion. While $3.5 billion in loans were newly delinquent, $3.2 billion were resolved.

CMBS delinquencies have historically been very low hovering around one-percent or less since this financing vehicle became popular in the 1990s. Indeed, delinquencies were exceedingly low most of last decade (around 1%) before surging with the collapse of the commercial real estate market coincident with The Great Recession in 2008. CMBS loans have recently experienced higher delinquencies than bank portfolio loans probably because most CMBS issuances were non-recourse to the borrowing entity.

By vintage year, 1999 delinquencies decreased by 500 basis points while 2002 rose a full 1,500 bps. All vintages except 1999, 2000, 2001 and 2006 rose with 2007 performing the worst.

REAL ESTATE AND ECONOMIC ROUNDUP

In its second estimate of Q2 2012 **Gross Domestic Product (GDP)** the Bureau of Economic Analysis reported that the economy expanded at a 1.7% seasonally adjusted annual rate. That is down from 2.0% in the first quarter and down from 2.3% in all of 2011. Recall that there are three estimates of GDP beginning with the "advance estimate" (+1.5%) that was delivered a month ago. Each estimate is based on more incoming data. Slowing growth in the second quarter, as compared to the first, is largely the result of rapid growth in consumer spending to virtually no growth. Last quarter, consumers invested heavily in durable goods, which, by definition are big ticket items such as autos, appliances and furniture, etc. Durable goods are expected to last three years or more. Growth in non-durables (consumables) also slowed in Q2. Spending rose again in July suggesting Q3 could move a bit higher.

Real gross domestic income rose a paltry 0.6% annualized in the second quarter in contrast to growth of 4.5% and 3.6% in the preceding two quarters.

Corporate profits were included in the second estimate. They grew at 0.5% over the quarter (not annualized) recovering part of the 2.7% decline a quarter earlier. In the first quarter, corporate profits were up 6.1% from a year earlier implying that businesses have the capacity to hire even though they are not.

The report showed that inflation rose at 0.7% which was substantially less than the +2.6% reading in the first quarter. This was largely due to falling energy prices. (Note that gas prices reversed course again and have been rising in very recent weeks.) Excluding food and energy, Q2 inflation slowed less dramatically from 2.2% to 1.8%. Inflation concerns remain low.

At 1.7% annualized growth, the economy continues to underperform its potential. That level of growth will not be enough to cause any measurable downward movement in unemployment.

Case Shiller Home Price Indices for the three month period ending in June increased modestly. The 20 city index gained 0.5% year over year. Similarly, the 10 city composite, representing the nation's largest cities rose 0.1% from a year ago. These are seasonally adjusted annual rates (SAAR). The unadjusted rates were larger (10 city = +2.2% and 20 city = + 2.3%) but there is significant seasonality in the numbers in the summer months. More metros had prices above year ago levels. Only San Diego, Los Angeles, Chicago, Las Vegas, New York and Atlanta experienced declines. Atlanta was the biggest loser at 12.1%. Alternatively, the biggest winner was Phoenix with a gain of 13.9%. The gains are the first since 2010 and that gain was driven by tax credits. Excluding the tax credit effect, the gains are the first since 2006. Robert Shiller, one of the creators of the indices, opined that housing may finally have hit bottom. Nevertheless, housing recovery is still fragile and housing is not yet out of the woods.

Pending Home Sales as reported by the National Association of Realtors rose 2.4% in July to their highest level since April 2010. The 2010 surge was home buyer tax credit induced. Nevertheless, the index is up 12.4% year over year. The Pending Home Sales Index (PHSI) is a leading indicator. It is based on contracts reported by Realtors and is reasonably indicative of closing activity in the short term future; usually two to three months.

Housing demands is beginning to move in the right direction and will likely to continue to do so barring any unforeseen shock to the housing sector or the broader economy. Foreclosure appear to be the most significant remaining obstacle.

SEPTEMBER 6, 2012

BEHIND THE NUMBERS ON NEW HOME SALES

Recently in this space we reported on new home sales during July 2012. Sales totaled 372,000 at a seasonally adjusted annual rate. As new home construction is so important to the nation's economy, it seems as though the subject deserves a bit more than a passing glance.

During this real estate cycle we have witnessed both extremes of new home sale volume. From August 2002 through November 2006 the seasonally adjusted annual rate was greater than one-million. Sales performed in that fashion for all but five months during that lengthy period. The peak occurred in July 2005 with 1.389 million sales on an annualized basis. That rate of growth was clearly unsustainable and was fuelled for reasons other than real demand. Investors, speculators and flippers entered the market. Prices soared and much of the new development at that time was to satisfy faux demand without regard to real demand driven by need for housing. Indeed, during the "bubble era" somewhere between 25% and 40% more homes were built than there were people to occupy them either by purchase or rental. As early as 2002 and 2003 prices were increasing faster that incomes and it became apparent to anyone willing to pay attention that decline was inevitable. Nevertheless building went on.

The bubble finally burst in late 2006 and sales steadily declined until they reached a low of 280,000 (annualized) in May 2010. The peak to trough decline (1,389,000 to 280,000) was nearly 80%. Since then sales have bounced along the bottom in the 200,000 and 300,000 ranges finally reaching a new multi-year high of 372,000 in July. Still, that "new high" is rather dismal when one considers that these are annualized numbers for the entire United States. Indeed, 372,000 sales is roughly equivalent to total volume in 1966, some 46 years earlier, when population and other demographics were far different than they are today.

Under normal economic circumstances, construction has a widespread and positive effect on the broader economy. In 2006 for example, new home construction contributed $1.195 trillion, to the nation's GDP (8.9%). At the cyclical low point, housing was a drag on the economy. By 2011 new construction contributed less than 5% to GDP. These figures are direct spending on new home construction and do not include any multiplier effect.

Construction employment was severely affected during the downturn. The sector lost 1.5 million jobs from December 2007 through June 2009, the declared dates of the recession.

The decline was 19.8% and reduced construction employment to a level last seen in 1998. The majority of the losses occurred during the last nine months of the recession when employment declined by 1.0 million jobs. Employment continued to decline after the recession was declared ended in June 2009. Many workers who had lost jobs in the residential sector moved to the commercial sector but eventually lost those jobs too as both sectors slowed. By 2010, construction unemployment exceeded 20%.

Different Data Different Perspectives. New home building permits, construction starts and new home sales are all measured monthly and each offers a different perspective of the all important housing sector. New home data tend to be forward looking, more so than existing home sales. That is largely because new home sales are counted when a contract is executed. With an existing residence, a sale is a closed transaction.

The data are also a good reflection of sentiment but among different groups and for different reasons. A new home sale is a good reflection of consumer confidence. New home construction starts however is more of a production number and perhaps a sign of builder confidence. Finally, building permits may be a reasonable sign of things to come.

Housing's multiplier (ripple) effect. A home purchase always has a ripple or "multiplier effect" in the economy. In other words, for each dollar that is spent, there is an additional amount spent over and above the initial investment that ripples through the economy. Multipliers take many forms but in housing, economists and policy analysts attempt to quantify three fundamental things: jobs, spending and tax revenues. These multiplier impacts tend to occur in two phases. The first is when the house is constructed and the second is throughout occupancy. While growth critics sometimes opine that housing doesn't pay its fair share, the reality is it almost always does, and then some except perhaps in times of severe recession.

An existing home sale produces a multiplier effect but certainly not as great as when a new home is constructed and sold. The first impacts in new home construction occur when the home is built. There is spending on the workers who build the homes as well as in the firms that support them. There are usually office staff, cost estimators, buyers accountants and more. This first layer of impact is typically referred to as *"direct impact."*

In addition to the direct impact of home construction, are the ripple effects; those that ripple through the local economy in some form or another. Generally two forms are measured. One is the *"indirect impact."* This is typically the jobs and spending created from businesses that are suppliers to the construction operation. This might include building supplies, architectural and engineering spending, cabinetry, flooring , decorating, financing and much more.

Finally there is *"induced impact"* when workers spend their wages in the local area such as at restaurants, retail, healthcare and other establishments. The induced spending tends to create additional new jobs at these consumer related businesses as well.

New home construction is extraordinarily important to the broader economy in many ways ranging from job creation, spending, tax revenue and potentially in many areas that have not even been mentioned here.

SEPTEMBER 7, 2012

HOUSING, MORTGAGE, FANNIE AND FREDDIE

Each week the **Mortgage Bankers Association (MBA)** surveys the largest mortgage lending firms to gain an understanding of how many mortgage loan applications are received for both purchase and refinance as well as on a composite basis. The survey is published each Wednesday morning and captures an estimated 40% of mortgage loan applications received the previous week. The survey is important as it signals the degree of confidence in residential real estate and the general direction of the market. Viewed weekly, the results can be volatile and the MBA makes no revisions. Over time, however, the surveys tend to reveal meaningful trends.

The composite index (purchase + refinance) slipped 2.5% last week. That is the fifth consecutive week of decline. Moreover, both components, purchase and refinance, retreated as well. The purchase index declined fractionally last week by 0.8%. It remains down 0.6% from four weeks ago and fractionally higher (0.5%) from a year ago. Refinance applications have led the way most weeks as a result of continuing record low interest rates. That component accounted for 78.7% of prospective loan volume as represented by applications. Nevertheless the volume of refinance applications still declined 3% from the previous week. Volume is down 21% over the last four weeks but still up 19.7% over a year ago. The refinance index accounts for around four out of five mortgage loan applications.

The purchase applications index is reflecting the residential real estate market as a whole and is struggling to gain traction. It has been virtually flat since hitting bottom in the middle of 2010 and remains near a 15 year low.

Fannie Mae and Freddie Mac are back in the black. In the second quarter, both companies turned profitable for the first time since being forced into conservatorship nearly four years ago. As housing shows signs of improvement, both government sponsored enterprises (GSEs) are as well. Roughly half the mortgages in both portfolios have been issued since 2008. That, combined with stabilizing housing values, more robust underwriting, lower loan to value ratios, write off of the worst of the worst and reversal of certain previous provision expense (reserves) which goes straight to the bottom line, both companies showed a solid profit. Fannie recorded a $7.8 billion profit in the first half of 2012 against a $16.9 billion loss a year ago. Freddie earned $3.6 billion against a loss of $5.3 billion last year. The cost to taxpayers of bailing out the two mortgage giants peaked at $151 billion at year end 2011. Today it is estimated at $142 billion and the Treasury Department estimates the bailout cost will total $28 billion a decade from now.

In a separate report, changes to the Treasury's bailout agreement with Fannie Mae and Freddie Mac may be quietly signaling the end to both companies as we knew them. The changes make it clear that neither company will be permitted to resume its former role. Each company will be required to wind down its portfolio by 15% per year rather than the previous 10% per year requirement. The new rules do not remove the federal government as the main guarantor of U.S. mortgages. The GSEs will continue to issue mortgage backed securities as long as private issuers stay on the sidelines. Treasury also made it clear that neither company would return to being private anytime soon, if ever. Instead

---

RECESSION CHRONICLES

they will continue to be run like public utilities and all profit will be returned to Treasury rather than being distributed as dividends.

AUGUST EMPLOYMENT WEAKER THAN EXPECTED

The much anticipated August jobs report proved to be weaker than expected. The report fell short of expectations with only 96,000 new payroll jobs having been created. In addition, June and July estimates were revised down. In the latest estimate, June was reduced to 45,000 new jobs from the last estimate of 63,000. That is the second downward revision for June which was originally reported at 69,000. The July gain was originally estimated at 163,000 but revised down to 141,000. Payroll job growth has averaged 94,000 over the last three months. That is above the recent low point in June but still about half the pace achieved early in the year. It is also less than half of what is necessary to reduce the nation's employment rate. Although the rate did decline slightly to 8.1% from last month's 8.3%, the underlying reason was not job growth but a decline in the size of the civilian labor force. While 96,000 new jobs were created, 368,000 persons dropped out. That ratio is 3.83 to one. In other words, for every new job created, nearly four people dropped out. The nation's unemployment rate has now been above that psychologically important 8% marker for 43 consecutive months.

Of the net 96,000 jobs added in August, 103,000 were private sector while the government sector lost 7,000 jobs. The government sector August decline brought the total jobs lost in the government sector in 2012 to 93,000. The breakdown is 61,000 state and local job losses and 32,000 federal.

Manufacturing has been showing signs of weakness in recent weeks. Inventories have risen while new orders have declined and exports have softened. The shifting dynamics have now shown up in manufacturing employment. The sector gained 23,000 jobs in July but lost 15,000 in August. That was the biggest about face in any sector and the weakness is concerning. Some, but certainly not all, of that change was linked to auto plant shut downs for new model retooling. For that reason, auto manufacturing employment can be volatile at this time of year and should bounce back, at least in part, next month. Fewer auto workers were laid off this year in July but fewer workers were also recalled in August. A complete rebound in manufacturing though, seems unlikely in the next few months as only 36.4% of manufacturing industries added workers in August; the fewest since late 2009 in the early months of recovery.

The chart to the left shows job change in the U.S. since 2001. The black bars are gains; the red lines are losses and the gray bars indicate periods of declared recession. Note that job losses have consistently been greater than the gains which clearly indicates widespread and continuing systemic labor market weakness.

Several industries added jobs in August. These included food and drinking establishments which gained 28,000 in August and 298,000 over the year. Professional and technical services gained 27,000 while healthcare gained 17,000. Finance and insurance gained 11,000.

All told, the economy has added 1.11 million jobs in the first eight months of 2012. That is an average of 138,750 per month. The private sector has added 1.21 million jobs. At the current pace the economy is on track to add 1.8 million jobs in all of 2012. That is less than the 2.1 million added in 2011. At the current rate of growth the unemployment rate will also continue to hover above 8% for the rest of the year.

The average workweek for private non-farm workers was unchanged at 34.4 hours. For production and non-supervisory workers, the work week was slightly shorter at 33.7 hours. The average hourly wage inched down fractionally to $23.52 per hour after having risen 1.7% year over year. Production and nonsupervisory workers saw an average hourly rate of $19.75.

The number of unemployed persons remains at about 12.5 million, changed only fractionally from the last three months. The number of long-term unemployed, which is defined by BLS as 27 weeks or more, remained virtually unchanged at about 5.0 million or 40% of total unemployed workers. Another 8.03 million workers were classified as involuntary part time. That is down from 8.25 million a month earlier.

RECESSION CHRONICLES

That group (involuntary part time) may have had hours reduced or for other reasons had accepted part time work when they could not find full time opportunities. Another 2.6 million workers were classified as marginally attached to the work force. That group includes persons who wanted and were available for work; had looked in the last 12 months but had not looked in the four weeks leading up to the survey. This category is about equal to what it was a year ago. Finally, another 844,000 workers were classified as discouraged. They believe there is no job available for them. When all these groups are tallied and added to the headline unemployment rate of 8.1%, the under- employment rate (alternative measure U-6) becomes 14.7%. That is little changed over the last few months but down from 16.1% a year ago.

While the overall continuing weakness in the labor market is concerning, three categories of data stand out. The first is the labor force participation rate which, at 63.5% in August, hit another cycle low. Indeed, that rate is also the lowest in 31 years. This figure represents the percentage of working age population who are actually in the labor force. The rate increased significantly for several decades beginning in the mid-1930s as women entered the work force in large numbers. A rate of 66-67% has been the norm for the last two decades but it began declining concurrent with The Great Recession. The decline appears to be the product of demographic movement as older workers retire or drop out as well as the lingering effects of the recession including extraordinary uncertainty in the broader economy. A companion statistic is the employment to population ratio which declined to 58.3% in August. This is a new low for the year and just above the cycle low.

The level of long term unemployment at 40% (5.03 million people) is also concerning. Although that rate is trending down from its cycle high and even over the month it remains obvious that workers who become unemployed tend to stay unemployed longer. This is clearly one of the leading labor market difficulties.

Similarly, the employment to population ratio in the 25-54 age group, though still higher than all age groups in aggregate, has declined significantly. This age group represents the most productive age group and should be around 80%. It has been hovering in the 74-75% range.

While many companies are flush with cash and some are pushing the limits of productivity most are reluctant to hire as they fear the impact of the fiscal cliff which could push the economy back into recession. Others are dealing with the uncertain aspects of health care legislation and new regulation that many fear will impact their businesses adversely. Clearly, the labor market continues to be plagued by structural rather than mere cyclical issues.

SEPTEMBER 24, 2012

HOUSING RECORDS STRONG PERFORMANCE IN AUGUST

Existing home sales volume increased 7.8% in August as compared to July. Sales volume was 9.3% higher than a year ago. At 4.82 million units on a seasonally adjusted annual basis (SAAR), August volume was the highest since May 2010 during the latter stages of the second stimulus program. The single family sector performed the strongest although both major sectors; single family and condo posted solid gains according to the National Association of Realtors (NAR).

The national **median price** for all housing types, including single family, condominium unit, townhouse and co-op was $187,400. That is 9.5% higher than a year ago and the strongest gain since January 2006 when the median price rose 10.2% year over year. Single family detached home sales rose 8.0% to a seasonally adjusted annual rate of 4.3 million units. That was about 89% of the total number of sales. The median single family sale price was $188,700, slightly higher than the all housing types figure. Existing condo and co-op sales increased about 6.1% to a seasonally adjusted annual rate of 520,000 in August. That was about 30,000 more units than a month earlier.

Distress sales, which includes foreclosures and short sales, declined modestly from 24% of all sales for the month to 22%. The distress sale total was about 1.06 million units. Approximately 12% of distress sales were foreclosures while 10% were short sales. The number of distress sales and the percentage of total are declining slowly but steadily which may be in large part responsible for the rising median price. Foreclosures sold for about 19% less than otherwise similar but non-foreclosed properties while short sales sold for about 13% less. All cash sales totaled 27% of all transactions or about 1.301 million units. Of that total, investors bought 18% or around 234,252 units; primarily in the lower price ranges.

Months of **inventory** declined to a relatively normal level of 6.1 months even though listings rose 2.9% month over month. Again, the increase in listings is the strongest gain since 2010. August inventory stands at about 2.47 million residential units. Inventory is broadly balanced around the country although there is some evidence of shortages in the South and West Census Regions. Listed inventory is down about 18.2% year over year. These shortages may also be contributing to a higher median price.

In August, the median **time on the market** was about 70 days. That is consistent with July but down 23.9% from the 92 days on the market a year ago. Thirty two percent of homes were on the market for fewer than 30 days while only 19% for more than six months.

Geographically by census region, the Northeast performed the best with volume rising 8.6% to an annualized pace of 630,000 units. The median price was $245,200. The Midwest gained 7.7% more sales in August, rising to a level of 1.12 million units on a median price of $152,400. Volume is up 17.9% over the year and median price is up 7.8%. In the South, existing home sales rose 7.3% to 1.90 million units on a 6.5% increased median price of $160,100. Finally, volume in the West rose 8.3% to 1.17 million units on a median price of $242,000 which is 16.3% higher than a year ago.

Outlook. Solid gains are always welcome but the outlook for robust housing recovery remains guarded. Employment remains weak with some 12.5 million Americans unemployed; over 5.0 million of them (40%) long term which is defined as longer than six months. Wages have stagnated and household wealth is still at a near record low point after being decimated during The Great Recession. Labor force participation is at 63.5% which is its lowest point in 31 years. Foreclosures continue and will likely keep a lid on prices for several more years. None of these indicators bode well for quick and robust housing recovery.

GDP DECLINES AGAIN
ECONOMY NEAR STALL SPEED

The U.S. economy remains dangerously close to stall speed as evidenced by the third estimate of second quarter 2012 Gross Domestic Product. The estimate showed growth at a very slow and disappointing 1.3% seasonally adjusted annual rate (SAAR). Expressed another way, the nation's economy grew 1.3% annualized. That is down from an also disappointing 2.0% in the first quarter and down from the first and second estimates of second quarter GDP at 1.5% and 1.7% respectively. The Bureau of Economic Analysis releases three estimates throughout each quarter as new information becomes available. These were previously referred to as the advance, preliminary and final estimates. Recently however, the terminology was changed to simply first, second and third estimate, presumably to be more descriptive and to recognize the reality that the estimates are never absolutely final.

The downward revisions were larger than usual and were led by declines in consumer service spending in finance and insurance as well as reduced spending on durable goods. Durable goods refers to those expected to last longer term such as automobiles and appliances. Spending on durables turned from rapid growth in the first quarter to no growth in the second. Similarly, spending on non-durable goods (largely consumables), as well as equipment and software also slowed during the quarter.

Real gross domestic income increased at 0.2% annualized which was a steep decline from readings of 4.5% and 3.6% recorded in the preceding two quarters. It is also a downward revision from the 0.6% growth reported previously in the second quarter.

The 1.3% rate of GDP growth is the slowest since Q3 2011. Over the past year, the economy has grown at about 2.1%. While growth has been positive, it has been, and remains, insufficient to either return the economy to its potential or reduce unemployment below that psychologically important 8.0% mark where it has been for 43 consecutive months.

The Great Recession technically ended in June 2009, but the economy still can't gain the necessary traction to resume robust growth. The economic wheels are spinning but little is happening. By nearly every measure, this recovery is the weakest following any of the 11 recessions since World War II.

In our view, this continuing and painful level of slow growth is a product of fiscal, political and regulatory uncertainty as well as the looming fiscal cliff, Middle East unrest and the lingering European debt crisis. Sadly, there are no leading indicators that suggest the economy will advance faster than near stall speed this year.

The same report also showed that inflation rose at 0.7% which is well below the first quarter rate of 2.5% and well within the Federal Reserve Board's tolerance zone. Inflation concerns remain small and are not likely to alter the Fed's loose monetary policy.

In a separate report, orders for durable manufactured goods plunged 13.2% after rising 3.3% a month earlier. That is significant because new orders had supported economic growth for the last several months. Most of the decline was in transportation which fell a staggering 34.9% with huge declines in aircraft, automobiles and parts. Part of that decline was expected as a result of auto plant closures for retooling plus 260 aircraft purchases in July which were not likely to be repeated. Excluding transportation, new orders fell much more modestly by about 1.6%. August data suggest slower contributions to GDP growth from business throughout the remainder of 2012.

SEPTEMBER 30, 2012

HOUSING REPORTS GENERALLY POSITIVE IN AUGUST

Last week we wrote about existing home sales in this space. The news was generally positive. Sales volume was 9.3% higher than a year ago at 4.82 million units. That was the highest volume of sales since May 2010. Inventories have returned to a relatively normal level and distressed sales are down slightly. We described our outlook as guarded only because the housing recovery remains fragile and some strong headwinds remain. The last week was a data rich one for housing as

---

several key reports were released. Here is a summary.

New Home Sales declined 0.3% to an annualized 373,000 units. Nevertheless, sales are up 28% from a year ago. The median price of a new home nationwide is $256,900 which is up approximately 17% year over year. New home pricing is notoriously volatile and subject to wild swings based upon product mix.

Inventory remained essentially flat at 141,000 available units. That is 12% less than a year ago. While builders still struggle to compete against much lower priced existing homes, particularly foreclosure transactions, new home prices rose sharply in August. That appears to be the product of tight inventories.

Geographically, new home sales have been uneven across the country. The Northeast recorded the largest gain surging 20% in August alone. Year over year, sales in the Northeast are up 57%. Conversely, the South was the only region to show deterioration as new home sales declined 5%. Year over year, sales are up 65% in the west and 12% in the South. The Midwest posted a solid gain with sales up 2% over the month and 17% over the year. We expect new home sales to languish at or near their current level for the remainder of the year and into 2013. Employment needs to pick up and foreclosures need to clear before new home sales volume can show any appreciable gains.

Existing home prices accelerated year over year in the three month period ending in July. That is according to the widely watched and highly regarded **S&P/Case-Shiller Home Price Index**. That is in comparison to the three month period ending in June. The 20 city index gained 1.2% year over year while the 10 city index gained 0.6% compared to year ago levels. The gains were widespread. A larger number of metropolitan areas covered in the release saw gains. Year over year price gains ranged from a fractional increase in Cleveland and Los Angeles to a soaring 16.6% increase in Phoenix; a previously overbuilt and troubled metro. Only Las Vegas, Chicago, Atlanta and New York experienced declines. Atlanta was by far the biggest loser with prices down 9.9% year over year.

House prices, as measured by the **Federal Housing Finance Administration (FHFA)**, continued to rise as well. The agency, which is also the conservator for mortgage giants Fannie Mae and Freddie Mac, reported that its purchase only index rose 0.2% in July. It is now 3.7% higher than July 2011. Monthly growth for June was revised down fractionally. Like the other indicators, the FHFA showed uneven results around the country.

The Pending Home Sales Index (PHSI) produced by the National Association of Realtors (NAR) declined 2.6% in August and gave back much of what it gained a month earlier. Nevertheless, the index is 10.7% higher than a year ago and trending near a two year high. Geographically, the Northeast was the only region showing an increase in pending sales. In the West, the index declined 7.2%. In the Midwest it fell 2.6% and in the South pending home sales fell 1.1%. All regions except the West showed results higher than a year ago.

OCTOBER 1, 2012

CMBS 60 DAY DELINQUENCIES DECLINE

The 60 day plus delinquency rate for commercial mortgage backed securities decreased to 9.7% in August from 10.06% a month earlier. Delinquency rates decreased for retail, hotel and multifamily but rose for industrial and office. August showed the first decline in the overall delinquency rate since January 2012 when the rate was 9.30%. Delinquencies were relatively flat throughout 2011 but began inching up again in early 2012 with renewed weakening of the broader economy and brisk European headwinds. Delinquency rates for each major property class are shown in the table at the bottom of this page.

The total volume of CMBS loans outstanding decreased in July to $548.1 billion from $553.6 billion in July. Outstanding balances have steadily declined in both the CMBS sector and in bank portfolios as few new loans are being made, resolutions are increasing and most new construction today is still not economically feasible; meaning its value when complete is often less than the cost to create it. Over the last year, shrinking outstanding balances have been largely the result of pay downs outpacing new originations. We expect that trend to continue at least into 2013. Outstanding balances have declined for 50 of the last 55 months after peaking at $793.5 billion in December 2007. That month was also the value peak for commercial real estate; the starting point from which CRE as a sector lost 50% of its value. Outstanding CMBS balances are down 31% since that time.

The total outstanding balance of delinquent CMBS loans fell by $2.5 billion in August to $53.2 billion. While $2.6 billion in loans were newly delinquent, $5.2 billion were resolved. Resolutions were unusually large in August. That level of decline is not likely to continue and we anticipate that overall delinquencies will resume their upward movement perhaps as early as September.

CMBS delinquencies have historically been very low hovering around one-percent or less since this financing vehicle became popular in the 1990s. Indeed, delinquencies were exceedingly low most of last decade (around 1%) before surging with the collapse of the commercial real estate market coincident with The Great Recession in 2008. CMBS loans have recently experienced higher delinquencies than bank portfolio loans probably because most CMBS issuances were non-recourse to the borrowing entity.

OCTOBER 8, 2012

SEPTEMBER EMPLOYMENT STORY MIXED UNEMPLOYMENT RATE DOWN, LABOR FORCE UP

The much anticipated September jobs report was mixed. Payroll employment rose by a net 114,000 jobs which was in line with expectations. Private sector payrolls increased by 104,000 jobs and government rose by 10,000. There was job growth in the state and federal government sectors but more decline in local government.

Job growth totals for July and August were also revised up. July was revised upward fractionally to142,000 while August was unexpectedly revised upward significantly to181,000 for a net increase of 86,000 jobs for the two prior months. The revisions are disconcerting because of their size and apparent volatility. The August revision, for example, was nearly double the originally reported total (96,000 to 181,000) increase. The government sector was largely responsible for the large revision. The first August report showed a loss of 7,000 government jobs. The revision showed a *net gain* of 45,000 which is an unusually large swing. Eventually the reasons for the extraordinary variance will become clear. At first glance, however, it appears to be a product of declining government job cuts and difficulty in the seasonal adjustment process. The summer and fall months are notoriously more volatile than other months.

Looking at payroll growth longer term, which is always preferable to just the early monthly estimates, shows that the average monthly gain thus far in 2012 was 146,000 as compared to 153,000 per month in 2011. Both are relatively anemic and unlikely to drive robust growth in the broader economy or return the unemployment rate to its long term average of around 5.7%.

Drilling deeper into the numbers shows that the private service sector added 114,000 jobs while the private goods producing sector lost 10,000 jobs. Manufacturing, which has been showing considerable weakness lately, shed 16,000 jobs with the largest declines being in computer and electronic products. Manufacturing weakness appears to be driven by equal parts of weak domestic and global demand.

In the service sector, healthcare gained 44,000 jobs over the month and 295,000 over the last 12 months. Transportation and warehousing gained 17,000 jobs in September and 104,000 over the year. Financial activities grew by about 13,000 jobs while professional and business services also added about 13,000 jobs. Sector growth was driven by modest improvement in real estate and credit intermediation.

The number of involuntary part time workers increased from 8.0 to 8.6 million in September. This too was a stunning increase and should be viewed cautiously. The number of persons unemployed long term (27 weeks or more) declined slightly to 4.8 million but the total is still historically high and represents some 40.1% of the 12.1 million unemployed persons. The labor force participation rate, which has been hovering at a 31 year low of 63.5%, was virtually unchanged at 63.6%.

Turning to unemployment, the headline or "official " unemployment rate fell to 7.8% which is the lowest it has been since January 2009. September ended a run of 43 consecutive months over 8%. Unemployment estimates are based on a separate and much smaller survey of households. In September, the number of unemployed persons declined by 456,000 to 12.1 million persons while total employment rose by 873,000 jobs. The underemployment rate which is the official rate (U-3) plus involuntary part time, marginally attached and discouraged (U-6 measure) was unchanged at 14.7%.

OCTOBER 24, 2012

EXISTING HOME SALES DOWN IN SEPTEMBER UP FOR THE YEAR

Existing home sales in September once again confirmed our view that the free fall in existing home sales is over but both sales and prices would continue to fluctuate within a fairly narrow range and probably for a rather lengthy period of time. Sales volume on a seasonally adjusted annual basis (SAAR) declined to 4.75 million units over the month in September. That is down 1.7% or 80,000 units from the fractional upward revision to the August total which is now 4.83 million units. In our view, longer term performance is more meaningful than the largely inconsequential and fractional monthly changes. Indeed, sales volume is up a meaningful 11% over the 4.28 million units recorded a year ago. The 4.75 million September unit total includes all housing types; single family detached, condominium and co-op units as well as townhouse units. The single family detached sector performed the strongest although both major sectors; single family and condo, posted solid gains according to the National Association of Realtors (NAR).

The national **median price** for all housing types was $183,900 in September. That too is down fractionally from $184,900 a month earlier but up a strong 11.3% from a year ago. September marked the seventh consecutive month of year over year increases. The last time the existing housing sector experienced a similar run was the seven month period at the top of the market between November 2005 and May 2006.

Single family detached home sales volume declined 1.9% over the month to 4.21 million units (SAAR). Nevertheless, the single family sub-sector remains 10.8% higher than the 3.8 million units recorded a year ago. The national single family median price was $184,300 in September. That is also up 11.4% year over year. Condominium and co-op unit sales were unchanged in September at a seasonally adjusted annualized total of 540,000 units. That is up 12.5% from the 480,000 year ago total. The median price was $181,000.

Total **inventory** fell 3.3% to 2.32 million units at the end of September. That represents a relatively normal 5.9 month supply. Nevertheless, inventories have been contracting and that has led to shortages in certain markets, especially in the west. Listed inventory is also down 20% from its year ago levels. The average time on the market was just 70 days in September. The inventory condition requires careful monitoring as isolated supply shortages are beginning to appear and they are pushing up the median price in some areas. In the west, for example, where the shortage is most evident, the median price rose 18.4% year over year to $246,300 as volume declined by 3.4% to 1.13 million units annualized.

Distress sales, which includes foreclosures and short sales, rose modestly from 22% to 24% of all sales in September. There were about 1.14 million transactions annualized in September. The breakdown was 13% foreclosure and 11% short sale. Distress transactions accounted for 30% of all transactions a year ago so the trend is in the right direction. Foreclosures sold for about 21% less than an otherwise comparable but non-distressed home while short sales sold at an average price of 13% less.

Housing markets are tightening as indicated by months of supply now being below the six month mark; a marker generally considered to be a normal level and consistent with a normally functioning market. Nevertheless, the housing market is still not functioning normally and we fully expect more short term fluctuations in both sales volume and median price until long absent equilibrium returns to the market. While the number of distress transactions appears to be slowing, that may be deceiving as there remains a huge number of seriously delinquent loans which servicers are struggling to push through the pipeline. We expect the number of distressed transactions to rise again later this year and into 2013 and that will contribute to yet more market volatility. Our outlook for housing is one of "guarded optimism."

WHY OUR VIEW OF HOUSING STILL REMAINS "GUARDED"

The housing freefall has ended. After six long years, including a double dip housing recession, the market (perhaps arguably) hit bottom a few months ago. It is now showing signs of slow but meaningful recovery. Nearly every recent housing report has contained at least some positive news. Barring an economic fall over the fiscal cliff early next year or some other currently unforeseen economic shock, we expect recovery to continue; albeit it in an agonizingly slow, inconsistent and sometimes painful fashion. Clearly the economy has experienced a housing recession like none other since at least The Great Depression of the 1930s some 75 years ago. Following that depression, it took housing 19 years to recover. There are still well defined weaknesses in the economic fundamentals that drive housing. Indeed, one or a combination of adverse events could derail or prolong housing recovery. Here are a few.

The Fiscal Cliff. While many consumers still appear oblivious to the personal consequences of the so-called fiscal cliff, the possible impact is real and severe. The simultaneous impact of nearly $500 billion in tax hikes and spending cuts would, according to the Congressional Budget Office (CBO), throw the U.S. economy into a relatively severe but possibly short lived recession in the first half of 2013. The CBO also reports that such a recession could cost the economy some two million jobs next year and keep unemployment above 8% through at least 2014. By extension, that may take a very large number of potential home buyers out of the market and keep many of them out until they regain confidence (which is already fragile). Indeed, the unemployed don't generally purchase homes and the concern over continued employment may hold others back.

Employment continues to be a threat to both recovery of the broader economy and the housing market. Aggregate job losses since the beginning of the down turn were deeper and broader than any recession since at least World War II. In addition, the recovery has been longer and it is still unclear when or even if the economy will recover all of the jobs that were lost since the last employment peak. The economy gained only 114,000 new payroll jobs in September bringing the average for the year to about 146,000 per month. That compares to an average of 153,000 per month for the full year 2011.

For illustration purposes, if the economy creates an average of 200,000 jobs per month, employment recovery (as measured by the pre-recession employment level) will be an August 2014 event. At 150,000 jobs per month, recovery will be a July 2016 event. At a mere 50,000 jobs per month, recovery will be an April 2020 event. We acknowledge the weakness in the simplicity of this illustration and also the fact that neither job creation nor recovery are precisely this linear. The point is that job recovery is still several years away.

New jobs being created today are too often lower pay or part time. For example, a number of well known service firms including Darden Restaurants, which operates Olive Garden, Red Lobster and a variety of other chains announced it is considering moving some full time workers to part time to avoid the financial obligation of health care. Other firms have already done that. Some have created two part time positions out of one full time position. Indeed, there was a stunning increase of around 600,000 workers who moved into the involuntary part time category reported by the Bureau of Labor Statistics in September. In addition to part time wages, such moves have an adverse effect on innovation, employee loyalty and much more. Employees who move from full time to part time wages will also find it difficult to purchase a home.

Additionally, wages have been stagnating for years. In addition to other evidence, a significant Pew Research study found that workers who lost a job early in the recession and who found new employment often received compensation around 20% less than the job they lost.

Long term unemployment. There is also growing evidence that those who become unemployed often stay unemployed longer. Indeed, long term unemployment (defined as 27 weeks or more) has been hovering in the 40% range for months. In September, the BLS reported that 40.1% of the 12.1 million unemployed workers, some 4.8 million workers, had been employed long term. This trend is expected to continue.

The nation's unemployment rate has averaged 5.7% since 1948. Recent research on the subject of the natural rate of unemployment by economist Edmund Phelps and others suggests that the "new unemployment rate" could be 6.5% to 7.5%. The following chart graphically depicts job losses from each recession since World War II. Losses are aligned at the depth of job losses and illustrates the months to recovery, which for this purpose, is a return to peak pre-recession employment. The pattern is revealing. In early recessions, most job losses were cyclical in that after the economy recovered, jobs were quickly added. All but the last three recoveries were "V" shaped which confirms that trend. Starting with the recession of 1990, job losses were more structural and were not replaced as quickly. The most recent recession, as depicted by the red line on the chart, is by far deeper, broader and more prolonged than any other. That leads us to the conclusion that, at best, recovery will be a mid-2015 event. Clearly, there are no employment indicators that bode well for housing by suggesting a quick or robust recovery.

Foreclosures have slowed over the last year but the problem has not been resolved. According to RealtyTrac, a leading provider of foreclosure information, there were about 1.5 million foreclosed homes nationwide in September. About 180,400 of them were newly foreclosed while around 80,800 others were sold during the month. One in every 730 dwelling units received some sort of foreclosure notice in September. The ratio is nearly double that in several of the hardest hit states such as Florida (1 in 318), California (1 in 361) and Arizona (1 in 398).

Perhaps more worrisome is the number of homes in the **shadow inventory**. These are homes where mortgages are 60 days or more delinquent, in foreclosure or which have been repossessed by banks. The research firm CoreLogic pegs that total at 2.245 million homes. That is down 10.2 % from a year ago (July 2001—2012) but still a daunting overhang. It is comprised of 1.0 million seriously delinquent mortgages, 900,000 in some stage of foreclosure and another 345,000 bank owned properties.

Delinquencies and Underwater Mortgages remain problematic. At the end of June about 6.3% of home mortgages nationally were delinquent according to the Mortgage Metrics Report published by the Office of Comptroller of the Currency (OCC). Delinquencies are uneven around the country. In Florida, for example, delinquencies soared to more than 15%, a level seen in other states hardest hit by the real estate crisis and recession. In addition, nearly 20% of all mortgages are underwater. In other words, more is owed on the loan than the property is worth. Like mortgage delinquencies, the rate doubles in some of the hard hit states. In Florida, for example, 37% of mortgages are underwater. Delinquencies and underwater mortgages are problematic in that the leading cause of foreclosure today remains negative equity.

As delinquent loans move to foreclosures (as most will) and foreclosed homes move through the pipeline and come back to market for sale, they will almost certainly have an adverse effect on prices and values. The National Association of Realtors recently reported on existing home sales for September. About 24% of the 4.75 million homes sold (1.14 million) were either foreclosures or short sales and they sold at prices significantly less than otherwise comparable non distressed properties. Foreclosures sold for 13% less and short sales sold for 11% less.

Household Wealth has risen since the depths of the recession when consumer balance sheets were crushed. Since the mid 2009 technical end of the recession, households have regained around 71% of lost wealth. That is good but not good enough to support robust and sustained spending. In aggregate, wealth remains about $4.7 trillion below its Q3 2007 peak.

Financing is still not available to a very large share of potential home buyers, especially those who have less than sterling credit and limited or no equity.

Add to these things a stunning loss in home equity as well as recession driven demographic changes, continuing fiscal, regulatory and tax uncertainty and the risks to robust and sustainable housing recovery continue to loom large. The recent sector good news is welcome but threats remain. Stay alert.

COMMERCIAL REAL ESTATE: CONDITION AND OUTLOOK

The U.S. economy continues to limp along in an environment shrouded by uncertainty as it performs far below its potential. While still in positive territory, second quarter GDP growth was a paltry 1.3% annualized. The recently announced first estimate of third quarter growth was not much better at 2.0%. Looking back, the economy has grown at around 2.3% over the last 12 months. Looking forward, there are no leading indicators to suggest significant improvement over the next 12 months. The economy needs a minimum of around 2.5% growth to move the needle on employment and start measurably reducing unemployment.

The labor force participation rate, at 63.8%, is just off its 31 year low. In addition, there are 102 U.S. metros with populations greater than 500,000. Eighty five of them lost jobs in the five years since the recession began in December 2007 and still have a deficit. Only 17 metros have gained jobs. The steepest losses were in some of the nation's historically prime areas for both job creation and real estate development. Los Angeles, for example, currently has a deficit of 333,300 private sector jobs. Chicago is down 204,300, Phoenix is down 150,800 and Miami–Ft. Lauderdale is down some 160,900 jobs.

The housing sector is beginning to emerge from six years of dismal performance. It has been a drag on GDP but is now starting to contribute positively, albeit very modestly. While a bottom likely occurred last July, and recent performance has improved, there are still reasons to be wary of the still fragile recovery.

Some of the uncertainty was lifted recently with the re-election of the President. Nevertheless, remaining uncertainty looms large in the form of the fiscal cliff which could push the nation into another recession in early 2013. Add to that a laundry list of new regulations in process and likely to emerge and businesses continue to have reason to remain fearful and not invest, hire or make other long term commitments.

Enter commercial real estate. Like the broader economy, recovery in commercial real estate is slow, uneven and still plagued by last decade's overbuilding, current foreclosure hangover, the European crisis as well as the usual suspects; tax, regulation and financing uncertainty. Last decade, the commercial real estate sector followed the same pattern as housing. There was unprecedented development and price growth, much of which was created by faux demand until prices peaked in late 2007. The sector quickly collapsed and prices fell roughly 50% from their peak. The fall was faster, steeper and significantly deeper than the housing crash. Moreover, there are perhaps two more conditions currently frustrating recovery. First, there is little measurable demand for new product. Second, most proposed new development today is not economically feasible. In other words, development is constrained in markets where new product is often worth less than it would cost to create.

It is difficult to discern sustained and robust recovery in any commercial real estate product sector other than rental apartments. That sector has been nothing less than hot for nearly three years. Nevertheless, it too is cooling and showing cracks in its most fundamental demand and value drivers. The following is a sector by sector look at current condition and outlook.

With the broader economy struggling to recover and GDP at roughly half of its long term growth rate, the **office market** continues to languish. The office sector became seriously overbuilt last decade as developer rushed to create space to serve the explosive housing growth they believed was coming. In deference to the 1989 Kevin Costner film, *a field of dreams* emerged. They built it but few came as the perceived housing demand turned out to be a mirage. Suburban office markets became seriously overbuilt.

Historically, suburban office markets have been among the first to recover after a recession. Recessions tend to create new entrepreneurs as displaced professionals create new businesses. They often fund startup businesses with home equity loans and locate in less expensive space in suburban locations. That is not the case so far in the current recovery. Today, entrepreneurs have less financial capacity with which to start businesses or expand. Even home equity is virtually non-existent today and financing a start-up is next to impossible.

As a result, office space in central business districts, which are largely dominated by larger and established companies, appears to be recovering at a faster pace than suburban office space.

The office sector is also facing demographic changes. The so-called *Millenial Generation* represents those persons born between roughly 1977 and 1997. That generation is some 88 million persons strong. They are digitally confident and tend to prefer telecommuting or working in large open spaces. Unlike previous generations, most millenials report they couldn't care less about earning the big corner office. This generation is now entering the work force and is leading the way to smaller workspaces and telecommuting; trends we expect to continue, thus reducing office space requirements.

Nationally, the office vacancy rate, according to research firm Reis, is 17.1%. That is about the 1993 level making the sector the slowest to recover. Average capitalization rates are hovering in the 7.8% range for central business district space and 8.4% for suburban.

Office Outlook. We expect the office sector to underperform its potential for the next two or three years. The sector continues to face significant structural and demographic headwinds. Lease expirations and maturing loans are also a growing risk that could bring more space to already over supplied markets.

The **retail sector** has been plagued by slow or no growth in consumer and retail spending as well as by low consumer confidence and an ever increasing internet retail presence. Many traditional retailers complain that consumers often look at products in their stores then buy on the internet.

The national retail vacancy rate is now 10.9% after peaking at 11%. Regional malls have performed better (9% vacancy) due the dominance of large national tenants who are perceived to have more staying power. That said, they are also quicker to pull the plug on underperforming stores. New construction has declined to near record lows with just 569,000 square feet constructed in the third quarter.

Outlook. The sector has clearly not recovered. Fundamentals such as household income, employment, confidence and spending will need to recover before is assured. New development will remain constrained as most is not economically feasible at this time and there is no leading indicator that suggests a short term change.

The **apartment sector** hast been hot for nearly three years. That begs the obvious question, *"how long can it remain hot."* The short answer is "not long." Indeed, the sector is now beginning to show cracks in its most fundamental demand and value drivers.

According to Reis the national third quarter vacancy rate was 4.6%. That is down from 4.7% a quarter earlier and it seems unlikely that it can decline any further. Occupancy gains are slowing significantly. The third quarter was the slowest gain since early 2010 and around half of what it was for the last few quarters. As the sector is bumping up against the highest level of sustainable occupancy, owners appear to be trying to achieve rent increases. That too could prove difficult in the face of stagnating incomes. Class "A" space has the most room for increase while Classes "B" and "C" have the least.

At this time absorption is still faster than inventory growth but that could change as there are about 130,000 units expected to come on line beginning in early 2013.

Capitalization rates have now dipped into the mid 6% range which is equivalent to 2006 levels. There is anecdotal evidence of a few ridiculously low rates under 6% but those appear to be exceptions. And certainly not the rule.

Outlook. The rental apartment market has clearly been the shining star of the broader CRE marketplace however cracks are beginning to appear in the fundamentals. With broader economic recovery softening while the apartment market is still heating up, it is our view that the recent pace of growth is not sustainable.

The **Industrial Sector** includes two broad sub-categories: Flex/ R&D and Warehouse/Distribution. The two sectors are behaving very much like we described for the office sector. After most recessions, the Flex/ RD sector is the first to recover as entrepreneurs bring new technology ventures to market. As pointed out previously, however, this recovery is different as entrepreneurs don't have the financial capacity to create new ventures. As a result, the warehouse / distribution sector is out performing so far in the current recovery.

The Flex /RD subsector recorded a national vacancy rate in the third quarter of 14.2% while warehouse/distribution did moderately better at 12.4%. At the same time average capitalization rates according to PWC (formerly Korpacz) were 8.65% for Flex/ RD and 7.33% for warehouse/distribution.

Containerized storage is also changing the warehousing dynamic. Port cities are scrambling to deepen channels. Most can accommodate Panamax container ships needing a 35 foot channel depth however newer and larger ships (from Asia) require 42 to 52 feet of channel depth.

Outlook. There is currently improved investor sentiment around the industrial property sector. Nevertheless, recovery is still a 2015 event.

NOVEMBER 19, 2012

HOUSING RECOVERY BEGINNING TO GAIN TRACTION

Existing home sales in October rose modestly (+40,000 SAAR) to 4.79 million units despite some modest regional impact from Super Storm Sandy. Sales of all housing types (single family detached, condo and coop units as well as townhouse units rose 2.1% over the month from a downwardly revised 4.69 million units in September. Over the year, sales rose 10.9% from the 4.32 million sales recorded a year ago. That marks the eighth consecutive year-over-year increase, a record last matched in the October 2005 to May 2006 time period. The **median price** recorded in October was $178,600 for all four property types. The single family detached sector dominated sales activity with 4.22 million units sold (SAAR) at a median price of $178,700. The median price was 10.9% higher than recorded a year ago.

First time homebuyers accounted for 1.48 million purchases or 31% of total. The ratio was 32% in September and 34% a year ago. **All cash sales** totaled 1.39 million or about 29% of all sales. That is up fractionally from 28% a month ago. Investors dominated the cash buyer category with 20% of all homes sold during the month.

Total **inventory** fell 1.4% to 2.14 million units at the end of October. That is a 5.4 month supply and is the lowest recorded inventory since

February 2006 when it stood at 5.2 months. Nevertheless, inventories have been contracting for several months and that has led to shortages in certain markets and has been putting upward pressure on prices in those areas. Listed inventory is also down 21.9% from its year ago levels. The average time on the market was just 71 days in September. The inventory condition requires careful monitoring as supply shortages are beginning to appear and they are pushing up the median price in some areas. In the west, for example, where the shortage is most evident, the median price rose 21.2% year-over-year to $242,100 as sales volume rose 4.4% to 1.18 million units; 3.5% higher than a year ago.

Distress sales, which includes foreclosures and short sales, remained flat at 24% of all sales in September. There were about 1.15 million distress transactions in October on an annualized basis. The breakdown was evenly divided at 12% foreclosure and 12% short sale. Distress transactions accounted for 30% of all transactions a year ago so the trend is in the right direction. Foreclosures sold for about 20% less than an otherwise comparable but non-distressed home while short sales sold at an average price of 14% less. These gaps changed only fractionally over the month.

Super Storm Sandy appears to have had only a modest impact on sales as it occurred at the very end of the month. Nevertheless, the storm impacted a very broad area encompassing around 16% of the nation's housing stock and 10.1% of the nation's households. The storm impacted area also represents about 13.2% of the nation's GDP.

Current condition and outlook. Housing markets are clearly tightening as indicated by months of supply now being slightly below the six month mark; a marker generally considered to be a normal level and consistent with a normally functioning market. Nevertheless, the housing market is still not functioning normally and we fully expect more short term fluctuations in both sales volume and median price until long absent equilibrium returns to the market. While the number of distress transactions appears to be slowing, that may be deceiving as there remains a huge number of seriously delinquent loans which servicers are struggling to push through the pipeline. We expect the number of distressed transactions to rise again later this year and into 2013 and that will contribute to yet more market volatility. Our outlook for housing is one of "guarded optimism." While housing recovery is underway and is steadily gaining traction, it remains erratic and will likely remain that way until employment rebounds.

NOVEMBER 28, 2012

NEW HOME SALES UP SOLIDLY YEAR OVER YEAR

Sales of new homes in the U.S. were little changed at 368,000 units (SAAR) in October after having risen in September by 5.7%; the fastest pace since April 2010. Sales increased 17.2% over the 314,000 recorded a year ago. The April 2010 sales volume was artificially inflated by home buyer tax credits at the time. The current pace, however, is unaffected by any form of stimulus. That, combined with strong existing home sales in October support our view that the housing market is finally beginning its long awaited recovery.

The median price of a new home sold in October was $237,700, up solidly from $212,300 recorded a year earlier. The seasonally adjusted estimate of new homes offered for sale at the end of October was 147,000 which represents a 4.8 month supply at the current sales pace. The current inventory as measured by months of supply is relatively healthy although the total sales volume is not, despite the impressive percentage gains over the last year. Volume closer to 700,000 units is widely considered to be a healthy sales pace.

Residential construction and permitting activity was strong in October suggesting that sales activity over the next few months will also be strong. Building permits increased 29.8% from the same period a year ago. Residential permits now stand at 866,000 of which 562,000 or 65% are single family units. Multifamily permits (buildings with five or more units) totaled 280,000 and declined slightly from September. Nevertheless, they rose 40% from a year ago. The multifamily sector remains strong at this time but fundamentals are beginning to show early signs of weakness.

Construction starts totaled 894,000 in October. That is up 3.6% from September and up 41.9% since last year at this time. There were also

772,000 completions in October. Completions were up a very solid 17.3% over the month and 33.6% over the year. The single family detached sector dominated at 542,000 completions at 61% or 542,000 total units.

Although new homes capture only a small portion of the nation's home sales, they have a disproportionate impact on the broader economy due to the multiplier effect. In other words, for each dollar spent there is an additional amount spent over and above the initial investment that ripples through the broader economy. In its broadest terms each home built creates an average of three jobs for a year and generates about $90,000 in tax revenue. Housing has been a drag on economic growth the last few years however the sector appears to be poised to turn the corner and contribute positively to GDP growth by mid-2013.

DECEMBER 5, 2012

CMBS DELINQUENCIES DECLINE, INVESTOR INTEREST RISES, RISK APPETITE GROWS

As CMBS delinquencies decline and more assets leave special servicing, investor interest in CMBS bonds has grown. Investors are once again taking on more risk in search of yield.

Delinquencies are still high by historic standards but improvement is evident. The 60 day-plus delinquency rate declined overall to 9.38% in October, the most recent month available. That is down from 9.57% a month earlier and was the third monthly decline. Delinquency rates decreased for all major property types except multifamily rental apartments. At the same time, total delinquencies fell $600 million to $51.5 billion. Approximately $2.1 billion in loans were newly delinquent while $2.7 billion were resolved during the month, clearly a move in the right direction. Total CMBS loans outstanding also declined in October to $544.5 billion. That is down from $548.7 billion a month earlier. Outstanding balances have steadily declined in both the CMBS sector and in bank portfolios as few new loans are being made, resolutions are increasing and most new commercial construction today is

---

still not justified by continuing weak demand nor is new development economically feasible; two conditions that are inseparable.

Over the last year, shrinking outstanding balances have been largely the result of pay downs outpacing new originations. We expect that trend to continue at least into 2013. The majority of loans backed by five year leases begun in 2007 have seen leases renegotiated at lower rates thus removing what could have been a huge downside risk, Outstanding balances have declined for 52 of the last 57 months after peaking at $793.5 billion in December 2007. That month was also the peak value month for commercial real estate; the starting point from which the sector lost 50% of its value. Outstanding CMBS balances are down over 31% since that time.

The large decline in CMBS delinquencies was driven primarily by a large increase in the value of loans leaving special servicing. The value of those loans far exceeded the value of incoming loan delinquencies. The remaining inventory of problem CMBS loans is more troublesome and most are not good liquidation candidates at the moment. While that has caused the volume to decline, the length of time loans remain in special servicing has increased. According to Fitch Ratings, the average time in special servicing rose to 18.6 months in June 2012. The duration was 14.8 months a year earlier and 10.8 months, two years earlier in June 2010. Again, the movement is in the right direction.

Investor risk appetite has been growing as investors quickly snap up new offerings; even those that include mortgages secured by assets with significant vacant space and underwriting based on projections. This type of underwriting was responsible in large part for many problems still being worked out today.

DECEMBER 7, 2012

WHO IS REALLY CREATING THE JOBS THIS RECOVERY

The Great Recession as it has come to be known was declared over at the end of June 2009. The economy has therefore been "recovering" for over three years. By historical standards, employment should have recovered and the economy should be robust or at least performing nearer its potential. Nevertheless, it is not. Despite numerous Federal Reserve and Administration attempts to stimulate the economy, nearly every sector from consumer spending, employment, housing and commercial real estate are all bouncing along the bottom in a recovery which is the weakest since at least World War II.

Conventional wisdom (or perhaps political mythology) suggests that small business is the engine of the economy and the contributor of most jobs. Indeed, that was true prior to The Great Recession. Today however, big business is leading the jobs recovery and that may help explain the mediocre job creation. It may also suggest that recovery may take much longer than is widely expected.

Data from the Bureau of Labor Statistics (BLS) suggest that small firms actually did better during the recession. BLS Employment Dynamics data show that small firms (companies with fewer than 20 employees) cut back about two-percent from peak to trough while companies with more than 1,000 employees cut back by nearly 14%. This is surprising since small firms tend to be more dependent upon bank financing than large firms and financing virtually dried up during the recession. Large firms usually have more avenues open to them to raise cash. These avenues may include corporate bonds, equity issuance and commercial paper. The data reveal that not only did small firms experience fewer job losses during the recession, they actually cut back less on hiring than did larger firms. Larger firms often implemented rigid hiring freezes while the smaller and nimbler entrepreneurial companies hired as resources permitted and opportunities arose.

Labor Dynamics changed post-recession. Larger firms have been hiring much more aggressively while smaller firms have languished. BLS data which is also confirmed by the payroll processing firm ADP, indicate that less than 30% of job gains since 2010 were the result of hiring by companies with fewer than 50 employees. The vast majority of new hires were by large companies. One explanation may be that since large companies in general cut deeper they have more to make up than smaller companies. Nevertheless, there are weaknesses in that theory too. Business dynamics data indicate that there are fewer new firms being formed today and those that are being formed are hiring fewer employees than they did historically. A study by the Hudson Institute, a Washington, D.C. based conservative think tank, shows that existing companies (big and small) tend to be net job losers averaging a net loss in aggregate of around 1.0 million jobs each year. New firms however, have historically gained 3.0 million jobs on average each year. Nevertheless even the size of a new firm has declined over the years. In 1998, the average size new firm has 6.4 employees. By 2011, the average size firm had fallen to 3.9 employees.

There appear to be numerous reasons for the change in labor dynamics and the shift to big companies being the predominant job creators. Reasons include the lingering effect of The Great Recession, business, tax and healthcare cost uncertainty, technology and cost saving techniques chipping away at employment, increased productivity and structural employment changes leading to more permanent than cyclical losses.

In our view, diminished home equity has also had a profoundly negative effect on small business. A significant amount of home equity has historically been used to fund entrepreneurial ventures. Today, in an era of seriously diminished home equity, entrepreneurs are often unable to start, or fund new ventures or grow existing small businesses. That leaves larger firms as today's primary job growth driver—at least for now.

DECEMBER 13, 2012

NOVEMBER EMPLOYMENT SUMMARY

The nation's labor market absorbed the impact of super storm Sandy much better than had been expected. Indeed, any adverse effect on job totals was negligible overall. While the storm, which made landfall in the Northeast on October 29th, was severe and caused billions of dollars in both damage and lost productivity, the probable reason for the negligible impact on jobs was in the measurement standard used by the Bureau of Labor Statistics. Workers were counted as unemployed only if they were off payroll for one pay period or more and were not paid. Many workers lost hours or days but were still counted as employed whether or not they were paid for the lost time. Moreover, it will probably take another month or two before the fog clears from around the

Sandy impact numbers. Regional and State employment estimates will be released on December 21st and that should show more granularly where the Sandy impact really was.

Sandy aside, total payroll employment also surprised on the upside. The economy added 146,000 net payroll jobs. The private sector added 147,000 while the government sector lost 1,000 jobs. Gains originally reported for September and October were revised down a total of 49,000 jobs to 138,000 and 132,000 respectively. The declines were largely government related. September was revised down from a gain of 20,000 to a gain of 10,000 and October was revised from a loss of 13,000 jobs to a loss of 51,000. In the private sector September and October revisions were offsetting.

By sector, construction employment declined 20,000 jobs which is likely the result of weather related delays including super storm Sandy. We expect the construction sector will begin to show a modest gain as early as December as Sandy recovery begins in earnest and new housing construction gains traction. Manufacturing changed little overall but gains and losses within the sector were mixed. Food manufacturing declined by 12,000 jobs and chemicals were down 9,000. These were in part offset by gains in motor vehicles and parts (+10,000) and wood products (+3,000). Other key sectors generally gained jobs.

The retail sector added 53,000 jobs. The sector typically shows gains at this time of year but the increase in November was larger than usual. That is probably a result of an earlier than usual Thanksgiving holiday which results in a longer holiday selling season. The retail sector has added 140,000 jobs over the last three months. The largest three month gains were in clothing and accessories (+33,000); electronics (+9,000) and general merchandise (+10,000). Healthcare added 20,000 jobs in November with noteworthy gains of 8,000 in hospitals and 5,000 in ambulatory care facilities. Professional and business services added an impressive 43,000 jobs with most of the gain in computer system design and related services.

Net job gains thus far in 2012 have averaged about 151,000 per month which is nearly the same as full year 2011. Private employers have averaged slightly more at 152,000 jobs monthly. Growth has generally been improving since mid year. The average, though positive, is indicative of modest economic recovery. The economy still needs around 125,000 new jobs per month just to keep up with population growth and double that to push the unemployment rate down significantly and drive more robust economic growth.

The headline **unemployment rate** declined from 7.9% to 7.7% in November, its lowest level in several years. Nevertheless, the decline was not the result of significant job gains but rather more workers dropping out of the work force. Over the month (October to November), some 350,000 more workers left the labor force. That also pushed the labor force participation rate down to 63.6% where it remains at its lowest level in 31 years. That is the share of the population actually working or looking for work. There are still 4.4 million fewer workers today than when the Great Recession Officially started in December 2007.

DECEMBER 18, 2012

CASE-SHILLER: HOME PRICES ROSE—GROWTH RATE SLOWED

The Case-Shiller national composite home price index, which covers all nine U.S. census regions, increased 3.6% in the third quarter of 2012 as compared to the same period in 2011. That is the strongest growth rate in over six years. It is also the sixth consecutive month of rising prices. Over the quarter (Q2 to Q3), the national index increased 2.2% after having risen 7.1% from the first quarter to the second. The 10 and 20 city indices also rose 2.1% and 3.0% respectively. Eighteen of the 20 cities covered in the composite 20 index saw annual price increases. Phoenix, which was one of the hardest hit major cities in the housing bust, soared back and is leading the recovery with a 20.4% annual growth rate. Miami, which was also hard hit experienced 7.4% annual growth in September while Tampa saw 5.9% growth and Las Vegas experienced a 3.8% rise. In the loss column were New York at –2.3% and Chicago at –1.5%. Both metros were negative month over month as well. Atlanta has been languishing with 26 months of annualized decline but it broke that string with fractional growth of 0.1% in September. The national composite index shows prices back at their mid 2003 levels.

Looking behind the numbers, price gains are both slowing but are becoming more geographically diverse. On a quarterly basis, the gains in the third quarter were only about half of what they were in the second. Nevertheless, appreciation was more diverse as prices increased in 111 of the 134 metropolitan areas covered by the national composite. Prices increased in all but two of the nine census regions. Gains ranged from a paltry 0.5% in the Mid-Atlantic Region to a stunning 21% in the Mountain Region. This recent string of increases supports our view that the housing market has bottomed. The volatility, however, supports our additional view that prices are still likely to fluctuate within a fairly narrow range and that there is still a high probability of modest but short lived price declines.

Foreclosures are improving significantly but are still casting a dark cloud over the housing market. According to RealtyTrac, foreclosure activity decreased three-percent month over month in November. Foreclosures are down a very significant 19% year over year. The decline in overall foreclosure activity was led by a 9.6% decline in pre-foreclosure filings. In fact, November marked a 71 month low in pre-foreclosure activity. Scheduled foreclosure auctions also fell 7.7% from the previous month and are now about 26% fewer than they were a year ago.

On the flip side, bank repossessions rose 10.6% between October and November and are now about 5.3% higher than a year ago. November marked the first increase in more than two years. Mortgage servicers are working through what is still a backlog of distressed properties and processing delays. As these homes move to bank REO (real estate owned), they are likely to renew the downward pressure on home prices. The recent uptick in repossessions implies that there may be modest near term price declines however they are likely to be very short lived as new foreclosure activity is declining.

Overall, housing is benefiting from both tightening inventories and fewer distressed properties coming to market in many parts of the country irrespective of the very recent uptick in repossessions. In general, housing is quickly moving from being a drag on the broader economy to contributing positively. While prices are rising and are clearly off their bottom, they are still climbing out of a very deep hole. Nationally, prices are still about 30% below their 2006 peak. Some of the hardest

---

hit geographies are still in a hole twice as deep where peak to trough declines were 50-65%. Much of the house price appreciation between 2002 and 2006 was artificial and clearly not true demand as it was not backed by consumer income levels or real purchasing power. As history has so painfully revealed, the growth was not sustainable.

DECEMBER 20, 2012

HOUSING RECOVERY SOLIDLY IN PLACE BUT RENEWED BOOM NOT LIKELY

Existing home sales in November rose solidly to 5.04 million units from the downwardly revised October total of 4.76 million units. Data are from the National Association of Realtors (NAR) and totals are at a seasonally adjusted annual rate. The November increase represents a 5.09% gain or 264,000 more sales. Similarly, sales are up over the year, by 14.5% or 640,000 units. The reported median price for all 1-4 family housing types including single family detached homes as well as condominium, townhouse and co-op units was $180,600. That is up 10.1% over the year. The median price was identical for the single family detached sector. Sales are now at their highest level since November 2009 when sales surged to 5.44 million units then retreated significantly. Moreover, November was the ninth consecutive monthly year over year price gain. The last time there was a similar gain was from September 2005 through May 2006 near the end of last decade's boom years.

Looking behind the numbers, **First time homebuyers** accounted for about 1.5 million purchases or 30% of the annualized total. The ratio was 31% in October and 35% a year ago. **All cash sales** totaled 1.5 million units or about 30% of all sales. That is up fractionally from 29% a month ago. Investors dominated the cash buyer category with 19% of all homes sold during the month.

Total **inventory** fell 3.8% to 2.03 million units at the end of November. That is the lowest since boom year 2005. Raw unsold inventory is only about 1.89 million units, the lowest it has been since December 2001.

Total inventory is a 4.8 month supply at the current sales pace and is the lowest recorded inventory since September 2005 when it stood at 4.6 months. Inventories have been contracting for several months and that has led to shortages in certain markets and has been putting upward pressure on prices in those areas. Listed inventory is also down 22.5% from its year ago levels. The average time on the market was just 70 days in November. Despite the increase in activity, the housing market is now in its Winter slow season and many potential sellers have taken their property off the market for the season. That too is reducing inventory and putting upward pressure on prices. Nevertheless, the inventory condition requires careful monitoring as supply shortages are beginning to appear and they are pushing up the median price in some areas. In the west, for example, where the shortage is most evident, the median price rose 23.9% year-over year to a median price of $248,300. Sales volume rose 4.4% over the year to 1.19 million units.

Distress sales, which include foreclosures and short sales, declined slightly to 1.1 million units or 22% of all sale transactions. The breakdown was divided between 12% foreclosure and 10% short sale. Foreclosures sold for about 20% less than an otherwise comparable but non-distressed home while short sales sold at an average price of 16% less. These gaps changed only modestly over the month.

Super Storm Sandy appears to have had only a modest impact on sales in the Northeast. The disruption it caused in the directly impacted areas was more than offset by gains in other areas of the Northeast. Nevertheless, the storm impacted a very broad area encompassing around 16% of the nation's housing stock and 10.1% of the nation's households. The impacted area also represents about 13.2% of the nation's GDP.

Current condition and outlook. In a commentary last May, we opined that housing had reached a bottom. We also opined that a renewed boom era was not imminent and that housing would experience ups and downs within a fairly narrow range. Indeed it has. While housing is recovering, it is still a work in progress. In our view the recovery is sustainable but we also caution that it is not yet functioning normally. We expect more short term fluctuations until long absent equilibrium returns to the market. Our outlook for housing still remains one of "guarded optimism."

2013
THE NEW NORMAL?

"More of the same" would describe economic recovery in 2013. Employment dynamics remained volatile but home prices accelerated. After a remarkable slowdown, new residential construction showed renewed signs of life.

Late in the spring, however, it appeared as through economic recovery had taken a spring break. Employment numbers turned dismal and retail sales also turned in a disappointing report. Those dynamic caused all consumer sentiment indicators to decline.

The 2013 experience may be the new normal.

JANUARY 3, 2013

NEW HOME SALES RISE WHILE CONSTRUCTION DECLINES

Sales of newly constructed homes rose 4.4% to 377,000 units in November from the revised October rate of 361,000 units. That is the greatest number of sales since early 2010 when sales activity was being fuelled by tax credits. As we saw then, however, the stimulus driven sales volume was not sustainable as sales plunged 80% to an all-time low of 280,000 units in May 2010 after expiration of the tax credits.

The November total of 377,000 units was 15% higher than November 2011 when sales totaled 327,000 units. Sales have also rebounded nearly 35% from the all-time low. While the percentage gains seem impressive, new home sales are emerging from a very deep trough and still have a very long way to rise before reaching a sales pace of around 700,000 units which is typically considered healthy. For historical perspective, new home sales reached an annualized high of 1,389,000 units in July of 2005 during the housing bubble before falling 80% to the trough of 280,000 units in May 2010.

The median price of all new homes sold in November was $246,200. The median is the point at which half the sales prices are higher and half are lower. The average of all sale prices was $299,700. For comparison, the median price of an existing home sold in November was much lower at $180,600. While distress sales (foreclosure and short sales) of existing homes have fallen sharply over the last year or so, builders of new homes still have difficulty competing with deeply discounted sale prices of existing homes. Nevertheless, strong and consistent sales of existing homes combined with slow but steadily improving new home sales performance support our view that the long anticipated housing recovery is finally in process and is sustainable. Despite meaningful recovery, sales are still likely to fluctuate within a relatively narrow range for the next couple of years. Moreover, sales of new homes are likely to languish until employment, income, home equity and household wealth show more robust improvement. The same metrics impact existing home sales but are more pronounced in the new home sector.

Residential construction and permitting activity grew modestly in November. Residential building permits rose to 899,000 from 866,000 units in November (+3.81%). Permitting activity a year ago was 709,000 the single family detached component declined slightly from a revised 566,000 units in October to 565,000 units in November.

Housing starts totaled 861,000 in November. That is down three-percent from the revised October figure of 888,000 but up 21.6% from a year earlier. The single family detached component declined 4.1% over the month to 565,000 units. The multifamily component (defined as buildings with five units or more) totaled 285,000. The multifamily sector has been and remains strong but is showing signs of weakening fundamentals. Owners have achieved what is arguably maximum occupancy approaching 96% and are now trying to sustain revenue growth by raising rents. That will be difficult to sustain in the face of stagnating wages.

Completions in November totaled 677,000 units and were 9.7% below the revised October total of 750,000 units. The single family sector dominated completions at 520,000 units or 30% of total completions

---

but it too was down fractionally from October. There were an estimated 150,000 multifamily completions in November.

The modest volatility does not appear to be a trend reversal. Instead, much of the downward movement is likely seasonal. There are some potential headwinds though; most specifically, persistently high unemployment.

JANUARY 23, 2013

EXISTING HOME SALES DIP SEASONALLY IN DECEMBER

Housing Recovery Still Solidly In Place

Existing home sales dipped slightly in December to 4.94 million units from a downwardly revised 4.99 million units a month earlier. Data are from the National Association of Realtors (NAR) and are at a seasonally adjusted annual rate (SAAR). The total existing home sale and median price numbers include single family detached homes as well as condominium, co-op and townhouse units. The December total is 12.8% higher than the 4.38 million-unit total recorded a year ago. The median price in December for all housing types was $180,800 which is 11.5% higher than a year ago. Single family detached home sales dominated total existing sales at 4.35 million units at a median price of $180,300.

NAR reports all monthly sales data at a seasonally adjusted annual rate. At the end of the year, however, total sales and median price are reported for the year without seasonal adjustment. The preliminary 12 month sales total for all housing types in 2012 was 4.65 million units. That is up 9.2% from the total of 4.26 million sales recorded in 2011 and is the highest sales volume since 2007 when 5.03 million sales were recorded. The 2012 rate of increase was also the strongest since 2004. The overall 2012 median price was $176,600. The annual totals will almost certainly be revised over the next month or two. Historically, however, the revisions have been within a fairly narrow range.

In our view, the slight dip in volume is not reason for concern. It appears to be seasonal and most importantly, housing recovery remains intact. Nevertheless, there are still headwinds that may shake recovery but not derail it. Indeed, the most significant threats continue to be historically high unemployment, diminished household wealth, foreclosures and shadow inventory, potential sequestration related job losses, stagnant wages and, of course, the impact of the largest one year tax increase in U.S. history which was driven by the fiscal cliff legislation and healthcare reform. Overall, our outlook for housing remains one of "guarded optimism."

Looking behind the December numbers, **first time homebuyers** accounted for about 1.48 million purchases or about 30% of the annualized total. The ratio was 31% in October and 35% a year ago. **All cash** sales totaled 1.43 million units or about 29% of all sales. That ratio has been consistent over the last few months and has changed only fractionally. The share of investor cash purchases rose slightly to 21% of all sales. The investor share was 19% a month ago but has hovered in a consistent range throughout 2012.

Total inventory fell 8.5% to 1.82 million homes available for sale. That is a 4.4 month supply at the current sales pace. Listed inventory is a significant 21.6% below a year ago. The current housing supply is the lowest since the peak of the housing boom in May 2005 when inventory represented a 4.3 month supply. Low inventory levels are clearly putting upward pressure on home prices. In December, the average time on market was 70 days. That too is consistent with where it has been for several months. We expect the tight inventory situation to abate during the spring and summer selling seasons as prices continue to rise and more potential home sellers enter the market. That should return inventory, price increases and marketing time to more normal and sustainable levels.

Distress sales, which includes foreclosures and short sales, ticked up slightly to 1.18 million units or 24% of all sale transactions. The breakdown was divided equally between foreclosure and short sale at 12% each. Foreclosures sold for about 17% less than an otherwise comparable but non-distressed home while short sales sold at an average price of 16% less. These gaps changed only modestly over the month. Shadow inventory (loans 90 days+ delinquent or in foreclosure) have declined to 1.8 million loans however that is still enough to keep foreclosures at higher than normal levels into the short term future.

STRUCTURAL UNEMPLOYMENT CONTRIBUTES TO VOLATILE EMPLOYMENT DYNAMICS

The Great Recession, as it has come to be known, profoundly changed the nation's employment sector. Today, nearly four years after the recession was declared over, employment and the broader economy still struggle to recover. The reasons, which are not at all obvious are both many and diverse and range from structural changes in employment dynamics, the darker side of technology, fiscal policy, law, regulation and much more.

Job losses during recessions. Have usually been cyclical and, when graphed, they resemble a "V" shape. Historically, jobs were lost then the economy or industry recovered and employees were rehired either by the same company or at least in the same or allied industries. That was the pattern throughout eight of the eleven recessions since World War II. That pattern began to change following the recession of the early 1990s. While the losses were not particularly deep, the "loss curve" flattened and it took about 32 months to recover. That is far longer than historical recoveries. The same pattern repeated itself following the relatively mild recession 10 years later in the early 2000s. It took about four years to recover lost jobs and during the recovery, wages stagnated. Enter the 2007 Great Recession. Job losses were much deeper than at any time since The Great Depression of the 1930s and have still not recovered.

The common element throughout the three recent recessions is technology. While technology has been chipping away at employment for decades, its effect became most pronounced in the early 1990s and, in our view, that was the leading cause of the shift from cyclical to structural job loss. Moreover, from the three most recent recessions, it has become apparent that many jobs—especially at lower levels—probably will not be replaced. Technology now does what people might have historically done. That means that to remain employed, many Americans must upgrade their skills and learn new ones. Retraining has become a huge need as has the need to better educate our children and better prepare them to compete in a more technological global economy. Workers are no longer mindlessly assembling so-called widgets. Robots now do that but people run the computers that run the robots and that takes an entire new skill set which goes far beyond the rote task of assembly.

As the economy recovers, global competition and skill based technological change will drive worker skill requirements even higher. If the level of educational achievement does not keep up—and it has not for nearly four decades—many workers will be left behind, wages will stagnate, long term unemployment will rise and wage inequality will widen further thus increasing the structural unemployment rate even more. Moreover, America's well recognized innovation advantage will suffer. A depressing sidebar is that the median wage for men with only a high school education has declined an inflation adjusted 46% since 1970. If that trend continues, the effect will ripple through the broader economy inhibiting spending. It may also lead to a widening gap between the wealthy and middle class and perhaps lead to cultural changes and even unrest such as we have seen in several European companies in recent years.

Duration of unemployment is another unwanted trend of recent vintage. Today, the average duration of unemployment has reached a disturbing 35 weeks which is the longest it has ever been. The longer someone is unemployed, the more their skills are likely to deteriorate and the less likely they are to find a comparable new job. The back story here is that many employers are reluctant to hire the long term unemployed and that is clearly exacerbating an already difficult employment recovery.

The nation's employment problem is exceedingly complex and certainly defies easy or traditional answers. Much of the traditional reasoning and rules of thumb no longer apply.

JANUARY EMPLOYMENT REPORT—A MIXED STORY

The January 2013 employment situation report offered up a mixed view of the U.S. labor market. Payroll employment grew by 157,000 jobs over the month. The private sector added 166,000 jobs while state and Federal government shed 9,000. At first blush, January looks like another in a long line of mediocre job reports. The bigger story, however, is the revisions for November and December as well as the annual benchmark revisions which showed more jobs having been added than originally reported throughout most of 2012. November payroll growth was revised up to +247,000 (from +161,000) while December was revised up to +196,000 (from +155,000).

The Bureau of Labor Statistics also performs an annual "benchmark revision" wherein the original monthly estimates for the previous year are revised using the full universe of data from the employment tax system. The level of non-farm payroll employment in March 2012 was revised up by 424,000 jobs (not seasonally adjusted) or +0.3%. All in, the increase to last year's payrolls was a highly significant +747,000 with a total of 600,000 jobs having been created in the last three months. That is a revised average of 200,000 new jobs per month since November. On average, payrolls increased by about 181,000 jobs monthly over the last year rather than the 153,000 average monthly gains previously estimated. As a result, 2013 is beginning with a little stronger employment foundation than originally thought. Nevertheless, the job market still faces widespread uncertainty and significant negative pressure.

Returning to the January numbers, the 157,000 net gains is underwhelming. By sector, health care continued its string of monthly job gains. Growth in ambulatory health care services such as physician offices and outpatient care centers grew by 28,000 jobs. That was partially offset by a modest loss in employment at residential care facilities resulting in a net gain of 23,000 jobs. The sector has added 320,000 jobs over the last year.

Employment in construction increased by about 28,000 jobs. The gain was almost equally divided between residential and non-residential specialty trade contractors. Since its trough in January 2011, the sector has added 296,000 jobs with about one-third of that gain occurring in just the last three months. The recent gain is largely the result of the housing sector beginning to rebound. Nevertheless, the construction sector remains about 2.0 million jobs below its peak level in April 2006 at the height of the housing bubble. Going forward, we expect the sector to continue to grow steadily but modestly as housing, particularly new construction continues its slow but steady recovery.

Service providing industries added about 130,000 jobs during the month. The gains were spread among a wide variety of industries. Retail trade also added about 33,000 jobs. Clothing stores led the way among retailers. That seems unusual given the weakness in consumer spending. The sector also lost 8,000 temporary workers. While the loss is typical in January as seasonal employees are released, the number is high by historical standards. It is unclear at this writing whether retailers over hired in anticipation of stronger holiday sales; are anticipating slower sales going forward or are dealing with the requirements of the affordable healthcare act.

Employment in wholesale trade rose by 15,000 jobs in January. The gain was largely in the non-durable goods component (consumables). The sector has added about 291,000 jobs since its cycle low in May 2010. At the same time employment in manufacturing, financial activities, professional and business services and leisure and hospitality were essentially unchanged over the month.

Transportation and warehousing declined. Couriers and messengers lost 19,000 jobs following strong seasonal hiring in November and December. That seasonal pattern of growth followed by decline is typical.

The government sector lost 9,000 jobs in local and federal government in January. Over half of the jobs lost were in public education. Total government payrolls have contracted by 74,000 jobs over the last 12 months. Most were in state and local government. The contraction is slowing and we expect the burden of job losses to shift to the federal government this year as sequestration takes a currently uncertain toll on defense and other federal government spending.

Total payroll unemployment was essentially unchanged at about 12.3 million in January. Those unemployed long term, which by Bureau of

Labor Statics definition is 27 weeks or longer was essentially unchanged at about 4.7 million persons or 38.1% of the unemployed population. Those working part time because their hours were reduced or they could not find full time employment remained at about 8.0 million workers. Those marginally attached to the workforce fell by 366,000 as compared to a year earlier although the total is still elevated at 2.4 million persons. That category also includes 804,000 discouraged workers which is a category of workers who have given up looking as they believe there is no job available for them. These categories total 22.7 million and represent the approximate number of Americans who are unemployed or under-employed.

The **unemployment rate** in January inched up 0.1% to 7.9%. Among the major worker groups, both adult men and adult women (age 20 and over) experienced an unemployment rate of 7.3%. The teenage unemployment rate (age 16-19) was 23.4%. By race or ethnicity, whites experienced a 7.0% unemployment rate while blacks experienced 13.8% and Hispanics experienced 9.7%. By educational attainment, those with less than a high school education experienced 12% unemployment. With a high school diploma, unemployment dropped to 8.1%. It dropped further to 7.0% with either some college or an associate degree and to 3.7% with a Bachelor's degree or higher. All rates are seasonally adjusted by the BLS.

The nation's official unemployment known variously as the headline unemployment rate or the U-3 measure was 7.9% in January. It has hovered at or near eight-percent for the last 50 months and there are no leading indicators to suggest the rate will decline significantly anytime soon. Moreover, the rate may even be deceptively low as it does not account for more than 5.0 million persons who have left the labor force since the technical end of the Great Recession in June 2009. The headline rate also does not account for persons moving from full time to part time employment. Indeed the raw number of jobs may rise even if full time employment declines but part time employment rises.

The better measure in our view is the so-called *U-6 measure of labor underutilization* as it offers a more comprehensive look at <u>un</u>employment and <u>under</u>employment. The U-6 starts with the official unemployment rate (U-3) then adds discouraged workers (sum = U-4), then adds all other marginally attached workers (sum = U-5) and finally adds involuntary part time workers resulting in the U-6 measure. The BLS asserts that the U-6 is not truly an "unemployment" rate as it includes some who are working such as the involuntary part time workers. Indeed, that is correct. It does, however, more precisely measure the effect of underemployment including those persons involuntarily moving from full time to part time. This issue will take on more significance going forward as more companies shed full time workers in favor of part time workers to avoid the need to provide health care benefits under the Affordable Care Act which is in the early stages of implementation.

The U-6 measure of labor underutilization in January was 14.4%. It has been stuck at that level (+) throughout most of the current post recession period making this the slowest employment recovery following any recession since World War II.

The **nation's labor force participation rate** was 63.6% in January. That is the lowest participation rate since 1981; some 32 years ago. It was 65.7% when the recession technically ended in mid 2009 and was also higher than the current rate throughout the last four recessions. Some will pass off the extraordinary low participation rate as more baby boomers retiring and leaving the labor force. According to the non-partisan Congressional Budget office, however, an aging and retiring population explains only about one-third of the downward change. The balance is the product of a troubled economy where Americans cannot find full employment. The employment to population ratio was 58.6% in January. It too was unchanged.

Looking forward at employment. The short term future for employment is mixed. While growth is far from robust, housing appears to have turned the corner. After being a drag on economic growth since the bubble burst in 2007, housing is now contributing positively. We expect that trend to continue and with it will come additional jobs. While new home construction and sales are far from robust, permitting activity, construction starts and sales have all risen and the multiplier effect of creating jobs in allied industries is significant.

On the down side, the labor force faces several new challenges this year. By some accounts, the economy could lose one-million jobs if Congress and the President fail to change the law that will make sequestration a reality in March or soon thereafter. Federal government spending cuts are already being felt. In addition, small businesses are being squeezed by slow economic recovery together with the effect of higher taxes plus the effect of the Affordable Healthcare Act. Indeed, small businesses are not creating the number of jobs they did during previous recoveries and that is clearly slowing the current recovery.

Notwithstanding the January payroll data revisions, we expect monthly job creation to remain in the 150,000 range for most of 2013. That will be enough to support population growth and new work force entrants but it is not likely to push the unemployment rate down measurably.

FEBRUARY 7, 2013

FISCAL POLICY AND REGULATION WEIGH HEAVILY ON EMPLOYMENT RECOVERY

As we've written previously, The Great Recession as it has come to be known profoundly changed the nation's employment dynamics. Today, nearly four years after the recession was declared over, employment and the broader economy still struggle to recover. In addition to recession related employment difficulties, the sector faces what can only be described as self-inflicted wounds; in other words, those created directly by fiscal policy, law or regulation. The following is a brief look at two emerging trends—sequestration and healthcare—that may soon trigger adverse economic consequences.

Sequestration, an odd government term used to describe automatic spending cuts agreed to by law after the so-called super committee failed in 2011. It will likely have a profoundly negative effect on employment, especially in the defense sector where the automatic cuts could total some $600 billion. Sequestration was originally scheduled to kick in on January 1st however Congress and the President, as part of the fiscal cliff law passed quickly over the New Year's holiday, booted implementation down the road until March 1st; a date that is now rapidly approaching. Unless, changed very significantly, sequestration may profoundly and adversely affect federal spending, employment, consumer spending and the broader economy. A recent study commissioned by USA Today, estimated that the steep defense cuts alone could eliminate one-million jobs. Those are direct cuts but the multiplier effect would be greater and would ripple through the broader economy.

Indeed, the anticipated effects may be showing up already. After a huge increase in federal spending in the third quarter of 2012 that contributed to unusually high GDP growth (+3.1%), defense spending declined 22% in the fourth quarter leading the GDP into negative territory (-0.1%).

The requirement to provide healthcare benefits or face fines under the affordable care act (also known as Obamacare) is weighing heavily on many small businesses and even large employers of modest wage workers. Historically, it was the employers' option to provide benefits to employees and the employees' option to accept or reject employment. Going forward, however, healthcare benefits will be mandatory for employers of 50 or more full time workers. Firms with fewer than 50 full time workers are exempt. New Treasury Department rules released in early January give employers until June 30th before their staffing levels begin to influence the fines they may incur beginning in 2014 for not providing legally required healthcare coverage. Those fines could be as much as $3,000 per Obamacare subsidized worker. Since the law exempts part time workers, which is defined in the law as those working fewer than 30 hours per week, the obvious strategy for some employers is to make more employees part time.

The effect of that strategy showed up in the January Employment Situation Report. The report showed that the number of retail payroll employees rose by 32,000 while the total hours worked actually declined. Indeed, the retail work week declined in January to 30.1 hours. Looking back further, aggregate hours worked was lower than it was a year ago even though the number of workers has increased by some 200,000. At the same time, the number of involuntary part time workers, which had been slowly declining in recent years, recently increased again by 212,000. While these changes are barely enough to move the needle at the macro level, they are significant at the firm level and will almost certainly grow over time.

Looking forward, we expect the trend toward part time employment to continue, especially in the retail sector which is the most likely sector to employ large numbers of modestly paid workers. The cost of healthcare compliance; or fines for non-compliance, is significant and clearly enough to break many firms. This is another trend that will have a lengthy and profound effect on employment dynamics.

FEBRUARY 11, 2013

THE NATION NEEDS JOBS BUT WHERE WILL THEY COME FROM?

Employment has improved since the depths of the recession. Indeed, in January 2009, the nation's economy lost an astounding 820,000 jobs. After annual benchmark revisions and large upward monthly revisions to last November and December job numbers, the economy added 181,000 per month on average throughout 2012. That's good but by no means good enough. In January there were still 12.3 million Americans unemployed. That includes some 4.7 million Americans who have been unemployed long term or, by Bureau of Labor Statistics (BLS) definition, 27 weeks or longer. In fact, the average duration of unemployment is now a staggering 35 weeks.

In addition to the personal tragedy of job loss, unemployment does not bode well for the broader economy. While unemployment compensation may cover some of the consumable necessities, the unemployed can't spend significantly. Generally, they don't buy homes. They don't remodel or buy furniture and appliances and they don't buy cars and other big ticket items that drive the economy.

Despite improvement in employment, there is still a long list of factors frustrating employment recovery. Some, such as structural changes in employment dynamics, will take time to resolve. Others, such as sequestration and healthcare, are self-inflicted by government in the form of law, policy and regulation and it will take a united government to undo the actions ... or perhaps not. We have shared our thoughts about some of these factors in recent commentaries. The big question for most of us today is *"where will new jobs come from"* in the short and mid-term future or is mediocre job growth accompanied by historically high unemployment just the new normal?

After six long years of housing distress, we think housing will ultimately return to being an important employment growth agent. The reason is not just housing but rather the huge multiplier effect the sector creates. A home purchase always has a ripple or "multiplier effect" in the economy. In other words, for each dollar that is spent, there are additional dollars spent over and above the initial investment that ripple through the economy. Multipliers take many forms but in housing, economists and policy analysts attempt to quantify three fundamental things: jobs, spending and tax revenues. These multiplier impacts tend to occur in two phases. The first is when the house is constructed. The second is throughout occupancy. An existing home sale produces a multiplier effect but certainly not as great as when a new home is constructed and sold.

The first impacts in new home construction occur when the home is built. There is spending on the workers who build the home as well as in the firms that support them. There are usually office staff, cost estimators, buyers accountants and more. In addition to the direct impact of home construction, are the ripple effects; those that ripple through the local economy in some form. Generally two forms are measured.

There is the *"indirect impact."* from jobs and spending created from businesses that are *suppliers* to the construction operation. This might include building supplies, architectural and engineering spending, cabinetry, flooring, decorating, sales, financing and more.

Induced impact is created when workers and others spend their wages. This might include restaurants, retail stores, healthcare and other establishments. The induced impact tends to create jobs for these consumer related businesses. Then, of course, are taxes which are paid throughout the process and continue to be paid long after construction is complete.

With the steadily improving housing market, we are already witnessing some indirect effects in home improvement stores, tools, transportation and even light truck purchases.

MARCH 12, 2013

EXISTING HOME SALES FLAT
NEW HOME SALES SURGE

All widely watched housing indicators suggest that the long awaited housing recovery is solidly in place and is gaining momentum. Existing home sales are approaching the 5.0 million mark (SAAR) while new home sales which had declined to an all time low have begun to rebound. That is all good news, not only for the housing sector, but also for the broader economy. Indeed, housing carries with it, a huge multiplier effect which will be an important agent of spending and employment growth.

Existing home sales, as reported by the National Association of Realtors, were essentially flat in January at 4.92 million units. That is a seasonally adjusted annual rate (SAAR) and is compared to December. That is about 12% higher than the 4.38 million sales volume recorded a year ago. For all of 2012, NAR has preliminarily estimated that there were 4.65 million units sold (not seasonally adjusted). That is up 9.2% from the 4.26 million total recorded a year earlier in 2011. Barring currently unforeseen economic shock, we expect existing home sales to trend upward modestly throughout the year and breach the psychologically important 5.0 million mark by the end of 2013. The last time sales volume passed the 5.0 million mark was in 2007 when 5.03 million sales were recorded. The rate of increase is also the strongest recorded since 2004.

The **median sales price** for all existing housing types (single family detached, townhouse, condominium unit and co-op unit), was $173,600. That is up 12.3% year-over-year and represents an annual price increase last seen in mid-2005 to mid-2006 during last decade's boom years. Nevertheless, the median price has declined in very recent months to its lowest level since last June when it was $188,800. In December the median price was $180,200. Volatility within a fairly narrow range is not reason for concern. The trajectory of year over year movement has been steadily upward. The single family detached sector recorded the largest number of sales at 4.34 million units or 88% of all transactions. The median price was also fractionally higher at $174,100.

First time home buyer activity was strong at 1.47 million units or 30% of the total units sold. **Cash purchases** were also strong at 1.38 million units or 28% of total purchases. **Investors** dominated cash purchases at about 21% of the total.

Distress sales, that is short sales and those sold after foreclosure, totaled about 23% of January sales or roughly 1.13 million units. The breakdown by volume was 14% sold after foreclosure and 9% short sale transactions. Foreclosures, on average, sold for about 20% less than an otherwise comparable property that was not in foreclosure while short sales sold for about 12% less. Those ratios are consistently trending down but the overhang of distress transactions is still great enough to keep a lid on price increases in locations not subject to low inventory levels.

Looking forward at distressed transactions, however, there may be another dark cloud moving in. Preforeclosure notices, the first step in the foreclosure process, surged in the second half of 2012. Many will turn to foreclosure then auction and the properties will likely come back to market at distress level prices perhaps beginning as early as mid-2013. In our view, the overall housing market has regained enough strength to withstand this modest storm and generalized price declines are not likely. Nevertheless, some metro areas could experience modest but temporary price decline.

S&P / Case-Shiller, another highly regarded and widely watched index also moved higher. Case-Shiller measures repeat sales over a lengthy period of time. The 10 city composite index in December (most recent) was up 5.9% over the year while the broader 20 city index was up 6.8%. Over the month, the gain for both was 0.9%. Not seasonally adjusted, the apparent gain was 0.2%. Most metro areas covered by the release are showing steady improvement. New York, where prices declined 0.5%, was the only metro covered by the release that showed a decline. Gains, however, were strong in many areas. They ranged from a 2.2% gain in Chicago to a stunning 23% gain in Phoenix, one of the hardest hit areas during the recession. Phoenix is also the only metro to show a gain greater than 15%. On a seasonally adjusted basis, no metro covered by the Case-Shiller release recorded a decline. Nevertheless, prices are still well below their pre-recession peak. Both the 10 and 20 city composites are still down around 30%. Several metros are still down much more. Las Vegas for example, remains 56.4% below its August 2006 peak. Miami is still down 45.8% from its December 2006 peak. San Francisco is still down 32.6% from May 2006 and the list goes on. Peak prices were artificially driven at the time and are not likely to return to those peak levels anytime soon. Following the Great Depression of the 1930s, it took 19 years for prices to rebound to pre-depression levels.

Finally, the **FHFA Purchase Only House Price Index** continued its upward movement as measured quarterly. The FHFA is the Federal Housing Finance Agency which is the regulator of and conservator for both Fannie Mae and Freddie Mac. The index measures prices of homes purchased with conforming loans; that is loans that conform to Fannie and Freddie property and underwriting standards. The index in December was up 5.8% over the year and increases were broad based.

While there are several additional indices, NAR, Case-Shiller and FHFA are perhaps the most widely watched and the ones we follow most closely. The Realtors existing home data measures the largest share while Case-Shiller is based upon repeat sales and the FHFA measures sales made with the benefit of conforming loans. All are moving together in the same upward direction and collectively suggest that the housing recovery is intact and likely to continue.

Total **inventory** as reported by NAR fell 4.9% to 1.74 million existing homes available for sale at the end of January. That is a 4.2 month supply at the current sales pace and is the lowest inventory reading since April 2005 when it was also 4.2 months. Inventory registered 4.5 months of supply last month and 6.2 months a year earlier. Listed inventory is down 25.3% over the year. Inventories are unusually low and that has led to upward pressure on prices especially in the West. Tight inventories there have constrained sales volume as well. Volume in the West was down 5.7% over the year.

The housing crash in 2006 and 2007 has left many would be home sellers underwater on their mortgages and therefore reluctant to put their homes on the market. According to research firm Core-Logic, roughly 20% of mortgages nationwide were underwater in Q3 2012 (latest data available). That surged to 37% in Florida which was one of the hardest hit housing crisis states. Even otherwise vibrant metro-Atlanta saw

50% of mortgages under water.

We will soon enter the stronger spring and summer selling season where more homes will likely come to market and more will be sold. The last few selling seasons have generally been disappointing. Conventional sales have followed the typical seasonal pattern while distress transactions occur throughout the year. That has led to distress sales having a larger overall negative effect. We anticipate that this year's selling season will be stronger as the overall volume of distress sales has declined.

Turning to **new home sales**, the number of new homes sold in January surged to 437,000 which is the strongest sales pace since July 2008. That is an increase of 15.6% from the revised December total of 398,000 units. It is also up 28.9% year over year. Sales in the West and Northeast Census regions were up a stunning 60% and 54% respectively (year over year) while the south and Midwest recorded gains of 17% and 14%. The overall month over month gain was the strongest since the early1990s. It was also broad based across all regions of the country.

The median new home price was $226,400 which is up 2.3% year over year. The price gain was smaller than other recent months. Pricing tends to be more volatile in the new home sector due to the broad product mix and smaller sample size. With respect to inventory, the estimated number of new homes for sale at the end of January was 150,000. Inventories have steadily tightened with the months of supply at the current sales pace now at 4.1.

Construction indicators were also strong in January suggesting that short term future sales could also be strong, barring, of course, unforeseen economic shock. Building permits rose to 925,000 at a seasonally adjusted annual rate. That is 1.8% above the revised December total of 909,000 units but a very strong 35.2% above the year ago level of 684,000. Single family permits dominated at 584,000 or 63% of the total. Multifamily building permits (buildings of five units or more) totaled 311,000 in January.

Housing starts were at a seasonally adjusted annual rate (SAAR) of 890,000 in January. While that is 8.5% below the revised December total of 973,000, it is 23.6% above a year ago. Housing completions also rose in January. Completions totaled 724,000 units (SAAR) which is 6.0% above the revised December total of 683,000 but over 33% higher than the year ago level of 542,000. The single family sector dominated at 565,000 completed units.

The new home sector is clearly recovering but it is doing so from an exceptionally low base. Sales volume peaked at 1.389 million units in July 2005. Sales exceeded 1.0 million units from August 2002 through November 2006. The bubble finally burst in late 2006 and steadily declined reaching a record low of 280,000 units in May 2010. Since them, the new home sector has struggled to gain traction but finally appears to be doing so.

Overall, the macro housing market appears to have turned the corner, moving from drag on the broader economy to being a driver.

MARCH 28, 2013

CASE-SHILLER: HOME PRICES ACCELERATED

Existing home prices rose strongly in the three month period ending in January according to the recent S&P/Case-Shiller Home Price Indices. The indices are highly regarded and widely watched largely because they track repeat sales over a fairly lengthy time period. On a seasonally adjusted basis, the 10 city composite index rose 7.3% year over year as compared to the 5.9% increase reported for the three month period ending in December 2012. The 20 city composite rose 8.1% over the year as compared to the 6.8% increase reported a month earlier. All 20 cities posted year over year price increases. Atlanta, Detroit, Las Vegas, Los Angeles, Miami, Minneapolis, Phoenix and San Francisco all reported double digit gains. Phoenix, which was very hard hit during the recent recession posted a stunning 23.2% year over year increase while Las Vegas, also hard hit, turned in a 15.3% year over year gain. Both composite indices are shown at the left. The percentage year over year gains are shown in parentheses. For the first time in over five years, all metro areas in the 10 and 20 city indices experienced year over year increases. New York, the last hold-out, is still weak but managed to post a small 0.6% gain. Prior to January, the New York metro area recorded negative annual performance for more than two years. Overall, both composite annual gains were the strongest since before the housing collapse which began in 2006.

Results on a month over month basis, that is, the three month period ending in January as compared to December were mixed. While the majority of cities recorded price increases, several posted small price declines. The eight cities recording declines were Chicago, Cleveland, Detroit, Minneapolis, Portland, San Diego, Seattle and Washington, D.C. In every case, the declines were fractional at less than one-percent. Given well documented seasonal patterns, weak month to month growth in the fall and winter is not surprising nor is it reason to suggest that the housing recovery is losing traction.

Despite the strong annual increases, prices are still significantly below their pre-recession highs. That too is not surprising since the run up during the middle of last decade was largely artificial and not supported by housing fundamentals such as real demand, demographics, income and more. As of January, both the 10 and 20 city composites are more than 29% below their peak levels as shown in the following table.

When will prices return to pre-crash levels? As we've written in this space several times over the last few years, it took over 19 years for prices to recover after the Great Depression of the 1930s. History, in this case, may provide a clue but the reality is no one knows for sure. Robert Shiller, Yale economics professor and co-creator of the Case-Shiller survey was asked that same question in a recent CNBC interview. He replied, *"30 years, maybe 50 years, no one knows for sure."*

In our view, the housing recovery is real. It appears sustainable, barring of course, currently unforeseen economic shock. That is not to say that all of the risks are behind us. Indeed, headwinds remain fairly strong. The housing market has not yet achieved true equilibrium and some metro level price increases are being driven by low inventory levels; indeed the lowest in 12 years. As more homes come to market for sale, the rate of increase will almost certainly level out. Moreover, mortgage interest rates are being maintained at artificially low levels. Finally, several metros are experiencing bubble like conditions. Bubbles always burst and can do so at any time. Our view is that moderate volatility will continue into the foreseeable future but the overall trajectory is up.

CURRENT HOUSING RECOVERY IS THE REAL DEAL BUT DOWNSIDE RISKS REMAIN

Each new monthly data release tells us that housing recovery has finally taken root. After several false starts over the last few years, what we are witnessing today appears to be the real thing. Home prices have been rising for at least the last six months. According to most widely watched measures, price appreciation has been in the 3-9% range on a year over basis. That has improved consumer sentiment and has contributed to greater home equity or less negative equity which is clearly driving potential purchasers back to the market. Indeed, 2012 was the best year for housing since 2005 with all major measures rising for the first time since the peak of the housing boom.

Fundamentals have clearly improved and we expect growth to be sustainable. For several years, housing was a drag on the broader economy as indicated by a negative contribution to the nation's Gross Domestic Product (GDP). That has changed and housing is becoming a driver of the broader economy. The fundamental reason is the shear size of the housing market and the inherent multiplier effect it carries with it. Typically, housing has led recession recovery; at least from 10 of the 11 recessions since World War II. Until now that has not been happening during this recovery. Today, however, we are seeing housing perform in a manner more consistent with previous recoveries. Both new and existing home sales are the strongest they have been since the tax credit fuelled pace of late 2009. Building permit issuance is roaring back. At the same time distress sales have declined and inventories have contracted. Similarly, the number of underwater homeowners declined in the fourth quarter according to Core Logic. The ratio of underwater mortgages compared to total mortgages outstanding nationwide was 21.5% as compared to 25.2% a year earlier. Some states, such as Florida are nearly double that rate but overall more homeowners are digging out of the negative equity hole.

Looking forward, the worst case in our view, is that housing will just chug along at a nominal sub-par pace. At best it will lead the way to broader economic recovery. The obvious and necessary caveat is that there will be no currently unforeseen economic shock that would derail the recovery or throw the fragile broader economy back into recession.

Despite all the indicators that bode well for the future of housing, there are still some downside risks. Fiscal policy continues to weigh heavily on both housing and the broader economy. The end of the payroll tax break affected not only high earners but raised the tax liability for an estimated 77% of working Americans. Additionally, higher marginal tax rates for high income individuals; a higher capital gains tax rate (15% to 20%) on high income households and the 3.8% tax surcharge on proceeds from a home sale for married couples earning more than $250,000 may take a bite out of the luxury or higher end home market and have negative implications for the jumbo mortgage sector. Overall, the impact is likely to be small.

Uncertainty over sequestration could pose a bigger threat in the form of job losses, particularly in the defense industry. A recent study commissioned by USA Today newspaper suggested that there may be upwards of 1.0 million job losses, primarily in states serving the defense industry. Only time will tell what the job losses will actually be but the uncertainty will weigh heavily and will likely dampen housing demand. With what we know at this writing, however, the overall housing market should survive sequestration successfully.

Although the share of distress sales has been edging down in recent months, they are still at historically high levels and may rise again, at least temporarily. Indeed, pre-foreclosure filings rose sharply in February (+10%) suggesting more distress properties may come to market later this year.

APRIL 18, 2013

ECONOMIC RECOVERY TAKES A SPRING BREAK

The U.S. economy appears headed for its fourth consecutive midyear slowdown. For reasons that are not entirely clear, the U.S. has developed a pattern of strengthening in the winter months and weakening in the summer. That has been the pattern for the last three years and judging by March and early April data, the pattern will repeat for a fourth time. The last few years, we've watched as energy prices, debt-ceiling debate and the natural disaster in Japan slowed growth. This year, the reason is shaping up to be self-inflicted wounds created by fiscal policy in general and the anticipated effect of budget sequestration in particular. Indeed, the economy has not faced this much fiscal pressure since government spending cuts and the military drawdown following World War II. The end of the payroll tax holiday in January combined with budget sequestration and other tax increases are likely to trim well over one-percent from calendar year 2013 GDP leaving annual growth in the low to mid one-percent range. As we've opined previously in this space, that is stall speed for the economy and it would not take much additional economic shock to push the economy over the edge into recession. The political wrangling and brinksmanship around raising the debt ceiling this summer could be the trigger.

March **employment** numbers released April 5th were dismal. The economy created only 88,000 new jobs, the fewest since June 2012 and less than half of the average for the last six months. Several industries cut jobs sharply. Retailers, for example, cut 24,000 jobs after averaging 32,000 monthly gains for the last three months. Manufacturers cut 3,000 jobs and financial services shed 2,000. The bigger story, however, was the 663,000 persons who dropped out of the workforce in March. That left the number of Americans not in the labor force at a record 90 million (89,967,000). Indeed, nearly 9.5 million Americans have dropped out of the workforce since January 2009. Some of those are retiring baby boomers, students going back to college and even those who have exhausted unemployment benefits. The largest share, however, is working age Americans who cannot find work and have simply dropped out. The labor force participation rate in March fell to an historic low of 63.3%. That's the lowest it's been in nearly 34 years. That many people dropping out of the labor force also had the perverse mathematical effect of reducing the headline unemployment rate to 7.6% simply because those who are not looking for work are also not counted as unemployed.

It is too early to assess the **job loss impact of budget sequestration**. Anecdotal evidence currently suggests that some government contractors have already pulled back but the full impact is not likely to be apparent in the macro numbers until the third and fourth quarters. Additionally, the **Affordable Care Act** may weigh heavily on job growth as firms that currently do not provide health insurance coverage and are nearing the mandated 50 employee threshold to do so or face fines, are holding back hiring. Payroll processing firm ADP data show that private payrolls of firms in this size range have weakened sharply recently. Similarly, there is anecdotal evidence that firms may be moving employees to part time status. While that is widely touted, such a move has not yet shown up in BLS (Bureau of Labor Statistics) data. Indeed, the number of persons working part time for economic reasons actually declined by 350,000 in March. The total, 7.6 million workers, however, remains high.

The large number of people no longer in the labor force, forced to work only part time or those who are discouraged or marginally attached, has led to a troubling economic and social back story. The Census Bureau reports that 46 million Americans, or 20% of the population not in the military, prison or nursing homes, received some kind of government assistance in 2011 (most recent full year numbers). Of those 46 million, 30.4% characterize themselves as disabled. Additionally, according to the Department of Agriculture, about 47.3 million (one in seven) Americans currently receive food stamps (formally known as the Supplemental Nutrition Assistance Program or SNAP).

Retail spending as reported by the International Council of Shopping Centers (ICSC) was similarly disappointing in March. The ICSC chain store index was up a paltry 2.5% over the year against expectations of a 5-6% gain and a 4.6% average year over year gain for the first two months of the year. The decline was not surprising given the tax increases earlier in the year and the dismal March employment report.

Fiscal uncertainty is also weighing heavily on **consumer confidence**. All major indices have declined recently, particularly those that are more heavily weighted toward expectations, such as The Conference Board. The University of Michigan survey for the first half of April also trended lower. With incoming data suggesting a slowing economy, consumer sentiment could remain weak into the short term future. Our overall view is that economic recovery is still intact but risks remain heavily skewed to the downside.

WILLIAM L. PITTENGER

CMBS DELINQUENCIES DECLINE

As commercial mortgage backed securities (CMBS) delinquencies decline and more assets leave special servicing, investor interest in CMBS bonds has grown. Investors are once again taking on more risk in search of yield.

CMBS delinquencies are still high by historic standards but improvement is clearly evident. The 60 day plus delinquency rate declined overall to 8.38% in July. That is the fourth consecutive monthly decline. It is also down fractionally from 8.51% recorded in June. Delinquency rates decreased for all major property types except hotel. At the same time, total delinquencies fell $1.496 billion to $43.49 billion. Total outstanding CMBS loan balances declined to $519.8 billion from $528 billion in June. The outstanding volume of CMBS loans has declined in all but five months over the last 66 months. CMBS loans outstanding peaked at $793.5 billion in December 2007 and have fallen 34% from there. December 2007 was also the cyclical peak month for commercial real estate values. The trough was 50% lower just a year later in December 2008. Most sectors have been recovering but doing so at a snail's pace since then. The exception has been multifamily which has seen dramatic improvement over the last four years.

By asset class delinquent CMBS loans secured by industrial properties fell to 11.21% in July from 11.25% in June. Industrial delinquencies are down only 14 basis points over the last 12 months. Multifamily (rental) secured loans declined to 10.73% from 11.05% a month earlier. Over the last 12 months, delinquencies have declined over 380 basis points. That is indicative of what has emerged as a very robust multifamily market over the last four years. CMBS office loan delinquencies declined to 9.43% in July from 9.63% in June. The office sector is down some 85 basis points over the year. Retail loans recorded the lowest 60 day plus delinquency at 6.91%. That is down fractionally from 6.96% a month earlier. It is also down 90 basis points from 12 months earlier. The only sector not reducing delinquencies was the hotel sector which remained at 9.16% as compared to June. Improvement, however, has been fairly dramatic with a reduction of 350 basis points over the last year.

Outstanding balances have steadily declined in both the CMBS sector and in bank portfolios as comparatively few new loans are being made. Loan volume in both sectors, is, however, picking up. At the same time resolutions of problem assets are increasing and much new commercial construction today is still not justified as a result of continuing weak demand and absence of economic feasibility; two conditions that are inseparable.

Over the last year, shrinking outstanding CMBS balances have been largely the result of pay downs outpacing new originations. We expect that trend to continue well into 2014. The majority of loans backed by five year leases begun in 2007 and 2008 have seen leases renegotiated at lower rates thus removing what could have been a huge downside delinquency risk.

The large decline in CMBS delinquencies has been driven primarily by a large increase in the value of loans leaving special servicing. The value of those loans far exceeded the value of incoming loan delinquencies. Indeed, roughly $2.88 billion in CMBS loans were resolved during July however another $1.42 billion in loans became delinquent. The remaining inventory of problem CMBS loans is more troublesome and most are not good short term liquidation candidates. Servicers report a wide array of legal problems and other issues that preclude immediate sale.

Investor appetite for CMBS bonds is clearly improving. The money on the sidelines together with a quest for yield and a once again increasing risk tolerance should enhance commercial real estate financing ability going forward.

SEPTEMBER 12, 2013

ANOTHER MEDIOCRE JOBS REPORT IN AUGUST

August was another month for mediocre job creation. The labor market added 169,000 net new jobs of which 152,000 were private sector and 17,000 were government. While the gain fell modestly short of the 180,000 net new jobs that were widely expected, the back story is more revealing and clearly more disturbing. Job growth in June was originally estimated to be 188,000. That was revised down to 172,000. Similarly, July job growth was originally reported at 162,000 but was revised down to 104,000. All told, 74,000 fewer jobs were created in June and July than originally thought. As adjusted, gains for the last three months have averaged 148,000 per month which is the lowest so far this year and barely enough to keep pace with rising population without even making a dent in real unemployment. Moreover, that level of job creation is not enough to grow the economy in a meaningful fashion which means that GDP (Gross Domestic Product) growth will continue to hover in the low two-percent range. That is barely above economic stall speed.

At the same time, the headline unemployment rate fell slightly in August to 7.3%. It was 7.4% a month ago and 8.1% a year ago. Regrettably, that decline was not the product of significant job creation but rather quite the opposite as more workers dropped out of the labor force. Approximately 312,000 persons left the labor force in August. That is nearly twice the number of net new jobs created (169,000). Since those persons are no longer in the labor force, they are also no longer counted as unemployed. In that sense, headline unemployment (also called the U-3 measure) can be a bit deceiving as mathematically the unemployment rate declines as workers leave the labor force. In our view, the more meaningful measure, though not widely reported, is the U-6 measure. It takes into account total unemployed, plus those marginally attached to the workforce (2.3 million persons in August) and involuntary part time workers (7.9 million persons in August). Those are workers who would prefer to be working full time but can only find part time work. On that basis, the unemployment rate in August was 13.7%. It was a full percentage point higher a year ago. Nevertheless, there are still 11.3 million Americans unemployed. That number surges to 21.5 million workers as measured by the U-6. components.

Despite job gains in most sectors, most of the August job weakness is the product of slower gains in the service sector; especially financial services and information technology. Information was the only sector to actually lose jobs in August. The sector declined by 22,000 jobs after gaining slightly (8,000) a month earlier. Additionally, construction contractors have stopped adding to payrolls. The latter appears to be a temporary construction labor plateau and we expect construction hiring to resume over the next few months, weather permitting.

With fewer persons in the labor force, the civilian labor force participation rate, which measures the share of working age Americans who are actually working, declined to 63.2% in August. That is the lowest since August 1978; some 35 years ago. The steadily declining participation rate is being driven by demographics, as an aging population retires and leaves the labor force and also by technology as many workers are being displaced. A very slow economic recovery is also weighing negatively on the labor force but that component is more difficult to quantify. What is clear, however, is that while layoffs are declining, employers in general have been remarkably slow to hire. Compared to the U.S. population, only 58.6% of persons are working. That is a troubling trend as it means that only slightly more than half the population is working as compared to record numbers dropping out.

NOVEMBER 2013

COMMERCIAL REAL ESTATE AFTER THE GREAT RECESSION

Economically, commercial real estate is secondary to residential which is regarded as primary. Expressed another way, everyone needs a place to live making housing primary but not everyone needs an office, a warehouse or a retail store. The commercial market therefore draws its demand from what happens in the residential sector. In a balanced market, when a subdivision is created, commercial space will eventually migrate toward it and create services needed by residents. Oftentimes during the recent boom, however, commercial developers *assumed* residential development would be coming and development got out of sync. Commercial development actually proceeded residential. When the music stopped and the housing market collapsed, developers and their lenders were left with extraordinary amounts of commercial space for which there was no demand and which could not be rented.

To meet the perceived demand, developers developed, lenders loaned, rents increased, capitalization rates plunged and prices soared. A field of dreams mentality emerged. They built it but no one came, or even cared. Predictably—like residential—the commercial market crashed.

The commercial real estate market peaked in late 2007. At that time aggregate CRE value was about $6.5 trillion against aggregate loan balance of $3.5 trillion. That was a comfortable margin until the market collapsed and CRE lost roughly 50% of its value leaving aggregate value and loan principal roughly equal. The adverse effect was compounded by the recession and little demand for commercial space.

While no sector escaped the commercial down turn, the office sector was the hardest hit. In the early part of last decade, there was a wide spread perception that large amounts of office space would be needed to accommodate the burgeoning internet technology market. Space was built at the peak of the market in about 2001. Nevertheless, the "dot. com" bubble burst and so did the office real estate market. Just three short years later, the housing bubble began to inflate again and there was another widespread belief that large amounts of office space would be needed to serve housing and allied industries such as construction, finance, sales and others. Once again, employment and inventory both peaked and the sector collapsed. Much of the expected demand never materialized.

Predictably, bank credit quality suffered as defaults surged. Late cycle loans originated in 2007 performed the worst. A stunning 35.6% by principal balance defaulted. After the collapse, all sectors suffered. Industrial and warehousing generally held up the best followed by multifamily (except condo) office and retail.

By 2012 and early 2013, vacancies were off their highs but all four key CRE product sectors remain under stress and are still struggling to recover. This despite pockets of growth around the country. The sectors are clearly not recovering at a consistent pace. All are suffering from the slow recovery of the broader economy and a general lack of confidence and economic malaise.

The exception is multifamily (apartments) which is currently benefitting from the housing collapse as one time owners who have been foreclosed upon become renters. Cap rates have dropped to a national average in the low 6% range and are largely being sustained by record low interest rates. Caution is in the air though as the current multifamily vacancy rate hovers around 4.2% and the sector is showing signs of overheating once again. It is unlikely that the vacancy rate can decline further so some owners are turning to raising rents to generate more revenue. Their success doing so may be frustrated by still stagnating wage growth.

While the pace of sale transactions is modest, there has been anecdotal evidence of rising prices driven by renewed cap (capitalization) rate compression. Some top tier properties are offered at dangerously low cap rates in the five-percent range (multifamily in particular). Owners of lower tier properties are seeing the low offered cap rates and are following suit although there is no widespread evidence they are actually fetching prices based on five percent cap rates. What is happening, however, is that high pricing is pushing owners to at least consider new development. There is very little evidence of development success, however, due largely to financing constraints.

When we consider the four broad categories of commercial real estate (office, retail, industrial and apartment), it is apparent that three of the four have a ways to go before declaring a sustainable and robust recovery. The multifamily sector is doing well. At the opposite end of the product spectrum, retail remains most vulnerable. There is little discernible retail development potential and national vacancy stands at about 10% (equivalent to 1991). In the middle are office and industrial. Office vacancy is now around 17% and possibly poised to move higher due to pending lease expirations. Industrial (including warehousing and flex) is now in the 13-15% range.

Demographic Shifts. The demographics driving commercial real estate are clearly not what they were as little as six or seven years ago in the pre-recession era. That change is largely the product of technology and the demands of the Echo Boomer generation; that group of people born between 1982 and 1995 which began reaching college age in 2000. That generation is now some 80 million people strong, and like the baby boom generation (post World War II) before it, is changing the face of business. Echo boomers, in general, don't have the number of possessions their parents had and they don't want them. They are also opting for smaller apartments. Unlike their parents, they like to live in cities rather than suburbs and prefer to both live and work close by. They are deferring marriage and starting families. They prefer open office spaces and telecommuting thus driving the office space requirement down from around 220 square feet per employee to 90. These demographic shifts are worth paying close attention to.

Standards of Functional Adequacy. The housing boom and bust has left its mark on commercial real estate product types. Over time, however, many projects built during the boom have experienced functional change. Here is a summary of functional issues to remain aware of and carefully evaluate:

Too much office space (especially in the suburbs) was created to serve what turned out to be faux demand driven by housing. Some of that space is now functionally obsolete. Current demand is for smaller offices, work stations, open space and non-traditional working environments. Too much retail space was also created to meet the faux demand of housing. Retail got ahead of housing and much of the space was "high end" and beyond what most retailers can justify today. Too much warehousing was also created to serve the demands of builders. Much of it too is now functionally obsolete. Today, cubic space is at least as important as floor space for container storage.

Real Estate Finance and Regulation. Commercial real estate credit is still a deep concern for the Federal Banking agencies. The OCC, for example now regulates all national banks and federally chartered thrifts. The addition of thrifts was the result of the 2010 Dodd-Frank Act which eliminated the separate thrift charter. Together, those two important sectors hold about $700 billion in commercial real estate loans and the total is about 14% of their aggregate loan portfolios. The concentration is even higher for community banks where commercial real estate accounts for about 37% of the total loan portfolio.

"Concentrations Kill." Commercial real estate loan concentrations have been troublesome for community banks in particular since the bubble began to inflate in the middle of last decade. While large banks generally had lower percentage CRE exposure than community banks, their portfolios also performed more poorly. The lower exposure was due largely to size and diversity of loan types but the poor performance appears to have been the product of out of market lending; more speculative loans and more loans made on a non-recourse basis.

Most community bank CRE weakness came from over exposure to CRE. Many banks became overly concentrated in CRE when they tried to imitate their big bank competitors and grow quickly with wildly speculative CRE loans and those for which they did not have the capital, infrastructure, personnel, background or knowledge to compete safely, soundly and profitably. In one particularly naïve and egregious example, a community bank in South Florida literally copied the strategic lending plan of a trillion dollar (asset) global bank and began engaging in small business, middle market, agricultural, asset based and capital markets lending (as well as other types) without the tools to effectively do so.

While large banks had fairly nominal exposure on a percentage of capital basis, many community banks were much higher at 400% to as much as 800% of capital allocated to commercial real estate. In a significant number of those cases, high concentrations were the direct cause of failure. The OCC (Office of Comptroller of the Currency) performed retrospective analyses of commercial loans and concentrations. Predictably, they found that construction and development loans were the worst performers by a very large margin and that high concentrations in that sector were a reliable indicator of eventual bank failure. The OCC points out that in March 2007, nearly 2,000 national and state community banks held construction and development loans that exceeded their capital. By September 2011, 13% of those banks had failed.

The federal banking agencies released guidance concerning CRE concentrations in late 2006. That guidance set thresholds of 300% of capital for total CRE and 100% of capital for construction lending. The OCC subsequently discovered that 23% of banks that exceeded the guidelines failed. When banks were within the guidelines only about 0.5% (one-half percent) failed.

Outlook: Our view of commercial real estate for the short and mid-term is positive but still guarded. First there is too little demand for most types of space and the little demand there is, is being frustrated by low confidence, a shifting employment dynamic, and a broader economy that is still struggling to recover.

Second, is technology and changing demographics that will dictate changing space requirements, in terms of the type of space, the amount of space required and its location.

Third, is financing constraints. Not only are lenders risk averse but new Basel III capital rules are likely to constrain lending even more. Among other far reaching effects of the new standards is a 150% risk weighting for a new category of loans called HVCRE or high volatility commercial real estate. That category is generally development and construction lending. For community banks, that requirement will become effective in January 2015.

AFTERWORD

July 2014. The Great Recession, as it has come to be known, ended in June 2009. As this Afterword is written, that is over five years ago. Expressed another way, June 2009 may have been when the economy reached its cyclical low point. Since that time the trend has been toward recovery but recovery has been painfully slow and uneven with numerous setbacks along the way. As some suggest—probably with good cause—the recession may not have truly ended in many sectors. Indeed, as you have read on the previous pages from 2009 forward, there is precious little evidence to suggest a rebound of much significance. Sure, we've seen some improvement in employment, housing and other important areas however it is far from robust. Some observers, including the author, would suggest that the economy has merely moved from great recession to great stagnation.

What we have witnessed is a technical end, as defined by the Business Cycle Dating Committee (BCDC) of the National Bureau of Economic Research (NBER). Nevertheless, many sectors of the economy are still being propped up by low interest rates, artificial stimulus and are recovering unevenly. Some current economic highlights:

Corporate profits are up and the stock market is on a tear largely due to the effect of quantitative easing; that is, the Fed's ongoing purchases of mortgage backed securities. Although the Fed has tapered its purchases from $85 billion per month to the current $35 billion, interest rates have not shown any upward movement. Indeed, the Fed is likely to continue to prop up the economy with sustained low interest rates for the foreseeable future. That suggests that the economy has not recovered to the point of being self-sustaining. While markets are up, business confidence is down. Firms are still reluctant to hire and make other long term investments in people, plants, software and equipment.

The housing market, which led us into recession in the first place, has shown improvement. Some observers were even making bubble predictions earlier in 2014 as prices once again grew past the point where they were affordable in many local communities. Double digit increases are not sustainable in the long run as they grow beyond what the local populace can afford. In my view, the growth was being driven largely by pent up demand, fewer distress transactions and low inventories; factors that will correct themselves as we proceed down the path to equilibrium and sustainability. At this writing, housing appears to be on spring break but likely to return soon in a slower but more sustainable and orderly fashion.

Nevertheless, there are factors that will constrain growth over the longer term; perhaps for the next two decades or so. Yes. I said decades. An interesting "factoid" is that following the Great Depression of the 1930s, it took housing a full 19 years to regain pre-depression price levels.

The U.S. economy has grown at around 3.5% annually since World War II. On average, it sustained that level of growth through 10 previous recessions (not including the one just passed); periods of high inflation in the late 1960s and early 1980s and extraordinary periodic defense obligations. Recessions of years past; indeed up to the recession of the early 1990s tended to be short lived cyclical interruptions of relatively constant and sustained economic growth. Many observers referred to them as being "V" shaped meaning that when they were graphed, the performance resembled the letter "V" with steep fall off, a short period on the bottom followed by a sharp rise. Beginning with the recession of the early 1990s, however, the pattern has become more "U" shaped with an elongated bottom, indicative of a much longer recession.

Historically, recessions also tended to be cyclical and were largely caused by economic shock or monetary policy gone awry. In terms of employment, for example, workers who were laid off were usually called back to the same or similar positions when the economy or industry recovered. Every recession since the early 1990s has followed a similar "U" shaped pattern and recovery has grown ever longer with each recession and its recovery. Most importantly however, the reasons for unemployment turned structural rather than cyclical. Many of the job losses in the last three recessions have been permanent and the result of structural changes in the economy. Most will never be recovered.

Despite higher than desirable unemployment, many jobs today go unfilled. Why? There is a huge skills gap. That gap will likely widen as the U.S. competes in an increasingly global marketplace.

Why are so many job losses permanent? Two words. Technology and demographics. More jobs are being performed robotically. The economy is less about mindless assembly of widgets as we talked about in business school years ago. Today, it is more about technology including robotics. Manufactures have less need for "widget makers" and more need for those who have the knowledge and skill to run the machines that assemble the widgets.

Demographically, retiring baby boomers have helped push the nation's labor force participation rate down to a near record low of 63.8% (June 2014). The population to employment rate is even lower at around 58%. Imagine the implications of roughly 63% of the labor force supporting an economy which includes funding a retiree population that is growing by 10,000 persons every day.

For there to be truly meaningful economic growth we must have growth in the size of the working age population and the workforce AND increased productivity. Neither appears likely. This new, or continuing era of slow growth has widespread implications including fiscal, social, political, monetary policy and much, much more.

In my view, average economic growth for most of the current decade will hover around half of the post war average rate leaving GDP growth at roughly 1.75 to 2.5% or the equivalent of perennial economic stall speed. Indeed, the economy actually declined by 2.9% in the second quarter of 2014 although we expect it to return to positive territory.

Perennial slow growth has a wide variety of unpleasant and troubling implications. Real household income (median), for example, has fallen significantly from $54,892 in 2006 to $51,017 in 2013. That's a 7% decline. Since the beginning of the Great Recession, median income has fallen 6% roughly where it remains today. That means less consumer buying power including spending on homes and since commercial real estate depends largely on what happens in housing (the multiplier effect) it extends to the commercial sector.

Innovation too has declined as has the number of entrepreneurial firms coming to market. Historically, many small entrepreneurial ventures were funded with home equity loans and even credit cards. Not today. Too little home equity and lack of other credit availability are problematic. Venture capitalists too have also grown weary since the 2008 meltdown and are less willing to fund, untried, untested ventures; the same type of ventures that led to some of the greatest technological and advances over previous decades.

Some have labeled this era of slow growth "*The Great Stagnation.*" Perhaps. But whether it is stagnation or just slower than golden era growth, the realities suggest that no one is totally immune from economic pressures and the challenge going forward will be one of doing business successfully and prudentially in a slower economy than the one we had become accustomed to.

20TH AND 21ST CENTURY U.S. RECESSIONS FROM THE GREAT DEPRESSION TO THE PRESENT

The Great Depression
Start: August 1929
End: March 1933
Duration: 3 years, seven months
Time Since Previous Recession: 1 year, 9 months
Peak Unemployment: 24.9% (1933)
GDP Decline, Peak to Trough: 26.7%

Proximate Cause: Stock markets crashed worldwide and a banking collapse followed in the United States. Extensive tariffs contributed to the extraordinary depth of the recession. The U.S. remained in recession until World War II.

Recession of 1937–38
Also Known As Recession In a Depression
Start: May 1937
End: June 1938
Duration: 1 Year, 1 month
Time Since Previous Recession: 4 years, 2 months
Peak Unemployment: 19.0% (1938)
GDP Decline, Peak to Trough: –18.2%

Proximate Cause: The Recession of 1937 is only considered minor when compared to the Great Depression, but is otherwise among the worst recessions of the 20th century. Three explanations are offered for the recession: that tight fiscal policy from an attempt to balance the budget after the expansion of the New Deal caused recession, that tight monetary policy from the Federal Reserve caused the recession, or that declining profits for businesses led to a reduction in investment.

Recession of 1945
Start: Feb 1945
End: Oct 1945
Duration: 8 months
Time Since Previous Recession: 6 years, 8 months
Peak Unemployment: 5.2% (1946)
GDP Decline, Peak to Trough: -12.7%

Proximate Cause: The decline in government spending at the end of World War II led to an enormous drop in gross domestic product, making this technically a recession. This was the result of demobilization and the shift from a wartime to peacetime economy. The post-war years were unusual in a number of ways (unemployment was never high) and this era may be considered a "*sui generis* end-of-the-war recession".

Recession of 1949
Start: July 1953
End: May 1954
Duration: 10 months
Time Since Previous Recession: 3 years, 9 months
Peak Unemployment: 6.1% (Sep 1954)
GDP Decline, Peak to Trough: -2.6%

Proximate Cause: After a post-Korean War inflationary period, more funds were transferred to national security. In 1951, the Federal Reserve reasserted its independence from the U.S. Treasury and in 1952, the Federal Reserve changed monetary policy to be more restrictive because of fears of further inflation or of a bubble forming.

Recession of 1958
Start: Aug 1957
End: April 1958
Duration: 8 months
Time Since Previous Recession: 3 years, 3 months
Peak Unemployment: 7.5% (July 1958)
GDP Decline, Peak to Trough: -3.7%

Proximate Cause: Monetary policy was tightened during the two years preceding 1957, followed by an easing of policy at the end of 1957.

The budget balance resulted in a change in budget surplus of 0.8% of GDP in 1957 to a budget deficit of 0.6% of GDP in 1958, and then to 2.6% of GDP in 1959.

Recession of 1960–61
Start: Apr 1960
End: Feb 1961
Duration: 10 months
Time Since Previous Recession: 2 years
Peak Unemployment: 7.1% (May 1961)
GDP Decline, Peak to Trough: –1.6%

Proximate Cause: Another primarily monetary recession occurred after the Federal Reserve began raising interest rates in 1959. The government switched from deficit (or 2.6% in 1959) to surplus (of 0.1% in 1960). When the economy emerged from this short recession, it began the second-longest period of growth in NBER history. The Dow Jones Industrial Average (Dow) finally reached its lowest point on Feb. 20, 1961, about 4 weeks after President Kennedy was inaugurated.

Recession of 1969–70
Start: Dec 1969
End: Nov 1970
Duration: 11 months
Time Since Previous Recession: 8 years, 10 months
Peak Unemployment: 6.1% (Dec 1970)
GDP Decline, Peak to Trough: –0.6%

Proximate Cause: The relatively mild 1969 recession followed a lengthy expansion. At the end of the expansion, inflation was rising, possibly a result of increased deficits. This relatively mild recession coincided with an attempt to start closing the budget deficits of the Vietnam War (fiscal tightening) and the Federal Reserve raising interest rates (monetary tightening).

1973–75 Recession
Start: Nov 1973
End: Mar 1975
Duration: 1 year, 4 months
Time Since Previous Recession: 3 years
Peak Unemployment: 9.0% (May 1975)
GDP Decline, Peak to Trough: –3.2%

Proximate Cause: A quadrupling of oil prices by OPEC coupled with high government spending because of the Vietnam War led to stagflation in the United States. The period was also marked by the1973 oil crisis and the 1973–1974 stock market crash. The period is remarkable for rising unemployment coinciding with rising inflation.

1980 Recession
Start: January 1980
End: July 1980
Duration: 6 months
Time Since Previous Recession: 4 years, 10 months
Peak Unemployment: 7.8% (July 1980)
GDP Decline, Peak to Trough: –2.2%

Proximate Cause: The NBER considers a very short recession to have occurred in 1980, followed by a short period of growth and then a deep recession. Unemployment remained relatively elevated in between recessions. The recession began as the Federal Reserve, under Paul Volcker, raised interest rates dramatically to fight the inflation of the 1970s. The early '80s are sometimes referred to as a "double-dip" or "W-shaped" recession.

Early 1980s Recession
Start: July 1981
End: Nov 1982
Duration: 1 year, 4 months
Time Since Previous Recession: 1 year
Peak Unemployment: 10.8% (Nov 1982)
GDP Decline, Peak to Trough: –2.7%

Proximate Cause: The Iranian Revolution sharply increased the price of oil around the world in 1979, causing the1979 energy crisis. This was caused by the new regime in power in Iran, which exported oil at inconsistent intervals and at a lower volume, forcing prices up. Tight monetary policy in the United States to control inflation led to another recession. The changes were made largely because of inflation carried over from the previous decade because of the 1973 oil crisis and the 1979 energy crisis.

Early 1990s Recession
Start: July 1990
End: Mar 1991
Duration: 8 months
Time Since Previous Recession: 7 years, 8 months
Peak Unemployment: 7.8% (June 1992)
GDP Decline, Peak to Trough: –1.4%

Proximate Cause: After the lengthy peacetime expansion of the 1980s, inflation began to increase and the Federal Reserve responded by raising interest rates from 1986 to 1989. This weakened but did not stop growth, but some combination of the subsequent 1990 oil price shock, the debt accumulation of the 1980s, and growing consumer pessimism combined with the weakened economy to produce a brief recession.

Early 2000s Recession
Start: March 2001
End: November 2001
Duration: 8 months
Time Since Previous Recession: 10 years
Peak Unemployment: 6.3% (June 2003)
GDP Decline, Peak to Trough: –0.3%

Proximate Cause: The 1990s were the longest period of growth in American history. The collapse of the speculative dot-com bubble, a fall in business outlays and investments, and the September 11th attacks, brought the decade of growth to an end. Despite these major shocks, the recession was brief and shallow. Without the September 11th attacks, the economy might have avoided recession altogether.

Great Recession

Start: Dec 2007
End: June 2009
Duration: 1 year, 6 months
Time Since Previous Recession: 6 years, 1 month
Peak Unemployment: 10.0% (October 2009)
GDP Decline, Peak to Trough: -4.3%

Proximate Cause: The subprime mortgage crisis led to the collapse of the United States housing bubble. Falling housing-related assets contributed to a global financial crisis, even as oil and food prices soared. The crisis led to the failure or collapse of many of the United States' largest financial institutions: Bear Stearns, Fannie Mae, Freddie Mac, Lehman Brothers, Citi Bank and AIG, as well as a crisis in the automobile industry. The government responded with an unprecedented $700 billion bank bailout and $787 billion fiscal stimulus package. The National Bureau of Economic Research declared the end of this recession over a year after the end date. The Dow Jones Industrial Average (Dow) finally reached its lowest point on March 9, 2009.

LARGEST MONTHLY JOB LOSSES IN AMERICAN HISTORY

Month and Year	Job Loss
Sep 1945	-1,966,000
Oct 1949	-834,000
Jan 2009	-741,000
Dec 2008	-681,000
Mar 2009	-663,000
Feb 2009	-651,000
July 1956	-629,000
Dec 1974	-602,000
Nov 2008	-597,000
Feb 1946	-589,000
Feb 1958	-501,000

SOURCE: *Bureau of Labor Statistics*

The decline in government spending at the end of World War II led to an enormous drop in gross domestic product, making this period technically a recession. This was the result of demobilization and the shift from wartime to peacetime economy. The post-war years were unusual in a number of ways (unemployment was never high) and this era may be considered a "*sui generis*"—end-of-the-war recession. There were four short recessions following World War II (1945, 1949, 1953, and 1958).

PEAK TO TROUGH MEDIAN HOUSE PRICES IN FLORIDA

MSA		Peak Date	Trough Price	Trough Date	% Change
State – Florida	$257,800	6/06	$130,900	1/10	-49.22%
Fort Lauderdale	$391,100	11/05	$180,000	1/10	-53.98%
Fort Pierce Port Saint Lucie	$269,400	9/05	$101,100	1/10	-62.47%
Melbourne Titusville Palm Bay	$248,700	8/05	$104,100	12/09	-58.14%
Orlando	$267,100	10/06	$123,500	1/10	-53.76%
West Palm Beach Boca Raton	$421,500	11/05	$227,500	11/09	-46.03%

Data Source: Florida Association of Realtors

GROWTH OF PART TIME EMPLOYMENT

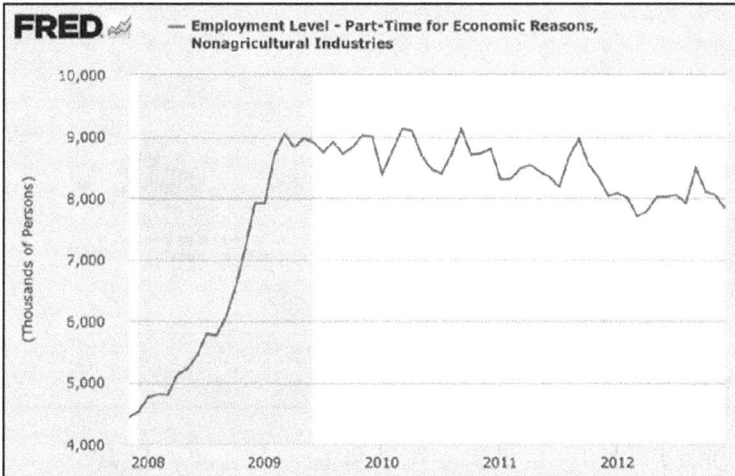

SOURCE: *Federal Reserve Economic Data – Federal Reserve Bank of St. Louis*

Part time employment for economic reasons, also referred to as "involuntary part time employment" surged concurrent with the start of the recession in late 2007. It reached a peak of over 9.0 million workers in 2009. The decline has been modest since the recession ended in mid-2009.

MEDIAN HOUSEHOLD INCOME

Real Median Household Income in the United States (MEHOINUSA672N)
Source: U.S. Department of Commerce: Census Bureau

US household income back to levels last seen in 1989.

www.mybudget360.com

Shaded areas indicate US recessions.
2013 research.stlouisfed.org

SOURCE: *Federal Reserve Economic Data | Federal Reserve Bank of St. Louis*

Median household income is now (2014) approximately $53,000 per annum. That is six-percent lower than 2007 when the recession started. U.S. Household income has returned to a level last seen in 1989.

Median per capita income is now (2014) approximately $28,000 per annum.

Only 4.6% of households make more than $200,000 per year and only 9.2% make more than $150,000.

Most Americans are not seeing income growth. That is a painful dilemma in our economy which is dependent on people spending and where roughly 70% of the economy is driven by consumer spending.

EXISTING HOME SALES PATTERN 2000-2014

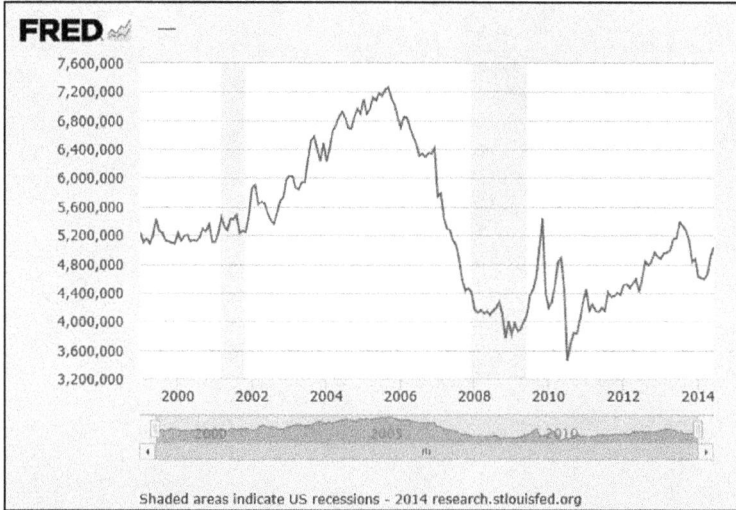

Source: Federal Reserve Economic Data | Federal Reserve Bank of St. Louis

U.S. existing home sales peaked in 2006 and hit a trough in 2010. The twin peaks in 2009 on the accompanying chart were the result of two home buyer tax credit programs. The first was designed for first time home buyers. The Administration deemed it a resounding success at the time and quickly expanded it. As the graph shows, however, the market gave all the gains back suggesting that demand was not there.

A

Absorption 4, 5, 9, 10, 11, 12, 13, 14, 17, 25, 26, 27, 28, 29, 49, 50, 51, 125, 127, 131, 171, 179, 183, 202, 203, 208, 209, 345

AIB 12

Architectural Billings 12, 48

B

Bailout 36, 76, 98, 264, 307, 308, 324, 400

Banking ix, xv, xx, xxiv, xxviii, 22, 36, 97, 102, 115, 123, 137, 142, 148, 188, 195, 199, 200, 222, 231, 232, 235, 239, 261, 311, 388, 389, 395

Bankruptcy 1, 36, 94, 147, 242, 264, 306

BCDC 2, 37, 56, 91, 184, 199, 247, 253, 254, 276, 278, 279, 280, 296, 297, 391

BLS 11, 18, 25, 26, 32, 33, 42, 53, 72, 161, 186, 200, 265, 294, 298, 326, 339, 351, 366, 367, 370, 381

Bubble xxviii, xxix, xxx, xxxi, xxxii, xxxiii, 7, 20, 22, 23, 30, 33, 83, 84, 100, 136, 140, 142, 146, 149, 162, 164, 165, 170, 172, 188, 189, 190, 191, 192, 205, 222, 223, 224, 225, 226, 229, 230, 233, 234, 239, 251, 265, 271, 275, 280, 292, 293, 302, 310, 321, 359, 365, 367, 376, 377, 386, 388, 391, 396, 399, 400

Bureau of Labor Statistics 11, 18, 25, 32, 42, 43, 45, 53, 60, 62, 72, 75, 78, 96, 112, 114, 129, 134, 158, 161, 168, 175, 181, 186, 200, 214, 220, 244, 246, 265, 276, 277, 294, 298, 299, 317, 339, 351, 352, 364, 370, 381, 401

Business Cycle Dating Committee xx, 2, 37, 56, 91, 159, 184, 199, 222, 247, 253, 254, 276, 278, 279, 280, 296, 391

C

Case-Shiller xxi, xxii, 178, 197, 263, 270, 277, 282, 283, 286, 287, 288, 290, 292, 304, 332, 354, 373, 374, 376, 377

Central Florida xv, 8, 14, 28, 29, 44, 256, 267

CMBS xx, xxi, xxii, 24, 47, 50, 52, 120, 121, 126, 140, 164, 193, 230, 231, 233, 286, 287, 305, 306, 310, 317, 318, 333, 334, 349, 350, 382, 383

Commercial Real Estate v, xiv, xvi, xviii, xxii, 1, 2, 8, 10, 11, 22, 23, 24, 25, 26, 37, 98, 120, 120, 121, 122, 128, 134, 139, 144, 149, 162, 163, 164, 165, 176, 188, 199, 207, 221, 226, 229, 230, 232, 234, 235, 236, 238, 240, 247, 254, 268, 286, 306, 307, 310, 318, 334, 342, 342, 343, 350, 351, 382, 383, 385, 385, 386, 387, 388, 389, 390, 393

Conference Board 3, 17, 22, 40, 47, 76, 93, 110, 137, 315, 316, 381

Consumer xv, xvi, xvii, xxviii, 1, 3, 15, 16, 17, 18, 21, 22, 30, 31, 33, 34, 37, 38, 39, 40, 41, 42, 47, 52, 53, 55, 56, 59, 61, 62, 66, 67, 68, 70, 76, 78, 79, 80, 81, 82, 86, 92, 93, 94, 97, 99, 102, 104, 106, 107, 108, 109, 110, 122, 123, 124, 125, 127, 128, 137, 138, 139, 157, 158, 159, 160, 163, 180, 185, 187, 190, 195, 200, 203, 207, 213, 223, 230, 232, 234, 236, 238, 249, 264, 268, 270, 272, 281, 291, 297, 307, 315, 316, 317, 319, 322, 323, 330, 341, 344, 351, 356, 358, 365, 368, 371, 378, 381, 393, 399, 404

Consumer Balance Sheet xvii, 106

Consumer Borrowing 33, 53, 55, 107

Consumer Confidence 3, 15, 17, 22, 37, 39, 40, 40, 42, 47, 70, 93, 99, 110, 110, 137, 138, 180, 187, 203, 207, 230, 232, 234, 236, 238, 270, 291, 297, 316, 322, 344, 381

Consumer Sentiment 40, 47, 53, 268, 315, 316, 358, 378, 381

Consumer Spending xxviii, 3, 15, 17, 18, 34, 37, 38, 39, 40, 42, 47, 55, 76, 79, 92, 102, 110, 122, 123, 124, 125, 127, 128, 139, 157, 160, 185, 195, 230, 249, 316, 317, 319, 351, 365, 368, 404

Consumer Stress xvi, 52

CRE xx, 122, 229, 230, 231, 232, 233, 238, 286, 307, 310, 318, 334, 345, 386, 388, 389

Credit xvii, xviii, xxv, xxx, xxxi, xxxii, xxxiii, 1, 2, 3, 15, 16, 17, 19, 20, 24, 30, 33, 34, 36, 37, 38, 41, 43, 45, 53, 55, 56, 57, 66, 67, 68, 71, 72, 76, 79, 80, 81, 82, 83, 86, 90, 92, 93, 99, 100, 105, 106, 107, 108, 109, 120, 121, 122, 124, 125, 127, 128, 132, 136, 137, 141, 142, 143, 146, 147, 148, 151, 157, 170, 172, 177, 179, 188, 192, 196, 198, 203, 204, 205, 206, 207, 209, 210, 213, 214, 221, 226, 232, 233, 234, 242, 243, 248, 251, 255, 258, 259, 266, 269, 272, 277, 290, 301, 307, 320, 335, 341, 378, 386, 388, 393, 405

Credit Card 16, 33, 34, 36, 67, 99, 107, 109, 307

Credit Card Debt 33, 34, 36

Credit Markets 3, 19, 24, 37, 43, 82, 86, 120, 122

Credit Quality xvii, xviii, 56, 66, 67, 79, 106, 108, 108, 146, 147, 206, 210, 213, 214, 232, 233, 248, 386

Cyclical xxxiii, 39, 46, 100, 152, 153, 159, 167, 176, 191, 199, 215, 224, 245, 265, 276, 294, 298, 299, 321, 328, 340, 352, 362, 382, 391, 392

D

Debt xxxiii, 15, 17, 20, 31, 33, 34, 35, 36, 47, 53, 65, 68, 71, 80, 83, 84, 85, 107, 142, 146, 162, 164, 165, 189, 222, 223, 234, 238, 281, 309, 331, 380, 399

Default 67, 71, 83, 84, 85, 88, 95, 108, 109, 110, 131, 164, 197, 211, 212, 214, 228, 272, 286

Discouraged Workers 72, 102, 112, 114, 133, 145, 152, 161, 167, 175, 181, 201, 215, 219, 236, 245, 366

Distress Sales 328, 359, 375, 378, 379

Dodd-Frank xxvi, 200, 268

Double Dip Recession 242, 244, 248, 254, 281

E

Employment xvi, xvii, xx, xxi, xxii, xxiii, xxviii, xxx, xxxiv, 1, 3, 11, 15, 18, 19, 25, 26, 27, 28, 29, 30, 31, 32, 33, 37, 39, 40, 41, 42, 43, 44, 45, 46, 47, 49, 50, 52, 53, 54, 59, 60, 61, 62, 63, 70, 72, 73, 74, 75, 76, 77, 82, 83, 89, 90, 91, 93, 94, 96, 97, 99, 101, 102, 103, 104, 112, 113, 114, 115, 116, 117, 123, 128, 129, 132, 133, 134, 138, 140, 142, 143, 144, 145, 148, 149, 150, 151, 152, 153, 154, 156, 157, 158, 159, 161, 162, 166, 167, 168, 169, 170, 174, 175, 176, 180, 181, 182, 186, 188, 190, 191, 192, 193, 194, 197, 199, 201, 203, 209, 210, 215, 216, 217, 218, 219, 221, 222, 224, 225, 229, 236, 237, 238, 240, 244, 245, 246, 249, 250, 257, 258, 265, 266, 267, 270, 273, 274, 275, 276, 277, 281, 292, 293, 294, 295, 297, 298, 299, 309, 316, 321, 322, 325, 326, 327, 329, 332, 334, 336, 338, 339, 340, 342, 344, 348, 350, 351, 352, 353, 358, 359, 362, 363, 364, 365, 366, 367, 368, 369, 370, 371, 372, 380, 381, 386, 389, 391, 392, 393, 403

Equilibrium xviii, 4, 5, 6, 7, 8, 65, 66, 89, 132, 136, 172, 192, 226, 249, 253, 268, 337, 347, 357, 377, 392

F

Fannie Mae xxx, xxxi, 36, 71, 92, 108, 131, 146, 209, 283, 290, 309, 324, 332, 374, 400

FDIC xx, 151, 187, 199, 226, 231, 233, 236, 238, 248

Fed 3, 18, 19, 22, 32, 36, 43, 55, 61, 62, 331, 391

Federal Reserve xxix, 16, 17, 18, 35, 55, 56, 61, 93, 106, 121, 127, 141, 142, 206, 209, 213, 234, 238, 248, 263, 307, 309, 331, 351, 395, 396, 397, 398, 399, 403, 404, 405

Fed Funds 18, 61

FHA 57, 211, 259, 272, 273, 290, 307, 308

FHFA xxx, 178, 283, 290, 332, 333, 374

Fiscal Cliff xxi, 300, 301, 317, 328, 331, 338, 342, 361, 368

Fiscal Policy xxii, 242, 362, 368, 380, 395

Flippers xxxi, xxxii, 58, 70, 71, 83, 163, 321

Florida v, ix, xiv, xv, xvi, xvii, xviii, xix, xx, xxiii, xxiv, xxx, xxxii, xxxiii, xxxiv, xxxv, xxxvi, 4, 5, 6, 8, 9, 10, 12, 14, 15, 20, 21, 26, 27, 28, 29, 38, 41, 43, 44, 46, 48, 49, 54, 57, 59, 60, 63, 64, 65, 66, 67, 68, 69, 70, 71, 73, 74, 77, 81, 82, 83, 87, 88, 89, 94, 95, 96, 97, 100, 101, 103, 104, 109, 114, 116, 118, 128, 129, 130, 134, 135, 137, 143, 144, 146, 147, 148, 150, 153, 154, 156, 160, 161, 163, 165, 166, 168, 169, 170, 171, 172, 175, 176, 177, 178, 183, 184, 191, 192, 193, 194, 196, 197, 199, 202, 204, 205, 210, 211, 212, 213, 216, 217, 219, 224, 225, 227, 228, 229, 230, 234, 236, 240, 243, 246, 251, 252, 253, 255, 256, 257, 258, 260, 261, 264, 267, 274, 275, 277, 285, 288, 292, 305, 313, 340, 341, 374, 378, 389, 402

Florida Employment xx, 43, 46, 54, 63, 73, 77, 103, 103, 116, 116, 128, 134, 176, 194, 246, 257, 258, 267

Foreclosure 7, 21, 38, 57, 58, 64, 65, 70, 74, 82, 83, 84, 87, 95, 108, 109, 118, 121, 131, 136, 146, 147, 148, 156, 180, 192, 197, 198, 210, 211, 212, 213, 225, 227, 228, 230, 232, 234, 242, 243, 252, 253, 254, 261, 262, 263, 264, 270, 271, 272, 273, 277, 288, 289, 290, 292, 293, 305,

37, 38, 39, 40, 41, 43, 44, 45, 47, 49, 52, 53, 54, 56, 60, 64, 65, 67, 68,
69, 71, 73, 74, 77, 81, 82, 83, 87, 88, 94, 95, 96, 99, 100, 108, 109,
117, 118, 120, 123, 124, 130, 135, 136, 138, 141, 142, 147, 148, 149,
150, 154, 155, 157, 160, 161, 162, 163, 166, 167, 169, 170, 172, 176,
178, 180, 182, 184, 188, 190, 191, 192, 195, 197, 199, 203, 204, 206,
209, 211, 212, 213, 216, 221, 222, 224, 225, 226, 227, 228, 229, 230,
232, 234, 240, 243, 244, 246, 247, 248, 249, 251, 252, 253, 255, 257,
258, 259, 260, 261, 262, 263, 264, 265, 266, 268, 269, 270, 271, 272,
273, 274, 275, 276, 277, 278, 279, 280, 281, 282, 283, 284, 285, 286,
287, 288, 289, 290, 291, 292, 293, 294, 295, 296, 297, 302, 304, 305,
307, 311, 312, 314, 315, 320, 321, 322, 323, 324, 328, 329, 331, 332,
336, 337, 338, 340, 341, 342, 343, 346, 347, 348, 349, 351, 353, 354,
355, 356, 357, 359, 360, 361, 365, 367, 371, 372, 373, 374, 375, 376,
377, 378, 379, 385, 386, 388, 391, 392, 393, 400

Housing Sector xvii, 8, 15, 16, 38, 64, 77, 87, 130, 161, 169, 251, 274, 276,
284, 287, 315, 320, 322, 336, 342, 365, 372

Housing Starts xvi, 6, 99, 260, 314

I

Industrial xvi, 10, 11, 12, 13, 22, 23, 37, 48, 105, 121, 122, 123, 162, 165,
195, 232, 240, 278, 305, 307, 318, 333, 345, 346, 382, 386, 387, 397,
400

IndyMac 35

Inflation xxx, 3, 15, 18, 19, 22, 30, 32, 40, 56, 59, 61, 62, 71, 140, 155, 158,
159, 162, 214, 234, 310, 316, 319, 331, 363, 392, 396, 397, 398, 399

J

Jobs xvii, xviii, xix, xxii, xxviii, xxxiv, 11, 18, 26, 32, 37, 39, 40, 41, 43, 44,
45, 46, 49, 50, 53, 54, 59, 60, 62, 63, 71, 72, 73, 74, 75, 77, 89, 90, 91,
92, 94, 96, 99, 100, 101, 102, 103, 104, 112, 113, 114, 115, 116, 120,
124, 128, 129, 132, 133, 134, 140, 142, 143, 144, 145, 148, 149, 150,
151, 152, 153, 160, 161, 162, 163, 167, 168, 169, 170, 171, 174, 175,
176, 177, 180, 181, 182, 186, 187, 190, 191, 193, 194, 200, 201, 210,
214, 215, 216, 217, 218, 219, 220, 221, 224, 229, 236, 237, 244, 245,
246, 247, 250, 256, 257, 258, 260, 265, 266, 267, 268, 276, 281, 293,
294, 297, 298, 299, 305, 321, 322, 323, 325, 326, 334, 335, 336, 338,
339, 340, 342, 349, 350, 351, 352, 353, 354, 362, 364, 365, 366, 367,
368, 369, 370, 371, 380, 383, 384, 392, 393

RECESSION CHRONICLES

L

Labor Market xvi, xxviii, 3, 18, 37, 40, 42, 45, 52, 53, 58, 59, 67, 75, 149, 186, 207, 219, 221, 250, 272, 279, 291, 296, 298, 299, 326, 327, 328, 352, 364, 383

Lehman 36, 163, 400

Loan Losses 232, 235, 269, 307

Loan to Value 57, 85, 122, 164, 212, 227, 228, 324

Lost Decade xviii, 141, 142, 143, 265

M

Manufacturing 11, 18, 41, 43, 44, 45, 46, 52, 53, 54, 60, 62, 63, 77, 90, 97, 101, 102, 103, 112, 113, 115, 116, 123, 144, 150, 153, 154, 158, 161, 167, 168, 174, 176, 182, 186, 201, 207, 214, 217, 218, 220, 237, 245, 248, 249, 258, 265, 267, 279, 281, 296, 302, 317, 325, 326, 335, 353, 365

Marginally attached 96, 102, 112, 114, 116, 133, 145, 152, 161, 167, 175, 181, 182, 187, 200, 201, 215, 216, 219, 236, 245, 294, 298, 299, 327, 336, 366, 367, 381, 384

MEW 41, 79

Mortgage Equity Withdrawal 41, 79, 80

N

National Bureau of Economic Research 2, 37, 56, 96, 99, 159, 184, 199, 247, 253, 276, 279, 280, 296, 391, 400

NBER 2, 37, 56, 91, 184, 199, 247, 253, 276, 279, 280, 296, 391, 397, 398

New Construction 1, 4, 5, 6, 64, 66, 89, 131, 173, 179, 180, 203, 209, 274, 308, 318, 321, 333, 365

New Home Sales xix, xx, xxi, xxii, xxix, xxxiii, 2, 15, 47, 64, 172, 178, 183, 202, 208, 208, 209, 236, 238, 248, 251, 255, 259, 271, 271, 275, 277, 284, 290, 302, 303, 303, 313, 313, 314, 320, 320, 322, 332, 332, 348, 358, 358, 359, 372, 372, 375

O

OCC 121, 285, 340, 388, 389

Office xvi, xviii, xxv, xxvii, xxx, 10, 11, 23, 24, 25, 26, 27, 28, 29, 48, 49, 50, 51, 52, 60, 120, 121, 122, 123, 125, 147, 162, 163, 165, 170, 171, 176, 190, 224, 229, 230, 232, 240, 285, 301, 305, 307, 308, 317, 322, 333, 338, 340, 343, 344, 345, 367, 371, 382, 385, 386, 387, 388, 389

Office of Comptroller of the Currency 121, 147, 285, 340, 389

OFHEO xxx

Outlook xviii, xx, xxi, xxii, 18, 32, 33, 39, 47, 61, 73, 76, 82, 91, 100, 108, 120, 121, 123, 127, 139, 145, 156, 178, 180, 198, 228, 258, 265, 273, 286, 288, 291, 299, 300, 305, 315, 329, 331, 337, 342, 343, 344, 345, 346, 347, 357, 361, 389

P

Part Time xxiii, 72, 75, 96, 102, 112, 115, 116, 133, 145, 152, 156, 161, 167, 175, 181, 182, 187, 200, 201, 215, 216, 219, 236, 245, 294, 298, 299, 326, 327, 335, 336, 339, 366, 367, 369, 381, 384, 403

Permits xvi, 1, 6, 7, 129, 172, 178, 179, 182, 183, 209, 260, 314, 322, 348, 359, 375

Productivity 3, 18, 22, 153, 168, 214, 215, 220, 250, 328, 352, 393

R

Recession v, viii, xi, xvi, xvii, xx, xxi, xxii, xxiv, xxv, xxvi, xxviii, xxx, xxxiii, xxxiv, xxxv, xxxvi, 1, 2, 3, 11, 15, 22, 30, 31, 32, 33, 35, 36, 37, 38, 39, 40, 41, 42, 44, 45, 46, 49, 56, 57, 60, 67, 72, 73, 74, 76, 77, 81, 85, 86, 90, 91, 92, 93, 94, 95, 96, 98, 99, 100, 101, 103, 104, 105, 107, 108, 111, 112, 113, 114, 115, 116, 118, 123, 125, 127, 128, 132, 136, 137, 139, 140, 141, 142, 144, 145, 148, 149, 150, 151, 152, 153, 154, 157, 159, 163, 166, 167, 168, 169, 171, 174, 176, 180, 181, 184, 185, 186, 187, 188, 189, 190, 191, 192, 198, 199, 200, 201, 204, 206, 209, 210, 214, 215, 218, 220, 221, 222, 223, 224, 225, 230, 232, 233, 236, 237, 238, 240, 241, 242, 244, 245, 247, 248, 250, 251, 253, 254, 255, 257, 265, 266, 268, 269, 270, 272, 273, 274, 275, 276, 277, 278, 279, 280, 281, 282, 286, 288, 293, 296, 297, 299, 300, 301, 306, 307, 308, 315, 316, 317, 318, 321, 322, 326, 327, 328, 329, 330, 334, 338, 339, 340, 341, 342, 343, 350, 351, 352, 354, 362, 366, 367, 368, 370,

S

V

W

www.ingramcontent.com/pod-product-compliance
Lightning Source LLC
Chambersburg PA
CBHW060528220326
41599CB00022B/3455